STUDENT HANDBOOK OF CRIMINAL JUSTICE AND CRIMINOLOGY

Cavendish
Publishing
Limited

London • Sydney • Portland, Oregon

STUDENT HANDBOOK OF CRIMINAL JUSTICE AND CRIMINOLOGY

Edited by
John Muncie
Professor of Criminology
Open University
and
David Wilson
Professor of Criminology
University of Central England, Birmingham

Cavendish
Publishing
Limited

London • Sydney • Portland, Oregon

First published in Great Britain 2004 by
Cavendish Publishing Limited

This edition reprinted 2006
by Routledge-Cavendish
2 Park Square, Milton Park, Abingdon, Oxon, OX14 4RN

Simultaneously published in the USA and Canada
by Routledge-Cavendish
270 Madison Avenue, New York, NY 10016

Reprinted 2006, 2007

Routledge-Cavendish is an imprint of the Taylor & Francis Group

© The Contributors   2004

British Library Cataloguing in Publication Data
Student handbook of criminal justice and criminology
1 Criminology
I Muncie, John II Wilson, David
364

Library of Congress Cataloguing in Publication Data
Data available

ISBN 10: 1-85941-841-4
ISBN 13: 978-1-85941-841-3

Printed and bound in Great Britain by
MPG Books Ltd, Bodmin, Cornwall

CONTENTS

List of Contributors *vii*

Editors' Introduction *ix*

PART 1 APPROACHING CRIMINAL JUSTICE AND CRIMINOLOGY

1 **CONTEMPORARY CRIMINOLOGY, CRIME AND STRATEGIES OF CRIME CONTROL** 3

 John Muncie

2 **THE POLITICS AND PROCESSES OF CRIMINAL JUSTICE** 21

 David Wilson

3 **RESEARCHING CRIME AND CRIMINAL JUSTICE** 35

 Gemma Buckland and Emma Wincup

PART 2 UNRAVELLING CRIMINAL JUSTICE AND CRIMINOLOGY

4 **CRIMINAL JUSTICE, PUBLIC OPINION, FEAR AND POPULAR POLITICS** 51

 Lynn Hancock

5 **MEDIA REPRESENTATIONS OF CRIMINAL JUSTICE** 67

 Yvonne Jewkes

6 **MINORITIES, CRIME AND CRIMINAL JUSTICE** 81

 Nadia Joanne Britton

7 **GENDER, CRIME AND CRIMINAL JUSTICE** 93

 Sandra Walklate

8 **VICTIMS, CRIME AND CRIMINAL JUSTICE** 105

 Graham Wright and Jane Hill

9 **ISLAM AND CRIMINAL JUSTICE** 123

 Basia Spalek

10 **REGULATION AND CORPORATE CRIME** 133

 Dave Whyte

11 **GLOBALISATION, HUMAN RIGHTS AND INTERNATIONAL CRIMINAL COURTS** 153

 Wayne Morrison

PART 3 DELIVERING CRIMINAL JUSTICE

12 **CRIME PREVENTION, COMMUNITY SAFETY, AND CRIME AND DISORDER REDUCTION**   169
Gordon Hughes

13 **POLICE AND POLICING**   183
Douglas Sharp

14 **SENTENCING AND COURT PROCESSES**   203
Anthea Hucklesby

15 **YOUTH CRIME AND YOUTH JUSTICE**   221
Barry Goldson

16 **PROBATION AND COMMUNITY PENALTIES**   235
Mike Nash

17 **THINKING ABOUT IMPRISONMENT**   249
Joe Sim

18 **RESTORATIVE AND INFORMAL JUSTICE**   265
Gerry Johnstone

19 **CRIMINAL JUSTICE IN SCOTLAND**   279
Anne Reuss

Index   295

LIST OF CONTRIBUTORS

NADIA JOANNE BRITTON is Lecturer in Applied Sociology at Sheffield University.

GEMMA BUCKLAND is Senior Policy Officer at Rainier and was formerly Research Associate at Kent Criminal Justice Centre, University of Kent.

BARRY GOLDSON is Senior Lecturer and Director of Research at the Department of Sociology, Social Policy and Social Work Studies at the University of Liverpool.

LYNN HANCOCK is Lecturer in Criminology and Criminal Justice and member of the International Centre for Comparative Criminological Research at the Open University.

JANE HILL is Senior Lecturer in the Faculty of Law and Social Science at the University of Central England.

ANTHEA HUCKLESBY is Senior Lecturer in Criminal Justice in the School of Law at the University of Leeds.

GORDON HUGHES is Senior Lecturer in Social Policy and member of the International Centre for Comparative Criminological Research at the Open University.

YVONNE JEWKES is Senior Lecturer and Director of Undergraduate Studies in Criminology at the University of Hull.

GERRY JOHNSTONE is Professor of Law at the University of Hull.

WAYNE MORRISON is Reader in Law at Queen Mary College, University of London and Director of the External Laws Programme of the University of London. He is also a Barrister and Solicitor of the High Court of New Zealand.

JOHN MUNCIE is Professor of Criminology and Co-Director of the International Centre for Comparative Criminological Research at the Open University.

MIKE NASH is Principal Lecturer in Criminal Justice and Associate Head of the Institute of Criminal Justice Studies, University of Portsmouth.

ANNE REUSS is Lecturer in Sociology at the University of Abertay, Dundee.

DOUGLAS SHARP is Professor of Criminal Justice and Director of the Centre for Criminal Justice Policy and Research at the University of Central England in Birmingham.

JOE SIM is Professor of Criminology in the School of Social Science, Liverpool John Moores University.

BASIA SPALEK is Lecturer at the Institute of Applied Social Sciences, Birmingham University.

SANDRA WALKLATE is Professor of Sociology at Manchester Metropolitan University and Honorary Visiting Research Fellow at the University of Bangor.

DAVE WHYTE is Lecturer in Criminology in the Department of Law at the University of Stirling.

DAVID WILSON is Professor of Criminology at the University of Central England.

EMMA WINCUP is Lecturer in Criminology in the School of Social Policy, Sociology and Social Research at the University of Kent.

GRAHAM WRIGHT is Senior Lecturer in the Faculty of Law and Social Science at the University of Central England.

EDITORS' INTRODUCTION

This book is explicitly designed to meet the needs of undergraduate students of criminal justice and criminology as they embark on their studies. It is a one-stop-shop for all of those wishing to learn more about the rational for, the operation and the effectiveness of criminal justice in contemporary society. It also provides tutors and lecturers with an invaluable resource from which a criminal justice curricula might be proposed and developed. To this end we have invited 21 of the leading criminology and criminal justice teachers and researchers in the UK to identify and explore critical issues in the delivery of criminal justice. We have deliberately included but also moved beyond a more traditional exposition of the key agencies, such as the police, courts, probation and prisons, to also include cutting-edge discussion in areas stretching from community safety partnerships to restorative justice and from corporate regulation to international criminal courts.

Criminal justice is a particularly complex process through which the state decides what particular forms of behaviour are to be considered unacceptable and then proceeds through a series of stages – arrest, charge, prosecution, trial, sentence, appeal, punishment – in order to 'bring the guilty to justice'. However, this book is not simply concerned to describe these powers and procedures but is intent on encouraging critical reflection on how they are used and implemented. Criminal justice always appears as controversial. Should it be directed at the anti-social and the threatening or restrict itself to those behaviours strictly defined as criminal by law? Do the police need more powers of stop, search and arrest? Are the courts too soft? Why do miscarriages of justice occur? Should the remit of criminal law be fully extended to incorporate a wide range of social harms such as wilful pollution, environmental damage, malnutrition, medical negligence, state violence, corporate corruption and so on? Do we need a separate system of justice for children and young people? Is the system institutionally racist? Do we imprison too many people? Are community penalties effective? Should we be devoting more of our energy on preventing rather than punishing crime? These issues, in a variety of guises, are not simply academic concerns; they are the daily diet of much of our media.

This book provides the reader with a wide range of relevant facts, figures, theoretical positions, research findings and positioned arguments from which they will be better placed to recognise the layers and nuances of criminal justice debate and better informed in order to participate in such debates themselves.

Part 1, *Approaching Criminal Justice and Criminology,* outlines three essential starting points in the study of criminal justice and criminology. Chapter 1 illustrates the linkages between criminological theory and major criminal justice strategies. Criminal justice is never a simple matter of policy and practice. Any criminal justice strategy – whether based on retribution, deterrence, rehabilitation, prevention or tolerance – is grounded in and driven by a particular theoretical or philosophical position. It is the push and pull between these positions that makes criminal justice such a complex but intriguing area to explore. Chapter 2 outlines the work of the various agencies of the criminal justice system in England and Wales and makes the important point that criminal justice is as much a *process* driven by political priorities and decision making than a fully integrated *system* in which all agencies are acting in tandem. Chapter 3 asks the fundamental question of how we come to know about the workings of criminal justice. What insights can be drawn from criminological research? Again, the essentially political nature of knowledge production, dissemination and implementation is underlined.

The next series of chapters in Part 2, *Unravelling Criminal Justice and Criminology*, are all concerned to interrogate the nature of 'justice' produced by formal systems of crime control. They also highlight some of the routine presences, inbuilt biases and notable absences both in criminology and in the operation of criminal justice systems. Chapters 4 and 5 look at the impact that public opinion and the media might have on the formulation of criminal justice policies. It has been widely shown that whilst criminal justice operates within formal principles of equality, it is also capable of producing discriminatory outcomes. Chapter 6 examines evidence of the differential treatment of minorities as suspects, perpetrators, victims and agents. Chapter 7 explores the key issue of gender and why it is that both criminological research and the work of the criminal justice system are dominated by particular conceptions of men and masculinity. Chapter 8 examines the adequacy of both academic and state responses to victims and the nature of victimisation. Further, Chapter 9 focuses on how religious faith and identity influence the ways in which crime, victimisation and criminal justice disadvantage are experienced by British Muslim communities. The part concludes with an examination of serious crimes and offences that often appear to be ignored by criminal justice systems. Chapter 10 looks at corporate offending and explores how this evades the punitive gaze of criminal justice. Chapter 11 pursues a similar line of enquiry in respect of state sponsored atrocities, genocidal massacres and crimes against humanity. In particular it assesses the possibilities and limitations of reform in this area with regard to the establishment of an International Criminal Court.

Part 3, *Delivering Criminal Justice*, returns to the rather more familiar criminal justice terrain of examining the role of such core agencies as local authority crime reduction partnerships (Chapter 12), the police (Chapter 13), the courts (Chapter 14), youth justice and youth offending teams (Chapter 15), probation (Chapter 16) and prisons (Chapter 17) in responding to crime and disorder. Most of these agencies operate within dominant assumptions that the role of youth and criminal justice is primarily to punish the offender in accordance with the rule of law. In contrast, Chapter 18 explores the new possibilities opened up by an alternative vision of justice in which the principles of restoration, redress, reparation and harm minimisation are uppermost. The book concludes with a vital reminder that the criminal justice systems of the UK are not all of a piece. Criminal justice in Scotland has a unique history and an identity distinct from that of England, Wales and Northern Ireland.

As befits what is primarily an aid to teaching and learning, each chapter opens with a brief summary of the issues to be discussed, together with a list of key terms and closes with recommendations for further in-depth reading. In order to facilitate debate, each chapter also highlights some key issues and questions designed to form the basis of any ensuing seminar-based discussion. The aim throughout is to encourage continual critical reflection on the particular and partial ways in which 'justice' is defined and put into practice.

Finally our thanks go to all of the contributors to this volume. We have been extremely fortunate in persuading such a wide range of experts, each at the head of their respective fields, to join us in this project. Needless to say none of it would have come to fruition at all without their willingness to give so freely in their time and without their generosity in sharing their academic knowledge and teaching skills.

They have all made our job as editors less arduous than it might have been. Whilst this has been a truly collaborative effort, much of the administrative burden was carried by Barbara McCalla at the University of Central England. Our greatest thanks are reserved for her.

John Muncie
David Wilson
May 2004

PART 1
APPROACHING CRIMINAL JUSTICE AND CRIMINOLOGY

CHAPTER 1

CONTEMPORARY CRIMINOLOGY, CRIME AND STRATEGIES OF CRIME CONTROL[1]

John Muncie

SUMMARY

This introductory chapter is designed to illustrate the linkages between criminological theory and some major criminal justice strategies. It does so in order to make the important point that theory matters. Most criminal justice policies are, either implicitly or explicitly, justified by and grounded in particular theoretical formulations. In turn, every theory put forward to explain crime is premised upon a variety of beliefs about the nature of criminal behaviour (and human nature) and offers potential solutions. In certain circumstances, crime control policies and strategies change as theorising about crime changes. However, we should not expect any criminal justice system to operate solely through any one philosophical principle or theoretical position. Rather, we are more likely to encounter the simultaneous existence of a number of crime control strategies working alongside, or against, each other. Similarly, we should remain mindful that certain policies may be based on erroneous theoretical connections and are driven as much by political motivation as by theoretical purity or scientific assessments of 'what works'.

The chapter introduces and discusses some of the major philosophical positions on crime control and explores their theoretical underpinnings. For ease of reference it does so under the generic headings of punishment, treatment, prevention and tolerance:

Punishment
Classicism and deterrence
Conservatism, incapacitation and retribution

Treatment
Individual positivism and rehabilitation

Prevention
Sociological positivism, left realism and social reform
Rational choice theory and situational crime prevention

Tolerance
Social construct theory, diversion and non-intervention
Critical criminology, decarceration and abolition

From the outset, it is important to register that none of these positions is likely to be found in pure or uncontested form. Criminal justice is a far more complex and hybrid affair. In most criminological literature, criminal justice is viewed as a technical or

---

1   This chapter draws on a framework first developed by Eugene McLaughlin, Gordon Hughes and myself for the Open University undergraduate course, *Crime, Order and Social Control*. I am indebted to them for allowing me to rework our collective ideas in this form.

policy issue rather than as a philosophical or theoretical one. In contrast, this chapter is designed to reveal how a critical appreciation of crime control philosophies and strategies is a prerequisite for understanding, explaining and challenging the current bewildering array of public and private responses to crime.

KEY TERMS

Positivism; neo-conservatism; abolitionism; just deserts; labelling; proportionality; tolerance; punishment; treatment; rehabilitation; deterrence; retribution; restorative justice; relative deprivation; welfare; crime control; classicism; rational choice; determinism; prevention.

PUNISHMENT

There would seem to be a near universal human belief that society has the right to react against those who transgress its behavioural borderlines. The 'common sense' response seems to be castigation and punishment. Punishment, however, has no rigid boundaries. Lacey (1988: 15) warns us that:

> There is no one neat, polished final justification for punishment: there are only arguments for and against it, which apply differently not only within different political systems but also according to the social and economic conditions holding in different societies in which the institutions exist.

Nevertheless, three essential ideas seem to be present in most modern definitions of punishment:

- It is deliberately administered by state officials on an individual who is legally defined as being subject to the laws of that state.
- Because it involves intentional deprivation and suffering, it requires some *normative justification* that the pain/deprivation/suffering is warranted.
- Its primary purpose is usually represented as being the instrumental one of reducing or containing rates of criminal behaviour.

The dominant philosophical justifications for punishment are typically to be found in incapacitation, retribution, just deserts and deterrence.

Classicism and deterrence

Understanding crime and its causes

A deterrent model of crime control was first formulated by the 18th century classical school of criminology. According to the classical school, crime is rational, self-interested and freely chosen behaviour. Human behaviour is shaped by the pursuit of maximum advantage, pleasure and happiness and the avoidance of pain, unhappiness and costs. Each individual can decide what is 'pain' or 'pleasure'. In line with a social contract theory of society, individuals *rationally determine* what is in their own *self-interest* and act accordingly. For classical criminology, the result of individuals seeking to satisfy their *instrumental* or *expressive* desires can impinge on the interests and, more importantly, the rights of others. It thus developed the utilitarian principle of 'the greatest happiness of the greatest number'. The primary purpose of criminal law is to protect the well-being of the community, not to punish offenders. Laws protect the community when they deter the commission of crime and minimise the severity of crimes committed. Hence, a well-ordered state would construct a criminal justice system that would persuade people that law-abiding behaviour was in their best interests. From these premises came the notion of psychological hedonism – we calculate pleasures and pains in advance of action and regulate our conduct by the results of such calculations. As a result, classicism constructs a penal philosophy based on the precise calculations of rational people (Beccaria, 1764).

Policy implications

The logic of classicism is that the individual who has committed a crime will find the punishment so unpleasant that the offence will not be repeated. In the long run, the individual's punishment serves a general deterrence. As a result, classicism looks to the prevention of *future* crime.

Deterrence is based on the premise of affording rational, self-interested individuals good reasons not to commit crimes. Since the punishment must be one that can be calculated, it must be the same for all individuals, regardless of age, mentality, social status or gender. It is a theory premised on equal treatment for all. Individual differences stemming from personal experiences or social factors are denied or ignored. It is the act that should be judged, not the individual. Clemency, pardons and mitigating circumstances are excluded. To do otherwise would violate the equal rights of all individuals. The punishment should fit the crime, not the individual (Roshier, 1989):

- the pain of possible punishment must exceed the potential pleasure of committing an offence;
- the less certain the punishment for a given offence, the more severe it should be; conversely, the more certain the punishment, the less severe it should be;
- punishment should avoid the evils of over- and under-punishing offences;
- punishment should be *public, prompt* and *certain* rather than necessarily severe. Punishment should publicly symbolise the offence, so that if a crime is committed the offender can be sure that punishment will follow; and
- preventing future crime is more significant than punishing past offences. Prevention requires that laws should be clear, simple and universally supported.

Such principles had a considerable impact on the reformation of the criminal justice system across Europe and the USA in the latter half of the 18th century and they continue to do so largely in the form of neo-conservative and rational choice theories (see below). Deterrence assumes two major forms, both of which are designed to make it clear that crime does not pay. General deterrence is aimed at controlling entire populations, whilst individual deterrence is targeted at the known offender. Its ultimate sanction is the death penalty. However, legislators have also found that insistence on the principle of strict proportionality could not be sustained for all. Groups such as children may not be able to fully calculate the 'pleasures and pains' of their actions and should therefore be excluded from the full rigours of the law. Neo-classical principles of punishment, although retaining the core doctrine of free will, came to acknowledge that proportionality should be adjusted to take account of individual circumstances. In this sense neo-classicism paved the way for positivist discourses about the causes of crime and the *treatment* of offenders (see below).

Conservatism, incapacitation and retribution

Understanding crime and its causes

Traditionally, conservatism has typically regarded crime as a violation or disturbance of the divine or moral order. It also rests primarily on the doctrines of free will and rational action. Like classicism, it assumes that human beings are free to choose between alternative actions and therefore deliberate wrongdoing should be requited by appropriate penalties. Contemporary conservative (or what has been termed neo-conservative) theorising on crime draws on this heritage but is also heavily informed by notions of moral culture, moral decline and parental permissiveness. Amongst its formative ideas are the following propositions:

- The search for the causes of crime in terms of predisposing social factors (deprivation, unemployment, poverty) is misguided because improvements in social conditions in the 1950s and 1960s did not herald a decrease in crime, but rather an increase (Wilson, 1975).

- Crime, essentially, has biological roots which are not amenable to individual treatment or social engineering. Wicked people exist; nothing avails but to set them apart from the innocent (Wilson, 1975). Thus, it is impractical to try and 'cure' crime (Wilson and Herrnstein, 1986).

- Individuals commit crime through rational choice. Lack of self-control and a lack of individual responsibility are at the root of all criminal responsibility (Gottfredson and Hirschi, 1990).

- Crime is a symptom of declining moral standards epitomised by 1960s permissiveness, welfare dependence, liberal methods of child-rearing, family breakdown, illegitimacy, single parenting and the lack of effective means of discipline. Collectively, these factors have been instrumental in the development of a dependent, demoralised and dangerous 'underclass' (Murray, 1990).

Neo-conservatism stresses the need for strong government and social authoritarianism in order to create a disciplined and hierarchical society in which individual needs are subordinate to those of the 'nation'. For neo-conservatives, most forms of mitigation act simply to absolve individuals of responsibility for their actions and offer a 'culture of excuses' for criminality. James Q Wilson (1975: 41–42), for example, argues that criminality is accounted for by the existence of rationally calculating 'lower class' people who attach little importance to the opinion of others, are preoccupied with the daily struggle for survival and are 'inclined to uninhibited, expressive conduct'. But in a later work, *Crime and Human Nature* (1986), he also forwards a bio-social explanation of behaviour. 'Personality traits', such as impulsiveness and lack of regard for others, are related to biological predispositions and cited as key factors in criminality, particularly when these traits are found in 'discordant families'. He continues to argue that criminality rests on choice – but it is a choice that is mediated by a genetic ability to develop a conscience. The criminal, as described by Wilson and Herrnstein (1986: 61), is a person without a conscience, but who is capable of reacting to a variety of influences in which 'the larger the ratio of the rewards (material and non-material) of non-crime to the rewards (material and non material) of crime, the weaker the tendency to commit crimes'. For Gottfredson and Hirschi (1994), the key factor underlying criminal behaviour is lack of self-control. Crime may not be an automatic consequence of low self-control, but is viewed as its primary distinguishing feature. In turn, self-control derives from effective socialisation. Thus, the major 'causes' of low self-control, it is argued, are ineffective child-rearing, poor parental supervision and discipline, working mothers and broken families: in short, a lack of self-control in the home.

In these ways, neo-conservatives contend that crime cannot be eliminated; it can only be reduced to socially acceptable levels. The state should target its efforts on repeat offenders and on specific high-crime neighbourhoods. Successful crime control requires tough and swift punishment for the targeted 'criminal class', with retribution and selective incapacitation as the most potent weapons that the state has available.

Policy implications

Incapacitation assumes that offenders will commit a certain number of crimes over a given time if they remain in society and that a substantial reduction in the total crime rate can be achieved through incarceration. This is the only theory of crime control, according to its supporters, that manifestly works. During the 1980s and 1990s, incapacitation became the dominant rationale particularly for the penal system in the United States. Right-wing commentators argued that 'prison works' because imprisoned criminals cannot victimise law-abiding citizens, and people who have been victims of crime have had the source of their fears removed from society. 'Tough on the criminal' policies have inspired habitual offender laws, such as 'three strikes and you are out', which permit courts to impose indefinite detention for repeated, however minor, offences. It has also been argued that life in prison should be made as stark as possible through establishing boot camps, eliminating privileges and by making prisoners work in chain gangs. In tandem, incapacitation has resulted in a massive private prison building programme in the United States and provided justification for the reintroduction of the death penalty (Zimring and Hawkins, 1995).

Retribution features prominently in Western notions of criminal justice because it is viewed as the most fundamental human response to crime and deviance. It is 'natural' to resent and to retaliate against any harm done or attempted against ourselves or against those with whom we empathise. Such ideas are deeply ingrained in many theological texts, such as the *lex talionis*, the Mosaic doctrine expressed in Exodus 21: 23–25, 'and if any mischief follows, then thou shalt give life for life, eye for eye, tooth for tooth, hand for hand, foot for foot, burning for burning, wound for wound, stripe for stripe'. Punishing the sinner is a positive moral duty. The moral order can only be restored or the violation atoned for by inflicting evil (generally pain) upon the guilty.

Retribution concentrates on the detection and sanctioning of the criminal act that has occurred. Unlike classicism, it is not interested in the future conduct of offenders or in crime prevention. An individual who deliberately violates the rights of others should and must be punished. The act of punishment restores the moral order that was breached by the wrongdoing. If an individual has been found guilty of a crime, then not only does the guilt make it possible to punish that individual, it makes it necessary to do so.

This focus disentangles the criminal justice system from the world of welfare and social problems. The system is rationalised by concentrating on its core task – identifying and removing from circulation those individuals whose continuing freedom threatens public safety and morality.

TREATMENT

In contrast to philosophies of punishment, a treatment model assumes that behaviour is determined by factors outside of the individual's control. Some theorists have focused on biological and psychological factors, thus locating the sources of crime primarily *within* the individual and bringing to the fore questions of individual pathology. This approach can be described as individual positivism. Other theorists have argued that more insights could be gained by studying the social context external to individuals; thus, crime is more a matter of social pathology. The latter can be described as sociological positivism. Of key importance remains the conviction that, once the aberrant condition can be identified, it can be treated and the problem resolved.

Individual positivism and rehabilitation

Understanding crime and its causes

The key features of positivism are:

- the assumption that 'criminality' is different to 'normality' and indicative of various *pathological states*;
- the abandonment of rationality as a causal factor;
- the attempt to establish 'cause and effect' relations scientifically and thus to increase the ability to *predict* criminality (when particular criminogenic factors can be identified);
- the assumption that, as criminals are abnormal, their behaviour is in violation of some widely held *consensus* in the rest of society;
- the *treatment* of causes with the ultimate goal of eliminating anti-social behaviour. As behaviour is involuntary and not a matter of choice for the offender, punitive responses are misplaced.

Positivism is the antithesis of classicism and conservatism. Positivists argue that it is possible to apply the rationale of experimental scientific investigation (observation, description, measurement) to uncover the causes of crime (biological, psychological, sociological) and to discover new systems of prevention and treatment to protect society from criminality. Positivism denies the connection between guilt, responsibility and just deserts through asserting the *scientific* principle of determinism rather than the *metaphysical* idea of free will. Human beings, including criminals, do not act of their own free will but are compelled to act by powerful internal or external forces and by circumstances beyond their control. If behaviour is the result of antecedent causes, then the individual cannot be held responsible for his or her actions. This rules out retribution, incapacitation and deterrent justifications in favour of rehabilitation.

Policy implications

For individual positivists, *treatment* of the criminal, rather than punishment, should be the aim of the criminal justice system. Treatment programmes, by addressing specific needs and problems, can prevent people from reoffending. Those who cannot be reformed and pose a danger to society should be segregated. Instead of the punishment fitting the crime, the treatment needs to match the individual offender. Positivism favours indeterminate measures on the grounds that it is reckless to decide at the moment of sentencing how long an offender needs to be detained, since this will depend on how responsive that person is to the treatment programme.

This shift to more individualised forms of penality first occurred in Britain in the late 19th century and the early decades of the 20th century. It is in this period that we find the origins of rehabilitation – a penal welfare model of crime control, premised upon ideas of determinism, individualism and pathology (Garland, 1985). A series of competing discourses and types of professional expertise – psychiatric, medical, social work, legal – now had a voice in judicial proceedings. This marked a radical departure from ideas of 'criminal justice', 'crime control' and 'full criminal responsibility' and a move towards a focus on welfare and therapeutic treatment to suit each individual. Cornish and Clarke (1983) have argued that it would be hard to overstate the influence of the medico-psychological model, particularly in the post-war period. A generation of social workers and probation officers were taught that the major determinants of delinquent behaviour were located firmly within the individual and, in particular, within emotional disturbances resulting from unsatisfactory human relationships.

However, by the late 1960s, doubts, which had never been totally assuaged throughout the period of rehabilitation's dominance, were voiced by critics on both the right and left. Cohen (1985) drew attention to the abuses that might occur in the development of forms of social control under the guise of 'benevolent treatment'; that a lack of due process and proportionality violated individual rights; and that, by appearing to be benign, recourse to criminal justice was encouraged. In other words, rehabilitation also involves punishment (Hudson, 1996). Further critique of rehabilitation came from evaluations which suggested that different types of treatment made little or no difference to the subsequent reconviction rates of offenders. The most widely quoted study was that of Martinson (1974: 25) who, after analysing 231 studies of particular treatment programmes in the United States, argued that 'with few and isolated exceptions, the rehabilitative efforts that have been reported so far have had no appreciable effect on recidivism'. The often-cited conclusion drawn from this study was that 'nothing works'.

In the wake of such criticisms, a 'modern retribution' or 'just deserts' model re-emerged. Von Hirsch (1976), for example, argued that rehabilitation encouraged excessive intervention and denied offenders their due rights. He advocated the reinstatement of the following (neo-classical) concepts at the centre of contemporary penal philosophy:

- proportionality of punishment to crime, or the offender is handed a sentence that is in accordance with what the act deserves;
- determinacy of sentencing and thus an end to indeterminate, treatment-oriented sentences;
- an end to judicial, professional and administrative discretion;
- an end to disparity in sentencing;
- equity and protection of rights through due process;
- the predication of penal philosophy on justice and not control.

Above all, in order to reinstate 'justice', the considerable bank of discretionary powers built up by the state needed to be rolled back.

The responses in the UK and the United States to the acceptance of the idea that 'nothing works' were varied. Certain practitioners and policy-makers have attempted to keep alive a modified rehabilitative ideal. McMahon (1992) has argued that community-based correctional programs should be expanded, not simply because they are just as effective as institutional ones, but because they are also less costly and more humane. Cullen and Gilbert (1982) contend that, at the very least, rehabilitation forces the state to recognise that it has an obligation to care for the offender's welfare and needs. Other defenders of rehabilitation have argued that, rather than being the defining rationale for the system, treatment efforts should be restricted to specific types of offenders such as young offenders and sex offenders. Indeed, rehabilitation and treatment programmes are now much more focused on 'what works' and on 'offender accountability' to ensure that they can withstand external critique. Vennard and Hedderman's (1998) review of contemporary risk assessment and risk management strategies suggests that successful programmes are those which:

- attempt a risk classification and target more intensive programmes at high risk offenders;
- target criminogenic needs, ie those factors which contribute directly to criminal behaviour, eg anti-social attitudes, drug dependency, low level of education and skills, poor cognitive and interpersonal skills;
- have high programme integrity;
- match teaching methods to offenders' learning skills;
- use a skills-based intervention which helps to improve problem-solving and social interaction, but which also addresses and challenges the attitudes, values and beliefs which support offending behaviour;
- are community based.

PREVENTION

The stated goal of crime prevention underlies numerous divergent crime control policies from deterrence to community action. However, by the 1980s, two strategies emerged which placed prevention at the centre of their respective agendas. *Situational crime prevention* is directed at designing out the opportunities for the commission of crime. *Social crime prevention* invokes elements of sociological positivism in its insistence that effective crime control should be directed at the social causes of crime and implemented through localised inter-agency crime reduction partnerships

Sociological positivism, left realism and social reform

Understanding crime and its causes

It has long been proposed that, as rates of crime are both regular and predictable, the causes of criminal behaviour must be generated by something more than purely individual motivation. Compared to individual positivism, sociological theories appear less interested in crime as a specific pattern of behaviour and more in *probabilistic* accounts of variations in crime rates given particular social, geographical and economic circumstances. They focus on general patterns of criminality rather than on individual motivations. Nevertheless, the concern remains to isolate key causal variables, such as lack of opportunity, thwarted aspirations, poverty, unemployment, social disadvantage and relative deprivation, to discover the extent to which such conditions *determine* rates of criminality. Numerous sociological theories have been directed at this task. In the inter-war period, the most notable were Merton's strain theory, which proposed that crime was the result of high aspirations being thwarted by the denial of opportunity, and Shaw and McKay's insight that criminality was dependent on the degree of community cohesion (Lilly et al, 1989: 47–81; Einstadter and Henry, 1995: 121–69). In the 1980s, left realism set out its crime control stall against neo-conservatives (and also abolitionists – see below) by arguing that the structural factors that give rise to offending – especially relative deprivation – must be acknowledged and confronted (Lea and Young, 1984). For left realists, 'good jobs with a discernible future, housing estates of which tenants can be proud, community facilities which enhance a sense of cohesion and belonging, a reduction in unfair income inequalities, all create a society which is more cohesive and less criminogenic' (Young, 1994: 115–16). It is not absolute deprivation and poverty, but the perception that resources are distributed in an unfair manner that causes crime.

Policy implications

Proponents of this approach would claim that little can be achieved to change individual behaviour through rehabilitation if the offender is simultaneously returned to the same social and economic circumstances that 'produced' his or her initial criminality. The focus then is on challenging the processes that cement disadvantage. The 1960s American project 'mobilisation for youth' (MFY), for example, was based directly on Cloward and Ohlin's (1960) opportunity theory and the assumed link between delinquency and lack of opportunities for lower class young people. The main aim of MFY was to expand job opportunities. However, to achieve such an objective it was also drawn to advocating community action to improve housing, welfare rights and fair rents: strategies which soon brought it into conflict with established power structures. Subsequent US criminal justice policy soon adopted rather less ambitious goals, for example, of rebuilding family ties and achieving reintegration through education and training.

Nevertheless, North American left realists such as Elliot Currie (1985; 1998) continue to advocate policies that would precipitate a move from a neo-liberal market society to what he describes as a 'sustaining society'. He advocates a number of both macro policies, based on full employment policies and a concerted strategy for reducing the extremes of social and economic inequality, and micro programmes, based on comprehensive child and family support. In short, an effective crime control strategy lies outside of the criminal justice system.

British left realists have been less forthcoming on the specific macro strategies they would use to tackle the roots of crime, in part to ensure that they cannot be accused of 'being soft on crime' (Matthews and Young, 1992). Typically, they have supported a variety of local authority-based policies based on:

- broad notions of community safety rather than simply crime prevention;
- efforts on the part of families, schools and social services to mobilise informal social controls;
- multi-agency partnerships and the co-ordination of responses by local authorities;
- locally based victimisation surveys to obtain a more accurate estimate of the true extent of crime and to deepen and democratise crime control strategies.

In the 1990s, some of this reasoning seemed to permeate criminal justice policy in England and Wales to the extent that New Labour could claim that its welfare to work and New Deal policies were driven as much by an anti-crime as an economic rationale. The problem remains though of slippage in the drive to recognise and implement institutional change. Such programmes are just as likely to degenerate into readings of family failure or of irresponsible parenting with the concomitant policy response being informed by the rather more neo-conservative notions of family and individual pathology.

Rational choice theory and situational crime prevention

Understanding crime and its causes

Policy-makers involved in crime control were faced with a considerable problem in the 1970s – a time when the rising crime rate was becoming a major political issue. Existing policies of rehabilitation and deterrence were challenged on the following lines:

- Retribution had nothing practical to offer the crime controller.
- There was no evidence to show that incapacitation had a significant effect on the crime rate (a reduction in the crime rate of just 1 per cent would require a 25 per cent increase in the prison population).
- Improvements in policing or increases in police resources had no real effect on the crime rate.
- Prevention through social reforms might be desirable but was not politically feasible.
- Despite the attempts of psychologists to refashion rehabilitation, too much effort had already been expended on unproductive attempts to change the criminal disposition of offenders.

Home Office researchers began to look at other pieces of social and psychological research for clues to what might work, including:

- ecological studies that concentrated on the places where crimes occur and the social and physical features of where offenders live;

- crime-specific research that analysed the spatial and temporal distribution of burglary, shoplifting or robbery;

- 'defensible space' theorising which asserted that good architectural design can engender a sense of territoriality among residents and greater opportunities for surveillance;

- theories of 'natural' victims which argued that targets (person and property) were more likely to be victimised when they were alluring (for whatever reason), not well-guarded and frequently exposed to potential offenders.

The focus on these issues moved attention towards the *circumstances* surrounding the commission of different criminal acts rather than attempting to deal with offenders after the offence. Underpinning this administrative criminology was rational choice theory.

Rational choice theory is based on the premise that most offenders are reasoning and normal, rather than pathological. Crime is understood as rational action performed by ordinary people (as in conservatism and classicism) but also by people acting under particular pressures and exposed to specific opportunities and situational inducements. Crime rates have increased in advanced industrial societies because opportunities have increased. For a crime to occur, two events must coincide: the opportunity for the commission of the criminal act must present itself; and the individual must decide that the gains to be had from taking the opportunity outweigh both the chances of being caught and the penalty should he or she be apprehended (Clarke, 1980; Felson, 1997).

Policy implications

It follows that society can successfully prevent crime by increasing the risks of crime, reducing the rewards of crime and removing the excuses for crime. Typically this is achieved through target hardening and surveillance. By the late 20th century, a range of surveillance techniques, such as CCTV and biometric scanning devices (smart cards, fingerprinting, iris scans, hand geometry scans, voice recognition, DNA testing and digitised facial recognition), had been removed from the realm of science fiction and adopted within the criminal justice system. The potential for national and international systems of intimate monitoring to classify individuals into appropriate spaces and times where they 'belong' rapidly became realised. By the mid-1990s, the UK had the highest penetration of CCTV cameras in the world. Pictorial databases of groups such as hooligans, political demonstrators, bank robbers, suspected illegal immigrants and environmental campaigners were established. Gated residential communities, privately policed shopping malls and fortified enclaves of private space have become commonplace.

Situational crime prevention approaches also have implications for how policing should be conceptualised. Wilson and Kelling (1982) used the image of 'broken windows' to explain how neighbourhoods descend into incivility, disorder and criminality if attention is not paid to their maintenance. Similarly, petty disorderly acts, which are not necessarily breaches of the criminal law, trigger a chain reaction that undermines community safety and pave the way for serious criminality. Much of this 'zero tolerance' logic underpins the drive to identify and combat anti-social behaviour and disorder (as well as crime) that has been relentlessly pursued since the passing of the 1998 Crime and Disorder Act in England and Wales.

TOLERANCE

Tolerance stands in antithesis to all approaches we have so far encountered in that it implies that social interventions of whatever form can be far more damaging than non-intervention or limited and less formal modes of intervention. Most social problems are not amenable to criminal justice definition and processing. There may be other, more effective, means to achieve conflict resolution.

Social construct theory, diversion and non-intervention

Understanding crime and its causes

Social construct theory emphasises the flexibility of individual responses to social situations. Social order is perceived as a set of fluid relationships embracing conflict and disagreement, as well as co-operation and consensus. A key concern is with understanding 'criminalisation', the process by which certain people and forms of behaviour are designated 'criminal'. Rather than viewing behaviour as determined by 'external' forces, social construct theory is more concerned with questions of voluntarism, negotiation and the variability of meaning in everyday life. Crime and deviance are not viewed as pathological acts that violate consensual norms, but rather as things that are created in the *process* of social interaction. Rather than asking behavioural questions such as 'who is deviant?', 'why do they do it?' and 'how might they best be controlled?', construct theory concentrates on definitional questions such as 'why are some behaviours and not others defined as deviant?', 'why are some people rather than others labelled as deviant?', 'who has the power to define another as deviant?', 'how does that person react to this designation?', and 'how are deviant roles subsequently adopted and played out?'.

Adopting this anti-positivist stance, an emergent *labelling* perspective of the 1960s argued that notions of crime and deviance will be forever problematic because deviance only arises through the imposition of socio-cultural judgments on others' behaviour, and such judgments are not universal but reflective of changing social conditions (Becker, 1962). In other words, deviance can never be an absolutely known fact because its existence depends on a series of transactions between rule-makers and rule-violators. Lemert (1967), for example, emphasises that social control is not simply a response to deviant activity but plays an active and propelling role in the creation and promotion of deviance. *Social control causes deviancy*. It is the labelling of individuals as deviant which 'causes' deviance since, in the process of being labelled, people are isolated, categorised negatively, stamped as morally inferior or unfit, and thus undergo a significant transformation of status and identity. A number of other key propositions follow:

- No act is intrinsically criminal.

- Criminal laws are created as a result of the activities of moral entrepreneurs leading moral crusades.
- Criminal definitions are enforced in the interests of powerful groups.
- An individual does not become a criminal by violation of the law but by the designation of criminality by the authorities.
- Because everyone conforms and deviates, individuals should not be separated into 'criminals' and 'non-criminals'.
- The act of 'getting caught' begins the labelling process.
- Age, socio-economic class, race and gender are the major offender characteristics that establish patterns of differential justice decision-making.

Policy implications

The phrase 'radical non-intervention' is widely attributed to Edwin Schur (1973). It is the logical policy implication of a labelling approach to understanding crime and deviance. If, as labelling theorists suggested, social reaction does not prevent offending but establishes deviant identities and careers, then the reach of state intervention should be reduced. In particular, it was argued that a range of 'victimless crimes' – drug use, gambling, juvenile status offences (truancy, promiscuity), pornography and so on – should be removed from the remit of criminal law. Criminalising drug users, for instance, not only creates a new class of criminals, but may also drive them to commit further offences to support their habits, as well as encouraging the development of organised crime and law enforcement corruption and redirecting resources away from health and treatment programmes. In short, the removal of many troubling behaviours from criminal law sanction has the potential to be a highly effective measure of crime reduction.

Radical non-intervention (and the labelling approach in general) grew in popularity during the 1960s and had a profound impact on social policy (Empey, 1982). A series of measures – decriminalisation, diversion and deinstitutionalisation – designed to limit the extent of the state's intrusion into offenders' lives were implemented to varying degrees and with varying success in most Western criminal justice systems. For example, in the Labour Party's (1964) report, *Crime: A Challenge to Us All*, it was argued that, although all children misbehave, it is only working class children that are likely to come to the attention of the authorities. It went on to argue that no child in early adolescence should face criminal proceedings, that criminal proceedings were unnecessary where the offence was trivial, and that serious offences indicated the child's need for skilled help and guidance. Hence the report proposed:

- *decriminalisation* by redefining the legitimate jurisdiction of the criminal court;
- *de-institutionalisation* by diversion away from the formal criminal justice system;
- *informality* in dealing with the problem overall; and
- the *de-stigmatisation* of working class children.

Indeed, such strategies were employed to a remarkable effect, particularly in the youth justice system during the 1980s which witnessed dramatic falls in the numbers being sent to court and to custody. They also continue to have a presence in some restorative justice initiatives, such as the constructive 'reintegrative shaming' involved in various forms of family group conferences and healing or sentencing circles that have emerged since the 1980s as alternatives to formal court processes (Braithwaite, 1989; Johnstone, 2002; McLaughlin et al, 2003).

Critical criminology, decarceration and abolition

Understanding crime and its causes

Critical and some feminist criminologies argue that formal criminal justice processes are less a solution, and more part of the problem to be explained. They contend that:

- economic policies lead to immiseration and force people to consider turning to crime as a viable survival strategy;
- criminalisation strategies are class, race and gender control strategies that are consciously used to depoliticise political resistance and to control economically and politically marginalised neighbourhoods and groups;
- moral panics about crime being out of control are used to deflect attention away from inherent structural conflicts;
- orthodox crime control strategies are incapable of tackling the crimes of the powerful and state crimes;
- legal categories which are claimed to be gender neutral are riven with male assumptions of what constitutes normal or reasonable behaviour.

Above all, it has been argued that crime control has grown into an industry, controlled by multi-national interests, which is more committed to developing, not reducing, its core business (Christie, 2000). Certain critical criminologists, particularly those in Northern Europe, have maintained that orthodox thinking about crime, criminality and crime control is fundamentally flawed because the harms associated with social life cannot, and should not, be regulated by the criminal justice system. Abolitionists remind us that the events and behaviours that are criminalised have nothing in common, other than the fact that they have been usurped by the criminal justice system. 'Crime' has no ontological reality independent of the definitional processes of the criminal justice system. Crime is not the object but the product of crime control philosophies and institutions (Hulsman, 1986). Social problems, conflicts, harms and antagonisms are an inevitable part of everyday life and their ownership is lost if they are delegated to professionals and specialists promising to provide 'solutions'. When professionals intervene, the essence of social problems and conflicts is effectively stolen from individuals and communities and re-presented in forms that only aid their perpetuation (Christie, 1977). As such, the criminal justice system is overwhelmingly counter-productive in relation to its objectives. It does not function according to the claims made by it, whether these be rehabilitation, retribution, deterrence or prevention. It does not attend to the needs of real people because it causes unnecessary suffering and 'steals' the conflict, offering little influence to those directly involved. It cannot protect people from being victimised and cannot control crime. Overall, it is not only unjust and ineffective but also counter-productive.

Policy implications

Abolitionists argue that alternatives can be found. First, the vocabulary of the traditional system, especially the concepts of crime and criminality, should be abolished. This would in turn undermine other concepts such as 'seriousness', 'dangerousness', 'evil', 'good', 'punishment' and 'guilt' as well as the philosophical premises of retribution, deterrence and rehabilitation. Abolitionists argue that we would do better to start with notions of negligence and accidents rather than intent and responsibility. 'Crimes' should be reclassified for what they really are: conflicts, troubles, disputes, problems and harms. Other bodies of law – economic, administrative, environmental, health, labour – rather than criminal law could be drawn on to resolve legal disputes. Abolition of the apparatuses of the criminal justice system would eliminate the problems specifically generated by the system, such as the fabrication of guilt, the stigmatising of prisoners, the marginalisation and exclusion of certain powerless groups, institutionalised discrimination, the dramatisation of conflicts by the mass media, and the reproduction and perpetuation of violence. Abolitionists argue that the agencies of the criminal justice system have a vested interest in making sure that crime remains out of control. Abolition of these expensive and ineffective agencies would also revitalise society by allowing other forms of conflict resolution – redress, restorative justice, peace-making and community justice – to be imagined and properly resourced. Here, the emphasis is not on punishment or legal processes but on opening up communication between offender, victim and community such that the 'dispute' is resolved to everyone's satisfaction. The crucial point for abolitionism is that inclusionary rather than exclusionary means should be utilised to respond to harmful behaviours (Hudson, 1996: 142–45).

Abolitionism continually attempts to transcend the social and political constructions of crime and organisational categorisations of the criminal justice system. Mathiesen (1974), for example, argues that abolitionists need a sophisticated political strategy to take account of the dynamics of change and continuity. He argues that reformers must always adopt a political strategy of 'the unfinished' – they must refuse to make 'the choice' and work with the concept of 'becoming'. The work of the abolitionist is by definition an unfinished process, as there will always be more to be abolished.

CONCLUSION

We have encountered a remarkable diversity and lack of consensus, not only on what constitutes crime, but also on how it might be controlled. There is thus a plurality of competing theories of crime control, with 'old' philosophies often running parallel with more recent ones. Furthermore, research studies on specific localities and programmes illustrate the tension between detailed empirical investigation of crime control and grand theoretical frameworks. Many of the perspectives are in constant dialogue (if not agreement) with each other, and it is possible to find elements of certain positions in others. One point above all unites them: they are all in their own way concerned with identifying the conditions, circumstances and institutional and cultural arrangements that will secure social order. Some understanding of the contradictory positions of each of these strategies is necessary if we are to begin to understand contemporary criminal justice systems (such as that associated with New Labour) that depend less on any one philosophically grounded and theoretically defensible position and more on a pragmatic 'pick and mix' of what is considered appropriate (politically, economically, electorally) at any given time (Muncie, 2000).

SEMINAR DISCUSSION TOPICS

- What advantages does a rehabilitative strategy of crime control hold over that of deterrence?
- Account for the enduring popular support for retribution and the death penalty.
- Why has abolitionism been largely ignored by policy-makers?
- Does New Labour have a theoretically consistent criminal justice policy?

KEY READINGS

Criminological Theory: Context and Consequences by Lilly, Cullen and Ball (Sage, 1989) and *Criminological Theory: An Analysis of its Underlying Assumptions* by Einstadter and Henry (Harcourt Brace, 1995) probably remain the most thorough attempts to 'relate theory to practice' and provide a more sophisticated analysis than has been possible here. Jock Young's chapter 'Thinking seriously about crime' in the edited collection by Fitzgerald, McLennan and Pawson, *Crime and Society* (Routledge, 1981) also sets out a useful framework for relating theory and policy. All of these deserve reading, as do the multiple entries on theory and practice briefly outlined in the *Sage Dictionary of Criminology*, edited by McLaughlin and Muncie (Sage, 2001). Those wishing to move beyond this brief introduction should consult *Understanding Justice* by Barbara Hudson (Open University Press, 1996; 2nd edn 2003).

REFERENCES

Beccaria, C (1764, reprinted 1963) *On Crimes and Punishments*, New York: Bobbs-Merrill.

Becker, H (1962) *Outsiders: Studies in the Sociology of Deviance*, New York: Free Press.

Braithwaite, J (1989) *Crime, Shame and Reintegration*, Cambridge: CUP.

Christie, N (1977) 'Conflicts as property', *British Journal of Criminology*, vol 17(1) pp 1–15.

Christie, N (2000) *Crime Control as Industry*, London: Routledge.

Clarke, RVG (1980) '"Situational" crime prevention: theory and practice', *British Journal of Criminology*, vol 20(2), pp 136–47.

Cloward, R and Ohlin, L (1960) *Delinquency and Opportunity*, London: Routledge.

Cohen, S (1985) *Visions of Social Control*, Cambridge: Polity.

Cornish, DB and Clarke, RVG (1983) *Crime Control in Britain: A Review of Policy Research*, Albany, NJ: SUNY Press.

Cullen, FT and Gilbert, KE (1982) *Reaffirming Rehabilitation*, Cincinnati, OH: Anderson.

Currie, E (1985) *Confronting Crime: An American Challenge*, New York: Pantheon.

Currie, E (1998) *Crime and Punishment in America*, New York: Henry Holt and Co.

De Haan, W (1990) *The Politics of Redress*, London: Unwin Hyman.

Einstadter, W and Henry, S (1995) *Criminological Theory: An Analysis of its Underlying Assumptions*, Fort Worth, TX: Harcourt Brace.

Empey, La Mar T (1982) *American Delinquency: Its Meaning and Construction*, 2nd edn, Chicago: Dorsey Press.

Felson, M (1997) *Crime and Everyday Life*, 2nd edn, Thousand Oaks, CA: Pine Forge Press.

Garland, D (1985) *Punishment and Welfare*, Aldershot: Gower.

Gottfredson, M and Hirschi, T (1990) *A General Theory of Crime*, Stanford, CA: Stanford University Press.

Hudson, B (1996) *Understanding Justice*, Buckingham: Open University Press.

Hulsman, LHC (1986) 'Critical criminology and the concept of crime', *Contemporary Crises*, vol 10(1), pp 63–80.

Johnstone, G (2002) *Restorative Justice: Ideas, Values and Debates*, Cullompton: Willan.

Labour Party (1964) *Crime: A Challenge to Us All*, London: Labour Party.

Lacey, M (1988) *State Punishment: Political Principles and Community Values*, London: Routledge and Kegan Paul.

Lea, J and Young, J (1984) *What is to be Done About Law and Order?*, Harmondsworth: Penguin.

Lemert, E (1967) *Human Deviance, Social Problems and Social Control*, Englewood Cliffs, NJ: Prentice Hall.

Lilly, R, Cullen, F and Ball, R (1989) *Criminological Theory: Context and Consequences*, London: Sage.

McLaughlin, E and Muncie, J (eds) (2001) *The Sage Dictionary of Criminology*, London: Sage.

McLaughlin, E, Fergusson, R, Hughes, G and Westmarland, L (eds) (2003) *Restorative Justice: Critical Issues*, London: Sage.

McMahon, M (1992) *The Persistent Prison: Rethinking Decarceration and Penal Reform*, Toronto: Toronto UP.

Martinson, R (1974) 'What works? – questions and answers about prison reform', *The Public Interest*, vol 35, pp 22–54.

Mathiesen, T (1974) *The Politics of Abolition*, London: Robertson.

Matthews, R and Young, J (1992) 'Reflections on realism' in Young, J and Matthews, R (eds) *Rethinking Criminology: The Realist Debate*, London: Sage.

Muncie, J (2000) 'Pragmatic realism?: searching for criminology in the new youth justice' in Goldson, B (ed) *The New Youth Justice*, Lyme Regis: Russell House.

Murray, C (1990) *The Emerging Underclass*, London: Institute of Economic Affairs.

Roshier, R (1989) *Controlling Crime*, Buckingham: Open University Press.

Schur, EM (1973) *Radical Non Intervention: Rethinking the Delinquency Problem*, Englewood Cliffs, NJ: Prentice Hall.

Valier, C (2002) *Theories of Crime and Punishment*, London: Longman.

Vennard, J and Hedderman, C (1998) 'Effective treatment with offenders' in Goldblatt, P and Lewis, C (eds), *Reducing Offending*, Home Office Research Study 187, London: Home Office.

von Hirsch, A (1976) *Doing Justice: The Choice of Punishments*, New York: Hill and Wang.

Wilson, JQ (1975, 2nd revised edn 1983) *Thinking about Crime*, New York: Basic Books.

Wilson, JQ and Herrnstein, RJ (1986) *Crime and Human Nature*, New York: Simon and Schuster.

Wilson, JQ and Kelling, G (1982) 'Broken windows', *Atlantic Monthly*, March, pp 29–38.

Young J (1981) 'Thinking seriously about crime' in Fitzgerald, M, McLennan, G and Pawson, J (eds), *Crime and Society*, London: Routledge.

Young, J (1994) 'Incessant chatter: recent paradigms in criminology' in Maguire, M, Morgan, R and Reiner, R (eds), *The Oxford Handbook of Criminology*, Oxford: Clarendon.

Young, J (1999) *The Exclusive Society*, London: Sage.

Zimring, FE and Hawkins, G (1995) *Incapacitation: Penal Confinement and the Restraint of Crime*, New York: OUP.

CHAPTER 2

THE POLITICS AND PROCESSES OF CRIMINAL JUSTICE

David Wilson

SUMMARY

This chapter describes the workings of the criminal justice system in England and Wales (see Chapter 19 for a discussion on the criminal justice system of Scotland) and critically analyses the philosophical basis on which the criminal justice system operates at a time when the Criminal Justice Act 2003, which followed the White Paper *Justice for All,* could transform the criminal justice landscape. In passing, it considers to what extent there is in fact a 'system' in the 'criminal justice system', if 'justice' is actually dispensed, or if there might be other ways to respond to the problem of crime.

KEY TERMS

Criminal justice agencies; paradigm; models of criminal justice; crime control; due process; just deserts; what works?; managerialism; restorative justice.

INTRODUCTION

The criminal justice system of England and Wales is responsible for catching and convicting offenders; ensuring that they have a fair trial; if they are found guilty, that the punishment they receive is fair and proportionate; and, finally, if they receive a custodial sentence, that they are helped to change their behaviour and can thereafter resettle in the community at the end of their sentence. Thus, various groups and agencies are centrally involved in running the criminal justice system, including the police, the courts (both the magistrates' court and the Crown Court), the Crown Prosecution Service (CPS), youth offending teams, Victim Support and the Witness Service, HM Prison Service and the Probation Service, with, in the absence of a Ministry of Justice, overall organisational responsibilities falling primarily between the Home Office and the Department for Constitutional Affairs. As such, as Gibson and Cavadino (2002: vii), for example, suggest, the criminal justice system 'encompasses all the procedures and practices which flow from the detection and apprehension of offenders'.

Yet even this simple, 'common sense' description of what the criminal justice system does and who is involved with it masks a variety of tensions and problems. The most obvious of these is that, despite all the resources that it attracts and the people that are involved with it, the criminal justice system has been unable to resolve the central problem at its heart – crime. Indeed, on this basis, Wilson and Ashton (2001: xvii) argue that the criminal justice system is a 'complete failure' and that 'if your gas central heating system worked like our criminal justice system, you would long ago have had to switch to oil, or you would have frozen to death'. And it is not just academics that have little faith in the ability of the criminal justice system to resolve the problem of crime; the public too seem to have lost patience in the criminal justice system. For example, in a Home Office study (2000: 3–10, 18) into attitudes to crime and criminal justice, based on findings from the 1998 British Crime Survey, 49 per cent of the public reported that judges were 'much too lenient' in the sentences that they handed down in their courts and 45 per cent that judges were 'very out of touch' with what 'ordinary people think'. Twenty-seven per cent of those interviewed thought that HM Prison Service was doing a 'poor or very poor job' and 25 per cent thought that the Probation Service was similarly failing to perform. Only the police were rated as relatively good at what they did, with, for example, some 61 per cent of the public believing that they did an 'excellent or good' job. As heartening at this is for the police, it is also quite clear that the public's perception is wrongly based on consistently over-estimating the amount of crime in the community – and the police's detection rate – and under-estimating current sentencing practice at magistrates' and Crown Courts. For example, although more people were aware in 1998 than in 1996 that recorded crime was falling:

- 59 per cent still thought that it had increased between 1995 and 1997, although in fact recorded crime fell by 10 per cent in that period;

- nearly four-fifths of respondents thought that 30 per cent or more of recorded crime was violent, whereas only about 8 per cent of recorded crime relates to serious wounding or sexual assaults; and

- 56 per cent thought that less than 60 per cent of convicted adult rapists are imprisoned, whereas 99 per cent of males aged 21 or over convicted of rape in England and Wales in 1997 received a custodial sentence.

Unsurprisingly, governments of both political parties – who give resources to and shape the policies and practices which guide the criminal justice system, and who have increasingly made crime a party political issue – have taken a close interest in how the criminal justice system operates. More recently, for example, New Labour published the White Paper, *Justice for All* (Home Office, 2002), which flowed from, although did not necessarily reflect the recommendations of, the Auld and Halliday Reports, which suggests that 'victims should be at the heart of the criminal justice system' and that the criminal justice system should be more 'joined up', with a new National Criminal Justice Board, a Criminal Justice Council and 42 local Criminal Justice Boards. At the heart of the strategy contained within the White Paper, and now in the new Criminal Justice Act 2003, is a desire to create 'a transparent, joined up system that commands the respect of the public it serves by delivering faster and more effective justice for victims and the wider community while safeguarding the rights of defendants'.

So, in one sense, we can see these proposals as a way of responding to the public's perception of the criminal justice system – even though this perception is often incorrect – and of the Government trying to resolve the historic inability of the criminal justice system to deal with the problem of crime. Through a strategy based on being 'tough on anti-social behaviour, hard drugs and violent crime', 'rebalancing' the criminal justice system in favour of the victim, and giving the police and prosecution more powers to 'bring criminals to justice', the Government hopes to improve the public's perception of what the criminal justice system does, help those who have been the victims of crime and manage better the agencies involved with operating the criminal justice system. It is of course too early to tell whether these initiatives will succeed or not, and as this book goes to press we now have the creation of the National Offender Management Service (NOMS) (see Chapter 16), but we should not let them pass without comment, despite the fact that they are often presented as 'common sense'. For example, one section of *Justice for All* is called 'Putting the sense back into sentencing'. However, this 'common sense' approach often masks ideological opinions as to who commits crime and how best to respond to them, and implementing policies based on these opinions could quite fundamentally affect the ancient principles that have guided our criminal justice system for centuries. For example, amongst a range of proposals, the right to trial by jury might disappear, a defendant's previous convictions might be presented before the court – thus implying guilt – and there may be exceptions to the 'double jeopardy' rule, which prevents someone being tried for the same offence twice, where there is 'compelling new evidence'. As James and Raine (1998: 11) have argued, changes such as these indicate that there are contrasting paradigms of criminal justice at work here, with a move away from a 'welfare' paradigm, which focused on why an offender committed a crime and how best to adjust his/her behaviour, to a 'justice' paradigm, which is more focused on the appropriate penalties for an offence. However, before discussing the underlying philosophical and sometimes competing rationales for the criminal justice system, it would also be helpful to build on the brief picture that has been painted as to what the criminal justice system looks like and what it aims to do.

A DAY IN THE LIFE OF THE CRIMINAL JUSTICE SYSTEM

In Annexe E of *Criminal Justice: The Way Ahead* (Home Office, 2001a), a snapshot of the work of the criminal justice system was presented, mostly derived from the annual reports of the various criminal justice agencies or from annual statistics that are collected, and this section has been adapted from that snapshot. We start with what has already been identified as the 'central problem' of the criminal justice system – crime.

Crime

For various reasons, most obviously because some victims choose not to report them, more crimes are committed than are ever recorded by the police. As such, we do not know how much crime is committed on any given day. However, based on evidence from the British Crime Survey for such offences as robbery, theft from the person, household theft, bicycle theft, vehicle-related theft, vandalism, common assault, wounding and burglary, we know that around 40,000 of these crimes are committed each day, of which only 39 per cent are reported. This 39 per cent is then subject to a sifting process, as not every allegation can be substantiated, and so the number of offences recorded by the police will be lower than the numbers of crimes reported to the police. Typically, the police will record some 14,500 offences on any given day; these are called 'notifiable' offences, given that the police are required to notify the Home Office about them. Of these 14,500, some 14 per cent will be crimes of violence, 58 per cent burglary or thefts, 3 per cent drug offences, and less than 1 per cent sexual offences. The police will also deal with large numbers of other offences on any given day, the most obvious of which will be related to motoring; typically, over 12,500 motoring offences will be dealt with each day.

The police

In 2002 there were just under 125,000 police officers in England and Wales, based in 2,099 police stations, of which some 600 were staffed on a 24-hour basis. On average, the police will respond to 25,500 '999' calls each day, of which some 15 per cent will require an immediate response. Officers on uniform patrol duty will carry out 2,235 'stop and searches' each day, with some 290 of these resulting in an arrest. Of the 14,500 'notifiable' offences that we have described above, only 25 per cent will be 'cleared up', with clearance success rates varying depending on the type of crime. Crimes such as murder, for example, have a much higher chance of being cleared up than house burglary. In the main, crime clearance follows the arrest of an offender and a decision to take some form of official action. Over 5,000 people will be arrested each day, either for a 'notifiable' offence or on a less serious matter, although it is estimated that no further action is taken against 950 of those who are arrested. Of the remainder, some 2,400 are charged or summonsed and 735 are cautioned.

The Crown Prosecution Service (CPS)

Once the police have begun proceedings, the case is passed to a CPS lawyer who will review the file and decide whether to proceed with, amend or drop the charge. There are around 1,400 CPS lawyers operating from 96 offices in 42 criminal justice areas, assisted by over 3,000 administrative staff, all helping to deal with a caseload that involves work in the magistrates' court and the Crown Court. In the former, the CPS finalises nearly 5,500 cases each working day, with the charges dropped in some 670 cases either before first appearance or at a latter stage. The vast majority of cases in the magistrates' court, just under 4,000, will result in a conviction, the greatest proportion (90 per cent) following a guilty plea. A further 350 will be committed to the Crown Court, either because the charges are so serious that they can only be dealt with there or because, in 'triable either way' cases, the magistrates decline jurisdiction or the defendant elects for a Crown Court trial.

Magistrates' courts

The vast majority of criminal cases in England and Wales (95 per cent) are dealt with in 430 or so magistrates' courts with their 1,620 courtrooms. On average, some 16,600 defendants appear in the magistrates' courts each day, of whom some 1,200 are defendants under the age of 18. The business of the magistrates' courts is conducted either by benches of lay magistrates, of whom there are currently 31,000 sitting for an average of 40 half days per year, or by professional District Judges, of whom there are 106 full time and 169 part time. On average, around 240 trials begin in magistrates' courts each day. Where the defendant is under 18, the youth court will deal with their case. Of the 7,500 or so defendants making their first appearance each day in the magistrates' court, around 4,175 have been summoned to appear, 2,840 arrested and bailed and 525 arrested and held in custody. Each day, just under 50 per cent of magistrates' court hearings result in an adjournment, and the average case is adjourned 1.2 times. Of those cases that reach a conclusion, involving some 5,300 defendants on each working day, 3,960 are fined, 524 receive community penalties and 232 receive an immediate custodial sentence.

The Crown Court

The volume of business in the Crown Court is much less than that of the magistrates' court, and the 78 Crown Court centres of England and Wales deal with just over 5 per cent of criminal cases. Typically, these are the more serious and complex cases and, on average, there are 365 courtrooms sitting on any working day. Some 350 defendants committed for trial make their first appearance in the Crown Court each working day and, of these, about 250 are given bail and 100 are remanded in custody. The eventual outcomes of their cases are as follows:

- 220 plead guilty;
- 45 are found guilty by a jury;
- 28 are acquitted by a jury;
- 7 are acquitted at the judge's discretion;
- 50 have their cases dropped before trial, written off, or they agree to a 'bind over', which involves an admission of guilt and represents a sanction against the offender.

Just over 300 defendants are sentenced each working day at the Crown Court and, of this total, 61 per cent receive an immediate custodial sentence, 27 per cent receive a community sentence and 4 per cent are fined.

Youth offending teams

Youth offending teams comprise probation officers, social workers, police officers, a health authority representative and someone nominated by the Chief Education Officer of the area. There are now 154 youth offending teams covering all of England and Wales, which are engaged with working with young people in a variety of ways, including assessing and managing their risk of reoffending, providing bail information and support services, preparing pre-sentence and other court reports, and supervising community sentences and reparation orders. Based on quarterly data provided by the Youth Justice Board, the scale of activity for the majority of youth offending teams comprises:

- 840 offences each day resulting in some form of substantive outcome, such as a sentence, a final warning or a reprimand;
- nearly 300 police reprimands or final warnings;
- nearly 300 young offenders sentenced; and
- 42 of the following types of orders imposed each day – parenting orders, reparation orders, compensation orders, fines imposed on parents and anti-social behaviour orders.

Victim Support and the Witness Service

On a typical day, the police will refer 3,000 victims to the organisation Victim Support, which is staffed by a mix of paid employees and volunteers. Victim Support will be successful in making contact with victims in 97 per cent of those cases which are referred, and victims can be helped in a variety of ways, such as receiving a visit from a Victim Support volunteer, or talking to a volunteer or member of staff on the telephone. Similarly the Witness Service, which comes under the umbrella of Victim Support, now exists in all Crown Courts and in many magistrates' courts to help those who are witnesses to crime – and who may also be the victims of crime – and who are required to attend court to give evidence. Help to this group may include pre-court familiarisation visits or advice or support on the day of the trial.

The Probation Service

Nationally, there are some 7,500 probation officers working from 948 offices, and the Probation Service carries out several key functions in the criminal justice system, including the preparation of reports to court to help the court arrive at an appropriate sentence, supervising offenders given community sentences, and supervising offenders released from custody. On a typical working day, the Probation Service prepares around 900 pre-sentence reports, some 485 convicted offenders begin community sentences supervised by the Probation Service, and around 171 offenders who served a custodial sentence of a year or more begin a period of supervision in the community on release from prison. Each day, some 218,342 offenders are under some form of supervision by the Probation Service, and the average caseload of a probation officer is 37 offenders on supervision.

HM Prison Service

There are 136 prisons in England and Wales, of different types, housing a range of convicted offenders or remand prisoners awaiting trial; the Prison Service employs around 44,000 staff. There are 41 Young Offender Institutions, of which eight can hold women, three are solely for juvenile males (15–17), and 10 hold juvenile males and young offenders. Around 375 prisoners under sentence enter prison each day and, of these, 347 are male (267 adults and 80 young offenders) and 28 female (23 adults and five young offenders). Similarly, there are around 336 remand prisoners sent to jail each day. In 1999, the average daily prison population was 64,770, of whom 51,690 were under sentence and 12,520 were on remand. The Prison Service seeks to engage prisoners in 'purposeful activity', such as education and training courses, sports and religious activity. In 1999–2000, the average time spent on purposeful activity was 23 hours per week – just over three hours a day. Not all convicted offenders remain in the criminal justice system, and so, for example, if the offender is suffering from a mental disorder, he or she will be transferred from prison to one of the three Special Hospitals in England and Wales or to a psychiatric hospital with a secure unit. On a typical day, four mentally disordered offenders are admitted from the courts to a special hospital, and one other is transferred there from prison.

This 'snapshot' does not identify any of the costs involved, and there are also other groups and organisations worthy of consideration. As far as costs are concerned, the figures are extraordinary. In 2002/03, for example, police funding of £7.777 billion accounted for just under 50 per cent of the total spending of the criminal justice system, with the next highest being Prison Service funding, which cost the taxpayer £2.577 billion, or 16.3 per cent of the total spend. Probation Service funding, on the other hand, accounted for just over 4 per cent of the total spent on the criminal justice system – some £637 million. Other groups or organisations that are important within the operation of the criminal justice system include the various inspectorate bodies, such as HM Inspectorate of Constabulary, HM Crown Prosecution Service Inspectorate, HM Inspector of Prisons and HM Inspector of Probation, as well as the Prisons and Probation Ombudsman. Similarly, the work of the Criminal Cases Review Commission (CCRC), based in Birmingham, is of note for a variety of reasons. Set up in 1997 under the Criminal Appeal Act 1995, in the wake of the overturning of a number of high profile convictions such as those of the Birmingham Six, it has 13 Commissioners and some 90 staff to review cases suspected of being 'miscarriages of justice' and to refer these to the appeal courts. Since it began its work, it has received over 4,000 applications and receives new applications at the rate of three per day, which suggests perhaps that, when speed and efficiency are prioritised by those who are working in the criminal justice system, mistakes are more likely to happen. In these circumstances, the criminal justice system does not dispense 'justice' at all.

MODELS OF CRIMINAL JUSTICE

This latter observation, that the criminal justice system might not dispense justice, should begin to make us question the underlying basis on which the criminal justice system operates; we have already considered above James and Raine's observation about there being a move away from a 'welfare' paradigm to a 'justice' paradigm. 'Paradigms' or, more broadly, models such as these help us to think more critically about the general characteristics, themes and principles that make up the criminal justice system at any one time and thus allow us to make sense of the often bewildering and complex array of government- or agency-inspired activities and initiatives that can take place in any given year. Perhaps the two most famous models were first identified by Herbert Packer (1968), who saw there being a 'crime control' model of criminal justice, which saw the efficient controlling of crime, and a 'due process' model, which stressed the importance of procedural safeguards and the rule of law. Packer's models were extremely influential and were further developed by Michael King (1981), who outlined six models and which are presented below in the form of a table.

Models of criminal justice

Social function	Process model	Features of court
Justice	Due process	Equality between parties; rules protecting defendants against error; restraint of arbitrary power; presumption of innocence
Punishment	Crime control	Disregard of legal controls; presumption of guilt; high conviction rate; support for the police; unpleasantness of the experience
Rehabilitation	Medical model (diagnosis, prediction and treatment)	Information collecting; individualisation; treatment; discretion of decision-makers; expertise of decision-makers; relaxation of rules
Management of crime and criminals	Bureaucratic model	Independence from political considerations; speed and efficiency; importance of records; minimisation of conflict; minimisation of expense; economical division of labour
Denunciation and degradation	Status passage model	Public shaming of defendant; court values reflect community values; agents' control over process
Maintenance of class domination	Power model	Reinforcement of class values; alienation of defendant; deflection of attention from issue of class conflict; differences between judges and judged; paradoxes and contradictions between rhetoric and performance

We now look briefly at each of these models to see if we can make sense of the many complexities within the criminal justice system. In turn, this might also help us to place new criminal justice initiatives within a broader context – a context that is often lost as we listen to politicians announcing each new policy development or direction.

The 'due process' model is an idealised version of how the criminal justice system should operate and is based on the rule of law. In essence, it incorporates and prioritises the defendant's rights and, as such, presumes innocence, the defendant's right to a fair trial and justice being 'seen to be done'. Perhaps the aphorism 'better the guilty go free than an innocent man be wrongly convicted' sums up the approach of the 'due process' model. On the other hand, the 'crime control' model has little time for the ideas behind this aphorism and is instead concerned with creating a criminal justice system that prevents and reduces crime by punishing the guilty. As such, the police and others are turned into 'crime fighters', ensuring that the guilty are brought to justice. This model has a great deal of popular, 'common sense' appeal, but how far should these priorities be pushed? For example, what if the police 'knew' but could not prove that a defendant had committed a crime? Should they invent evidence to secure a conviction? Or should they be allowed to torture a suspect to gain a confession? The 'rehabilitation' model reminds us that some offenders are not 'responsible' for their actions as a result of, for example, mental illness. In these and other circumstances, a rehabilitative approach would attempt to treat the condition that has caused the defendant to commit the crime, and in this way crime overall is eventually reduced. Thus, rather than prioritising crime fighting, the rehabilitation model emphasises the needs of the specific offender and, as such, allows 'experts' a great deal of discretion. The 'bureaucratic efficiency' model, on the other hand, puts pressure on criminal justice officials to follow rules and procedures to ensure that defendants are tried and sentenced speedily and efficiently. Thus, as should be becoming obvious, these models are often in competition with each other, and thus, for example, the interests of justice do not always sit easily with ideas of speed and efficiency. Similarly, the fifth model – 'denunciation and degradation' – suggests that the criminal justice system performs an important social function by reinforcing social values about crime being 'wrong', and therefore that the guilty should be ashamed of what they have done. However, this conflicts with the 'rehabilitation' model, which has recently found favour through the concept of 'reintegrative shaming' (Braithwaite, 1989). Finally, our sixth model asks us to question who makes the law and in whose interests, more broadly, does the criminal justice system serve.

To these six models Davies et al (1995: 23) remind us to add a seventh – the 'just deserts' model. This combines elements of punishment for offenders with concerns to respect the accused or defendant and prioritises the punishment of offenders in relation to their culpability and the seriousness of the offence that they have committed. As such, it does not seek crude revenge, but instead emphasises the wrongfulness of their act.

We have discussed these models as being in competition with one another, or as there being a tension between them. However, to complicate matters further, we could argue that these models do not separate like oil and water, but that, instead, aspects of one model can seep from one to another so that hybrid models emerge. Thus, for example, we could argue that, whilst there has been an overall trend to move away from a 'due process' model of criminal justice to one of 'crime control', a process that is becoming more obvious with the Criminal Justice Act 2003, there are also aspects of rehabilitation being emphasised with, for example, HM Prison Service being asked to provide a range of treatment courses for sex offenders in prison. We could also see aspects of different models being used in the Government's approach to young offenders, which has often had conflicting and overlapping rationales in dealing with young people (Muncie, 1999). For example, the Crime and Disorder Act 1998, which introduced a Youth Justice Board to give strategic direction to the youth justice system as a whole, viewed children as responsible for their actions and thus deemed them criminally liable from the age of 10 and allowed for local child curfews to be imposed. As well as these 'control' mechanisms, the Act also emphasised a popular punitiveness towards young people – reflecting the social need to 'denounce' their behaviour – as well as 'care' procedures such as parenting orders.

In all of this, we can discern a trend by governments of both political parties to implement polices which 'work'. Indeed, the 'what works' debate and, in particular, managerialism – or, to be more specific, new public managerialism – have sought to reorganise the delivery of criminal justice. New Labour has, for example, sought to implement 'joined up' managerialisation across the agencies of the criminal justice system, with an emphasis on aims and objectives, target-setting, the development of an evidence-led approach to the allocation of resources, a culture of performance management and the establishment of partnerships – sometimes with the private sector. The drive behind managerialisation may be linked to 'crime control' or has perhaps reached a stage in its development when it has become almost a separate phenomenon. However, what seems to be more pressing here is the question of whether managerialisation, 'what works', or any of the models that have been outlined have led to a reduction of crime – the problem that we have described as being at the heart of the criminal justice system, or whether there might be other ways of settling disputes and tackling crime.

RESTORATIVE JUSTICE

Conflict and trouble – more broadly, 'crime' – is part of everyday life, and, as we have seen, not every crime that is committed gets reported to the police. Quite simply, most people can resolve disputes in a variety of ways without resorting to the expertise and skills of the agents of the state – the criminal justice 'professionals'. As such, in the true story of Rose and Susie, we include below an example of a crime that was committed in Oxfordshire but which was resolved through a 'restorative justice conference' and which was reported in *RJ News*, published by the Thames Valley Partnership – the major initiative in restorative justice in England and Wales, which became operational for young offenders in April 1998.

Restorative justice, which emerged from the traditional and non-state systems of justice practised by the indigenous peoples of New Zealand, Australia and Canada, focuses on the relationship between the victims of crime, offenders and the wider community and attempts to reconcile these different interests by healing the rift between them (see also Chapter 18). It sees crime not as a violation of an abstract law but rather as an inter-personal harm, which in turn creates obligations on the part of the offender to the victim of the crime. Thus, in the example we provide, Susie stole a significant sum of money from Rose, and, whilst this theft hurt her greatly, Rose chose to attempt to rectify the situation by meeting with Susie and talking about how the crime had affected her and what could be done to put that matter right.

Rose and Susie

Rose got embroiled in the criminal justice system after a young friend of the family let herself into her home and stole Rose's savings. It was a large sum of money and the betrayal of trust affected her deeply, but Rose didn't want to go to court. That didn't mean that she wanted the matter dropped – and a restorative justice conference provided a welcome answer.

'I was very hurt when I found out who had stolen my money,' says Rose, 'but from the start, my only thought was for Susie. She had done wrong, but money isn't everything. The important thing was to put her back on the right road.'

Rose and her daughter came together with Susie and her parents at a restorative justice conference arranged by the local youth offending team. Each party was invited to speak about what the crime had meant to them, and how they thought the situation could be improved. For an hour people spoke eloquently, and agreed at the end that they would all look forward.

'After Susie stole the money, it was awkward because I love her, but I didn't know what to say to her,' says Rose. 'But we must have the confidence to put this behind us. Susie knows that I have forgiven her. Now we must all support her.'

For Rose, and other older people, the world is very different to the one of their youth. 'There was a lot more discipline when I was younger, but there was a lot of love too,' says Rose. 'Of course, some children got into trouble, but it was usually because they were hungry. It's not children's fault that the discipline's gone, though – and if we don't talk to them about right and wrong, they'll never know. I think that coming together to talk in a conference is the finest thing. It was the only thing that could possibly have helped Susie. It's a funny old world we live in now. But there is a lot of good and we have to look for that. The next generation is so important – young people are our future.' Peter Wallis, restorative justice manager for Oxfordshire Youth Offending Team, says: 'Older people can get frightened, but they often say that they think people are more important than possessions and are very forgiving.'

'Some of our schemes give kids a chance to make direct amends – befriending older people and helping them at home. It benefits both sides. Older people love having youngsters around, and it can be very helpful for kids to see the courage with which older people overcome their disabilities and live their lives.' (*RJ News*, Spring/Summer 2003, Thames Valley Partnership, p 6)

This might seem like an easy option, especially for Susie, but we should not only consider how difficult it is for offenders to meet with the victims of their crimes and to hear how their offending has affected their lives (the process that we have seen Braithwaite describe as 'reintegrative shaming'), we should also remember that resolving this crime in this way allowed the process to remain in the hands of the victim rather than with courts, barristers, police officers or probation staff. Rather than being a small part of the process of reconciling this theft by turning up at court and giving evidence, Rose was the key player from beginning to end. Indeed, in Australia, conferences such as the one engaged in by Rose and Susie are not just used in cases involving theft or with young offenders but involve adult offenders who have committed violent crimes. As yet, it is still too early to determine with any certainty whether restorative justice will work at reducing crime overall, and, as Hughes (2001: 247) has described it, restorative justice is a 'capacious concept'. However, an evaluation by the Home Office of restorative justice schemes in West Yorkshire suggested that they produced a 'small, but statistically significant reduction in reconviction rates' with some types of less serious offenders (Home Office, 2001b: 46). In the Thames Valley in 2000, some 5,000 cases were dealt with by using restorative justice schemes, involving mediation of some kind. Thus, at least in England and Wales, it is seen as an alternative within the criminal justice system – a way of siphoning off less serious offences (and note in the example we provide that a member of the youth offending team was centrally involved), rather than representing a challenge to the criminal justice system *per se*.

CONCLUSION

In this chapter we have outlined the work of the various agencies and groups that make up our criminal justice system and suggested at least six models that might help us to view the underlying direction of that system. We have further suggested that the criminal justice landscape might be about to change dramatically through the Criminal Justice Act 2003. Indeed, we have argued that, in broad terms, we are moving from a criminal justice system based on 'due process' to one that is based on 'crime control'. Nonetheless, we have argued that the central problem of our criminal justice system is that it seems to be unable to resolve the problem of crime, and thus we have instead offered an example of a restorative justice initiative as a way of suggesting different and non-state directions that could be attempted.

SEMINAR DISCUSSION TOPICS

- Take any recent criminal justice initiative that has been announced and see if it is possible to discern how this fits into an overall model of criminal justice.
- What 'works' in criminal justice?
- Discuss Rose and Susie's story – was this a fair way to resolve the theft?

KEY READINGS

For a standard introduction to the criminal justice system in England and Wales, see Davies, M, Croall, H and Tyrer, J (1995) *Criminal Justice: An Introduction to the Criminal Justice System of England and Wales*, London: Longman remains a useful starting point, whereas James, A and Raine, K (1998) *The New Politics of Criminal Justice*, London: Longman is a more recent critical account. For a broad attack on the criminal justice system and the political processes that have grown to dominate it, see Wilson, D and Ashton, J (2001) *What Everyone in Britain Should Know About Crime and Punishment*, Oxford: OUP.

REFERENCES

Braithwaite, J (1989) *Crime, Shame and Reintegration*, Oxford: OUP.

Davies, M, Croall, H and Tyrer, J (1995) *Criminal Justice: An Introduction to the Criminal Justice System in England and Wales*, London: Longman.

Gibson, B and Cavadino, P (2002) *Introduction to the Criminal Justice Process*, Winchester: Waterside.

Home Office (2000) *Attitudes to Crime and Criminal Justice: Findings from the 1998 British Crime Survey*, Home Office Research Study 200, London: Home Office.

Home Office (2001a) *Criminal Justice: The Way Ahead*, Cm 5074, London: Home Office.

Home Office (2001b) *An Exploratory Evaluation of Restorative Justice Schemes*, Crime Reduction Research Series Paper 9, London: Home Office.

Home Office (2002) *Justice For All*, London: Home Office.

Hughes, G (2001) 'Restorative justice' in McLaughlin, E and Muncie, J (eds), *The Sage Dictionary of Criminology*, London: Sage.

James, A and Raine, J (1998) *The New Politics of Criminal Justice*, London: Longman.

King, M (1981) *The Framework of Criminal Justice*, London: Croom Helm.

Muncie, J (1999) *Youth and Crime: A Critical Introduction*, London: Sage.

Packer, H (1968) *The Limits of the Criminal Sanction*, Stanford, CA: Stanford UP.

Wilson, D and Ashton, J (2001) *What Everyone in Britain Should Know About Crime and Punishment*, Oxford: OUP

CHAPTER 3

RESEARCHING CRIME AND CRIMINAL JUSTICE

Gemma Buckland and Emma Wincup

SUMMARY

This chapter offers an introduction to the development and practice of empirical research on crime and criminal justice. Throughout the chapter, we highlight both the diverse influences on criminological research and identify some of the key issues which criminologists need to consider when conducting research. In particular, we attempt to identify whether the issues criminological researchers are confronted with are distinctive. We begin by elucidating the foundations of qualitative and quantitative research traditions within criminology and draw links between these approaches to research and theoretical perspectives in criminology. Blurring the boundaries between qualitative and quantitative research traditions, we emphasise the importance of combining methodologies, where appropriate, in contemporary criminological studies. The influences of macro and micro political processes on criminological research are then documented. We acknowledge the diversity of responses to the question – is criminological research political? – and argue that criminological research can never be anything but political. To support our argument, we draw attention to the influence of political contexts on shaping the research process, from the generation of the research problem to the stages of publication and dissemination of findings.

The nature of criminological research requires a measured consideration of research ethics and safety to protect the interests of both participants and researchers. Key ethical principles such as intrusion, consent and confidentiality are introduced, and we highlight some of the complexities involved in navigating these delicate yet crucial aspects of the research process. The paradox of criminologists researching risk and danger yet failing to address the issue of research safety in an adequate manner is also examined.

KEY TERMS

Confidentiality; consent; critical criminology; dichotomy; disclosure; empirical research; ethics; ethnography; evaluation; evidence-based policy; moral statisticians; positivism; politics; privacy; qualitative; quantitative; risk; safety; symbolic interactionism; triangulation.

THE DEVELOPMENT OF CRIMINOLOGICAL RESEARCH

Criminology, as a field of academic study, is held together by a substantive concern: crime (Walklate, 1998). Consequently, it is multi-disciplinary in character, and for this reason it is helpful to view criminology as a 'meeting place' for a wide range of disciplines including sociology, social policy, psychology and law. Partly due to this diversity of theoretical and methodological approaches, charting the development of criminological research is problematic. Whilst there is a substantial literature on the maturation of criminology as an academic discipline, there are competing interpretations of the history of the discipline, leading to 'confusion over both its birthday and parentage' (Coleman and Norris, 2000: 24). To summarise briefly the debate, criminologists are divided as to whether the 18th century classical school is the first identifiable school of thought in criminology because, as Garland (2002: 11) argues, classicism 'made no distinction between the characteristics of criminals and non-criminals, and had no conception of research on crime and criminals as a distinct form of inquiry'. Others disagree (for example, Hughes, 1998) and propound that Garland's definition of criminology as an empirically grounded scientific understanding is too restrictive. Consequently, Garland's critics reject his claim that criminology was 'born' in the 19th century out of the convergence between the work of 'moral' statisticians and individual positivists: schools of thought we will describe in the following section.

The focus of this chapter is on empirical research, but it is important to note that criminological research exists in both theoretical and empirical forms. Both require different skills and training, and it is inappropriate for a 'pragmatic division of labour' (Bottoms, 2000: 15) to be fully adopted. All empirical researchers need to acknowledge that theory is an essential element of the data collection and analysis process. Similarly, theorists need to draw upon and understand empirical research as one means of testing the ability of their theoretical account to explain the social world.

The emergence of the quantitative tradition

The quantitative tradition is closely allied to a theoretical perspective known as positivism. Researchers who adhere to this approach aim to explain crime and predict future patterns of criminal behaviour. Emulating the analysis by natural scientists of causal relationships, positivists are concerned with developing objective knowledge about how criminal behaviour is determined by either individual or social pathology. Identifying the exact moment when positivist criminology became apparent is difficult (Muncie, 2001), but it is typically associated with the work of French and Belgian 'moral' statisticians in the 1820s. The publication of national crime statistics, beginning in France in 1827, provided these scholars with a dataset to be analysed. Studies following in this tradition have examined the impact of social, economic and environmental factors on crime rates (Durkheim, 1895; Shaw and McKay, 1842; Quetelet, 1842) and have suggested that crime rates are regular and predictable.

Contemporary criminologists who wish to conduct quantitative research now have access to wide range of data sources. As Maguire (2002: 324) argues, there has been a 'data explosion' in the last quarter of the 20th century, partly due to rapid development of electronic data storage. Alongside official statistics, researchers can make use of local, national and international victimisation surveys and studies of self-reported offending behaviour which have been conducted to uncover the 'dark figure of crime'. Collectively, they provide a clearer picture about the nature and extent of offences committed across England and Wales but are less revealing about possible causes of offending behaviour. Better data in this respect can be gleaned from longitudinal studies which are used by developmental criminologists to explore the evolution (or not) of criminal careers. Criminologists working in this tradition attempt to identify risk factors which make individuals vulnerable to offending and protective factors which make offending less likely (see Farrington, 2002, for an overview). By advancing complex explanations of offending and taking care not to estimate the explanatory power of one factor in isolation, this approach responds to some of the fierce criticisms to which positivism and the quantitative tradition have been subjected since the 1960s. Critics have argued that it is highly questionable to translate statistical association into causality. Quantitative work in criminology continues to be conducted but no longer adheres to a narrow positivist research tradition. Instead, quantitative work seeks to understand the complexity of social behaviour through examining a wide range of factors which influence trends in crime (for example, Hale, 1999). In addition, quantitative research techniques have also been used to explore the workings of the criminal justice system, for example, to identify whether there is evidence of discrimination in the courtroom (for example, Hood, 1992).

Quantitative research received a new impetus in April 1999 when the Crime Reduction Programme was launched. It ran for three years with an overall budget of £250 million (£25 million of this was dedicated to research). The programme comprised a series of diverse initiatives dealing with a wide range of offences and every aspect of the criminal justice process. The aim of the programme was to establish *what works* in reducing crime as part of a commitment to evidence-based policy and practice. As a result, funding was made available for independent evaluation which always involved the collection of quantitative data to assess whether particular interventions were influential in producing lower than expected reconviction rates, with some acknowledgment of the difficulties of relying on this measure of effectiveness. Many of these programmes had multiple components, making it difficult to isolate their 'active ingredients' (Farrington, 2002: 662) and to advance anything other than tenuous links between risk factors and crime reduction programmes. Rarely did the evaluators use quantitative approaches in isolation but coupled them with qualitative methods which provide rich and detailed data to flesh out the bare skeleton provided by quantitative data.

The emergence of the qualitative tradition

The qualitative tradition in criminology developed in the United States and owes a great deal to the work of the Chicago School. It made important theoretical and methodological contributions and bequeathed a tradition of conducting sociological research on crime and deviance which was distinctive in that they used ethnographic techniques to explore groups on the margins of urban industrial society in the 1920s and 1930s. Included in the long list of Chicago School ethnographies are studies of gangs, prostitution and homelessness. Ethnography can be defined as the study of groups of people in their natural setting, typically involving the researcher being present for extended periods of time in order to collect data systematically about their daily activities and the meanings they attach to them (Noaks and Wincup, 2004). The second Chicago School, which developed in the post-World War II period, continued to be dominated by ethnographies of deviance. Undoubtedly, the most well-known of these is Becker's study of marijuana users (Becker, 1963). Influenced by symbolic interactionism and its anti-statistical stance, Becker turned his attention away from the causes of crime and explored the process by which crimes are created and social reactions to crime. He emphasised the importance of human agency, consciousness and meaning in social activity, and highlighted the plurality of norms and values relating to 'normal' and 'deviant' behaviour. Whilst symbolic interactionist work has been subjected to vehement criticism for paying insufficient attention to the exercise of power by feminists, Marxists and critical criminologists, these theoretical approaches have continued to support the use of qualitative methods.

The ethnographic tradition came alive in the UK in the mid-1960s when the control of positivist criminology was threatened. Ethnography rejects the idea that social phenomena can be studied in the same way as natural phenomena, stressing the importance of deep involvement in the everyday lives of research participants and offering a commitment to understanding the meanings human beings attribute to their actions. The National Deviancy Conference of 1968, with the benefit of hindsight, marks a watershed in British criminology. Dissatisfaction with positivism, coupled with a lack of faith in symbolic interactionism, created the intellectual space for alternative theoretical frameworks to develop. These critical criminologists adopted a more politicised approach than earlier sociologists of deviance. Ethnography was championed in rhetoric, but the reality was that few papers based on ethnographic research were presented at subsequent colloquia (Hobbs, 2001).

As a means of conducting research on crime and deviance, ethnography faces many challenges. Unsurprisingly, as Maguire (2000: 121) notes, 'criminologists nowadays spend surprisingly little of their time talking to "criminals"'. Similarly, Parker (1996: 282) points out that British criminology has 'largely retreated from qualitative, ethnographic community-based studies of subculture and deviant lifestyles'. It would be wrong to give the impression that criminologists do not spend any time talking to offenders. They do, but in many respects their research does not resemble the ethnographic studies of previous decades. Criminologists often tend to access offenders through criminal justice agencies, particularly through police forces, prisons and young offender institutions, probation areas or youth offending teams. These constitute artificial settings, and institutional timetables and resources influence the type of research methods which can be utilised. Characteristically, this is a formal interview. More often than not, these interviews are likely to focus not on offending behaviour, but on an offender's experience of being arrested, remanded in custody, undertaking a community punishment order or other aspects of the criminal justice process. It is not difficult to imagine why criminologists have been reluctant to commit themselves to conducting ethnographic work. The ethical and personal safety dilemmas criminologists face (discussed later in this chapter) are heightened in ethnographic research.

Combining traditions

Whilst we have just presented quantitative and qualitative traditions within criminology separately, we are mindful of the dangers of drawing too sharp a distinction between the two traditions. For Silverman (1998), the qualitative/quantitative research dichotomy is acceptable as a pedagogical device to aid understanding of a complex topic, but such dichotomies are dangerous because they tend to locate researchers in oppositional groups. The reality is that many researchers make use of both qualitative and quantitative approaches, sometimes within the same research study. The process of combining both qualitative and quantitative methodologies is one aspect of triangulation. Triangulation can be defined simply as 'the use of different methods of research, sources of data or types of data to address the same research question' (Jupp, 2001: 308).

By combining both qualitative and quantitative approaches, criminological researchers are avoiding 'methodological pigeonholing' (Bottoms, 2000: 21). This can be defined as 'the tendency to assume that certain sorts of research methods "go with" particular kinds of theoretical approach, to the exclusion of other kinds of data' (2000: 21). Bottoms suggests that some qualitative researchers have set up mental barriers against the use of quantitative data, and similarly some quantitative researchers have been reluctant to make use of qualitative data. For Bottoms, these unjustifiable mental barriers have been some of the most unhelpful features of the British criminological landscape in the last quarter of the 20th century. He proposes that these barriers are now being overcome, leading to a healthier approach to criminological research.

As one of us (Noaks and Wincup, 2004) has advocated elsewhere, researchers need to adopt a pragmatic and theoretically coherent approach to the data collection process, using appropriate methods to answer their research questions. Researchers need to guard against the tendency to keep adding research techniques to their research design in an eclectic manner with the blind hope that it will produce a better thesis, report or other publication. A multi-method approach should only be pursued if it adds value to the study by enhancing understanding of the criminological issue of interest. Sometimes, there may be little to be achieved by using different methods. As Jupp (2001) argues, some combinations of methods do not work well because they are founded on different assumptions about the nature of the social world and how it can be explained. There are often pragmatic reasons (for example, the time and resources available) for considering carefully whether a number of methods should be utilised.

THE POLITICS OF CRIMINOLOGICAL RESEARCH

The term 'political' has multiple meanings attached to it in both lay and academic discourse, and consequently it is important for us to be explicit about our understanding of the term. We have adopted an inclusive and catholic working definition:

> Criminological research is a political endeavour in two senses. Firstly, the political context inevitably shapes, to varying extents, all stages of the research process because criminologists are researching a social problem, which politicians seek to explain and control. Secondly, criminological researchers inevitably become embroiled in micro-political processes because research often seeks to understand the standpoints of different, sometimes opposing, groups. (Noaks and Wincup, 2004, p 21)

This definition captures the different ways in which criminological research can be perceived as political. Inevitably, the nature and extent of political influences will vary from project to project and are dependent on a wide range of factors, including the subject matter, the theoretical framework adopted, funding arrangements and the timing of the research. Nonetheless, it is possible to claim that criminological research is inevitably part of a political process because it is shaped by a wider political context. Most criminologists are willing to acknowledge, sometimes reluctantly, that this is the case. Few will hold on to the traditional notion that research can be value-free (see May, 2001, for an overview of this debate). The question about whether research should be political has also been asked (see Hammersley, 1995, for a more detailed discussion). Certainly, some criminologists, for example, critical criminologists, have taken the political nature of crime as their starting point.

The politics of fieldwork

The political context impacts on both the process of gaining access to fieldwork settings and the task of managing relations within them (Noaks and Wincup, 2004). Whilst this provides data to be gathered, it makes conducting fieldwork a challenging task. A recurring theme in the literature is whether it is possible to be neutral at the data collection stage. Howard Becker's 1967 essay, entitled 'Whose side are we on?', continues to offer a major contribution to the debate. Described by Delamont (2002: 149) as a 'manifesto on values and methods', Becker's starting point is that neutrality is a myth shattered by the reality that personal and political sympathies inform research. The focus of Becker's essay was on research with deviant groups, chosen because researchers who focus on this group frequently have to answer to the charge that siding with deviant groups leads to distortion and bias. Becker suggests that a 'hierarchy of credibility' (1967: 241) operates in deviancy research and that credibility and the right to be heard are distributed differentially throughout the hierarchy. Researchers interested in deviant groups concentrate on those whose voices are normally unheard, and hence challenge what Becker (1967: 243) terms the 'established status order'. According to Becker, accusations of bias are levelled only at researchers who focus on deviants, rather than those concerned with criminal justice professionals. For Becker, researchers always have to take sides, and their challenge is to ensure that unavoidable sympathies with their research participants do not render their work invalid.

Remarkably, over 35 years after its publication, Becker's essay continues to be revisited by social researchers. In her article on prisons research, Liebling (2001: 473) argues that 'it *is* possible to take more than one side seriously, to find merit in more than one perspective, and to do this without causing outrage on the side of officials or prisoners' (emphasis in original). She does note, however, that this is a precarious business and risks encountering the wrath of criminologists who are sceptical of any attempt to understand officialdom. For Liebling, taking more than one side seriously does not lead to impartiality; instead, attempts to synthesise different or competing perspectives within the prison world at the analysis stage help to sharpen our focus, and consequently this is a valuable analytic task.

Many criminological researchers, regardless of whether they adopt Becker's position, find themselves in the precarious position of trying to keep everyone happy. This is particularly true for those conducting research within criminal justice agencies who have to strive to avoid alienating opposing groups, for example, prisoners and officers.

Publication and dissemination

The political context continues to influence the research process beyond the data collection stage. Submission of a research report of some kind is a requirement of all funders of criminological research. What happens next varies, but all require a final report, which may be sent to academics with specialist expertise in the area to review. For government-funded research, the draft is also scrutinised by policy-makers. Researchers are then asked to respond to the comments, and sometimes this process is repeated. It would be unfair to suggest that this practice is unhelpful. Receiving constructive comments on a draft often leads to a more polished report. Similarly, observations from policy-makers can produce a more user-friendly, policy-relevant publication. However, the whole process can also be frustrating, not least because it can lead to immoderate delays and challenges to the independence of the research. At the extreme, state-funded research may be subjected to censorship. This leaves the researcher with an ethical dilemma, but a 'publish and be damned' attitude is unwise if researchers seek to receive future funding, not least because research contracts forbid the publication of any findings without permission.

ETHICS AND THE RESEARCH PROCESS

We now turn our attention to ethical issues, which Welland and Pugsley describe as the 'messy realities' of social research (2002: 3). In the context of criminology, these 'realities' can be particularly 'messy', in the sense that there are many sensitive areas to navigate when researching crime, offenders, victims and the criminal justice system. Each research project raises distinct ethical issues, and here we offer an introduction to key ethical principles which guide research. It is important to note that ethical practices should permeate all stages of the research process (see Social Research Association, 2002, section 6, for an overview of issues at each stage). By reflecting on potential ethical problems that may arise in advance, measures can be devised to effectively minimise the impact of the research on participants. However, unaccounted ethical dilemmas may emerge whilst in the field, requiring more impromptu resolution.

The British Society of Criminology (2003) offers a framework for the consideration of ethical principles in terms of responsibilities. These responsibilities are directed towards criminology as an academic discipline, colleagues, sponsors and participants. More comprehensive guidance, which broadly correlates to these responsibilities, is provided by the Social Research Association (2002). For both organisations, the term 'ethics' encompasses general professional obligations regarding the production of high quality, methodologically sound research, the dissemination of research findings, and the prevention and correction of its misrepresentation. Professional judgment is required in balancing the commitment to ethical principles and the day-to-day practicalities of planning, conducting and promoting research. Whilst addressing these ethical considerations is desirable for good practice, rigid interpretation is not necessary (or encouraged) and can be counter-productive.

Gaining the approval of research ethics committees is increasingly required for criminological research, and this includes small-scale studies conducted by undergraduate and postgraduate students. These committees provide an independent assessment of the adequacy of measures taken to minimise ethical concerns. The medical model of research ethics broadly inspired the development of such committees, and it can be argued that, whilst their work is valuable, some aspects of the medical model are inappropriate to social research methodologies. The inflexibility of these committees and the extent to which they are independent has been particularly criticised (Coomber, 2002; Truman, 2003). For instance, Coomber uses the example of requiring signed consent forms when researching offenders to suggest that ethics committees can be unreasonably restrictive and may compromise the ability of the researcher to protect participants.

Intrusion, vulnerability and harm

Intrusion into the lives of participants is omnipresent in criminological research. At its simplest, this can mean making additional demands on busy criminal justice practitioners through to the risk of causing psychological or emotional harm to research participants. The extent to which intrusion occurs can be reduced by: careful consideration of research methods; the depth, breadth and nature of questions; impingement on time; and warning participants of potentially intrusive content. Sometimes, simple practical measures can be undertaken to minimise the intrusive nature of the research. For example, since 1994, the British Crime Survey has made use of computer assisted self-interviewing to explore sensitive topics such as domestic violence. The use of payments in the form of cash or vouchers is a useful strategy to lessen more generic exploitation, although this is not without its criticisms (see McKeganey, 2001). Feminist researchers have been instrumental in drawing attention to the impact of research on participants and have advocated the need for debriefing following disclosure of painful experiences, for example, by advising participants on sources of support or information.

Whilst all offenders could be argued to be vulnerable in terms of their lack of agency in the criminal justice system, criminologists often work with a range of groups who may be considered particularly vulnerable. Children, victims, women offenders and those with mental health, drug or alcohol problems and learning disabilities have been advocated as cases for carefully measured treatment. In contrast, Walklate (2000) contends that specific groups, in her case victims, need not be afforded special status, rather that respect for any participant is achieved through the appropriate choice of methodology and analysis techniques.

Informed consent

Criminological research is generally based on the principle of informed consent, though there have been examples where covert research has been justified (Adler, 1993; Calvey, 2000). Informed consent is defined by the British Society of Criminology as 'explaining as fully as possible, and in terms meaningful to participants, what the research is about, who is undertaking and financing it, why it is being undertaken and how any research findings are to be disseminated' (British Society of Criminology, 2003, section 4iii).

Ensuring that consent is fully informed is not straightforward. Barriers may include the difficulties of finding a common language with participants and potential participants giving agreement before listening to a full explanation in order to escape the boredom of institutional life within prisons and hostels (Smith and Wincup, 2000). Researchers may encounter particular problems in gaining the informed consent of some offenders, and a range of communication strategies may be required. For example, those with poor literacy skills may find it difficult to read information leaflets or listen to detailed explanations. Interpreters or signers may be required for foreign nationals or those with hearing impairments. It is rare that the use of alcohol, drugs (or some forms of prescribed medication) or mental health problems would wholly prevent someone giving informed consent, but in such cases it may be necessary to time approaches carefully. The extent to which the choice to consent is constrained by the research setting should also be considered. Some offenders may feel coerced into participation because they are fearful of possible reprisals from criminal justice agencies if they refuse to take part. Others may perceive incorrectly that their co-operation is directly beneficial to themselves.

Confidentiality and disclosure

The legal obligations of criminological researchers towards both research participants and the interests of society are far from clear, particularly in relation to the disclosure of criminal offences. This has been further complicated by developments in human rights and data protection legislation since 1998 that have strengthened the rights of research participants (see the Economic and Social Research Council guidelines on copyright and confidentiality).

Feenan (2002) offers a detailed account of legal and moral constraints that have influenced researchers' judgments in respecting privacy at various points in the criminological research process. For example, strategies can be taken to avoid the disclosure of criminal offences in the first instance, including not asking questions about offences, warning participants not to discuss offences for which they have not been convicted and only interviewing those who have been convicted. These nevertheless place limitations on the scope of criminological research. Where disclosure is unavoidable, researchers have minimised the risk of being ordered to expose identities by anonymising the data or consulting with the Crown Prosecution Service or police prior to fieldwork (Feenan, 2002). It is interesting to note the scarcity of guidance available to researchers regarding disclosure of child abuse, in contrast to that offered to practitioners and volunteers in the criminal justice system.

Limitations to confidentiality must be carefully considered and again clearly articulated to research participants. Researchers also need to be sensitive to the possibility that offenders' perceptions of the term 'confidential' may not accord with their own. Experiences such as a history of feeling disappointed by the 'system', coupled with an era when information sharing between criminal justice and partnership agencies has become the norm, may engender mistrust of authority. Encountering suspicion about their presence in the field is not uncommon for researchers, including being questioned about whether they are working for the police or the media. These assumptions can also extend to scepticism from non participants over participants' motivations for involvement in research, for example, questioning whether they are acting as informants.

SAFETY IN CRIMINOLOGICAL RESEARCH

Despite the plethora of literature that exists which raises awareness of risk of harm in relation to research participants, there is limited consideration of the risks researchers themselves may encounter in conducting criminological research. Some researchers have revealed their exposure to physical and psychological risk of harm that has arisen during empirical research (Hoyle, 2000; Sharpe, 2000; Wardhaugh, 2000). There is, however, little by way of guidance in this area with the exception of the Social Research Association (2003) code of practice for the safety of social researchers.

Risks encountered by researchers may be perceived as 'occupational hazards' and therefore taken for granted and only considered in retrospect. Consequently, many researchers are afforded little by way of measured protection from harm whilst in the field. It does not take much common sense to understand that researching criminal behaviour can bring particular risks. The extent to which these risks are systematically and explicitly recognised, acknowledged and managed at each stage in the research process is often unclear. Under health and safety legislation, employers have a duty of care towards the safety of their employees (Social Research Association, 2003). Establishing clear lines of accountability for the safety of researchers is not always straightforward. Ultimate liability may lie with personnel or other staff with particular remit for health and safety or with the research manager or grant holder. The researcher, as employee, also has some responsibility for his or her own safety in the field. External institutions or agencies that provide access to participants may also have obligations towards the safety of those working on their premises.

Safety in the field

Safety considerations will vary depending upon the research site. Criminal justice institutions are unlike many other research settings in the sense that they have their own safety measures and procedures to protect staff. Familiarisation with such practices is essential, but it is important to recognise that relying on the measures taken by staff can lead to a false sense of security. For example, we are currently conducting research in probation hostels and are aware that, despite agreed protocols, some staff do not routinely carry personal alarms. Staff within criminal justice agencies can offer useful information on risks and precautions that may need to be taken with particular individuals. However, the role of a researcher is distinct from that of criminal justice staff, and there are correspondingly different risks to which they may be exposed. It is also important to be aware that, over a period of time, familiarity with the research setting can lead to safety concerns becoming neglected.

Where research is not specifically facilitated by, or conducted in, criminal justice or other agencies, researchers are arguably exposed to a greater level of risk. Particular concerns have been raised about vulnerability where interviews or observation takes place in the home or within unfamiliar communities (Jamieson, 2000; Sharpe, 2000). Strategies that have been advocated to minimise risk include interviewing in public places such as parks or cafes, keeping mobile phones on and visible, indicating that colleagues know your whereabouts and leaving immediately if safety feels compromised.

The issue of safety has important implications for funding. The Social Research Association guidelines (2003) distinguish between infrastructure costs for all research projects and those peculiar to a specific project. The former include mobile phones, identity cards, risk assessment training and mechanisms for maintaining contact with researchers in the field (including outside normal office hours). For individual projects, researchers may need to budget for the cost of appropriate overnight accommodation, safe transport and training for appropriate ways to deal with, for example, violence and aggression. The nature of some criminological research may also necessitate counselling for researchers, for example, those who are exposed to disclosures of abuse.

Recognition of the importance of safety concerns in criminological research, or indeed any form of social research, has implications for the appropriateness of training available routinely provided to researchers. One option is to tap into professional training offered for criminal justice professionals, for example, on dealing with challenging behaviour, although the approach towards the management of risk taken in other professions may not be appropriate for researchers. For example, the National Probation Service promotes the interviewing of particularly high risk or dangerous offenders in pairs, which may not always be feasible for research projects in terms of costs, time and human resources.

CONCLUSION

In this chapter we have drawn attention to the multi-disciplinary nature of criminology and the range of methodological and theoretical approaches within it. Consequently, within the body of knowledge collectively labelled as 'criminological research', there is considerable diversity. Presented in the sanitised form of books, journal articles and reports, an uncomplicated picture of the process of conducting criminological research is offered. The reality is much messier, and the authors of these studies share common experiences of negotiating and conducting research in a political world, often on politically sensitive topics. Invariably, criminological researchers have faced ethical dilemmas and, often, encounters with risk, vulnerability and danger. These issues are not peculiar to criminological research, but it should be apparent from reading this chapter that studying crime and criminal justice does raise distinct issues, and consequently we need to ensure that we pay attention to these issue when designing our research and carrying it out. There are no clear-cut solutions, but careful examination of risks to the interests of society, participants and researchers throughout the research process can ameliorate some of the potential for harm.

SEMINAR DISCUSSION TOPICS

- What are the strengths and weaknesses of developing research designs which combine qualitative and quantitative methodologies? You might find it helpful to consider this question in relation to the following criminological problems: young people and illegal drug use, racism in the police force and the effects of overcrowding in prisons.
- Can criminological research ever be anything other than political?

- Consider the following scenario which one of us (Wincup) experienced. You are conducting research on the process of waiting for trial. One of the remand prisoners you interview shows you a small razor blade but reassures you that he will not use it to harm himself. He has told you this information in confidence. You are aware that he has been remanded in custody in order for a psychiatric report to be prepared. What are the ethical issues involved? How would you react in this situation?

- Imagine you are doing a victimisation survey about burglary and plan to interview people in their own homes. What measures would you take to protect yourself? If you were doing the same survey with passers-by in the street, what different measures would you take?

KEY READINGS

British Journal of Criminology, vol 41(3), 2001 is a special issue dedicated to the process of conducting criminological research.

Jupp, V, Davies, P and Francis, P (eds) (2000) *Doing Criminological Research*, London: Sage. This text offers a detailed and practical discussion of research in criminology and criminal justice.

Keynon, E and Hawker, S (1999) 'Once would be enough?: some reflections on the issue of safety for lone researchers', *International Journal of Social Research Methodology*, vol 2, pp 313–27. A rare discussion of research safety and suggestions of best practice.

King, R and Wincup, E (eds) (2000) *Doing Research on Crime and Justice*, Oxford: OUP. This text brings together reflections on the research process from both established criminologists and those at the beginning of their academic careers.

Lee-Treweek, G and Linkogle, S (eds) (2000) *Danger in the Field: Risk and Ethics in Social Research*, London: Routledge. A unique collection which offer first-hand accounts of conducting 'dangerous' fieldwork in criminological and other settings.

Noaks, L and Wincup, E (2004) *Criminological Research: Understanding Qualitative Methods*, London: Sage. An introductory text which develops many of the discussions in this chapter but with a particular emphasis on qualitative research.

REFERENCES

Adler, P (1993) *Wheeling and Dealing: An Ethnography of an Upper-Level Drug Dealing and Smuggling Community*, New York: Columbia UP.

Allen, D (2002) 'Research involving vulnerable young people: a discussion of ethical and methodological concerns', *Drugs: Education, Prevention and Policy*, vol 9, pp 275–83.

Becker, H (1963) *Outsiders: Studies in the Sociology of Deviance*, New York: Free Press.

Becker, H (1967) 'Whose side are we on?', *Social Problems*, vol 14, pp 239–48.

Bottoms, A (2000) 'The relationship between theory and research in criminology' in King, R and Wincup, E (eds), *Doing Research on Crime and Justice*, Oxford: OUP.

British Society of Criminology (2003) *Code of Ethics for Researchers in the Field of Criminology*, www.britsoccrim.org/ethics.htm.

Calvey, D (2000) 'Getting on the door and staying there' in Lee-Treweek, G and Linkogle, S (eds), *Danger in the Field: Risk and Ethics in Social Research*, London: Routledge.

Coleman, C and Norris, C (2000) *Introducing Criminology*, Cullompton: Willan.

Coomber, R (2002) 'Signing your life away?: why Research Ethics Committees (REC) shouldn't always require written confirmation that participants in research have been informed of the aims of a study and their rights – the case of criminal populations', *Sociological Research Online*, vol 7, p 1.

Economic and Social Research Council (2001) *Guidelines on Copyright and Confidentiality: Legal Issues for Social Science Researchers*, www.esrc.ac.uk.

Delamont, S (2002) 'Whose side are we on? Revisiting Becker's classic ethical question at the *fin de siecle*' in Welland, T and Pugsley, L (eds), *Ethical Dilemmas in Qualitative Research*, Aldershot: Ashgate.

Durkheim, E (1895) 'The normal and the pathological', abridged extract in McLaughlin, E, Muncie, J and Hughes, G (eds) (2003) *Criminological Perspectives: A Reader*, London: Sage.

Farrington, D (2002) 'Developmental criminology and risk-focused prevention' in Maguire, M, Morgan, R and Reiner, R (eds), *The Oxford Handbook of Criminology*, Oxford: OUP.

Feenan, D (2002) 'Legal issues in acquiring information about illegal behaviour through criminological research', *British Journal of Criminology*, vol 42, pp 762–81.

Garland, D (2002) 'Of crime and criminals: the development of criminology in Britain' in Maguire, M, Morgan, R and Reiner, R (eds), *The Oxford Handbook of Criminology*, Oxford: OUP.

Hale, C (1999) 'The labour market and post-war crime trends in England and Wales' in Carlen, P and Morgan, R (eds), *Crime Unlimited: Questions for the 21st Century*, Basingstoke: Macmillan.

Hammersley, M (1995) *The Politics of Social Research*, London: Sage.

Hobbs, D (2001) 'Ethnography and the study of deviance' in Atkinson, P, Coffey, A, Delamont, S, Lofland, J and Lofland, L (eds), *Handbook of Ethnography*, London: Sage.

Hood, R (1992) *Race and Sentencing*, Oxford: OUP.

Hoyle, C (2000) 'Being "a nosy bloody cow": ethical and methodological issues in researching domestic violence' in King, R and Wincup, E (eds), *Doing Research on Crime and Justice*, Oxford: OUP.

Hughes, G (1998) *Understanding Crime Prevention: Social Control, Risk and Late Modernity*, Buckingham: Open University Press.

Jamieson, J (2000) 'Negotiating danger in fieldwork on crime: a researcher's tale' in Lee-Treweek, G and Linkogle, S (eds), *Danger in the Field: Risk and Ethics in Social Research*, London: Routledge.

Jupp, V (2001) 'Triangulation' in McLaughlin, E and Muncie, J (eds), *The Sage Dictionary of Criminology*, London: Sage.

Liebling, A (2001) 'Whose side are we on? Theory, practice and allegiance in prisons research', *British Journal of Criminology*, vol 41, pp 472–84.

McKeganey, N (2001) 'To pay or not to pay: respondents' motivation for participating in research', *Addiction*, vol 96, pp 1237–38.

Maguire, M (2000) 'Researching "street" criminals' in King, R and Wincup, E (eds), *Doing Research on Crime and Justice*, Oxford: OUP.

Maguire, M (2002) 'Crime statistics: the "data" explosion and its implications' in Maguire, M, Morgan, R and Reiner, R (eds), *The Oxford Handbook of Criminology*, Oxford: OUP.

May, T (2001) *Social Research: Issues, Methods and Process*, Buckingham: Open University Press.

Muncie, J (2001) 'Positivism' in McLaughlin, E and Muncie, J (eds), *The Sage Dictionary of Criminology*, London: Sage.

Noaks, L and Wincup, E (2004) *Criminological Research: Understanding Qualitative Method*, London: Sage.

Parker, H (1996) 'Young adult offenders, alcohol and criminological cul-de-sacs', *British Journal of Criminology*, vol 36, pp 282–98.

Quetelet, A (1842) 'Of the development of the propensity to crime', abridged extract in McLaughlin, E, Muncie, J and Hughes, G (eds) (2003) *Criminological Perspectives: A Reader*, London: Sage.

Sharpe, K (2000) 'Sad, bad, and (sometimes) dangerous to know: street corner research with prostitutes, punters, and the police' in King, R and Wincup, E (eds), *Doing Research on Crime and Justice*, Oxford: OUP.

Shaw, C and McKay, H (1842) *Juvenile Delinquency and Urban Areas*, Chicago: Chicago UP.

Silverman, D (1998) 'Qualitative/quantitative' in Jenks, C (ed), *Core Sociological Dichotomies*, London: Sage.

Smith, C and Wincup, E (2000) 'Breaking in: researching criminal justice institutions for women' in King, R and Wincup, E (eds), *Doing Research on Crime and Justice*, Oxford: OUP.

Social Research Association (2002) *Ethical Guidelines*, www.the-sra.org.uk.

Social Research Association (2003) *A Code of Practice for the Safety of Social Researchers*, www.the-sra.org.uk.

Truman, C (2003) 'Ethics and the ruling relations of research production', *Sociological Research Online*, vol 8, p 1.

Walklate, S (1998) *Understanding Criminology: Current Theoretical Debates*, Buckingham: Open University Press.

Walklate, S (2000) 'Researching victims' in King, R and Wincup, E (eds), *Doing Research on Crime and Justice*, Oxford: OUP.

Wardhaugh, J (2000) '"Down and outers": fieldwork amongst street homeless people' in King, R and Wincup, E (eds), *Doing Research on Crime and Justice*, Oxford: OUP.

Welland, T and Pugsley, L (eds) (2002) *Ethical Dilemmas in Qualitative Research*, Aldershot: Ashgate.

PART 2
UNRAVELLING
CRIMINAL JUSTICE
AND CRIMINOLOGY

CHAPTER 4

CRIMINAL JUSTICE, PUBLIC OPINION, FEAR AND POPULAR POLITICS[1]

Lynn Hancock

SUMMARY

The first major poll carried out to assess people's perceptions of crime, the courts, sentencing and prisons in the UK was conducted by the Prison Reform Trust in 1982 (Shaw, 1982). In the 20 or so years that have followed, academic researchers, government departments, pressure groups, and the print and broadcast media have carried out frequent surveys to explore the range and depth of public feelings about the 'fear of crime', law-breaking and the adequacy of criminal justice responses. Whilst such research has become ever more sophisticated, 'public opinion' remains more often invoked than understood in much the same way in the current period as it was in 1982. Sentencers, politicians, practitioners, penal reformers and criminologists, writing from a variety of perspectives, with a greater or lesser degree of informed research, remain apt to make assessments about what the public will or will not tolerate where penal policy and criminal justice disposals are concerned. Governments in the UK and the USA, for example, have justified harsher penalties, more austere regimes and the removal of rights from suspects, defendants and prisoners on the grounds that they are satisfying public opinion. While some professional interests, pressure groups and academic criminologists have been articulate in their opposition to such shifts towards punitiveness and populism, nevertheless a tendency to view public opinion in an undifferentiated way remains. In many senses this is surprising: recorded crime statistics, their changing trends and the explanations offered for them receive regular interrogation, yet such a response is often conspicuously absent when public opinion polls and surveys are discussed. Also, and perhaps less surprisingly, while many of the same commentators have advocated or supported greater degrees of public involvement in criminal justice processes *in principle*, there remains widespread scepticism about and suspicion of public involvement in such decision-making.

The aim of this chapter is to 'unpack' some key ideas about public opinion in the sphere of criminal justice. The chapter first outlines how the importance of public perceptions concerning crime and criminal justice institutions has grown over recent years. The view that the swing towards more punitive criminal justice policies accords with public preferences in any simple way is questioned through a review of arguments and evidence across several jurisdictions. The ways in which public opinion is expressed and the problems associated with conventional methods to assess and measure public responses are examined, and some of the key influences that shape public views about crime and criminal justice are discussed. The evidence suggests that whilst harsh penal and criminal justice policies may not be supported by the general public as a means to control crime, it is clear that many members of the

---

1   This chapter has drawn upon ideas generated through discussions with Roger Matthews during our collaborative work over recent years and also, more recently, with colleagues in the ICCCR at the Open University.

public want *something* be done to address problems confronted by many members of the public, whether they are associated with crime, disorder or wider social problems to which they are often related.

KEY TERMS

Public opinion; public attitudes; punitiveness; public participation; involvement; fear of crime; vigilante activity; community action.

THE GROWING IMPORTANCE OF PUBLIC PERCEPTIONS

It is clear during the 1980s and 1990s that 'public opinion was not always sufficiently understood or taken into account by the politicians and policy makers and, conversely, that the public were generally not well informed' about crime or criminal justice responses. As a consequence, there 'was the potential for misunderstanding, distortion, misinterpretation and misinformation in both directions' (James and Raine, 1998: 65). However, since the election of the New Labour Government in 1997, we have witnessed attempts to furnish the public with more information about crime, the criminal justice system and how it operates. The frequency and size of the British Crime Surveys have increased so that the survey now takes place each year in England and Wales, and the sample has been extended to include interviews with 40,000 people aged over 16. Scotland and Northern Ireland each have separate surveys. These surveys are expected to provide more accurate information about public experiences of victimisation, fear of crime and perceptions of criminal justice. They are also expected to inform policy formation and to play a part in evaluating the effectiveness of government policies to reduce crime, fear of crime and to increase public confidence in the criminal justice system. The use of other ways of gathering and reflecting public opinion on crime and criminal justice matters is greater than ever in the current period, as identified in the proliferation of focus groups, 'consultation' exercises and other forms of public participation which have been drawn upon by local authorities in the UK in order to comply with the Crime and Disorder Act 1998 and to institute 'best value' regimes. In turn, the number of local crime surveys has grown rapidly since the mid-1980s. Though variable in quality, they have been given a fresh impetus by measures introduced by the New Labour Government.

We have also witnessed greater attempts to 'involve' the public in criminal justice. These include, for example: Police Community Consultative Groups (PCCGs); independent custody visiting (formerly lay visitors) in police stations (see Weatheritt and Vieira, 1999), which was given statutory status by the Police Reform Act 2002; 'community representatives' in restorative justice and youth offending board activities (including mentoring and youth offender panels, for example); and lay inspectors of the Crown Prosecution Service (see Billington, 2002). There have been reforms to existing sites of public involvement, such as Independent Monitoring Boards in prisons and immigration detention centres, formerly Boards of Visitors and Visiting Committees respectively (see Home Office, 2003). In addition, arguments that the representativeness of other lay members of the criminal justice system – such as jurors and lay magistrates (Justices of the Peace) – have been advanced (see Auld, 2001;

Morgan and Russell, 2000, for example) and reforms introduced (see Department for Constitutional Affairs, 2003).

There are three main reasons for gathering information from the public about their experiences and perceptions of crime and criminal justice, disseminating information to the public and securing their involvement in a range of institutional settings:

- In order to secure (or re-secure) the legitimacy of, and consent for, the organisation or institution seeking their involvement by providing an ostensible accountability mechanism.

- In order to make 'better' decisions, thereby improving efficiency and saving money. This becomes increasingly important as institutions become larger, more bureaucratic and subject to tighter financial regimes.

- To re-engage the public with a sense of 'citizenship' and civic involvement.

These reasons are not, of course, mutually exclusive. Some attempts to 'consult' the public have been viewed as cynical attempts to secure legitimacy. The introduction of PCCGs in the early 1980s was widely viewed in this way, for example (see Uglow, 1988; Jones and Newburn, 1997). Arguably, public involvement in each of the sites indicated above is primarily symbolic: an attempt on behalf of governments to secure the legitimacy of the authorities or agencies in question. However, it is also clear that criminal justice (and other) institutions increasingly require more and better information from the public, as well as the public's involvement and participation, to carry out their functions effectively. First, it is widely accepted that the advantage of developing trust relationships between the police and public, for example, is that greater willingness to report crime will follow, and witnessing is pivotal to securing convictions and clear-up rates. Increasing public participation and involvement may help to secure trust relationships between the general public and the criminal justice system more generally (Edwards, 2002). Secondly, for criminal justice agencies, such as the police, obtaining better information regarding the experience of victimisation, levels of risk and views about criminal justice, for example, through victim and residents' surveys, citizens' panels and focus groups can play an important role in targeting agencies' scarce resources and avoiding costly mistakes. Thirdly, the criminal justice system in England and Wales is hugely dependent upon the direct participation of lay labour to function, whether in the form of lay magistrates, Victim Support volunteers (Gill and Mawby, 1990) or in another capacity (see above), and this dependence is likely to increase. We should also note that the importance of responding to and reflecting the views of the general public in principle – as an end in itself – has been expressed by Home Secretaries Blunkett and Straw in the UK over recent years.

REFLECTING AND RESPONDING TO PUBLIC OPINION

For many writers, criminal justice policies and judicial decision-making have become increasingly punitive over recent decades. The evidence for this is found in such initiatives as 'three strikes' laws, the criminalisation of a growing number of behaviours and activities, longer sentences, 'truth in sentencing', the introduction of boot camps and 'zero-tolerance' policing. Commentators observe that policy-makers are responding to public preferences, and recent measures, such as these, accord with what the public wants (Garland, 2001; Ryan, 2003). However, some have suggested that less punitive criminal justice responses are now gaining favour in the USA as the American public has become more concerned with addressing the 'causes' of crime and promoting rehabilitative policies. This more recent shift in public opinion is reflected in the withdrawal of some 'three strikes' laws and the promotion of treatment programmes, alternatives to custody and restorative justice (see Doble, 2002). Against both of these views, Doble (2002) suggests that American public opinion has remained fairly constant over the last couple of decades: punitive and liberal attitudes co-exist and a variety of sentencing goals have been and continue to be favoured (see Chapter 1). For Doble, these positions are not inconsistent; rather they reflect the way that ordinary people may 'frame' questions of crime and justice differently to policy-makers and pollsters.

The shift towards more populist and punitive criminal justice and penal policies in the UK has been seen as part of a general shift underpinned by successive governments' attempts to manipulate the public's fear of crime as part of a more general project aimed at managing political or economic crises. Other commentators have suggested, however, that there has been a break under New Labour from 1997 (Ryan, 1999; see also Ryan, 2003; Pratt, 2002). New Labour's emphasis on 're-engaging the public's voice' represents such a departure (Ryan, 1999: 14), which has been brought about because the Government recognises that the public have become increasingly marginal to politics in general, and to the criminal justice process in particular (Ryan, 2003). New Labour has sought not only to 'reference' the public or to 'legitimise' the politics of law and order, but to re-engage the public in 'active citizenship' in a range of 'crime prevention' initiatives (Ryan, 1999, and see Chapter 12). The important point here is that re-engagement is seen to be necessary and real, rather than symbolic (see Ryan, 2003).[2] However, it is also worth noting that there are contradictory forces at play, which could limit public involvement at the very time when it is being promoted.[3]

There are a number of problems that arise, potentially at least, from advancing the view that criminal justice and penal policy *will* respond to public perceptions and opinions: there is the risk that more illiberal, counter-productive and socially divisive crime and criminal justice policies are developed and implemented. A decline in public confidence becomes a real possibility when public expectations (which may be elevated in this context) are not able to be met, or because the expressed views of the public may differ from and conflict with other targets and policies pursued by government. Insufficient funding for the public's priorities may result in a failure to deliver policies set around 'community' preferences. Indeed, while there have been measures aimed at decentralising and democratising policy-making and service delivery in a number of policy fields over recent years, there have been a number of others geared towards strengthening accountability towards central government and non-local bodies (such as the Audit Commission). The growing emphasis on

---

2   In June 2003, the Home Secretary launched the Government's 'Civil Renewal Agenda' and proposed a number of wide-ranging reforms to a number of public bodies, although policing and criminal justice were at the heart of the Home Secretary's proposals (see Blunkett, 2003).

3   For example, the representativeness and involvement of lay participants in the criminal justice system has been promoted, but there have been several attempts to limit jury trials in England and Wales over recent years and there remain a number of obstacles which limit the full participation of a range of social groups as jurors and lay magistrates (Matthews, Hancock and Briggs, 2004; Morgan and Russell, 2000).

efficiency, officially sanctioned views of 'what works' to reduce crime, and value for money may be at odds with public preferences and community-based views.

PUBLIC PUNITIVENESS AND LIBERAL UNEASE

A number of commentators have expressed a distinct sense of unease when considering an enhanced role for public opinion in criminal justice (see Ryan, 1999; Ryan, 2003; NACRO, 2001). Underpinning these feelings is the general belief that punitive attitudes thrive among the public in England and Wales (and in other jurisdictions), though many writers would also concur with the view that, in principle at least, it is important to secure more democratic involvement and accountability. In sum, extending public participation and recognising public preferences in criminal justice responses invokes fear of increasing levels of public intolerance and even harsher penal policies, of which unpopular and excluded minorities will bear the brunt. Collective expressions of intolerance and the spectre of vigilante activity have compounded concerns about involving the public in criminal justice in England and Wales and elsewhere. One of the most cited examples of activities that have crystallised the fears of liberal commentators in the UK came in 2000, when a series of protests and violent attacks were directed at people suspected of sexual offences against children. Public protests began on the Paulsgrove estate in Portsmouth, but a number of violent attacks were made in other cities in the UK. They were sparked by a campaign by the *News of the World* to pressure the Government to inform the public about the whereabouts of convicted paedophiles. The campaign for 'Sarah's law', modelled on Megan's law in the United States, followed the murder of Sarah Payne in Sussex. The *News of the World's* campaign involved the printing of pictures and names of convicted paedophiles.

There is little doubt that, for many liberal commentators, these events served to reinforce views of 'communities' as sites of tyranny, containing frenzied and often ill-informed responses to law-breakers. We will explore the extent to which such views are justified below. It is, however, noteworthy that expressions of public anger such as these raise a number of other issues that we should bear in mind. First:

> ... their emergence reflects a dissatisfaction with the existing criminal justice and penal systems, which seem too remote and non-responsive to the interests of ordinary people; a sense of vulnerability, and perceptions that the state's own penal solutions to crime and social problems cannot keep them in check. (Pratt, 2002: 189)

Secondly, such events reflect the way that some social and spatial groups are less able than others to protect themselves by purchasing security through the market when the state is no longer able or willing to guarantee to security of citizens (Pratt, 2002). This was not only manifest in the kinds of sites where the protests took place (such as Paulsgrove) but in the reactions of politicians and different sections of the news media who accused those who criticised protesters of 'snobbishness' (see Ryan, 2003). Thirdly, and importantly, they raise questions about changing levels of 'toleration' among community groups and the conditions that may underpin them (see Hancock and Matthews, 2001).

Despite (or perhaps because of) print, broadcast media and academic interest in high profile public protests, we know relatively little about the day-to-day responses to law-breakers of varying degrees of seriousness. Certainly, there are 'loud voices' and ones that are clearly eager to be 'involved' in crime control activities. However, there are other 'voices' that require us to at least ask different kinds of questions in order to uncover the nature of public priorities (Hancock, 2001). Without doubt, public opinion cannot be viewed as a homogenous 'thing'. In the same vein, we need to be wary of generalising about growing public punitiveness across different societies, which, it is claimed, has given rise to a new 'culture of control' (Garland, 2001; Young, 2002). Differences between societies (see O'Donnell and O'Sullivan, 2003) and the importance of context, place, culture and the history and nature of social relations within them need to be recognised (Hancock, 2001; Walklate and Evans, 1999). The following section discusses further reasons why we should be sceptical about generalising from public opinion data sets.

PUBLIC OPINION AND CRIMINAL JUSTICE

What is public opinion?

At its most basic, 'public opinion' refers to the expressed opinion of the public. We therefore need to consider: (a) how is this opinion expressed?; and (b) how adequate are the tools used to assess and measure public responses? When thinking about these questions, several points need to be borne in mind. First, 'loud voices', like those associated with 'spontaneous protests' of the like witnessed in Paulsgrove, can distort our perceptions of public opinion. Secondly, although some writers have acknowledged different 'publics' (Ryan, 2003), there often remains a tendency to view the public as an undifferentiated mass. Systematic research exploring differences and divisions in public opinion and the conditions that give rise to them is fairly limited and somewhat inconsistent. Thirdly, while improvements have been made to the ways in which public views are gathered and measured, the use and profile of the more sophisticated tools, and the studies employing them, have remained rather patchy.

Those writers who are familiar with the more advanced techniques for assessing public attitudes and opinions have urged researchers and policy-makers to exercise care when drawing upon data in opinion surveys, particularly when they are concerned with trying to assess public sentencing preferences and attitudes towards punishment. As Durham (1993) argued, there are several reasons why the validity of findings from many public opinion polls and surveys should be treated with caution. Durham summarises the problems as follows: the highly specific nature of the stimulus used to invoke a response (often a suggested sentence) from an interviewee; respondent lack of familiarity with the scenario in question; the time constraints of the interview; questions about the respondent's understanding of vignettes and the impact of their own ideological positions. Respondents may not have spent much time prior to the interview, or are unable to spend sufficient time during it, to consider the issues in detail. They may modify their views about crime and punishment when they are given more information. As a consequence, there are questions concerning the extent to which there are 'solid opinions in the minds of citizens regarding appropriate punishment for crime' (Durham, 1993: 8).

In Durham's view, the use of filter questions would be useful as an aid to interpreting the results from opinion poll data: researchers could ask respondents about the extent to which they have thought about the topic in question, 'instead of merely asking what sentence the robber in a crime vignette would receive' (1993: 10). Durham was writing in the North American context about the numerous surveys on crime and punishment now conducted, but the key points are relevant to many surveys in the UK where respondents are often unable to offer responses that reflect their complex, nuanced and perhaps ambiguous views about crime and punishment. This is important because, as Durham has argued, 'the complexity of opinions held by individual citizens resists simplistic characterisation' (1993: 9).

When researchers have employed more sophisticated methods, they have been able to reveal something of these complexities. For example, in Applegate, Cullen, Turner and Sundt's study (1996) of the 'three strikes and you're out' laws in Ohio, the researchers found that 'global' attitudes towards life-sentence incarceration for third time felons were prevalent when respondents were asked:

> As you may know, several states have recently passed laws commonly known as 'three strikes and you're out' laws. These laws say that anyone with two serious felony convictions on their record who is convicted of a third serious crime must be given a sentence of *life* in prison. Do you support or oppose passing a 'three strikes and you're out' law in Ohio?

Respondents were then asked whether they supported its implementation strongly, somewhat, opposed it somewhat or opposed it strongly. The authors noted that such a question is not atypical in public opinion surveys assessing support for 'three strikes' laws. Nor were their findings dissimilar: 88.4 per cent of their sample supported implementation strongly or somewhat strongly (Applegate et al, 1996: 525). However, when they assessed 'specific' support using vignettes, where a range of disposals of varying degrees of severity were on offer, they found that:

> The difference between the levels of global support and specific support was not only statistically significant ... but enormous. Although a large majority of respondents stated that they favoured passing a three-strikes law, when they were confronted with a specific situation only a small minority indicated that a life sentence was appropriate for the offender described. Moreover, 72.2% of the individual respondents answered the two questions inconsistently. (Applegate et al, 1996: 525)

Applegate and colleagues note how public attitudes appear to be less punitive when the methods used to gather public opinion 'dig deeper'. They conclude that 'basing policy on global attitudes alone can lead to correctional policies that the public does not necessarily support (or support strongly) in specific situations' (1996: 530). Their research illustrates a number of themes that have been revealed in other studies in a variety of jurisdictions. It reveals the importance of employing research methods that can uncover the range and, importantly, the 'depth' of public attitudes; it also shows that given the opportunity to think through some of the issues – using carefully researched, grounded scenarios and vignettes, for example – people respond with more sophisticated, reasoned and less punitive responses. Cullen et al (2002), for example, have demonstrated continuing support for rehabilitation or treatment-oriented sanctions in the USA, and a number of studies have established that providing the public with more information about criminal justice, sentencing and so on can have a positive impact on public opinion (see Doble, 2002; Hough and Park, 2002; Mirrlees-Black, 2002). As Hough and Roberts put it:

When asked about sentencing in general, the public think of the worst kinds of offenders (recidivists) and the worst crimes of violence, although these represent a small minority of the total offender population. When presented with a concrete description of an actual case, the public tend to be less punitive. As well, when given adequate information about the range of legal punishments available, the public are less likely to endorse the use of imprisonment. In other words, the more detail that people are given about any given crime and the available penalties, the more their sentencing preferences converge with actual sentencing decisions. (1999: 23)

Hough and Roberts note that, in large part, this derives from the kinds of (mis)information the public receive via the news media; they remember atypical sentences (often lenient) for the kinds of crimes and offenders indicated in the quotation above, and they are not aware of the range of sanctions available to the courts. As a result, people tend to regard judges as being 'out of touch'. Consequently, public confidence in sentencing is undermined, fuelling demands for harsher punishments.

SHAPING PUBLIC OPINION

Knowledge, experience and involvement

When members of the public have been provided with information and accorded more opportunity to think through criminal justice issues, positive effects concerning the way that people understand, evaluate and assess the criminal justice system have followed (Mirrlees-Black, 2002). The direct experience and involvement of the general public in the criminal justice system can have a similar impact. Matthews, Hancock and Briggs (2004) examined how the experience of jury service shaped people's perceptions, understanding, confidence and satisfaction with the jury system. Of the 361 jurors interviewed, 58 per cent said that the most positive aspect of their service was that they acquired a greater understanding of the criminal trial or that it was a positive learning experience. In contrast to Hough and Roberts' (1999) findings (see above), most people left jury service with positive impressions of judges, based on their experiences. Indeed, the majority (63 per cent) of those engaging in jury service had a more positive view of the jury trial system after their service than they did before. Moreover, amongst those who had not performed jury service in the past, over two-fifths (43 per cent) left jury service with a higher level of confidence in the court system; less than one-fifth left with lower levels of confidence. This research found that confidence in the jury system was closely associated with the perceived fairness of the process, adherence to due process, respect for the rights of defendants and, above all, the importance of juries being drawn from people from a range of socially diverse backgrounds. However, the overwhelming majority expressing strong support for jury trials also often had qualifications to make, and those who were more critical often recognised the qualities and strengths of this mode of trial. Rarely were attitudes one-dimensional or without qualification. In addition, those who had visited a court in the past, either as victims or witnesses, were more likely to leave with a higher level of confidence.

Media influences

Prior to their jury service, the respondents in Matthews, Hancock and Briggs' research indicated that television and newspapers were the main source of information about jury service and the criminal court system more generally.[4] The experience of being a juror prompted a number of respondents to comment that the reality of engaging in a court case was a long way from popular media depictions. As one respondent said:

> It [jury service] does give you an insight into how cases are dealt with in reality and it is very different compared with TV.

In a similar vein, another observed:

> The legal system is old fashioned and inefficient but I have a clearer idea of the reality rather than the fiction. The real legal profession are not as fickle or as entertaining as they are on TV. (Matthews, Hancock and Briggs, 2004: 33)

While many respondents expressed a healthy level of scepticism towards the media following their jury service, for those members of the public for whom direct contact with the criminal justice system has been limited or absent, there is evidence to suggest that the system is widely regarded with scepticism, contempt and cynicism (Gillespie and McLaughlin, 2002; 2003). Gillespie and McLaughlin's research on the role of the media in shaping public attitudes towards crime and punishment has suggested that, whilst people's attitudes are not unyielding and perceptions may be shaped in different ways by a range of media, people's personal experiences of crime, or the victimisation of others they know, can shape the way media representations are interpreted. Attitudes often remain deeply entrenched.

Some television programmes, such as *Crimewatch* in the UK, were likely to invoke more punitive responses from viewers. Moreover, respondents who tended to watch news and current affairs programmes, for example, were not necessarily more informed about the criminal justice system than those who watched fictional dramas. Soap operas provided key sources of information for the public as far as crime and offenders were concerned. Indeed, their analysis, based on focus group discussions, suggests that, because this type of programme can provide more information about an offender's background, the crime, as well as the opportunity to assess different perspectives, the potential exists to generate more empathetic responses to offenders. Nevertheless, knowledge about the criminal justice system in general and actual sentencing practices in particular remained limited for these viewers and for the sample as a whole (Gillespie and McLaughlin, 2002).

The role of the media in shaping public opinion is crucial, though not simple (see Chapter 5 and also Reiner, Livingstone and Allen, 2000). The news media provide key sources of information, but, as Indermaur and Hough (2002: 202) note, 'they do this in a particular way, reflecting the commercial (or quasi-commercial) pressures to retain their audiences and thus their revenue'. As such, media interests can be regarded as actors in their own right, as well as the vehicles through which politicians, interest

---

4   Fifty-five percent reported that their views and perceptions of the court system were shaped by the television news, 49 per cent said that drama and soap operas were influential, while the same percentage said that newspapers were important. Films were another important external influence for 14 per cent of respondents. Other influences included prior experiences or those of friends and family and, for a small minority (9 per cent), the education system. Respondents were permitted to acknowledge more than one influence where they found difficulty distinguishing one from another (Matthews, Hancock and Briggs, 2004).

groups and 'the public' convey themselves and their viewpoints to each other. It is through the media that each group acquires its knowledge of each other's views and standpoints. This is particularly the case for politicians and 'policy elites', whose sense of distance from 'public opinion' makes them particularly receptive to the 'window' into 'public opinion' offered by the media (Indermaur and Hough, 2002: 204).

Thus, it is not surprising that:

[t]here is something of a comedy of errors in which policy and practice are not based on a proper understanding of public preferences and opinions and those same opinions are not based on a proper understanding of policy and practice. In fact evidence from the USA and elsewhere suggests that the proportion of the population who tell pollsters that the system is too soft remain fairly static however harsh the system becomes. (Allen, 2002a: 6)

Nor is it unexpected that, despite recent falls in the recorded crime rate, many people perceive crime to be increasing, given that the figures have been widely reported to have been doing so for a number of decades (Hough, 2002; Pratt, 2002; Young, 2003). In this context, we can expect public fears about crime to continue in much the same way, not least because of the frenetic increase in the number of surveys reported in the news media along with the use of highly selective official statistics (see Young, 2003). However, this is not to suggest that public support for punitive criminal justice policies is simply 'conjured up' by manipulative media interests and politicians, or that the public are simply muddled and misinformed (Garland, 2001). That said, we need to remember that some interests are not best served by the crime drop and any (rational) corresponding reduction in resources that might imply (Young, 2003).

Fear, anxiety and worry about crime

Many commentators have agreed that worry about crime, and lack of public confidence in criminal justice agencies' abilities to respond to crime, is a reflection of wider insecurities and fragilities experienced in contemporary society (in the labour market and family life, for example). There is, however, disagreement in the literature regarding the kinds of social groups who are more likely to be receptive to or push for more punitive criminal justice and penal policies. Garland (2001) argued that the professional middle classes have been the most influential group in the shift towards more illiberal penal policies in the USA and the UK. Other commentators have questioned this view (Young, 2002). Indeed, as we have already noted, some social groups are much less able to purchase security through the market (see Hope, 2000; Pratt, 2002). The gap between those who are able to do so and the less affluent has grown over recent years in the UK: 1991 to 2001 saw the gap between the rich and poor widen significantly. Analysis of the 2001 Census showed that 'wealthy achievers' increased from 19 per cent to 25 per cent of the population, while those of 'moderate means' and the 'hard pressed' grew to 37 per cent (15 per cent and 22 per cent respectively) (Doward, Reilly and Graham, 2003: 7). Given that the experience of criminal victimisation is greatest in areas suffering the most from economic disadvantage (Hope, 2003), and that it is not clear that disadvantaged groups have benefited from the general fall in crime in England and Wales (Hope, 2003; Young and Matthews, 2003), it would be surprising to find that the need to 'do something' about crime and disorder did not find more resonance in those areas of cities occupied by the most economically marginal sections of the working class.

The British Crime Survey (BCS), administered by the Home Office, has examined various aspects of the 'fear of crime' (who is more likely to be concerned about crime, how worried are they, and about what) since 1984 (Kershaw et al, 2001). It specifies several types of property crime, such as burglary and theft of and from cars, and personal crimes, such as physical attack and rape, and asks respondents to say whether they are 'very worried', 'fairly worried', 'not very worried' or 'not very worried at all' (Kershaw et al, 2001: 36). The 2001 BCS found that:

- women are more worried than men about burglary and violent and sexual assault;

- the less affluent, those who live in social housing and people employed in unskilled or semi-skilled occupations, are more likely to be concerned about crime;

- those who live in inner-city and council estates and areas with high levels of victimisation and social/physical disorder (which refers to teenagers hanging around, graffiti, vandalism and so on) are also more fearful.

In this context, if 'outrage and anger are the culture's antidotes to fear and anxiety' (Garland, 2001: 145), it is not unreasonable to expect their expression to be found in these localities, or for it to take a punitive form. That said, when researchers have approached 'fear of crime' using different methodological approaches and standpoints (for example, Walklate, 1998; Walklate and Evans, 1999; Pain, 2000 and 2001; Gilchrist et al, 1998), more nuanced findings have emerged, and ones that raise different questions and problems for policy-makers. In the same way that some people are managing their fears, developing trust relationships, enjoying a sense of belonging and feeling less fearful, there are others whose lives are clearly disrupted by crime and disorder in their communities (see Walklate and Evans, 1999).

Interestingly, and perhaps counter-intuitively, however, some research has suggested that even victims of crimes such as burglary are not necessarily more punitive when compared with non-victims (Hough and Roberts, 1999; Mayhew and van Kesteren, 2002). Cross-national surveys have generated mixed results regarding the relationship between 'fear of crime' and 'punitiveness' (see Mayhew and van Kesteren, 2002). The research evidence regarding the kind of demographic groups which are more likely to favour punitive responses (favouring imprisonment, 'three strikes' laws and the like) is inconsistent too. Applegate et al (1996), for example, did not find any significant relationship between respondents' socio-demographic characteristics (including sex, age, race, education, income, marital status, and conservatism) and 'global support' for 'three strikes' policies. As far as 'specific support' for 'three strikes' laws is concerned, only 'conservatism' appeared to be related to support for this policy. Some studies have shown that younger people are more punitive in Western countries (Mayhew and van Kesteren, 2002) though other research has suggested otherwise (Allen, 2002a; Hough and Park, 2002). The more educated appear to be less punitive, and more likely to be adaptable in their views when given more information (Hough and Park, 2002), but it is important to recognise that comparing the results of different studies conducted within countries, as well as across them, generates a series of additional problems for the analyst.

LOCAL PRESSURE GROUPS AND COMMUNITY ACTION

While some sections of the general population do not appear to be particularly punitive, this should not be read as suggesting that they necessarily wish to exercise 'toleration'.[5] Rather, it is very likely that many people who perceive problems associated with crime and disorder in their neighbourhoods want *something* to be done. Perhaps in part because of the high profile nature of vigilante action, or perhaps because local pressure group activity has not traditionally received much research attention, even from political scientists (Stoker and Wilson, 1991), there has been little interest on behalf of the media and academic criminologists regarding the ways that people respond to crime and disorder on a daily basis. It is not that there is an absence of activity in urban communities in the UK (see Hancock, 2001) and elsewhere (see Podolefsky and Dubow, 1981; Skogan, 1988): collective, grass roots activities are not rare events. Podolefsky and Dubow distinguished 47 different types of anti-crime activities in their study of 10 neighbourhoods, in three cities, in the USA. Many would have been missed had *a priori* categories been used by the researchers. The limited research available suggests that community groups do not wish to 'isolate crime from the myriad of social problems' in a locality (Podolefsky and Dubow, 1981: 223; see also Hancock, 2001). It also indicates that it is not the prevalence of crime problems or fear of victimisation that encourages local activities; the presence of existing community groups or a history of community organisation is more influential. Other contextual factors, such as degrees of 'social solidarity', including the definition of 'out-groups' and 'local theories about the causes of crime' (1981: 15) that flow from the local 'social-cultural context', are significant. Hancock (2001) discusses further the key influences upon community mobilisation around crime and disorder and the factors that can undermine and promote activity. What is important to note is that, while some of the new mechanisms for involving communities in crime control and criminal justice (indicated in the introductory sections of this chapter) may enable some groups to address their goals through these forums (crime and disorder reduction partnerships, for example), they bring with them a number of risks as far as community action is concerned. Although they can act as 'structures of opportunity', where these bodies share definitions of problems with community groups and there is agreement between the parties regarding strategies for addressing them, the goals of organised groups are often transformed through participatory arrangements, definitions and strategies become disconnected from their social context, and the expectations of activists are modified as they come to realise the limits of what is achievable (see Podolefsky and Dubow, 1981; Hancock, 2001, Chapter 6). Solutions to crime problems often become much more narrowly defined even though crime and victimisation tend not to be seen as being separate from, or unrelated to, other neighbourhood conditions, such as neighbourhood instability, poor housing, the presence or absence of facilities and opportunities for young people and so on. Crimes are often not the most salient problems in disadvantaged communities. Indeed, even at a more general level, Allen (2002b) has shown in a review of available evidence that few people favour criminal justice sanctions as a means to reduce crime. Rather, better parenting, more police beat officers, better discipline in schools and finding ways to constructively engage young people in local activities are favoured in surveys of the general public.

---

5   'Toleration' generally refers to 'the deliberate choice not to interfere with conduct or beliefs with which one disapproves' (Hancock and Matthews, 2001: 99).

CONCLUSION

In this chapter we have observed how public perceptions of, and involvement in, criminal justice institutions have developed over recent years. Some of the key reasons that have been put forward to explain governments' attempts to involve and respond to the public and their preferences have been outlined. Drawing upon arguments and evidence from research in several jurisdictions, we have questioned the extent to which more punitive criminal justice policies accord with public preferences. The chapter considered the variety of ways in which public opinion is expressed and the problems associated with the methods frequently used to assess and measure public attitudes (see also Chapter 3). When the nature of public attitudes is explored in depth using sophisticated research methods, quite different results emerge compared to the often-cited rudimentary surveys. Some of the key influences that may shape the public's views about crime and criminal justice have been considered. In so doing, the importance of people's direct experience/involvement, the role of the media, and fear, anxiety and worry about crime have been discussed. The evidence has suggested that many members of the public are demanding that *something* be done to address crime, victimisation, fear of crime and other neighbourhood problems. However, there is little evidence to support the view that harsh penal and criminal justice policies are favoured as a means of addressing offending behaviour.

SEMINAR DISCUSSION TOPICS

- What are the advantages and disadvantages of (a) enhancing public involvement in criminal justice, and (b) responding to public preferences in criminal justice policy-making?
- What are the key factors that shape public opinion about crime and criminal justice? List the key factors outlined in this chapter and consider whether there are other factors that could be added to your list.
- Is it inevitable that greater public involvement will result in more punitive penal policies? What steps need to be taken in your view to develop more 'tolerant' criminal justice responses?

KEY READINGS

The most common means of measuring 'public opinion' on matters of crime and criminal justice is through victim surveys. Mattinson and Mirrlees-Black's (2000) *Attitudes to Crime and Criminal Justice*, gleaned from the British Crime Survey, is indicative. Hough and Roberts' (1998) Home Office Report, *Attitudes to Punishment*, reveals wide disparities between public perceptions and actual court practices. Such sources, however, should be read against those more attuned to 'global' and 'specific' attitudes, such as Applegate et al (1996) and to localised contingencies such as Hancock (2001). Roberts and Houghs' (2002) edited collection, *Changing Attitudes to Punishment*, is a useful overview of the many methodological complexities involved.

REFERENCES

Allen, R (2002a) 'What does the public think about prison?', *Criminal Justice Matters*, vol 49, Autumn, pp 6–7 and 41.

Allen, R (2002b) *What Does the Public Think about Prison?*, London: Esmée Fairburn Foundation (Research briefing), June.

Applegate, BK, Cullen, FT, Turner, MG and Sundt, JL (1996) 'Assessing public support for three strikes and you're out laws: global versus specific attitudes', *Crime and Delinquency*, vol 42(4), pp 517–34.

Auld, Lord Justice (2001) *Criminal Courts Review*, London: The Stationery Office.

Billington, A (2002) 'Inspecting the CPS', *Criminal Justice Matters*, vol 49, Autumn, pp 22–23.

Blunkett, D (2003) 'Civil renewal: a new agenda: the CSV Edith Kahn Memorial Lecture', 11 June.

Cullen, FT, Pealer, JA, Fisher, BS, Applegate, BK and Santana, SA (2002) 'Public support for correctional rehabilitation in America: change or consistency?' in Roberts, JV and Hough, M (eds), *Changing Attitudes to Punishment*, Cullompton: Willan.

Department for Constitutional Affairs (2003) *National Strategy for the Recruitment of Lay Magistrates*, London: Department for Constitutional Affairs, October.

Doble, J (2002) 'Attitudes to punishment in the US – punitive and liberal opinions' in Roberts, JV and Hough, M (eds), *Changing Attitudes to Punishment*, Cullompton: Willan.

Doward, J, Reilly, T and Graham, M (2003) 'Census exposes unequal Britain', *The Observer*, 23 November.

Durham, A (1993) 'Public opinion regarding sentences for crime: does it exist?', *Journal of Criminal Justice*, vol 21, pp 1–11.

Edwards, L (2002) 'Public involvement in the criminal justice system', *Criminal Justice Matters*, vol 49, Autumn, pp 16–17.

Garland, D (2001) *The Culture of Control: Crime and Social Order in Contemporary Society*, Oxford: OUP.

Gilchrist, E, Bannister, J, Ditton, J and Farrall, S (1998) 'Women and the fear of crime', *British Journal of Criminology*, vol 38(2), pp 283–98.

Gill, M and Mawby, RI (1990) *Volunteers in the Criminal Justice System*, Buckinghamshire: Open University Press.

Gillespie, M and McLaughlin, E (2002) 'Media and the shaping of public attitudes', *Criminal Justice Matters*, vol 49, Autumn, pp 8–9 and 23.

Gillespie, M and McLaughlin, E (2003) *Media and the Shaping of Public Knowledge and Attitudes Towards Crime and Punishment*, London: Esmée Fairburn Foundation (Research briefing), June.

Hancock, L (2001) *Community, Crime and Disorder: Safety and Regeneration in Urban Neighbourhoods*, Basingstoke: Palgrave.

Hancock, L and Matthews, R (2001) 'Crime, community safety and toleration' in Matthews, R and Pitts, J (eds), *Crime, Disorder and Community Safety*, London: Routledge.

Home Office (2003) *Independent Monitoring Boards in Prisons and Immigration Removal Centres*, London: Home Office.

Hope, T (2000) 'Inequality and the clubbing of security' in Hope, T and Sparks, R (eds), *Crime, Risk and Insecurity*, London: Routledge.

Hope, T (2003) 'The crime drop in Britain?', *Community Safety Journal*, vol 2(4), pp 14–16.

Hope, T and Sparks, R (2000) 'Introduction: risk, insecurity and the politics of law and order' in Hope, T and Sparks, R (eds), *Crime, Risk and Insecurity*, London: Routledge.

Hough, M (2002) 'Populism and punitive penal policy', *Criminal Justice Matters*, vol 49, Autumn, pp 4–5.

Hough, M and Park, A (2002) 'How malleable are attitudes to crime and punishment? Findings from a British deliberative poll' in Roberts, V and Hough, M (eds), *Changing Attitudes to Punishment*, Cullompton: Willan.

Hough, M and Roberts, J (1999) 'Sentencing trends in Britain', *Punishment and Society*, vol 1(1), pp 11–26.

Indermaur, D and Hough, M (2002) 'Strategies for challenging public attitudes to punishment' in Roberts, JV and Hough, M (eds), *Changing Attitudes to Punishment*, Cullompton: Willan.

James, A and Raine, J (1998) *The New Politics of Criminal Justice*, London: Longman.

Jones, T and Newburn, T (1997) *Policing After the Act: Police and Magistrates' Courts Act 1994*, London: PSI.

Kershaw, C, Chivite-Matthews, N, Thomas, C and Aust, R (2001) *The 2001 British Crime Survey, First Results, England and Wales*, London: Home Office.

Matthews, R, Hancock, L and Briggs, D (2004) *Jurors' Perceptions, Understanding, Confidence and Satisfaction in the Jury System: A Study in Six Courts*, London: Home Office, Online Report 05/04.

Mattinson, J and Mirrlees-Black, C (2000) *Attitudes to Crime and Criminal Justice: Findings from the British Crime Survey*, Research Findings No 111, London: Home Office.

Mayhew, P and van Kesteren, J (2002) 'Cross-national attitudes to punishment' in Roberts, JV and Hough, M (eds), *Changing Attitudes to Punishment*, Cullompton: Willan.

Mirrlees-Black, C (2002) 'Improving public knowledge about crime and punishment' in Roberts, JV and Hough, M (eds), *Changing Attitudes to Punishment*, Cullompton: Willan.

Morgan, R and Russell, N (2000) *The Judiciary in the Magistrates' Courts*, London: Home Office and Lord Chancellor's Department.

NACRO (2001) *Youth Crime Briefing*, London: NACRO, December.

O'Donnell, I and O'Sullivan, E (2003) 'The politics of intolerance – Irish style', *British Journal of Criminology*, vol 43, pp 41–62.

Pain, R (2000) 'Place, social relations and the fear of crime: a review', *Progress in Human Geography*, vol 24(3), pp 365–87.

Pain, R (2001) 'Gender, race, age and fear in the city', *Urban Studies*, vol 38(5 and 6), pp 899–913.

Podolefsky, A and Dubow, F (1981) *Strategies for Community Crime Prevention: Collective Responses to Crime in Urban America*, Springfield, IL: Charles C Thomas.

Pratt, J (2002) *Punishment and Civilisation*, London: Sage.

Reiner, R, Livingstone, S and Allen, J (2000) 'No more happy endings? The media and popular concern about crime since the Second World War' in Hope, T and Sparks, R (eds), *Crime, Risk and Insecurity*, London: Routledge.

Roberts, J.V and Hough, M (2002) 'Public attitudes to punishment: the context' in Roberts, JV and Hough, M (eds), *Changing Attitudes to Punishment*, Cullompton: Willan.

Ryan, M (1999) 'Penal policy making towards the millennium: elites and populists; New Labour and the new criminology', *International Journal of the Sociology of Law*, vol 27, pp 1–22.

Ryan, M (2003) *Penal Policy and Political Culture in England and Wales*, Winchester: Waterside.

Shaw, S (1982) *The People's Justice: A Major Poll of Public Attitudes on Crime and Punishment*, London: Prison Reform Trust.

Skogan, WG (1988) 'Community organizations and crime' in Tonry, M and Morris, N (eds), *Crime and Justice: a Review of Research, vol 10*, Chicago: Chicago UP.

Stoker, G and Wilson, D (1991) 'The lost world of British local pressure groups', *Public Policy and Administration*, vol 6(2), Summer, pp 20–34.

Uglow, S (1988) *Policing Liberal Society*, Oxford: OUP.

Walklate, S (1998) 'Crime and community: fear or trust?', *British Journal of Sociology*, vol 49(4), pp 550–70.

Walklate, S and Evans, K (1999) *Zero Tolerance or Community Tolerance: Managing Crime in High Crime Areas*, Aldershot: Ashgate.

Weatheritt, M and Vieira, C (1999) *Lay Visiting to Police Stations*, Home Office Research Study 188, London: Home Office.

Young, J (2002) 'Searching for a new criminology of everyday life: a review of "the culture of control"', *British Journal of Criminology*, vol 42, pp 228–43.

Young, J (2003) 'Winning the fight against crime? New Labour, populism and lost opportunities' in Matthews, R and Young, J (eds), *The New Politics of Crime and Punishment*, Cullompton: Willan.

Young, J and Matthews, R (2003) 'New Labour, crime control and social exclusion' in Matthews, R and Young, J (eds), *The New Politics of Crime and Punishment*, Cullompton: Willan.

CHAPTER 5

MEDIA REPRESENTATIONS OF CRIMINAL JUSTICE

Yvonne Jewkes

SUMMARY

This chapter explores media constructions of criminal justice. Although the discussion is broad in scope, a recurring theme throughout the chapter concerns the biases – especially racial biases – that permeate media discourses concerning crime and justice. In other words, while the chapter provides an overview of the relationship between media representations and public misconceptions about criminal justice in general, the differential treatment of black and Asian people provides a unifying theme within a broader argument that the media taps into psycho-social fears about 'others' and is one of the primary sites of social inclusion and exclusion.

KEY TERMS

Media; constructionism; fictional and factual portrayals; representation and misrepresentation; newsworthiness; bias; prejudice; offenders; victims; 'others'; outsiders; inclusion; exclusion.

INTRODUCTION

Several writers have examined the proposition that the media present crime stories – both factual and fictional – in ways which selectively distort and manipulate public perceptions, creating a false picture of crime which promotes stereotyping, bias, prejudice and gross over-simplification of the facts (Chibnall, 1977; Hall et al, 1978; Box, 1983; Schlesinger and Tumber, 1994; Kidd-Hewitt and Osborne, 1995; Jewkes, 2004). Their conclusion is that it is not just official statistics that misrepresent the picture of crime, but that the media are also guilty of manipulation and fuelling public fears. Studies carried out in the UK and the USA indicate that crime reporting in the press is more prevalent than ever before, and that interpersonal crimes, particularly violent and sexual crimes, are consistently over-reported in relation to official statistics (Ditton and Duffy, 1983; Smith, 1984; Schlesinger and Tumber, 1994; Naylor, 2001; Greer, 2003). Some studies have also found that newspaper readers over-estimate the proportion of crimes solved, and that the police sometimes reinforce journalistically-produced concerns about a 'crime wave' by feeding reporters stories based on previously reported incidents (Roshier, 1973; Fishman, 1981). This can sometimes provoke fear of a crime surge at a time when, statistically, incidents of that crime are on the decrease. Meanwhile, the media treat stories about erratic or 'light' sentencing decisions as highly newsworthy and ongoing evidence of a 'world gone mad'. The result of these combined (mis)representations is that, in general, public perceptions reflect the media's construction of a continually spiralling crime rate and a criminal justice system that is ineffective and 'soft on crime' (Hough and Roberts, 1998; Gillespie and McLaughlin, 2003).

The reasons for the media's preoccupation with certain types of crime – ie those involving sex, violence, women and children in any combination thereof – may be largely pragmatic and economic. They are, after all, in the business of selling newspapers and gaining audience ratings, and it is serious crimes involving women and children (as perpetrators or victims) which are most uncommon and therefore most 'newsworthy'. However, the dual outcomes of their portrayals of crime and violence, especially against vulnerable individuals, are heightened public anxieties and a greater public mandate for increasingly punitive forms of justice. It is the latter that this chapter will take as its primary focus. In other words, it will explore the role of the media in promoting a conservative consensus which, in matters of crime and deviance, emphasises deterrence and repression and voices support for more police, more prisons and a tougher criminal justice system. This agenda is often characterised by newspapers such as *The Sun* and the *Daily Mail* as a defence of the 'British way of life', a fiercely nostalgic sentiment which may now only appeal to a minority (ironically, usually termed the 'moral majority') of British citizens. Despite claiming to be the voice of the people, the criminalisation of certain individuals and activities by these newspapers highlights the general perceived intolerance towards anyone or anything that transgresses an essentially conservative agenda. It is also partial explanation for the vigorous policing and punishment of so called 'victimless crimes': asylum seeking and illegal immigration, recreational use of drugs, sexual permissiveness, especially among young people, public displays of homosexuality and lesbianism, anti-establishment demonstrators exercising their democratic rights to protest, and spectacular youth cultures. All are activities that are subject to continuous, and sometimes overblown, repression.

In addition to the generalised climate of conservative responses to crime and justice, it appears that political process in Westminster and media discourses are increasingly indistinguishable and mutually constitutive. The symbiotic relationship between the media and politicians is illustrated by the support that the press has given to the current Government, and the previous Conservative administration, in matters of law and order. For two decades a version of 'populist punitiveness' has characterised British governments' attitudes to penal policy, a stance which is replicated in the United States and in many other countries around the world. To put it bluntly, there seems little opposition from any political party in the UK to proposals to incarcerate ever younger children, to introduce curfews on young people, to bring in legislation to prevent large 'unauthorised' gatherings, and to introduce new and harsher measures against immigrants, protesters, demonstrators, the homeless, the mentally ill and the young unemployed. It is, in effect, a policy of crime reduction through criminalisation – a course of action which is uncritically communicated to the public at large by the mass media.

The 'self' and 'other'

In recent years notions of 'self' and 'other' have started to permeate criminological discourse (Garland, 1996; Jefferson, 2002; Jewkes, 2002; 2004), and there are many examples of mediated 'outsiders' – 'the threatening outcast, the fearsome stranger, the excluded and the embittered' (Garland, 1996: 461) – who provide the 'others' against whom we measure ourselves. As Foucault (1988) suggests, we judge the criminal, not the crime, and for all our 'postmodern' sophistication, the beginning of the 21st century finds us still falling back on the positivist discourses of 19th century criminology. By attributing irrationality, criminality and lesser reasoning to women, children, adolescents, those who lead 'unconventional' lifestyles, people from different ethnic backgrounds to our own and people with mental illnesses, it is perhaps not surprising that it is these groups who are most consistently demonised by the media as these ascribed attributes then become the lens through which we view crime and violent behaviour. No one who lives in today's media-saturated society is immune to the circulation of ideas about 'self' and 'other'. As far as the British media are concerned, 'we' are the civilised, law-abiding 'moral majority', while 'they' or their offspring are the dangerous classes who must be identified, controlled and contained. It is within this winner-loser/self-other/insider-outsider culture that laws are made and justice done. Little wonder that, to many of Britain's citizens and visitors, the police and criminal justice system are viewed as, at best, ineffective and, at worst, discriminatory and threatening (Reiner et al, 2001).

Our pre-modern responses to postmodern problems are also evident in the media's overwhelming tendency to denounce acts as 'evil' (Stokes, 2000). Since Stanley Cohen (1973) popularised the notion of the 'folk devil' three decades ago, the symbolic potency of that image has been weakened and has, in recent times, been replaced by a more powerful icon – the 'evil monster'. When serious offences are committed, the evil nature of the act is projected onto the perpetrators and 'evil' comes to be seen not as the element that sets the crime apart as an abnormal and isolated event, but as the common factor in all crimes that can be reported as components of a single moral panic (Franklin and Petley, 1996; Stokes, 2000). Furthermore, the concentration of news media on the criminal and deviant activities of people from the lower socio-economic strata and from religious, ethnic and cultural minorities serves to perpetuate a sense of a stratified, deeply divided and mutually hostile population. Some politicians have been quick to galvanise the support of an anxious and fearful public, and have undoubtedly contributed to negative reporting which has agitated social tensions. By simultaneously focusing attention on hapless victims of serious crime and calling for tougher, more retributive punishment, politicians not only promote a conservative agenda, but also deflect attention from other serious social problems. In addition, the generalised climate of hostility to marginal groups and 'unconventional' (to the dominant culture of journalists, at least) norms spills over into racism and xenophobia. The moral concerns over mugging in the 1970s were focused on young men of African Caribbean descent; the inner-city riots of the 1980s were frequently attributed entirely to black youths; and recent media coverage of the immigration into Britain of people from other countries frequently demonstrates a shocking disregard for others' human rights and the media's inability (or unwillingness) to differentiate between political refugees and illegal immigrants. Even people from ethnic and/or religious minorities born and raised in this country may be prone to overwhelmingly negative press, and recent years have seen Asian Muslims in the UK subjected to disapproving and sometimes hostile reporting, even when cast as victims.

Victims and offenders

The identification of alienated and demonised 'others' alerts us to the media's differential construction of victims. Quite simply, as far as the media are concerned, some victims are more deserving than others. For example, when an individual goes missing (whether or not foul play is immediately suspected), the likelihood of the national media lending their weight behind a campaign to find the missing person depends on several inter-related factors. If the individual in question is young, female, white, middle class and conventionally attractive, the media are more likely to cover the case than if the missing person is, say, a black, working class boy. Even in cases where abduction and/or murder is immediately suspected, the likelihood of media interest will vary in accordance with the background of the victim. If the victim is male, working class, of African Caribbean or Asian descent, a persistent runaway, has been in care, has drug problems, is a prostitute, or has been victimised by a close relative (or any combination of these factors), reporters perceive that their audience is less likely to relate to, or empathise with, the victim, and the case gets commensurately lower publicity. The compliance of the victim's family in giving repeated press conferences and making themselves a central part of the story is also a crucial factor in determining its newsworthiness, as is their willingness to part with photographs and home video footage of their missing child. Hence, the disappearances of Sarah Payne, Milly Dowler and the 'Soham girls', Holly Wells and Jessica Chapman, were all eminently newsworthy stories: attractive, photogenic girls from 'decent', middle class homes with parents who quickly became media-savvy and were prepared to make repeated pleas for help on behalf of the police (and, in the case of the Paynes and the Dowlers, have continued to court the media, even after the story would normally be 'closed', in order to publicise public safety campaigns established in the names of their murdered children).

Even the relatively high profile case of the murder of 10-year-old, Nigerian-born schoolboy Damilola Taylor in Peckham, South London was, initially at least, constructed very differently to the murders of the girls mentioned above. For over a week, the victim remained virtually invisible as media reports concentrated almost exclusively on issues of community policing and the levels of violent crime on the streets. It was not until Damilola's father flew into the UK from Nigeria (and made press statements and television appearances) and CCTV footage was released to the media that this little boy became a person in his own right – a person worthy of media attention and public mourning and remembrance. Nevertheless, the public grieving for Damilola failed to reach the near hysterical outpourings of anger and sadness that accompanied the deaths of Sarah, Milly, Holly and Jessica. Another example that illustrates the racial bias of a predominantly white, ethnocentric media concerns the case of eight-year-old Victoria Climbié, who was tortured and killed by her aunt, Marie Therese Kouao, and her aunt's boyfriend, Carl Manning, in 2000. Although her death resulted in an inquiry by Lord Laming, and new legislation designed to protect children (including the appointment of the first government Minister for Children), the circumstances of Victoria's life and death, her family background and the motivations of her killers have received only a fraction of the media attention and public mourning extended to some of the other cases mentioned. Like Damilola Taylor, Victoria had only been in England for a few months (she was sent by her parents from the Ivory Coast 'for a better life') and she was black. In addition, she met her death at the hands of a close female relative, another factor which conspired to make the shocking and brutal details of her short life non-newsworthy. Put simply, the story could not be constructed within the terms of the current moral panic over paedophiles – ie as the random yet inevitable murder of a white, middle class child from a 'respectable' home at the hands of an 'evil monster' with previous convictions for child abuse.

Just as the media shape public ideas about 'deserving' victims, they also influence notions of 'undeserving' offenders and, once again, race and ethnicity are key components of media constructions of criminality. When reporting crimes, the press and news media tend only to mention a suspect's race if they are non-white, a strategy that may generate fear of, or hostility towards, people from all minority ethnic backgrounds. One of the worst culprits is *Crimewatch UK*, which tends to over-represent crimes involving black offenders and under-represent black victims, especially males in both categories. In an analysis of the major crimes reported and/or reconstructed in three separate editions of the programme (Jewkes, 2004), it was discovered that, in cases where the ethnicity of the suspect was known, four offences involved white people, while 10 concerned non-white individuals (in two of the cases, both white and non-white offenders were involved). *Crimewatch UK* also frequently fails to distinguish between different ethnic and national groups, homogenising offenders' 'otherness' with phrases like 'North African appearance', 'Mediterranean appearance' or 'Kosovan appearance'. In the three programmes analysed, only one serious crime featured a female offender, and she was Asian. Meanwhile, in the segments of the show which rely on photographs and CCTV footage, black males outnumbered their white counterparts by a ratio of nearly three to one. *Crimewatch UK* also constructs offenders as the exact antithesis to victims. While victims are firmly located within family structures and are thus 'legitimised' as innocent and tragic casualties, the same contextualisation is never extended to offenders, who are invariably anonymous, constructed as individuals, and exist in isolation of social and familial ties (Jermyn, 2003; Jewkes, 2004).

Media representations of the criminal justice system: police, courts and prisons

The police have become increasingly visible in the factual news media, and dramatic portrayals of the police have to some extent reflected 'real life' events (many of which have been 'negative' in essence). Significant milestones in the recent, mediated history of the police include stories of police corruption (most notoriously within the West Midlands Serious Crime Squad in the 1970s, which resulted in the wrongful conviction of the 'Birmingham Six'); the inner city riots of the early 1980s, which led to a transformation in public order policing from inexperienced officers trying to protect themselves with dustbin lids to trained and 'tooled up' professionals – dubbed 'Robocops' by the media; the bungled investigation of the Yorkshire Ripper case during which the police were led up a blind alley by a hoaxer with a North-East accent; the murder of WPC Yvonne Fletcher at the Libyan Embassy in London; the Miners' Strike of 1984, in which the police were involved in bloody clashes and mocked as 'Maggie's boys' by miners protesting at the closure of their pits by a government led by Margaret Thatcher; the inquiry into the death of black teenager, Stephen Lawrence, in 1999, in which the Met were found to be 'institutionally racist'; and a BBC1 documentary shown in 2003, in which a journalist went undercover as a trainee police officer and secretly filmed racist behaviour and language among his colleagues so shocking that it led to several of the officers losing their jobs.

There has been very little research on the extent to which media representations inform public opinions about the police, and even less about the impact that the media have on the police, but such work as there is in this area suggests that the general public and older police officers who have served for a number of years hold dear the nostalgic image of *Dixon of Dock Green* and a force in which the police were men of pride and principle (Stick, 2003; Jewkes, 2004; cf Reiner, 2000). Younger (male) officers, on the other hand, have expectations of the police based on their mediated perceptions of excitement, glamour and car chases in the mould of 1970s cop shows such as *The Sweeney* and *Starsky and Hutch*. The archetypal 'rogue cop' and private eye are also stalwarts of television and cinema and are popular with viewers, even if they bear little relation to the reality of policing. Meanwhile, most serving police officers maintain that the most 'realistic' of the fictional television dramas is ITV's *The Bill*, largely because it does at least illustrate some of the bureaucratic demands made on today's police officers and it is deemed accurate in its portrayal of 'cop culture' and the language used by police officers (Leishman and Mason, 2003; Stick, 2003).

When it comes to factual representations of the police, eg in news or news-based television programmes, forces are increasingly espousing 'open' communications and transparency. This is partially achieved via the raft of employees working for the police at local, regional and national levels, who include press officers, marketing professionals, public relations officers and corporate identity specialists, or what are collectively known as police 'image workers' (Mawby, 2003). Concerns have been raised about the extent to which image workers are able to manipulate the media and imbue the work of the police with a positive 'spin'. However, this does not mean that there are insufficient muckrakers and whistleblowers working within the media to challenge the general picture of a democratic, accountable police service. The police may publicly congratulate themselves on their carefully managed openness and accountability, but they are not impermeable to outside attempts to highlight their ongoing, internal, structural deficiencies, as witnessed by the broadcast of *The Secret Policeman* (BBC1, 21 October 2003). This documentary exposé proved to be a public relations disaster for the police service. The programme showed the results of secret filming by an undercover journalist posing as a trainee police officer over a period of seven months at a national police training centre in Cheshire. In an eerie echo of a simulated racist attack by the young men suspected of murdering Stephen Lawrence (also filmed covertly), rookie police officers were shown voicing extreme racist opinions, and one was seen wearing a makeshift Ku Klux Klan hood. Like all covertly filmed 'documentaries', important questions arise concerning the ethics of secret filming, the opportunities for journalists to ask leading questions with the intention of 'entrapment', the processes by which hundreds of hours of film are edited down to an hour's material for broadcast, and so forth (see Chapter 3). Yet, however one views the ethics of the methods used, the findings of *The Secret Policeman* shocked many, including senior police officers who believed that they were succeeding in rooting out racism from within their ranks following the 1999 Macpherson Report, which highlighted institutional racism within the Metropolitan Police. But this programme demonstrated that, nationally, there is still a long way to go, especially in the areas of recruitment and training. Among the most surprising aspects of the exposé was that racial awareness training for new recruits appeared to consist of them being told there are four words they must not use: 'nigger', 'wog', 'paki' and 'coon'. To this extent, while superficially the programme might be interpreted as reinforcing the notion of a 'few bad apples', it actually hinted at more widespread, structural problems at the heart of the police.

For all the control they try to exercise over their image, then, the police remain a relatively open and publicly accessible organisation. In some respects, they are therefore easy targets for those who wish to test their accountability. Although the undercover journalist who infiltrated the police training college was arrested on charges of deception and damaging police property, the charges were quickly dropped when the impact of public shock was felt.

By contrast, the Contempt of Court Act 1981 prohibits the views of jury members from being disclosed publicly and, of all the institutions of the criminal justice system, it is arguably courts which remain most shrouded in mystery. An editorial in *The Guardian* argues that 'no great powers of deduction are needed to conclude that if racism is rife in society, it must be at work in the jury system ... [which] even more than in the police or the CPS, carries the potential to wreak serious miscarriages of justice' (Dyer, 2003). However, despite the fact that we are unlikely to see an undercover media exposé of racism in the jury box, courts and court trials are a perennial favourite of the media and are represented across all genres, from local newspapers to TV soaps. The reasons why court trials feature so prominently in local and regional news reporting are largely pragmatic. Courts are a relatively easy source of information about crime for journalists, and such stories are frequently used as 'fillers' in local newspapers. Within the national press, court trials are a predictable source of material insofar as newspaper editors and reporters can plan their coverage before the event has actually occurred, estimating the time that a criminal case will remain in court and deploying personnel and equipment accordingly. When high-profile offenders come to court, it also gives media organisations the chance to report for the first time (often in salacious and slavering detail) the minutiae of a criminal case that legally they have not yet been able to disclose.

The reasons for the predominance of court trials in fictional media genres such as soaps and dramas are perhaps less obvious. Whatever uppercrust intrigue one might anticipate finding at the criminal Bar is exploited to the maximum in TV shows like *Judge John Deed* (BBC1) which, regardless of the criminal cases featured, fulfils its quota of sex, infidelity and corruption from within the ranks of the barristers and other criminal justice professionals! In fact, court trials have been a staple of television drama since the introduction of commercial television in the 1950s. A pioneering 'court trial' programme was Granada Television's *Crown Court* (based on an earlier show by the same TV company called *The Verdict Is Yours*), which ran from 1972 until 1984. A half-hour programme shown thrice weekly at lunchtime, it presented viewers with fictional cases at 'Fulchester Crown Court' which were played out from beginning to end over the three episodes each week. While all other participants in each programme were actors, the jury was made up of ordinary members of the public from the Granada region, and the verdicts they reached on the Friday show were 'real' and unscripted. *Crown Court* remains widely respected among critics, not least for accurately recreating the stuffy and claustrophobic atmosphere of the courtroom and for the producers' bravery in tackling subjects that were controversial for any television genre, not least daytime drama. Among the difficult cases that came before the jury at Fulchester were attempted murders, armed robberies, rapes, racist attacks, terrorist acts and assaults on police officers. With its primitive form of audience interaction via 'real people', *Crown Court* was ahead of its time, and a similar format that exploits the immediacy and interactivity of new technologies is shortly to be launched by former *Brookside* executive producer, Phil Redmond. Like its predecessor, the new show will be a daytime drama series based on court cases, but viewers will be able to act as jury from home and will text in their 'verdicts' at the end of each programme. On the final day of the week, they will be able to watch a re-enactment of the crime to see whether their judgment was right.

Court trials also provide great storylines for soap operas, Hollywood films and American 'reality TV' shows such as *Judge Judy* (a cross between Jerry Springer-style audience participation shows and courtroom dramas in which a 'real life' judge presides over minor disputes and petty claims, usually involving former friends or members of the same family). The popularity of criminal trials in all these genres may go beyond the fact that, for many viewers, courts are shrouded in mystery and mystique. The courtroom provides the moral certainties that are craved by audiences and are frequently held to be lacking in the real world of criminal justice. Each case has a beginning, a middle and an end and all the characteristics of drama, but with a real and seemingly just resolution. It might also be argued that such shows provide a postmodern version of the gallows in which viewers can tune in to see justice done and individuals humiliated (literally, in the case of reality TV and 'infotainment' style shows). For some critics, this is simply one aspect of a wider phenomenon in which the mass media have come to replace visible punishment (Sparks, 1992). For others, the media's inclination to cover the details of violent, serious and sexual crimes in lurid detail, while devoting less attention to the processes of justice, and less still to punishment, points to a wanton refusal on the part of those who work within the media to acknowledge or challenge the punitive acts of the state (Mason, 2003).

When it comes to prisons, the relationship between media representations and public opinion is even more complicated. In fictional genres, especially films and TV dramas, the prison is often used as a backdrop for a tale about individual perseverance and the indomitable human spirit. In contrast to factual portrayals of criminals, fictional genres often present a more humanistic representation, in which the viewer is encouraged to empathise with the convicted offender and share in the highs and lows of his or her journey of self-discovery. The central protagonist may have been wrongfully convicted, but even when this is not the case, 'fictional' prisoners are often portrayed as old-style romantic heroes struggling to beat (or at least survive) the system. Yet in factual media, prisoners are virtually ignored, and the grim and frequently inhumane conditions of their incarceration only reach public attention if accompanied by a soundbite from a statement by Her Majesty's Inspector of Prisons in language that will appeal to the popular press. Occasionally, a television drama about prisons will emerge to challenge stereotypical assumptions about incarceration shaped by the cosy prison culture of *Porridge* or the familiar *Cell Block H*-meets-*Brookside* formula of *Bad Girls*. For example, David Wilson has said that the critically acclaimed Channel 4 drama series *Buried* prompted more discussion of the prison system than any academic study (Wilson, 2003). However, its influence on public opinion can hardly have been as significant as the programme arguably warranted, given that it averaged one million viewers and an 8 per cent audience share in its 10.35 pm Tuesday night slot. Even programmes about prisons and imprisonment which purport to have a public information imperative, but are actually rather sensationalised and voyeuristic, do not claim the viewing figures that one might expect, given the general assumption that the public has an insatiable appetite for information about 'true crimes'. One example is Channel 4's *Lifer: Living With Murder*, a programme in which film-maker Rex Bloomstein returned to talk to lifers two decades after first interviewing them for television. The second two-part series, broadcast in 2003, spliced footage from the original series with the new material in an attempt to discover how individuals come to terms with their offences and with serving a life sentence in prison. In pursuit of the former, they were encouraged to relate the details of their crimes (mostly rape and murder) in detail so vivid that it bordered on the pornographic. While such an approach might be expected to appeal to an audience used to tabloidesque treatment of serious crimes, the programme attracted only 1.7 million viewers, while even Channel 5's 1988 movie repeat *Tequila Sunrise*, shown at the same time, was watched by 2.1 million (http://mediaguardian.co.uk/overnights).

The conclusion that has to be drawn from such viewer apathy is that, for all the success of the familiar and unchallenging portrayals of prison in sitcoms and soaps, when it comes to 'real' or 'realistic' representations of imprisonment, which many inmates experience as brutalising, dehumanising and intolerable, public indifference prevails and some of the worst atrocities go unnoticed and unchecked. While the statistics on prisoner self-harm and suicide provide graphic evidence of the damage that prisons do to some of society's most vulnerable members, the popular view of prisons as holiday camps offering an array of 'luxuries' such as in-cell television to an undeserving and dangerous underclass continues to circulate, especially in the popular press (Jewkes, 2002). Meanwhile, other trends in incarceration are also virtually absent from the media agenda. The fact that the number of children under 15 in custody in England and Wales has increased by 800 per cent over the past decade (NACRO, 2003), and that twice as many children are incarcerated in this country as in Belgium, Portugal, Spain, Denmark, Sweden, Finland, Austria, France and the Netherlands put together (Goldson, 2003), is not at the top of the agenda for a media which persists in peddling stories about persistent young offenders and the justification of imposing sanctions on children for 'anti-social behaviour'. Furthermore, in an echo of earlier comments concerning the police and juries, the Prison Service has been accused of institutional racism. Following the murder of Zahid Mubarek by his white cellmate at Feltham Young Offenders Institute in March 2002, the Chair of the Commission for Racial Equality concluded that his death had been caused by a 'lethal combination of racism and systematic neglect' and that, had the victim been white, he would almost certainly still be alive (CRE, 2003). In the light of this revelation, one is compelled to wonder what a black journalist covertly posing as an inmate might uncover in the prisons, young offenders institutions and asylum centres of Britain.

Public ignorance and assumptions about criminal justice

Research conducted by Gillespie and McLaughlin (2003) has found that the viewing and reading public understand far less about sentencing and punishment than they do about crime and policing, and that as much information is learned from TV dramas and soaps as from factual programmes – although tabloid newspapers are most influential in shaping overtly punitive attitudes. Alternatives to custody, such as community sentences, are virtually invisible in all media genres, and, when they do feature on the media's agenda, they tend to be viewed as an illustration of a criminal justice system that is over-lenient and ineffective (Gillespie and McLaughlin, 2003). Yet many people are aware of the problems caused by a rapidly rising prison population and express concerns about the ineffectiveness of prisons as a deterrent to crime. Such individuals might view alternative sentences favourably in these contexts but do not have the resources available to make informed decisions about them. In Gillespie and McLaughlin's research, some respondents indicated that the electronic tagging of offenders could usefully be portrayed in a positive light in a popular drama – an opinion clearly shared by the writers of *Coronation Street*, who introduced tagging as part of a comic storyline involving Les Battersby who, on release from prison, was thwarted in his pursuit of a new romance by the tag around his ankle which required him to return home by 7 pm.

Gillespie and McLaughlin's findings about fictional characterisations of offenders also provide an interesting counterpoint to the dominant representations of criminals in factual media. For example, it was noted earlier that programmes such as *Crimewatch UK* reinforce the impression of the offender as 'outsider' with no ties to domesticity or 'normality'. Because *Crimewatch UK* and its ilk can only show cases where there are no significant leads or suspects (for fear of prejudicing a trial), the offender is frequently not seen in the programme's reconstructions at all, or he or she may be represented only symbolically as a figure in extreme long-shot, either walking or running near the scene of the crime or as a shadowy figure at the wheel of a vehicle. These representations-at-a-distance contrast with other television genres where knowledge about the background of offenders and the context of their crimes elicit a very different response (Gillespie and McLaughlin, 2002). For example, in focus group discussions of soap operas, the overtly punitive opinions that many had previously expressed about offenders were challenged, and ultimately reconfigured, in line with what they 'knew' about the character. In accordance with early media studies which proposed that media content had a more significant impact on audience members if they could, in some way, 'identify' with the character being portrayed, Gillespie and McLaughlin found that, where respondents could empathise with the offender on the basis of what they knew about him or her, a less punitive attitude was adopted. This 'deeper knowledge' of the background of the offender and the crime is precisely what is missing from most 'factual' or 'infotainment' media, where sympathy, empathy or understanding are simply not options. Popularly conceived as a 'breed apart', many offenders are judged within a moral framework which constructs them as morally deficient malcontents who must be dealt with punitively and taught the lesson of individual responsibility (Surette, 1994). In presenting offenders as 'others' and their crimes as senseless and random, programmes like *Crimewatch UK* stimulate sentiments of revulsion and repugnance towards offenders and reinforce populist ideas about punishment (Gillespie and McLaughlin, 2002).

CONCLUSION

It is increasingly being recognised that the media are situated within, and fully interwoven with, many other social practices, to the extent that crime, criminals and criminal justice cannot be separated from their representations in television, film and the press (Sparks, 1992; Ferrell, 2001). We should be wary of making sweeping claims about media 'effects' or about the media being responsible for 'causing' crime or fears about crime (Jewkes, 2004). Yet we can certainly look at the ways in which the media is integral to the processes of meaning-making by which we make sense of our everyday lives (Jewkes, 2002). Misrepresentations concerning the extent of certain types of crime and the effectiveness of the criminal justice system are bound to create a skewed picture of the 'problem' of crime and its solutions. This chapter has demonstrated that there are significant differences and divergences in the representations of crime and justice in factual and fictional media. Yet the media industries as a whole are complicit in failing to cover systemically all forms and expressions of crime, victimisation, sentencing and punishment, and are collectively guilty of pandering to the most voyeuristic and punitive emotions of the audience. Meanwhile, they promote little discussion of the many injustices perpetrated by the criminal justice system, not least the fact that those groups who are most vulnerable in our society – children, women, people from ethnic minority backgrounds, those with personality disorders and mental illnesses, and people whose lives have been blighted by sexual abuse, childhood neglect, alcohol and drug dependence – are the very individuals who are grossly over-represented in the police cells, courts and prisons of Britain.

SEMINAR DISCUSSION TOPICS

* This chapter has suggested that media and political institutions are so intertwined that penal policy is increasingly degenerating into a form of crude penal populism. What evidence is there to support or refute this claim?

* How have factual and fictional media representations of the police changed or evolved over the last 50 years?

* What are the arguments for and against the live television transmission of court trials in the UK, as has been happening in the United States for some time now?

* How would you characterise the relationship between mediated representations of imprisonment and the reality of prison for the various groups mentioned in this chapter?

KEY READINGS

The forthcoming *Media and Crime* by Jewkes (Sage, 2004) is a more wide-ranging analysis of many of the issues covered in this chapter, and includes a detailed examination of the news values which shape reporting of crime and criminal justice, as well as thorough analyses of the media coverage of the trials and punishment of children and women who commit very serious offences. Robert Reiner has written extensively on police and the media, including his chapter 'Media made criminality: the representation of crime in the mass media' in Maguire et al (eds), *The Oxford Handbook of Criminology* (OUP, 2002) and 'Mystifying the police: the media presentation of policing' in Reiner, *The Politics of the Police* (OUP, 2002). An excellent recent addition to this literature is Leishman and Mason, *Policing and the Media: Facts, Fictions and Factions* (Willan, 2003), and Paul Mason has also written about cinematic representations of prisons in his edited collection, *Criminal Visions: Media*

Representations of Crime and Justice (Willan, 2003), which follows his earlier chapter, 'Prime time punishment: the British prison and television' in Kidd-Hewitt and Osborne, *Crime and the Media: The Post-Modern Spectacle* (Pluto, 1995).

REFERENCES

Box, S (1983) *Power, Crime and Mystification*, London: Tavistock.

Chibnall, S (1977) *Law and Order News*, London: Tavistock.

Cohen, S (1973) *Folk Devils and Moral Panics: The Creation of Mods and Rockers*, St Albans: Paladin.

Commission for Racial Equality (CRE) (2003) *The Murder of Zahid Mubarek: A Formal Investigation by the Commission for Racial Equality into HM Prison Service of England and Wales Part 1*, www.cre.gov.uk.

Ditton, J and Duffy, J (1983) 'Bias in the newspaper reporting of crime news', *British Journal of Criminology*, vol 23(2), pp 159–65.

Dyer, C (2003) 'The dirty dozen', *The Guardian*, 28 October.

Ferrell, J (2001) 'Cultural criminology' in McLaughlin, E and Muncie, J (eds) *The Sage Dictionary of Criminology*, London: Sage.

Fishman, M (1981) *Manufacturing the News*, Austin, TX: University of Texas Press.

Foucault, M (1988) *Politics, Philosophy, Culture: Interviews and Other Writings, 1977–1984*, London: Routledge.

Franklin, B and Petley, J (1996) 'Killing the age of innocence: newspaper reporting of the death of James Bulger' in Pilchar, J and Wagg, S (eds), *Thatcher's Children? Politics, Childhood and Society in the 1980s and 1990s*, London: Falmer Press.

Garland, D (1996) 'The limits of the sovereign state: strategies of crime control in contemporary society', *British Journal of Criminology*, vol 36(4), pp 445–71.

Gillespie, M and McLaughlin, E (2002) 'Media and the making of public attitudes' *Criminal Justice Matters*, vol 49, Autumn, pp 8–9.

Gillespie, M and McLaughlin, E (2003) *Media and the Shaping of Public Knowledge and Attitudes Towards Crime and Punishment*, London: Esmée Fairburn Foundation (Research briefing) June.

Goldson (2003) 'Tough on children … tough on justice', presentation to the European Group for the Study of Deviance and Social Control Conference, *Tough On Crime … Tough on Freedoms*, Centre for Studies in Crime and Social Justice, Edge Hill College, Liverpool: 22–24 April.

Greer, C (2003) *Sex Crime and the Media: Sex Offending and the Press in a Divided Society*, Cullompton: Willan.

Hall, S, Critcher, C, Jefferson, T, Clarke, J and Roberts, B (eds) (1978) *Policing the Crisis: Mugging, the State and Law and Order*, London: Macmillan.

Hough, M and Roberts, J (1998) *Attitudes to Punishment*, Home Office Research Study No 179, London: HMSO.

Jefferson, T (2002) 'For a psychosocial criminology' in Carrington, K and Hogg, R (eds), *Critical Criminology: Issues, Debates, Challenges*, Cullompton: Willan.

Jermyn, D (2003) 'Photo stories and family albums: imaging criminals and victims on *Crimewatch UK*' in Mason, P (ed), *Criminal Visions: Media Representations of Crime and Justice*, Cullompton: Willan.

Jewkes, Y (2002) *Captive Audience: Media, Masculinity and Power in Prisons*, Cullompton: Willan.

Jewkes, Y (2004) *Media and Crime*, London: Sage.

Kidd-Hewitt, D and Osborne, R (eds) (1995) *Crime and the Media: The Postmodern Spectacle*, London: Pluto.

Leishman, F and Mason, P (2003) *Policing and the Media: Facts, Fictions and Factions*, Cullompton: Willan.

Mason, P (2003) *Criminal Visions: Media Representations of Crime and Justice*, Cullompton: Willan.

Mawby, R (2003) *Policing Images: Policing, Communication and Legitimacy*, Cullompton: Willan.

NACRO (2003) *A Brighter Future: Annual Review 2002/03*, London: NACRO.

Naylor, B (2001) 'Reporting violence in the British print media: gendered stories', *Howard Journal*, vol 40(2), pp 180–94.

Reiner, R (2000) *The Politics of the Police*, 3rd edn, Oxford: OUP.

Reiner, R, Livingstone, S and Allen, J (2001) 'Casino culture: media and crime in a winner-loser society' in Stenson, K and Sullivan, RR (eds), *Crime, Risk and Justice: the Politics of Crime Control in Liberal Democracies*, Cullompton: Willan.

Roshier, B (1973) 'The selection of crime news by the press' in Cohen, S and Young, J (eds), *The Manufacture of News*, London: Constable.

Schlesinger, P and Tumber, H (1994) *Reporting Crime: the Media Politics of Criminal Justice*, Oxford: Clarendon.

Smith, SJ (1984) 'Crime in the news', *British Journal of Criminology*, vol 24(3), pp 289–95.

Sparks, R (1992) *Television and the Drama of Crime: Moral Tales and the Place of Crime in Public Life*, Buckingham: Open University Press.

Stick, N (2003) 'An examination of the nature and influence of media representations of policing on the police themselves', unpublished MA thesis, University of Hull.

Stokes, E (2000) 'Abolishing the presumption of *doli incapax*: reflections on the death of a doctrine' in Pickford, J (ed), *Youth Justice: Theory and Practice*, London: Cavendish Publishing.

Surette, R (1994) 'Predator criminals as media icons' in Barak, G (ed), *Media, Process, and the Social Construction of Crime*, New York: Garland.

Wilson, D (2003) 'The perception and the reality of crime', presentation to NACRO conference, *Crime Watching: Crime, Public Perception and the Media*, British Library, London, 19 November.

CHAPTER 6

MINORITIES, CRIME AND CRIMINAL JUSTICE

Nadia Joanne Britton

SUMMARY

The criminal justice system follows the principle that all citizens are equal before the law and that everybody has equal access to justice regardless of their ethnic or racial background. This means that it is one of the most important institutions of the state in determining the extent to which minority groups are treated equitably in British society. The main aim of this chapter is to discuss the experiences of people from minority groups as suspects, perpetrators, victims of crime and agents of criminal justice. Available evidence suggests that their experiences of criminal justice are very different from those of the white majority (cf Crow, 1987; NACRO, 1991; Fitzgerald, 1993). This chapter will provide a summary of the evidence that both criminologists and successive governments have collected to describe and explain these experiences and will give an overview of the debates that criminologists have engaged in to explain elevated offending and imprisonment rates for certain minority groups.

The chapter will consider evidence of discrimination throughout the criminal justice system (see also Chapter 2). Many criminologists refer to this system as a process in order to emphasise the importance of considering how one part of it feeds into the others and affects the final outcome. For example, what the police decide to charge somebody with, and indeed if they decide to press charges, greatly affects if and where the accused stands trial and the likelihood that he or she will receive a custodial sentence. The chapter shows that we cannot fully understand minority groups' experiences of criminal justice unless we consider what happens as they pass through each stage of the process. Discriminatory outcomes are likely to be the result of a process of cumulative disadvantage at the different stages.

The chapter examines minority experiences of crime and criminal justice under the following headings:

- Suspects
- Perpetrators
- Victims
- Agents

These reflect the four main ways in which people come into contact with the system. For ease of reference, the term 'Asian' is used to refer to people originating from the Indian sub-continent, and the term 'black' refers to people of African-Caribbean origin. 'Minority groups' is used to refer to people of both Asian and black origin. The chapter also includes the term 'racialisation' which may be unfamiliar to some readers. This refers to the social process through which discourses of race are employed to label, constitute and exclude different groups.

KEY TERMS

Racialisation; criminalisation; criminality; discrimination; stereotypes; Asian; black; white; multi-cultural society; gun violence; drugs; disturbances; occupational culture; sentencing; imprisonment; victimisation; racist attacks and harassment; Macpherson; institutionalised racism; recruitment.

SUSPECTS

Over the years much criminological attention has been paid to explaining statistics that have consistently shown higher rates of arrest and imprisonment for people of African-Caribbean origin. For example, government statistics show that black people are five times more likely than whites to be arrested even though they are no more likely than whites to be charged with an offence following arrest (Home Office, 1998: 5–20). Criminological debates have focused on the extent to which higher rates are indicative of unfair targeting and treatment, particularly by the police, or above average levels of criminality within this particular population. In short, are African-Caribbeans a criminalised or criminal sub-population? In attempting to answer this question, criminologists have sought to establish conclusively that African-Caribbeans are treated differently from white people when all other relevant variables have been accounted for. This is very difficult, not least because isolating and excluding all relevant variables is extremely complex, and an adequate explanation of what constitutes discrimination is also a matter of contention. Despite this, there is a range of qualitative and quantitative research evidence that indicates differential treatment of African-Caribbeans at various stages of the criminal justice process. This section will summarise the evidence that indicates differential treatment of African-Caribbeans when they encounter the criminal justice system as suspects. First and foremost, the greater proportion of studies has suggested that the police are more proactive in the policing of African-Caribbean people. For example, a Home Office study discovered that the police were more likely to have initiated contact with black people than with white or Asian people (Home Office, 1994a). This raises the question of whether higher arrest rates for African-Caribbeans are a consequence of differential policing or are related to social disadvantage generally. The distinction between these legal and extra-legal variables, and the relative salience of each, has been another important aspect for investigation in this area of criminological research (Landau, 1981; Waters, 1990; Cook and Hudson, 1993; Fitzgerald, 1993). However, criminological theory has been criticised for its focus on a high level of social deprivation as an important factor in explaining apparent higher rates of criminality among African-Caribbeans. This argument involves the tenuous assumption that because people are poor they are more likely to commit criminal offences and also ignores certain types of crime, such as the white-collar variety, in which African-Caribbeans are under-represented. In addition, it can reinforce the cultural pathologising of young black men and the black family because it infers that African-Caribbean ways of life are somehow responsible for their supposed increased criminality. Until recently, criminological theory was dominated by the debate about how to explain elevated rates of offending among certain groups, but it is increasingly acknowledged that this debate is exhausted and that criminologists should concentrate instead on the lived experiences of minorities (Britton, 2000b; Phillips and Bowling, 2003: 270).

A more plausible explanation as to why the police are more proactive in policing African-Caribbean communities lies partly in the history of the relationship between these two groups. Historically, crime has been a consistent theme in the construction of ideologies and policies towards people from minority groups. In short, the racialisation of immigrants has consistently involved newly-arrived groups being portrayed as inherently predisposed towards criminality. It is therefore unsurprising that the areas into which post-war immigrants from the Caribbean moved rapidly became associated with crime-related behaviour (Keith, 1993; Solomos, 2003: 118). Evidence suggests that by the 1970s, young African-Caribbeans were portrayed as a serious social problem and crime-prone group, and that this problem was being framed in terms of police-community relations (Solomos, 2003: 123–24). It was at this time that the Government and media drew public attention to the apparent disproportionate involvement of young black men in various forms of street crime, or 'mugging' as they are collectively and commonly known. This criminalisation of African-Caribbeans served to reinforce the racialised link between minority groups and crime and so the social and political construction of the black population as a problem and significant threat to the social and moral order (Hall et al, 1978; Field, 1984; Gaskell, 1986). It also provided popular justification for the proactive policing of areas with a large black population. For example, cumulative statistical evidence over many years has shown that young black men are on average five to eight times more likely to be stopped and searched by the police than their white counterparts. However, there is also a great deal of evidence to show that they are no more likely than white people to be arrested having been stopped, implying that there is no justification for disproportionately targeting them.

In recent years, the issue of gun-related violence has reinforced racialised stereoptypes of young black men, whilst reflecting real problems that have developed in some deprived urban areas (Bowling and Phillips, 2001). It has sustained the criminalisation of young black men by further denoting mugging as an apparent black crime that is indicative of the pathological nature of black culture. The involvement of so-called Yardie gangster gangs from Jamaica in drug-trafficking and gun-smuggling has served to reinforce the notion that young black men and their apparent anti-social, alien culture are responsible for the proliferation of drugs and guns on British streets. Politicians and the media have blamed black music such as rap and hip-hop for supposedly condoning and glamorising a gun culture. Arguments such as these serve to reinforce the link between black people and criminality, whilst glossing over the complex reasons why gun crimes are really on the increase. They provide continued justification for proactive policing of black communities and added weight to black communities' claims of unfair, disproportionate policing.

In fact, the serious civil disturbances that occurred in several British cities during the 1980s had in common that police-black relations were a trigger in almost every case and were interpreted by black communities in particular as the culmination of many years of discriminatory policing. Lord Scarman's Report on the 1981 Brixton riots acknowledged the desperately poor state of police-black relations, arguing that the police, as highly visible representatives of the state, had become a symbol of black people's exclusion from British public and social life and the related sense that they were second class citizens (Mason, 2000: 109). The Scarman Report became the basis for a number of policy initiatives aimed at addressing the problems highlighted by the disturbances. However, its failure to accept that institutional racism in the police played a part meant that policy initiatives focused more on tackling social deprivation in inner city communities. In addition, changes to the law provided the police with greater stop and search powers, greater powers to deal with various forms of civil unrest and increased funding to adopt a more military style of policing to cope with any future disturbances. In other words, the police were provided with the ways and means to more proactively police problem, or arguably black, areas. This meant that the Government's response to the disturbances did not adequately address black people's sense of injustice regarding their treatment by the police, nor did it properly acknowledge that their grievances were justified.

During the 1990s and into the new century, the site of the most serious civil disturbances moved from the inner cities to northern towns and cities with large Asian populations, such as Bradford, Burnley and Oldham. These disturbances were quickly labelled 'race riots' because they largely involved young men of Bangladeshi and Pakistani origin. Although the reasons for the disturbances are complex and multi-faceted, the increasing criminalisation of young Asian men and associated proactive policing is likely to have played a part. These young men are subjected to racialised stereotypes associating them with religious extremism and an apparent rigid patriarchal culture. They encounter various forms of racism in everyday life that results in their exclusion from mainstream social and political life. Like young African-Caribbean men, they are racialised in a way that results in them being seen as a threat to civil society and therefore a problem to be managed.

Another important reason why the police are more proactive in policing minority communities lies in operational police work generally and the police occupational culture specifically. Over many years, studies of the police occupational culture have provided considerable evidence that rank and file police work is racialised (Lambert, 1970; Cain, 1973; Holdaway, 1983; Smith and Gray, 1983; Chan, 1997). Examples involving racialised stereotyping, name-calling and verbal abuse, and the unfair targeting and harassment of individuals from particular minority groups, have given weight to the argument that black people experience a different kind of policing from the white majority. In fact, it has been forcefully argued that race is a key categorising and defining principle in everyday police work (Holdaway, 1996). Despite this, rank and file police officers have been shown to share a perspective of law and order incorporating the assumption that, in principle, the police are a neutral social institution designed to protect the rights of all citizens. Their presented role therefore incorporates the ideal that the police are dispassionate and impartial during the course of their work (Britton, 2000a). This means that there is little room for acknowledging and addressing that everyday police work can involve discriminatory practices and procedures. As a result, the proactive, racialised policing of minority communities cannot be comprehensively challenged.

All of the above research evidence helps to explain why black people have also been shown to have an expectation of unfair treatment when they are involved in, particularly police-initiated, encounters with the police (Britton, 2000b). This lack of confidence in the police to protect their rights is compounded by the small but disproportionate number of black deaths in police custody. These have been found to result from a number of factors, ranging from the misdiagnosis and inadequate treatment of symptoms of illness arising from insensitive and careless supervision, to aggravated suicides and the violent treatment of black detainees by police officers (Benn and Worpole, 1986; IRR, 1991; Johnson, 1998). However, concerns about these deaths have contributed to the fear that the differential policing of black people continues behind closed doors after arrest and thus during the next stage of the criminal justice process.

PERPETRATORS

There is a good deal of evidence indicating that black people are treated differentially at the sentencing and imprisonment stage of the criminal justice process. For example, government statistics show that the representation of black people in the prison population is six times greater than their representation in the population as a whole (Home Office, 1998: 5–20). There is evidence that black people graduate to a custodial sentence more quickly than whites and that they are more likely to receive a harsher, and indeed custodial, sentence. They are also more likely than whites to be charged with indictable-only offences and therefore tried at Crown Court, less likely to be the subject of a pre-sentence report and more likely to be found not guilty (Gordon, 1983; Waters, 1990; Hood, 1992; Home Office, 1998). There is similar evidence suggesting black people's lack of confidence in the system, as they are more likely than whites to opt for a trial at Crown Court, and therefore by jury, rather than magistrates' court; also, they are more likely to plead not guilty (Home Office, 1998).

Black people's lack of confidence is compounded by what is often viewed as a general lack of public concern over so called black-on-black crime. As I noted in the section on suspects, the escalating perpetration of gun-related violence, often involving gangs trading in crack cocaine and other hard drugs, has become an increasing issue of concern within the black community. However, both the police and the wider public's response to this issue has arguably been racialised. For example, in 1998, after several shootings in the Lambeth and Brent areas of London, Scotland Yard set up Operation Trident to investigate gun crime in the black community. This initiative was crucial in helping to address criticism that the police were uninterested in gun crime precisely because the victims, as well as the perpetrators, tended to be black. Its success in achieving a clear-up rate for murders of 80 per cent has further helped to ease tensions between black communities and the police. In 2003, the initiative was expanded after a seven-year-old girl, Toni-Ann Byfield, became the youngest known victim of gang-related gun violence. Despite her murder, wider public concern over gun crime was arguably only aroused after shootings in the provinces and countryside involving white victims. In other words, the issue of how to reduce the perpetration of gun crime only became of general public concern when it was perceived to directly affect the white majority.

Similarly, in 2003, over 10 per cent of Britain's growing female prison population was made up of Jamaican drug couriers, or 'drugs mules', who had swallowed packets of cocaine and attempted to smuggle them into the country (*The Guardian*, 30 September 2003). The women's involvement is usually a consequence of poverty and deprivation, and they play a very small role in drug trafficking into this country. Their imprisonment is often costly and lengthy and does nothing to address the much bigger problem of the gangs who supply the drugs. Confiscation of discovered drugs and deportation, rather than prosecution, is increasingly being advocated as a way of relieving the burgeoning female prison population, but again this is an issue that has received little attention outside of black communities.

There is little publicly available information about differential treatment in the Prison Service generally (although see Wilson and Moore, 2003). However, the case of Zahid Mubarek, who was killed in 2000 by his overtly racist prison cellmate, highlighted the inadequacy of the service's policies and procedures in accommodating minority inmates. In 2003, the law lords ruled that there should be an independent public inquiry into the young man's death. This ruling was issued in a climate in which all criminal justice agencies had become the subject of much closer scrutiny following the publication in 1999 of the Macpherson Report, the details of which are explored in the next section.

VICTIMS

Studies have shown that people from minority groups are more vulnerable to many types of criminal victimisation than white people and, even when social and demographic factors are taken into account, the risks are still higher. Asian people are particularly at risk of vandalism, robbery and theft from the person (Aye-Maung and Mirrlees-Black, 1994). In addition, since the 1980s, there has been increasing recognition that people from minority groups face substantial risk of racial harassment and attack (Virdee, 1995: 12–13). The third report of the Home Affairs Committee on Racial Attacks and Harassment expressed a deep concern for the estimated growing number of 'racial incidents' and questioned the ability of the police and other agencies to effectively formulate policies and allocate resources when they are unaware of the extent and nature of the problem (Home Office, 1994b). In fact, it is consistently claimed that the criminal justice system fails people from minority groups when they are victims of crime.

This failure is partly due to the massive under-reporting that is believed to be characteristic of racist attack and harassment in particular. 'Racist attack and harassment' refers to a range of offences and anti-social acts, from verbal abuse and graffiti on property to more serious physical violence and, at worse, murder. They have in common a pervasive or partial racial motive and as such raise important questions about the social context in which minorities live and how legislators and policy-makers should respond (Holdaway, 1996: 45). Victims fail to report these crimes for a number of reasons, but fear or dislike of the police and a severe lack of confidence in their response have been found to be significant dissuading factors (Home Office, 1981 and 1994b; Aye-Maung and Mirrlees-Black, 1994; Runnymede Trust, 1994a). This lack of trust is unsurprising given that delays in responding to requests for assistance, denial of a racist motive and an unwillingness to prosecute perpetrators have all been reported as familiar aspects of the police response (Gordon, 1990). The failures of the police have been compounded by other criminal justice agencies such as the Crown Prosecution Service and the courts which, for example, have failed to prosecute and convict individuals charged with incitement to racial hatred. By 1994, an extremely low number of prosecutions had been authorised under the Public Order Act 1986 and, out of 14, only seven prosecutions had resulted in a conviction (Runnymede Trust, 1994b).

In recent years, the most well-known example of a racist attack was the murder of Stephen Lawrence. In 1993, Stephen was murdered by a gang of white youths whilst waiting at a bus stop in south London. The police mishandled the subsequent murder investigation, particularly because they did not accept a racial motive for quite some time, and this eventually resulted in the failure to successfully prosecute those widely believed to be responsible. The case was well-reported in the media, not least because of the effort and persistence of Stephen's parents to obtain justice. It resulted in widespread condemnation of and accusations of racism within the Metropolitan Police. When New Labour came to power in 1997, it launched a public inquiry into Stephen's murder, which resulted in the publication of the Macpherson Report in 1999.

The Macpherson Report was ground-breaking, and indeed controversial, because, unlike Lord Scarman's Report on the Brixton riots almost two decades earlier, Sir William Macpherson accepted that institutionalised racism was a significant problem in the police. The report defined institutionalised racism as:

> The collective failure of an organisation to provide an appropriate and professional service to people because of their colour, culture or ethnic origin. It can be see or detected in processes, attitudes and behaviours which amount to discrimination through unwitting prejudice, ignorance, thoughtlessness and racist stereotyping which disadvantage minority ethnic people. (Macpherson, 1999)

The scope of the report was wide as it included recommendations for changes to a range of policy arenas both within and beyond the criminal justice system (Solomos, 2003: 90–91).

It will be some time before changes introduced by the police and other criminal justice agencies following the publication of the Macpherson Report can be adequately assessed. Following the urban disturbances and subsequent Scarman Report of the 1980s, a commitment to reform was relatively quickly replaced by complacency and inactivity (Benyon and Solomos, 1987). One promising sign is that the current Government appears to be more committed than its predecessors to addressing racial discrimination. For example, it strengthened the 1976 Race Relations Act with the Race Relations (Amendment) Act 2000, so that all public authorities now have a statutory duty to promote racial equality. It is the case that, since the murder of Stephen Lawrence, the number of racist incidents reported to and recorded by the police has substantially increased. In 1998/99, 23,049 were reported, which was an increase of 66 per cent on the previous year (Commission on the Future of Multi-Ethnic Britain, 2000: 127). The reasons for the increase are unknown, but suggested contributory factors include improved police recording methods, increased confidence of Asian and black people to report incidents and a real increase in the number of attacks (Commission on the Future of Multi-Ethnic Britain, 2000: 127).

The Stephen Lawrence case is an example of a miscarriage of justice involving a black victim, but there are also incidents of miscarriages in which people from minority groups have been wrongly convicted of an offence. In both cases, minority groups' mistrust of the criminal justice system has been reinforced. Perhaps the most infamous case in recent years has been that of Winston Silcott, whose conviction for the murder of PC Keith Blakelock during the Broadwater Farm riots of 1985 was quashed in 1991. The portrayal of Winston Silcott in the media consistently played on the invidious racialised stereotype of the inherently criminal, threatening black male and was conveniently supported by his conviction for a separate murder. Silcott's case has become a cause célèbre for both groups highlighting institutionalised racism in the police and groups advocating the rights of victims of crime.

Since the 1990s, the police and other public bodies have also drawn attention to the growing number of victims of offences arising from the distinctive cultures of minority groups. These have provided a timely reminder of the challenge for the police and other criminal justice agencies in ensuring justice for an increasingly diverse, multi-cultural population. The two most prominent examples are forced marriages and so called 'honour killings', usually but not exclusively involving women of Asian origin. For example, in 2003, a Kurdish man, Abdalla Jones, was convicted of murdering his daughter because he believed that she had brought dishonour on her family by pursuing a 'Westernised' lifestyle, which included dating a man of another culture. Cases like this have highlighted the difficulties faced by criminal justice agencies in achieving a balance between respecting the cultural practices of minority groups and protecting individual human rights. The Metropolitan Police's Racial and Violent Crimes Task Force has been investigating 'honour killings', and several police forces have undertaken specific initiatives to liaise with local minority groups in an effort to understand such practices. These have helped to demonstrate the post-Macpherson commitment of the police to effectively and fairly policing minority communities.

AGENTS

The recruitment of police officers from minority groups has long been regarded as a key component of effectively policing a multi-cultural society and essential in improving police-minority relations. Recommendations in the Scarman Report of 1981 were based on the assumption that the composition of the police must reflect the society from which they are drawn (Scarman, 1981: 76; Holdaway, 1996: 139). This assumption has since formed the basis for successive recruitment initiatives aimed at attracting people from minority groups to a career in the police. For example, following the publication of the Macpherson Report (1999), the Home Secretary set new targets for minority recruitment based on the size of local minority populations. In 2003, Mike Fuller became Britain's first black Chief Constable, an achievement that should be indicative of the police's increasing success in recruiting and retaining minority officers.

However, none of the recruitment initiatives to date have succeeded in significantly increasing the number of Asian and black police officers. In 1999, only 2 per cent of police officers nationally were of minority ethnic origin (Home Office, 1999). All of the research evidence included in this chapter helps to explain why people from minority groups remain reluctant to join the police. The persistence of unequal, discriminatory treatment and institutionalised racism provides a clear message that police constabularies are unwelcome workplaces for minorities. Indeed, research has shown that minority officers experience poor treatment at the hands of their colleagues, ranging from racist jokes and name-calling to overt harassment (Holdaway, 1997). In addition, minority officers' acceptance by their colleagues is based on their willingness to participate in the occupational culture, even though other officers may not allow them to do so (Holdaway, 1997).

Recruitment initiatives have been criticised as 'window dressing' and mere tokenism because increasing minority representation provides an appearance of progress without seriously tackling issues of racism within the police. Indeed, Asian and black officers have been found to be particularly critical of and opposed to initiatives that approximate to any kind of positive action which can render them second class recruits (Holdaway, 1996: 195; Cashmore, 2001). This raises the question of how minority recruitment to the police can seriously be improved. Suggestions include compelling chief constables to take primary responsibility for the development of policy and practice to deal with race issues both in recruitment and in other areas of their organisation (Holdaway, 1995: 175–76). Another is to implement policies aimed at enhancing the career opportunities available to minority officers so that more achieve senior positions (Cashmore, 2001: 338).

The National Black Police Association was formed to support and advance the interests of Asian and black officers. In recent years, it has been particularly vocal in supporting minority officers who have been the targets of unfair disciplinary action. This is unsurprising given that minority officers are five times more likely to face disciplinary hearings than their white colleagues (Muir, 2003). There have been several high profile cases in which minority officers have been subjected to false accusations that have resulted in internal investigation and, in some cases, prosecution. These cases have arguably severely damaged police efforts to recruit more minority officers. In 2003, the Metropolitan Black Police Association withdrew its support of minority recruitment initiatives as a result of this state of affairs. Evidence of the discriminatory treatment of minority officers indicates that police forces have not yet made substantial progress in addressing the Macpherson Report's highlighting of institutionalised racism.

Like the police, other agencies of criminal justice are still overwhelmingly white and minorities are particularly under-represented at the more senior levels (Commission on the Future of Multi-Ethnic Britain, 2000: 135). They have also been criticised for having discriminatory practices and procedures which deter minorities from applying and hinder the career progress of those who do. For example, research has shown evidence of institutionalised racism in the Crown Prosecution Service (Denman, 2000). Another example is the lack of transparency in the system of appointing judges, or 'secret soundings' as it is commonly known, which has attracted much criticism in recent years and is the target of reform. The experiences of minority employees are relevant to the study of race, crime and criminal justice because challenging the discrimination they face is an essential part of addressing institutionalised racism in the system as a whole.

CONCLUSION

This chapter has demonstrated that there is evidence of discrimination throughout the criminal justice system and that minorities cannot be guaranteed fair and equitable treatment, regardless of the nature of their encounters with it. In accordance with the Macpherson Report's definition of institutionalised racism, this amounts to a collective failure to deliver an appropriate and professional service to minorities. It is therefore understandable that people from minority groups have a profound lack of confidence in the system's capacity to deliver equitable access to justice. Key criminological debates within this research area, such as the link between race and crime, are exhausted. In addition, criminologists have produced a lot of detailed research evidence that discrimination occurs but much less empirical evidence explaining how and why discriminatory outcomes are likely. The challenge still facing criminologists is to fully investigate and explain the processes that result in these outcomes. One suggestion is to place the experiences and understanding of Asian and black people at the centre of empirical investigation as their voices have been notably absent from many studies (Britton, 2000b). Another is to develop minority perspectives in criminology in a similar fashion to how feminist perspectives have developed (Phillips and Bowling, 2003). Both could help to properly explain and address minority groups' lack of confidence in the criminal justice system.

SEMINAR DISCUSSION TOPICS

- To what extent is gun proliferation a 'black problem'?
- Account for the increasing criminalisation of young Asian men.
- How useful is the concept of institutionalised racism in helping us to explain the discriminatory experiences of minority groups?
- How can people from minority groups be encouraged to join the police and other agencies of criminal justice?

KEY READINGS

Race and Racism in Britain, 3rd edn, by Solomos (Palgrave Macmillan, 2003) has a chapter that provides a good introduction to race and policing, and *The Racialisation of British Policing* by Holdaway (Macmillan, 1996) is a comprehensive study of this area. *Race and Ethnicity in Modern Britain*, 2nd edn, by Mason (OUP, 2000) includes a brief chapter on crime and criminal justice, and the report of the Commission on the Future of Multi-Ethnic Britain (Profile Books, 2000) is a good source of information about research and statistics on police and policing and the wider criminal justice system. The Macpherson Report on the murder of Stephen Lawrence (HMSO, 1999) is essential reading because of its importance in informing policy developments in the new century. Bowling and Phillips' *Racism, Crime and Justice* (Longman, 2001) is useful in moving beyond introductory reading.

REFERENCES

Aye-Maung, N and Mirrlees-Black, C (1994) *Racially Motivated Crime: A British Crime Survey Analysis*, Home Office Research and Planning Unit Paper 82, London: HMSO.

Benn, M and Worpole, K (1986) *Death in the City: An Examination of Police Related Deaths in London*, London: Canary Press.

Benyon, J and Solomos, J (eds) (1987) *The Roots of Urban Unrest*, Oxford: Pergamon Press.

Bowling, B and Phillips, C (2001) *Racism, Crime and Justice*, Harlow: Longman.

Britton, NJ (2000a) *Black Justice? Race, Criminal Justice and Identity*, Stoke-on-Trent: Trentham Books.

Britton, NJ (2000b) 'Examining police/black relations: what's in a story?', *Ethnic and Racial Studies*, vol 23(4), p 692–711.

Cain, M (1973) *Society and the Policeman's Role*, London: RKP.

Cashmore, E (2001) 'The experiences of ethnic minority police officers in Britain: under-recruitment and racial profiling in a performance culture', *Ethnic and Racial Studies*, vol 24(4), pp 642–59.

Chan, J (1997) *Changing Police Culture, Policing in a Multicultural Society*, Cambridge: CUP.

Commission on the Future of Multi-Ethnic Britain (2000) *The Future of Multi-Ethnic Britain, The Parekh Report*, London: Profile Books Ltd.

Cook, D and Hudson, B (eds) (1993) *Racism and Criminology*, London: Sage.

Crow, I (1987) 'Black people and criminal justice in the UK', *Howard Journal*, vol 26, pp 303–14.

Denman, S (2000) *Race Discrimination in the Crown Prosecution Service*, London: HMSO.

Field, S (1984) *The Attitudes of Ethnic Minorities*, Home Office Research Study 80, London: HMSO.

Fitzgerald, M (1993) *Ethnic Minorities and the Criminal Justice System*, London: HMSO.

Gaskell, G (1986) 'Black youth and the police', *Policing*, vol 2, pp 26–35.

Gordon, P (1983) *White Law: Racism in the Police, Courts and Prisons*, London: Pluto.

Gordon, P (1990) *Racial Violence and Harassment*, London: The Runnymede Trust.

Hall, S, Critcher, C, Jefferson, T, Clarke, J and Roberts, B (1978) *Policing the Crisis: Mugging, the State and Law and Order*, London: Macmillan.

Holdaway, S (1983) *Inside the British Police: A Force at Work*, Oxford: Basil Blackwell.

Holdaway, S (1996) *The Racialisation of British Policing*, Basingstoke: Macmillan.

Holdaway, S (1997) 'Responding to racialized divisions within the workforce: the experience of Black and Asian officers in England', *Ethnic and Racial Studies*, vol 20(1), pp 69–90.

Home Office (1981) *Racial Attacks*, Report of a Home Office Study, London: HMSO.

Home Office (1994a) *Race and the Criminal Justice System*, publication under s 95 of the Criminal Justice Act 1991, London: HMSO.

Home Office (1994b) *Racial Attacks and Harassment*, 3rd Report of the Home Affairs Committee, London: HMSO.

Home Office (1998) *Statistics on Race and the Criminal Justice System*, London: HMSO.

Home Office (1999) *Race Equality. The Home Secretary's Employment Targets: Staff Targets for the Home Office, the Prison, the Police, the Fire and the Probation Services*, London: HMSO.

Hood, R (1992) *Race and Sentencing: A Study in the Crown Court*, Oxford: Clarendon.

Institute of Race Relations (IRR) (1991) *Deadly Silence: Black Deaths in Custody*, London: Institute of Race Relations.

Johnson, G (1998) 'Out of harm's way', *Police Review*, 10 July, pp 28–29.

Keith, M. (1993) *Race, Riots and Policing: Lore and Disorder in a Multi-Racist Society*, London: UCL Press.

Lambert, J (1970) *Crime, Police and Race Relations*, Oxford: OUP.

Landau, SF (1981) 'Juveniles and the police: who is charged immediately and who is referred to the Juvenile Bureau', *British Journal of Criminology*, vol 21, pp 27–46.

Macpherson of Cluny, Sir William (1999) *The Stephen Lawrence Inquiry: Report of an Inquiry by Sir William Macpherson of Cluny*, London: HMSO.

Mason, D (2000) *Race and Ethnicity in Modern Britain*, 2nd edn, Oxford: OUP.

Muir, H (2003) 'Racist from the inside out', *The Guardian*, 16 September.

NACRO (1991) *Black People's Experience of Criminal Justice*, London: NACRO.

Phillips, C and Bowling, B (2003) 'Racism, ethnicity and criminology – developing minority perspectives', *British Journal of Criminology*, vol 43, pp 269–90.

Runnymede Trust (1994a) *Racially Motivated Attacks and Harassment*, submission to the Home Affairs Committee, London: The Runnymede Trust.

Runnymede Trust (1994b) *Multi-Ethnic Britain: Facts and Trends*, compiled for the conference on 'The future of multi-ethnic Britain: challenges, changes and opportunities', University of Reading, 1994, London: The Runnymede Trust.

Scarman OBE, Rt Hon the Lord (1981) *The Brixton Disorders, 10–12 April 1981*, London: HMSO.

Smith, DJ and Gray, J (1983) *Police and People in London IV: The Police in Action*, London: Policy Studies Institute.

Solomos, J (2003) *Race and Racism in Britain*, 3rd edn, London: Palgrave Macmillan.

Virdee, S (1995) *Racial Violence and Harassment*, London: Policy Studies Institute.

Waters, R (1990) *Ethnic Minorities and the Criminal Justice System*, Aldershot: Avebury, Ashgate.

Wilson, D and Moore, S (2003) *'Playing the Game': The Experiences of Young Black Men in Custody*, London: The Children's Society.

CHAPTER 7

GENDER, CRIME AND CRIMINAL JUSTICE

Sandra Walklate

SUMMARY

It is now some 45 years ago that Wootton (1959: 32) made the observation that, 'Yet, if men behaved like women, the courts would be idle and the prisons empty'. Despite the intervening years, some would say that it is still a moot point whether or not criminology, or her sister discipline, victimology, has as yet managed to take Wootton's observation to heart. As Cain (1989: 4) commented, 'this is because the criminological gaze cannot see gender: the criminological discourse cannot speak men and women'. Some would say that, current theoretical and empirical agendas notwithstanding, criminology (and victimology; see Chapter 8) still struggle with the question of gender (see, for example, Walklate, 2001). The purpose of this chapter is to try to unravel some of the issues associated with this perennial disciplinary blindspot. In order to do this, it will first of all introduce the student to the ways in which varieties of feminism have considered this question. It will then consider the different ways in which thinking about men and masculinity can be traced within the discipline. Finally, it will offer a brief overview of how the question of gender may be pertinent in understanding the work of the criminal justice professionals and the formation of criminal justice policy. In doing all of this, the central question of this chapter will be: 'when is gender the salient variable in facilitating our understanding of crime and criminal justice?'

KEY TERMS

Gender; victimology; feminism – liberal, radical, socialist, postmodern; essentialism; sex role theory; categorical theory; hegemonic masculinity.

SEX OR GENDER: WHAT IS THE DIFFERENCE?

Braithwaite (1989: 44) suggests that the first 'fact' any theory of crime should fit is that males are disproportionately the offenders. Home Office figures for 2001 showed that 81 per cent of known offenders were male (Home Office, 2002). This is a figure that has remained remarkably stable over the last 10 years. Home Office figures provide considerable detail on the differences between men and women in relation to their known offending behaviour, their experience of the criminal justice system and their presence as workers in the criminal justice system. So, for example, in 2001, women sentenced to custody received shorter sentences than men, women made up just over 5 per cent of the prison population, and 42 per cent of women homicide victims, compared with only 4 per cent of men, were killed by a current or former partner (for further information, see Home Office, 2002). Before we go on to offer some understanding of these differences, it is important to clarify what they are referring to.

These statistics are statistics relating to sex differences, ie differences that can be observed between the biological categories, male and female: they are not necessarily a product of gender. Gender differences are those that result from the socially ascribed roles of being male or being female, ie masculinity and femininity. In order to make this clear, let us return to the first 'fact' that Braithwaite comments on. Males are disproportionately the offenders. This 'fact' is presented as an observed difference between the sexes. The explanation for this 'fact' may lie in the different behaviour of the sexes and the social response to that behaviour (qua Wootton, 1959). In other words, it may be a product of the socially ascribed values of masculinity and femininity to the behaviour of the sexes. So, returning to criminology (and victimology) as disciplines, it could be said that they both have a tradition of being attuned to sex differences but have failed to explore those differences as a product of gender. As Cain has said and was quoted above, 'The criminological gaze cannot see gender'.

What follows is an attempt to explore why this has been the case and what efforts criminologists and victimologists have made to overcome this blindspot. This will be done under four main headings. First of all, we shall consider the contribution of work emanating from the feminist movement. Secondly, we shall consider the work of those who have been concerned to address the question of masculinity. Thirdly, we shall explore some questions relating to gender in the criminal justice professions. Fourthly, we shall consider the same question in relation to criminal justice policy. But, first, what has feminism had to say about criminology and her sister discipline, victimology?

FEMINISM, GENDER, CRIMINOLOGY AND VICTIMOLOGY

There are four clearly identifiable strands to feminist thought: liberal feminism, radical feminism, socialist feminism and postmodern feminism, though not all of these have had the same impact on the discipline and its studies. I shall make some observations on the utility of each of them in turn.

Liberal feminism argues for equality between the sexes. In the context of criminology, this stands for empirical equality, that is, ensuring that sex differences are explored empirically so that any sexist bias and/or sexist practice might be eliminated. Arguably, much empirical work within criminology has concerned itself with this precise theme, from the work of Pollak (1950) focusing as it did on the role of chivalry in masking the female offender, through to the more sophisticated analysis of differential sentencing practices in relation to the female offender offered by Hedderman and Gelsthorpe (1997). Work like this yields a wealth of information concerning the ways in which different factors interact to produce different outcomes for different female offenders as compared with male offenders committing the same offences. However, sexism does not only apply to women. It also applies to men (see for example, the work of Allen, 1987, on the interaction between the sex-based assumptions of psychiatry and the law), and the recognition of this fact sometimes makes it difficult to understand precisely what factors are contributing to people's experiences of the criminal justice process. However, if an interest in 'fair play' is key to liberal feminism, then that interest has clearly been present within criminology.

So, it is perhaps fair to say that women *per se* have not been systematically neglected by criminology. It is also fair to say that a focus on sexism itself presumes that if criminological theory and/or practices were emptied of sexism, then the theories and practices would in and of themselves prove to be sound, and, given that sexism also applies to men, such an assumption would not only fail to explore gender, it would also be unsound. It is at this juncture that some value can be found in exploring the agenda offered by radical feminism.

Radical feminism takes as its central focus of analysis men's power over women: patriarchy. So radical feminist analysis recasts our understanding of all our social relationships from the private life of the family to the public life of politics in terms of the power that men assert over women. Crucial to this kind of analysis is the question of sexuality. Thus, radical feminism presumes the oppression and control of women by men through their sexuality. In the context of criminology, this agenda has had its greatest impact on what might be termed 'victim studies', and it is this avenue that we shall explore here.

Much work conducted under the umbrella of radical feminism has concerned itself with women's experiences of the control of their sexuality by men, and much of that work has been conducted outside the disciplinary boundaries of criminology. It is work that much prefers the use of the term 'survivor' than 'victim', since 'survivor' implies a more positive and active role for women in their routine daily lives. It focuses on women's strategies of resistance and survival. In this vein, much radical feminist work has concerned itself with sexual violence and has redrawn the boundaries on sexual harassment, rape (including marital rape and date rape), domestic violence, child abuse and sexual murder. This work has consequently challenged conventional understandings of what counts as being criminal (violence between intimates as well as violence between strangers) as well as the locus of criminality (the home as well as the street). It also carries with it profound implications for the sub-discipline of victimology.

Victimology, as an area of analysis, reflects a similar, though younger, history than that of criminology but has been clearly influenced by very similar presumptions that Miers (1989) labelled 'positivistic' victimology. This identifies victimology's historical concern with patterns of victimisation and a wish to classify victims who have contributed to their own victimisation. One of the central concepts of victimology has been 'victim precipitation', and it was the extended use of this concept to explain incidents of rape that radical feminism took a particular dislike to. However, it is not the only concept within the victimological framework that reflects problematic (and gendered) assumptions. The widespread deployment of Hindelang et al's (1978) lifestyle exposure model as a way of explaining patterns of victimisation to be found in criminal victimisation survey data implicitly accepts a very male view of what counts as a high risk place: the street. Assumptions such as these have led to the observation that victimology has contributed to a gendering of the victim in a similar way that criminology has gendered the offender, ie making women (and children) visible as victims and men invisible as victims (see Walklate, 2003). However, it has to be said that much (radical) feminist work, focusing as it does on the nature and extent of male violence towards women, also results in the gendering of the victim in a similar, though unintended way (see below and also Newburn and Stanko, 1994). Nevertheless, recasting the 'safe haven' of the home as a place in which much criminal behaviour occurs, and which is perpetrated by men towards women (and children), does mean taking gender seriously. However, the campaigning voice of radical feminism that shouts 'all men are potential rapists' belies some difficulties inherent in this position.

Radical feminism presumes that all men have the same power and control over not only women's lives, but also their own lives. In addition, it presumes that all men share in the same relationship with their masculinity: that is, in its expression through the use of sexual violence against women. These two assumptions are derived from the problem of essentialism. Essentialism refers to the assumption that there are natural and unchangeable differences between men and women that all men and women share in common. The difficulties associated with such an assumption can be easily grasped by reflecting upon one's own experience. Put simply, the claim for sameness (all men?) denies difference (what about individual men?). Such claims also make the same error in relation to women.

Such difficulties notwithstanding, the work of radical feminism, both without and latterly within criminology, has clearly reset the criminological agenda both in terms of what we understand as being criminal and how such activities might be better explained. In this latter respect, radical feminism certainly played a crucial role in centring the importance of men and masculinity in the criminological arena. We shall return to this question in due course. There is a further danger in centring men in our understanding of the relationship between gender and crime. Such a process can overlook the importance of other variables. This is the position of socialist feminism.

Socialist feminism is interested in the complex ways in which gender and class (along with race) interact with each other to effect people's life chances and life experiences. In the context of criminality, this involves exploring the ways in which gender and class interact to produce different types of criminal behaviour and different opportunities for engaging in such. Carlen (1994), for example, comments that women in prison represent those whose criminalisation has been over-determined by the threefold effect of racism, sexism and classism, none of which is reducible to the other. In other words, the relationship between these variables is a compounding one, not a linear one. Criminology (and victimology) still struggles to make sense of this conundrum which is no great surprise given its origins in positivism and modernism (see Chapter 1). However, the implications of the work of people like Carlen clearly connect the criminological agenda with a social justice agenda and also challenge the essentialism of radical feminism.

Socialist feminism has had a limited impact on criminology. The same can be said in some respects of postmodern feminism. Postmodern feminism, with its origins in French literary circles, celebrates difference. It puts to the fore the notion of woman being 'the other' and sets out to put a positive understanding on this 'otherness'. This 'otherness', then, represents openness, plurality, diversity and difference and makes it highly problematic to denote 'all men' or 'all women'. It is an intellectual perspective that seeks to give voice to all those who are rendered silent by the constraints of existing discourses. So, in the context of criminology, as Young (1992: 76) states, 'Woman is always criminal, always deviant, always censured. This condition is utterly normal'. Hence, female criminality is by definition, because of its difference, always beyond the criminological gaze and in a different way returns us to the question: what is at the centre of criminology? We shall address this question again in the conclusion to this chapter.

Each of the branches of feminism discussed here poses different questions for criminology and the criminological enterprise. It has been argued that feminism and criminology are a contradiction in terms, but this largely depends on what version of feminism is being discussed. Liberal feminism has certainly left its mark on the criminological agenda, given its associated history in the exploration of sexism. Radical feminism, on the other hand, sits much less comfortably within the criminological domain, although its importance, along with socialist feminism, lies in its effort to place men and masculinity much more squarely on the criminological map. Postmodern feminism's resistance to universal statements renders criminology's attachment to the policy agenda very difficult. So herein lies a real contradiction. Much the same could be said for the questions posed by feminism for victimology.

However, if the maleness of crime is a central problem for criminology (and victimology), a statement which much feminist inspired work seems to suggest, it will be useful at this juncture to reflect upon how criminology (and victimology) have thought about men.

THEORISING MASCULINITY, GENDER, CRIMINOLOGY AND VICTIMOLOGY

It is fair to say that men have certainly not been absent from criminological thinking. Indeed, the activities of young urban males have preoccupied criminologists since the delinquency studies of the 1940s and 1950s. However, what criminologists have paid less attention to is the extent to which the behaviour with which they have been concerned was a product of those young males' understanding of themselves as men. This leads to one central question: to what extent is criminal behaviour a product of masculinity? As with feminism, there are a number of different theoretical frameworks that could be invoked to answer this question. Here we shall consider three: sex role theory, categorical theory and 'doing gender'.

Sex role theory refers to the ways in which, through the process of socialisation, boys and girls learn what is expected of their behaviour in relation to their sex. The work of the social theorist Talcott Parsons (1937) was especially influential in the 1950s and 1960s in introducing the idea that boys engaged in compensatory compulsory masculinity. Put simply, this refers to the idea that boys, surrounded as they are in childhood by female role models, reject all that is feminine in the construction of an understanding of their own masculine role. Much of the work on juvenile delinquency in the 1950s took this view of the socialisation process on board. Cohen (1955) argued, for example, that the lack of a readily-available male role model for boys in the home resulted in a sense of anxiety for them. Unsure of how to be 'good', this anxiety was resolved for them through membership in the street gang. Here, the assertion of physical prowess, and the thrill and excitement of rule-breaking, not only provided routes into delinquent behaviour, but also offered them an expression of themselves as young men.

The attractions of sex role theory are threefold. First, it moves us beyond biology. The roles that Parsons discusses are learned through socialisation. Secondly, this learning process becomes the route through which social structure impacts upon individual personality and so provides an opportunity for exploring the relationship between social structure and individuality, rather than presuming such characterisations as being biologically given. Thirdly, in this way, it provides an avenue for understanding the processes of social change. As a result, sex role theory carries with it significant theoretical and practical power. However, as Connell (1987) has pointed out, it also carries with it the resilience of the biological category of sex. As he argues, this theory tacitly treats the sex roles as if they were equal and as if they were non-problematic. However, experience tells us that sex roles are not like this. They are fragile, tentative and negotiated in character and certainly not equal.

Drawing on feminism, Connell (1987) suggests that, in order to overcome these inherent difficulties, it is necessary to draw on an understanding of gender relations that understands the categories of men and women as two opposing categories. This he calls 'categorical theory'.

In criminology, this approach to understanding gender, as the previous discussion has highlighted, has had its most profound effects in the analysis of sexual violence. However, again, as was noted in the discussion earlier, it would be a mistake to presume that all the perpetrators of sexual violence are male and all its victims female. This false universalism, as Connell calls it, presumes that there is one static form of masculinity on the one hand, and one static form of femininity on the other. The work of feminism in putting the question of men and their relationship with masculinity should not be under-estimated. It certainly put this on the criminological agenda and, without this stage of theorising, others like Connell and Messerschmidt would not have gone on to explore the gaps between masculinism, the ideology that supports male dominance, and masculinity(ies), the individually negotiated and fragile identities constructed by men. It is within this gap that an exploration of 'doing gender' has emerged.

Understanding how people do gender is the problem of understanding how people construct any social action: balancing the interplay between social structure and social action. The key theme to the work that might be put under this heading is an exploration of how gender is organised as an ongoing concern. Both Connell and Messerschmidt, differently influenced by the work of Giddens (1984), have endeavoured to explore how we do this. Connell (1987) argues that there are three socio-structural locations that constitute the background in which gender is constructed: the gender division of labour, the gender relations of power, and sexuality. These structures define the conditions under which expressions of masculinity and femininity are constructed. They may change over time and space, but they nevertheless offer a level of continuity to those constructs that Connell (1995) defines as 'hegemonic masculinity'. In late modern society, hegemonic masculinity is characterised normatively as being white, heterosexual masculinity. This serves not only to equip individual men with a sense of themselves as more of a man or less of a man in relation to it, but also to downgrade other versions of masculinity (like homosexuality, for example) as well as to downgrade femininity. This accepted framework underpins the sense that we have of ourselves as gendered subjects and simultaneously offers templates for individual action.

In this sense, as Messerschmidt (1993: 79) states, 'gender is an accomplishment'. In other words, it is something that we all have to work at. This view leads Messerschmidt to construct an understanding of how men differently construct a sense of themselves in different locations: the street, the workplace and the home. So, whilst the business executive might use his position and power to sexually harass his female secretary in perhaps more subtle ways than the pimp, the effects are the same.

The women concerned are subjugated, and the men concerned are affirmed as normatively heterosexual men.

As was commented on above, much victimological work has also traditionally presumed that victims are not likely to be male, from the early concept of victim proneness developed by von Hentig (1948) to the later work of the criminal victimisation survey industry. That was until researchers began to think a little more closely about why men's vicitimisation might be hidden. It is self-evident that men can be victims, but how they understand and experience their victimisation does not readily fit with the available conceptual framework of victimology. What helps make better sense of men's experiences may again be the notion of hegemomic masculinity. Men see their victimisation in relation to understandings of themselves as men reflected aptly in the everyday saying 'boys don't cry' (see Goodey, 1997). So, an understanding of themselves as men and their relationship with notions of masculinity is proving to be an increasingly fruitful avenue of exploration in understanding men's experiences of victimisation, including their experiences of sexual violence (see Lees, 1997).

However, later work by Messerschmidt in particular has become much more focused on the way in which gender, ethnicity and class interact with one another to reproduce particular hegemonic forms. Other work has turned to psychoanalysis to explore in greater detail the question of difference within this frame of criminological explanation. Indeed, as the debate between Miller (2002) and Messerschmidt (2002) illustrates, it may be that the dualism of gender inherent in the hegemonic masculinity thesis is itself too restrictive a framework for understanding what it is that people are doing with their sense of identity. This has led some to talk of a 'crisis in masculinity'. However, this, as Jefferson (2002) observes, may be more of a crisis of late modernity in which individuals are driven to seek biographical solutions to systemic problems (Bauman, 2000).

Here again, in the context of criminology, we hit the tension generated by the criminological commitment to modernism and its desire for a universal explanation. There is a tendency in some of the literature that centralises masculinity and crime to seek to explain all kinds of criminality by reference to that masculinity, from joyriding to state terrorism, a desire that denies other features of criminality, such as age, class and ethnicity. It also betrays the discipline's inherent heterosexism, an argument that is fully explored by Collier (1998). Both of these issues will be returned to towards the end of this chapter.

Questions of gender are not only pertinent in encouraging us to think a little more critically about offending behaviour and the processes associated with victimisation. A gendered analysis may also help us to think a little more critically about the nature and experiences of criminal justice professionals and the nature of criminal justice policy. We shall discuss some features associated with each of these in turn.

GENDER AND THE CRIMINAL JUSTICE PROFESSIONAL

Home Office figures for 2001 show that women are well-represented throughout the criminal justice system, though not in senior management positions. Women practitioners make up more that 50% of probation officers, Crown Prosecution Service lawyers and magistrates. However, they are particularly under-represented in the police service, in the judiciary and as barristers and as prison officers, though in the whole range of voluntary sector services that supports the work of the criminal justice system the representation of men and women is fairly equal. So, in all areas of criminal justice work, it is likely that gendered assumptions relating to the workplace may be operative.

The general observations made here certainly resonate with observations that can be made about men and women in the workplace as a whole. Those observations characterise the world of work as being stratified in two ways: horizontally and vertically. 'Horizontally' refers to the way in which certain jobs are known as men's work and others as women's work. In this context, it is useful to reflect upon the sex differentials between the probation service and policing, for example. 'Vertically' refers to the way in which the higher up anyone moves in a particular organisation, the more likely it is to be male dominated. However, despite the obvious concerns that having few females involved in the judiciary might raise, much of the critique and analysis around gender and the criminal justice professionals has been focused on policing.

Policework is both male membered and male dominated, and this fact has put policing at the forefront of those gendered analyses that have been conducted of criminal justice work. This work began with Ehrlich Martin's (1980) early understanding of how policewomen devise their own strategies of survival in the policing environment, developed in the UK context by Jones (1987). This work explored the extent to which working within a male dominated organisation resulted in policewomen either becoming *police*women (putting themselves as police officers first and women second) or becoming police*women* (putting themselves as women first and police officers second). This kind of analysis has been taken further by Heidensohn (1992), who offers an interesting gendered analysis of policing in the broader context of understanding control, and by Westmarland (2001), who explores policing in relation to a gendered analysis of the sociology of the body. However, as Walklate (2001) has observed, there is much more work to be done in understanding the gendered nature of work within the criminal justice system.

As Naffine (1987) has argued, the 'man of law' is the middle class entrepreneur. He 'wins' by intellectual stealth, rather than by brute force, but his masculinity pervades the day-to-day operation of the criminal justice process that takes its toll on both men and women. This kind of exploration of gender in the criminal justice system is as yet under-utilised. Thinking about the pervasiveness of this version of masculinity offers one way of thinking not just about the adversarial process of the Crown Court (where establishing truth is sidelined in the interests of winning), but about the success or otherwise of those practitioners who do not embrace this way of doing their work and the likely outcome of partnership working between, for example, a probation service committed to 'reflective practice' and a police force embedded in militarism. So, there are some, as yet, under-explored questions to pursue that a gendered lens might cast some light on. The same could also be said about criminal justice policy.

GENDER AND CRIMINAL JUSTICE POLICY

An exploration of how gender works systematically across the full arena that we might call criminal justice policy is not possible in the space available here, though we do know a considerable amount about how different aspects of the law operate with gendered assumptions (for example, on the magistrates' court, see Eaton (1986); on the role of psychiatry, see Allen (1987); on female offenders, see Worrall (1990); and, on rape, see Lees (1997)). Understanding the way in which gender operates systematically within the law has led some to claim that there is a case for a feminist jurisprudence (see Naffine, 1990; Smart, 1989). Others have argued that recognition of such a systematic process might better serve the criminal justice process by recognising, as Eaton (1993: 16) does, that the 'disciplined subject is also a gendered subject', and so a 'woman-wise penology' (Carlen, 1990) might offer justice to both men and women, as might Sim's (1994) analysis of punishment as 'taking it like a man'. Such observations and debates notwithstanding, it is self-evident that tough criminal justice policy is equated with prison and that soft criminal justice policy is equated with community sentencing. A more detailed analysis of how and why such distinctions exist and for whom, from a gendered lens, would prove an interesting addition to the literature cited above.

GENDERING THE CRIMINAL AND THE VICTIM OR GENDERING CRIMINOLOGY AND VICTIMOLOGY?

This chapter has explored the different ways in which assumptions concerning the concept of gender have been made more or less visible within the general criminological enterprise. However, it should be noted that not all of this work has had the outcome that was intended by it. Snider (2003), for example, offers an analysis of the ways in which feminist work within and without the criminal justice system has been used in the interests of an increasingly punitive society. So, whilst for her much of the feminist-inspired work referred to in this chapter challenges the universalism of science by constructing the 'Resistant [female] Subject' and thereby the 'Fallible Expert', what it has failed to do is 'challenge the punitive, cost-cutting agendas of the neo-liberal state' (Snider, 2003: 371). So, not all of this work has resulted in what might be considered as 'progress' by those engaged in it. In addition, and of central concern the question here, remains the issue of how much there is to be learned about crime, its causation and the processes of criminalisation and victimisation, by rendering the question of gender explicit in the way the work referred to here has tried to do.

It is clear that much has been learned about the places in which crime occurs and who commits it from feminist-inspired work concerned with exploring the nature and extent of sexual violence. It is also clear that recasting some of this behaviour in terms of masculinity has provided an increasingly perceptive insight into some aspects of its causal mechanisms. The question that remains, as raised above, is: 'when is gender the salient variable in criminality and or victimisation?' The later work of Messerschmidt (1997; 2003) points up the importance of understanding the interplay between ethnicity class and gender. Walklate and Evans (1999) would make the same point about the important mediating effect of people's relationships in their community. Hagan and McCarthy (1997) raise the same question in their study of youth crime and homelessness. Put very simply, is the opportunist burglar expressing his manhood or something else? And, as I have argued elsewhere: 'A gendered lens certainly helps us see some features of the crime problem more clearly perhaps; but under what circumstances is that clarity made brighter by gender or distorted by it?' Criminology and victimology need to consider this question in a much more self-critical and self-reflexive manner before it may be possible to answer it. They need to be recognised not only as disciplines with gendered subject matter, but also as disciplines that are membered in a gendered way. Starting here may lead to some more fruitful areas of investigation and will most certainly lead to the asking of different questions that may in and of themselves help us towards an understanding of when gender does and does not matter.

SEMINAR DISCUSSION TOPICS

- How, and in what ways, are men victims?
- What impact does the 'man of law' have on the workings of the criminal justice system and for whom?
- How and under what circumstances is gender the salient variable in criminal behaviour and criminal victimisation?

KEY READINGS

For a good selection of articles by feminist working within and without criminology, see Gelsthorpe, L and Morris, A (eds), *Feminist Perspectives in Criminology* (Open University Press, 1990). See also Rafter, N and Heidensohn, F (eds), *International Feminist Perspectives in Criminology* (Open University Press, 1995). For an understanding of developments in masculinity theory, see Connell (1995), and, as applied to criminology, see Messerschmidt (1997). Also look at the *Sage Dictionary of Criminology*. This offers a sound definition of hegemonic masculinity in particular. For a more detailed analysis of the issues addressed in this chapter, see Walklate, S (2001) *Gender, Crime and Criminal Justice* (2nd edn forthcoming).

REFERENCES

Allen, H (1987) *Justice Unbalanced! Gender, Psychiatry and Judicial Decisions*, Milton Keynes: Open University Press.

Bauman, Z (2000) *Liquid Modernity*, Oxford: Polity.

Braithwaite, J (1989) *Crime, Shame and Reintegration*, Cambridge: CUP.

Cain, M (1989) 'Feminists transgress criminology' in Cain, M (ed), *Growing Up Good*, London: Sage.

Carlen, P (1990) 'Women, crime, feminism and realism', *Social Justice*, vol 17(4), pp 106–23.

Carlen, P (1994) 'Why study women's imprisonment? or anyone else's?', *British Journal of Criminology*, vol 34, Special Issue, pp 131–40.

Cohen, AK (1955) *Delinquent Boys*, New York: Free Press.

Collier, R (1998) *Masculinities, Crime and Criminology*, London: Sage.

Connell, RW (1987) *Gender and Power*, Oxford: Polity.

Connell, RW (1995) *Masculinities*, Oxford: Polity.

Eaton, M (1986) *Justice for Women? Family, Court and Social Control*, Milton Keynes: Open University Press.

Eaton, M (1993) *Women After Prison*, Buckingham: Open University Press.

Ehrlich Martin, S (1980) *Breaking and Entering: Policewomen on Patrol*, Berkeley, CA: University of California Press.

Giddens, A (1984) *The Constitution of Society*, Oxford: Polity.

Goodey, J (1997) 'Boys don't cry: masculinities, fear of crime and fearlessness', *British Journal of Criminology*, vol 37(3), pp 401–18.

Hagan, J and McCarthy, B (1997) *Mean Streets*. Cambridge: CUP.

Hedderman, C and Gelsthorpe, L (1997) *The Sentencing of Women*, Home Office Research Study 170, London: HMSO.

Heidensohn, F (1992) *Women in Control? The Role of Women in Law Enforcement*, Oxford: OUP.

Hindelang, MJ, Gottfredson, MR and Garofalo, J (1978) *Victims of Personal Crime: An Empirical Foundation for a Theory of Personal Victimisation*, Cambridge, MA: Ballinger.

Home Office (2002) *Criminal Statistics, England and Wales 2001*, London: Home Office.

Jefferson, T (2002) 'Subordinating hegemonic masculinity', *Theoretical Criminology*, vol 6(1), pp 63–88.

Jones, S (1987) *Policewomen and Equality*, London: Macmillan.

Lees, S (1997) *Ruling Passion*, London: Sage.

Messerschmidt, J (1993) *Masculinities and Crime*, Lanham, MD: Rowman and Littlefield.

Messerschmidt, J (1997) *Crime as Structured Action*, London: Sage.

Messerschmidt, J (2002) 'On gang girls, gender and structured action theory; a reply to Miller', *Theoretical Criminology*, vol 6(4), pp 477–80.

Messerschmidt, J (2003) *A Mystery in Broad Daylight*, Boulder, CO: Westview Press.

Miers, D (1989) 'Positivist victimology: a critique', *International Review of Victimology*, vol 1, pp 3–22.

Miller, J (2002) 'The strengths and limits of "doing gender" for understanding street crime', *Theoretical Criminology*, vol 6(4), pp 461–76.

Naffine, N (1987) *Female Crime*, Sydney: Allen and Unwin.

Naffine, N (1990) *Law and the Sexes*, London: Allen and Unwin.

Newburn, T and Stanko, EA (1994) *Just Boys Doing Business*, London: Routledge.

Parsons, T (1937) *The Structure of Social Action*, New York: McGraw-Hill.

Pollak, O (1950) *The Criminality of Women*, New York: AS Barnes/Perpetua.

Sim, J (1994) 'Tougher than the rest' in Newburn, T and Stanko, B (eds), *Just Boys Doing Business*, London: Routledge.

Smart, C (1989) *Feminism and the Power of Law*, London: Routledge.

Snider, L (2003) 'Constituting the punishable women; atavistic man incarcerates post-modern woman', *British Journal of Criminology*, vol 43(2), pp 354–78.

von Hentig, H (1948) *The Criminal and his Victim*, New Haven, CT: Yale UP.

Walklate, S (2001) *Gender, Crime and Criminal Justice*, Cullompton: Willan.

Walklate, S (2003) 'Can there be a feminist victimology?' in Davies, P, Francis, P and Jupp V (eds), *Victimisation: Theory Research and Policy*, London: Palgrave.

Walklate, S and Evans, K (1999) *Zero Tolerance or Community Tolerance? Managing Crime in High Crime Areas*, Aldershot: Avebury.

Westmarland, L (2001) *Gender and Policing: Sex, Power and Culture*, Cullompton: Willan.

Wootton, B (1959) *Social Science and Social Pathology*, London: George Allen and Unwin.

Worrall, A (1990) *Offending Women*, London: Routledge.

Young, A (1992) 'Feminism and the body of criminology' in Farrington, DP and Walklate, S (eds), *Offenders and Victims: Theory and Policy*, selected papers from the British Criminology Conference, 1991: British Society of Criminology, ISTD.

CHAPTER 8

VICTIMS, CRIME AND CRIMINAL JUSTICE

Graham Wright and Jane Hill

SUMMARY

Criminology, for most of its formative development, retained a narrow-minded attitude to the study of crime by concentrating on the offender and the causal factors associated with the offence. This chapter will examine how criminology and the emergent discipline of victimology have developed and sustained a series of false dichotomies: criminal versus non-criminal; criminal versus victim; victim versus non-victim; visible victim versus invisible victim; blameless victim versus culpable victim; deserving victim versus undeserving victim; crime victim versus victimless crime. It will do so by exploring the relationship between criminology, victimology and criminal justice through discussion of (a) the ways in which victims have been variously constructed, and (b) the links between theoretical perspectives within criminology in general and theoretical perspectives that have informed debates about the study of victims. We will illustrate these debates by considering specific types of crime and victimisation, which, in turn, will lead us to raise questions about the role of politics and the state in deciding who is deserving of justice.

We will begin with an exploration of different conceptualisations of 'victim'. It may seem, perhaps, rather obvious to point out that, just as that which is to count as crime can be seen to change over time, so, therefore, those who are to be perceived as criminals and victims will vary from time to time and from place to place. We will look at early debates about victims that stem from the work of von Hentig (1948) and Mendelsohn (1947). Whilst von Hentig was concerned with the question of why some people are more likely to become victims, Mendelsohn was concerned with the more divisive question of whether victims can be said to be responsible for their victimisation.

Next, the chapter will explore the different ways of gaining knowledge about victimisation. There are many perspectives within victimology, just as there are in the study of crime in general. However, for the purposes of this chapter, we will simplify the debates by discussing the three main theories of knowledge (*epistemologies*) that have underpinned social research in general. We call these positivist (or orthodox), interpretivist and critical theories of knowledge into which categories the wide number of theoretical perspectives on crime and victims (and indeed all aspects of social life) can be placed. This schema quite closely follows that provided by Walklate (1998), although we will identify some important points of difference.

Finally, we will illustrate the ways in which different theories of knowledge have been used in relation to the consideration of victims by examining two important areas of victimisation: domestic violence and corporate crime. It is through the consideration of these issues that we will question the notion that the state takes all victimisation equally seriously.

KEY TERMS

The false dichotomies of the 'victim'; victimology – the positivist, interpretivist and critical approach; domestic violence; justice for victims.

INTRODUCTION: CONCEPTUALISATION OF THE TERM 'VICTIM'

It is taken for granted that the term 'criminal' is the product of various processes and institutions involved in the term's social construction (Heidensohn, 1989). The traditional representation of the criminal is restrictively associated with demonic images of urban working class youth, such that the notion of criminality becomes synonymous with youth. Yet, however misconceived this association, it has consistently informed criminal justice policy. The messages inherent in a policy which so closely associates crime with young people support the construction of a 'discourse of difference', which articulates 'youth' as a problem to adult society rather than as citizens (Brown, 1998 and see Chapter 15). In other words, policy-makers can employ the term 'criminal' to confer not just a legal but also a social status in order to isolate and socially exclude those labelled.

Similarly, the term 'victim' is also the product of social construction. It too confers a status and assigns a role for those so labelled. The term carries very significant social messages associated with vulnerability, powerlessness and passivity within interpersonal relationships. 'Victim' is a word which Quinney (1972) notes is loaded with meaning, and 'concern with the victim has become a powerful motif in contemporary western societal responses to crime' (Bottoms, 1983: 172). The common sense meaning projects an idealised image of the young, the old and the infirm. Those members of society who fit this idealised image as 'innocent victims' are those most able to claim legitimacy as victims and thus entitlement to sympathy, support or compensation. 'The ideal victim is, in my use of the term, a sort of public status of the same type and level of abstraction as that for example of a "hero" or "traitor"' (Christie, 1986: 18). 'Ideal' victims in fact exist only at the margins of a wide spectrum of complex social categorisation which can variably present the victim not just in an idealised form as 'innocent', but also as less than innocent, where the victim is deemed to be the instigator, the precipitator or the contributor to the criminal behaviour. Indeed, the early studies on victims created typologies of victim types which served to establish that some responsibility for the crime lay with the victim as a result of the victim's susceptibility to victimisation or the victim's participation in the events which led to the crime. These studies created a climate within which policy-makers could obviate some of the responsibility for crime causation through a process of victim blaming.

Whereas today, the status of the victim of crime is central to both policy-making and academic research, for most of the time that criminology was evolving during the 20th century, that status was, at best, peripheral. The criminal justice system was primarily concerned with victims as complainants and witnesses, and criminologists focused almost exclusively on the motivations of offenders, ignoring the significance of offender-victim relationships and creating what amounted to a 'black hole' for criminological theory (Mawby and Gill, 1987). Yet despite this collective myopia, the term 'victimology' had been in use from the late 1940s to describe a discipline which did acknowledge the importance of the role of victim and acknowledged the need to research victimisation. The American psychiatrist Frederick Wertham (1949), having described the murder victim as the 'forgotten man', went on to assert (at 259) that: 'One cannot understand the psychology of the murderer if one does not understand the sociology of the victim. What we need is a science of victimology.'

WAYS OF GAINING KNOWLEDGE ABOUT VICTIMS

Walklate (1998) talks of positivist, radical and critical approaches to victimology. Whilst we largely accept Walklate's description of positivist and critical approaches to victimology, we believe that, when it comes to distinctions between her second category, the radical perspective, and her third, the critical perspective, there is some confusion. This is, we think, because debates about theories of knowledge need to be separated from debates about differences in theoretical perspective; although the two are related, they are not the same. We define theories of knowledge (or epistemologies) as different positions on the debate about *how* knowledge should be produced. Theorists working within any one given perspective may sometimes differ in the assumptions that they make regarding the question of how knowledge should be produced (see below).

Perspectives that are underpinned by positivist epistemology operate with what is now considered by many social scientists as an outmoded view of science. The main assumption within positivism is that research can be carried out in a value-neutral way and that value-neutrality equates with objectivity. The main concern of this approach is the discovery of causal relationships, which are discovered through large-scale representative studies of a quantitative nature.

There are many criminological perspectives that have informed the study of victims. These perspectives, like all theoretical perspectives on social phenomenon, are underpinned by basic assumptions about (a) the nature of the social world itself, and (b) how knowledge that is convincing can or should be produced. The former are sometimes called ontological assumptions, and the latter are called epistemological assumptions. Social researchers differ in terms of these two sets of assumptions.

Assumptions about the nature of the social world are important to the study of victims because victims are not constructed in the same way at all times and in all places. Assumptions about how we should obtain knowledge are important because we need to understand how theories of knowledge affect the sorts of questions that are asked as well as the sorts of knowledge that are produced.

There are three key theories of knowledge: positivism, interpretivism and critical social research. It is often the case that social scientists in general talk about either positivism (by which is meant an approach to the study of the social world that closely resembles natural science and that is concerned with causal relationships) or interpretivism (by which is meant an approach that eschews science on the grounds that it is inappropriate for the study of thinking and 'feeling' human beings, and that is concerned with interpretation). The former is often associated with quantitative methods and the latter is associated with qualitative methods. It is also usually assumed that the former equates value-freedom with objectivity and that the latter is an altogether more subjective enterprise. This oppositional way of thinking about ways of gaining knowledge has been widely criticised not least because one side of the opposition, interpretivism, is often subordinated to the other, positivism, on the grounds that it is not 'scientific' (see, for example, Brunskell, 1998). However, the point to be emphasised here is that each theory of knowledge will produce different types of important information about the same phenomenon.

There is, however, another theory of knowledge called critical social research that challenges the dualism of such an either/or conceptualisation of research (see also Chapter 3). Critical social research does not necessarily eschew science, although it does not define it as a value-neutral activity, nor does it eschew interpretation. This means that critical researchers will often use a variety of methods to produce an array of evidence that will aid theoretical understanding of a social issue. Critical social research attempts to reveal the hidden processes through which ideologically dominant understandings of the world are constructed and maintained. It is an approach that is underpinned by the view that, as Muncie (Chapter 1) puts it, 'theory matters'. Theory matters because it is so easy in everyday life to forget its existence. Theories can enter our common sense knowledge and, once this happens, we are unlikely to question that knowledge. That is, certain aspects of our social world appear to be 'natural' or 'universal' and thereby not amenable to question or change. In simple terms, we fail to see that all knowledge is socially produced.

Critical approaches to the study of the social world seek to inform actions by drawing attention to the theoretical mechanisms that can serve to hide and maintain oppressive practices. As Mawby and Walklate (1994) have argued, critical victimology needs to point out the relationship between epistemology (a theory of knowledge), methodology and the political agenda. So, for example, orthodox victimology, underpinned by positivism, has operated with a taken-for-granted assumption that the notion of a victim is neutral and that politics should remain outside the operation of 'objective science'. This, in itself, makes the assumption that objective science can (or should) be carried out in a value-neutral way. However, this view of science is not one that is held by everyone. Indeed, critical social researchers would claim that *all* research is underpinned by a set of values, but only some researchers make these values explicit (Harvey, 1990).

It is important to note that even some of the most radical theories on crime and victims may not necessarily challenge the assumptions of positivistic science. We do not therefore reproduce Walklate's (1998) delineation between positivist, radical and critical approaches to victimology; rather we prefer to talk about positivist, *interpretivist* and critical. This is because we believe that such delineations provide a clearer distinction between theories of knowledge and theoretical perspectives, the latter of which are too numerous to discuss in a chapter of this type. We will explore these different theories of knowledge later in the chapter in relation to the issue of domestic violence.

POSITIVIST VICTIMOLOGY

Since its inception, victimology has predominately developed along paths parallel to positivist criminology. It was, and largely remains, concerned with exploring:

- the aetiology of victimisation through the construction of victim typologies in order to categorise victims, to distinguish them from non-victims and to explain why some people appear to be more prone to victimisation than others (for example, Mendelsohn, 1947; von Hentig, 1948; Sparks, Genn and Dodd, 1977);

- the nature of the relationships between criminal and victim which might indicate the extent to which a victim can be considered to be responsible for the victimisation, for instance, by in some way precipitating the events which led to their victimisation (for example: Wolfgang, 1958; Amir, 1971; Mawby and Firkins, 1986; Mawby and Gill, 1987);

- the extent, type and patterns and impact of victimisation from data obtained through national and local victim surveys.

Miers (1989) has characterised positivist victimology by its assumption that there is a social consensus as to who victims are and what victimisation is. The term 'victim' is therefore not seen as problematic, and victims are deemed to be readily identifiable. Positivist victimology 'is a view of the data-gathering process which privileges traditional conceptions of science and scientific objectivity' (Walklate, 2000: 185). It seeks to explain victimisation, located almost entirely within the context of crimes of interpersonal violence, through the study of these identifiable victims:

> The standard questions of positivist victimology are: what socio-cultural factors are most likely to produce victims, and why are some people victimised? These questions are answered by examining the values, beliefs and behavioural patterns displayed by victims; by analysing how victims differ from non-victims and by trying to identify those factors that increase a person's susceptibility to victimisation. (Miers, 1989: 4)

These questions were addressed in the earliest of studies of victimisation. From interviews with clients in his law practice, Mendelsohn (1947) noted the significance of understanding the inter-relationship between the criminal and the victim and called for a 'victimology' which would study that relationship. He developed typologies of victim culpability, which assigned victim-types along a moral continuum from the morally innocent to the morally guilty according to their responsibility for the crime. This is typical of the early victim studies, which emphasised the ways that victims can contribute to their victimisation and began to construct a controversial perspective, which saw the victim as sharing responsibility with the criminal for the criminal behaviour.

The most influential early study was Hans von Hentig's *The Criminal and his Victim* (1948), which provided an analysis of the relationships between murderers and their victims by categorising victims according to their behaviour and vulnerability. Central to this analysis was the view that the role of the victim was not as a passive sufferer, but that the victimisation could be a result of the victim's own precipitation of, or proneness to, the crime. Empirical support for von Hentig's analysis was provided by Wolfgang's *Patterns in Criminal Homicide* (1958), a classic study of 588 murder cases in Philadelphia, which concluded that in 26 per cent of the murders, the victims had initiated the events that led to their death. Wolfgang, by referring to this involvement as 'victim precipitation', both elevated the status and role of the victim in the dynamic of criminal behaviour and confirmed the need to consider the victim as being a significant factor in all subsequent crime analysis. These early studies are significant as they exposed the artificiality of the divisions between criminal/non-criminal and criminal/victim which are generated by the formalities of the criminal law and the criminal justice processes.

However, many of the subsequent studies, which sought to apply the concept of victim precipitation to a variety of interpersonal crimes, merely furthered a 'blame the victim' perspective. This perspective was presented most controversially by Amir in his study *Patterns of Forcible Rape* (1971), when he adopted a broader and more imprecise concept of victim precipitation in an analysis of the victim-offender relationship in rape cases. The implications of an analysis of rape that moves from an explanatory assessment of risk to an attribution of responsibility and blame to the victim were identified and strongly condemned by feminists. Such an approach perpetuates the insidious myth that women invite rape (or invite other forms of victimisation such as domestic violence, as we shall discuss below) and impacts upon the legal processing of such cases. Some psychiatric discourses have also played a part in perpetuating such myths. For example, Gayford's (1978) victim typologies in his study of battered wives could be said more to reflect the sexist assumptions that have served to undermine rape and domestic violence than to explain victimisation.

The 'Ipswich Rape Case' (*R v Allen* (1982) unreported) is a well-documented example of how criminal responsibility can be displaced when perspectives which perpetrate such myths are accepted. The trial judge, Richards J, suggested that, by hitch-hiking at night, the girl complainant had been 'guilty of a great deal of contributory negligence' in relation to her rape, and that the case had been a tragedy *for the defendant* (Jeffreys and Radford, 1984: 155) That case involved a stranger-rape, but the far more common nature of rape is that it is a crime involving people who are acquainted. Acquaintance rape, date rape and marital rape cases are now more frequently reported to the police and prosecuted, and there is therefore more scope for a 'victim-blaming' sceptical or dismissive approach to cases where the complainant and the accused might have talked, danced, shared a taxi, or were sexually intimate before the offence took place. Thus, although the concept of victim-precipitation was supposedly designed to provide a value-neutral explanatory model of homicide, it has been more recently criticised as a dangerous concept by feminists (Clark and Lewis, 1977; Walklate, 1998: 4–5). This is because it has been adapted to promulgate a male-conceived view of sexual and violent crimes in which female victims can be criticised for inviting victimisation, be categorised as either 'blameless' or 'culpable', and be viewed as either 'worthy' or 'unworthy' recipients of the label 'victim'.

Whereas victimology was a marginal aspect of social science when it began to develop a concern with the theoretical aetiology of individual victimisation, the past 30 years have seen the discipline transform as it became both more applied and politicised and developed a more macro, indeed global, perspective. Victimology emerged as an area of significance for social science and political activity largely as a result of (a) the work of feminist researchers, such as Carol Smart, who were especially interested in the ways in which female victimisation was hidden from view, and (b) the development of crime surveys, most notably by left realists (note, however, that much of the victimisation resulting from corporate crimes continued to remain hidden, not least because of the different official response that is made in relation to such crimes).

These surveys provided new and more detailed crime data, which could be employed to expand the study of crime. The first victim surveys were conducted in America from the mid-1960s and in 1977 the findings of the first British survey to explore unreported crime, conducted by Sparks et al in London, were published (Sparks, Genn and Dodd, 1977). Although since 1972 the General Household Survey had included a question on domestic burglary, it was the establishment of the British Crime Survey, conducted regularly since 1982, which provided the impetus for the growth in the interest in victimisation (Hough and Mayhew, 1983).

By the 1980s, alongside national British Crime Surveys, a considerable number of local crime and victim surveys were being conducted which focused upon the experiences of victims of crimes at a community and at an individual level. The increasing use of crime surveys to assess hidden levels of crime (the 'dark figure' of unreported crime) began to elicit detailed information which related to the nature and extent of victimisation (for example, Kinsey, 1985; Jones, Maclean and Young, 1986; Painter, Lea, Woodhouse and Young, 1989).

By disclosing some of the less visible areas of criminality and victimisation, these surveys challenged the traditional representations of the prevalence and distribution of crime. Whereas traditional official crime statistics were indices of conventional policing and reflected areas of discretion in the criminal justice process through their construction (Kitsuse and Cicourel, 1963), victimisation surveys provided specific information on areas of social behaviour, such as domestic violence, rape, and abuse of both children and the elderly, which had been beyond the reach of official investigation (see, for example, Dobash and Dobash, 1980; Hall, 1985; Painter and Farrington, 1998; Morgan and Zedner, 1991; Brogden and Nijhar, 2000). These developments maintained a radical edge in left realist thought.

However, whilst creating a new locus of academic and political interest through the provision of data on patterns and regularities of victimisation and on typologies of victims, initial empirical findings of victimisation surveys remained within the descriptive tradition of positivist criminology. Hudson has described this process as 'the unreflexive production of technicist information for legislators, criminal justice planners and practitioners' (Hudson, 2002: 235). As such, the findings from such data were employed to substantiate and sustain criminological and political positions across the whole spectrum of opinion.

A right realist perspective which had emerged firstly in America (Wilson, 1975; Wilson and Kelling, 1982; Wilson and Herrnstein, 1985) had linked a routine activity approach to the analysis of victimisation (Cohen and Felson, 1979) with a more general examination of the lifestyle of victims which correlated modes of lifestyle with levels of risk of victimisation (Hindelang, Gottfredson and Garofalo, 1978; Garofalo, 1986). Although the early victim surveys had found a homogeneity between criminal and victim which should have obfuscated this distinction, the functionalist lifestyle-risk approach reinforced the traditional criminological concern with the perception of urban male youth committing conventional crimes in the public domain against idealised victims. It also fed a political agenda which sought to manage criminal behaviour through the implementation of reactive, preventative policies. In Britain, this manifested itself with the emergence of what Young has described as an 'administrative criminology' (Young, 1988) and the key role taken by the Home Office in promoting policies of situational crime prevention and rational choice theories which explained crime as opportunistic (Cornish and Clarke, 1986). Hughes (1998) has pointed out that, although situational crime prevention and rational choice theories acknowledge the point of view of the victim, they do so mostly in terms of precipitative behaviour.

In recent years, both 'old Conservative' and 'New Labour' policies on criminality and victimisation have closely mirrored the positions of right realists. Young has noted how the pronouncements of the Labour Government on crime mirror the right realist discourse: '[A]t times Blair's recent pronouncements on crime look like literal transcriptions from JQ Wilson's *Thinking About Crime* (1975)' (Young, 2002: 463–64).

Early analysis of the British Crime Survey findings suggested that those who felt most vulnerable, women and the elderly, were those least likely to become crime victims, and therefore their feelings of vulnerability were dismissed as irrational. One of the many outcomes arising from the findings of the British Crime Survey was a particular focus on fear of crime and the debate around whether its effect on lifestyles meant that such fear was more socially damaging than crime itself. These views were ascribed by Young (1991) to an 'objectivist' tendency in contemporary victimology, which he distinguished from the 'subjectivist' tendency which saw fear of crime as rational because what people fear is based on real and often undisclosed experiences of victimisation. Young argued for a left realist position which avoided generalisations about the experience of crime or the assessment of rationality of fear of crime based upon statistical averages risk rates. A left realist approach values the findings from victim surveys as disclosing the 'lived realities' of different social groups in different social areas and, in doing so, emphasises the racial and gender dimensions of victimisation. However, it should be noted that the age dimension is still not adequately theorised. Much violence and financial abuse that is perpetrated against the elderly, for example, takes place within the private sphere. As Pain (1999) has argued, these issues continue to be marginalised by criminologists and victimologists. This therefore should raise questions about the notion of equal victims.

The left realist approach fixes the victim in the equation of the 'square of crime', a model which explains the crime rate as a consequence of the interaction between (a) the agencies of social control, such as the police, and (b) the offender, (c) the public and (d) the victim. By calling for an 'accurate victimology' (Young, 1986: 23–24) and claiming to take the experiences of victims of crime seriously, realists avoid the positivist tendency to indulge in victim-blaming. The concept of the 'square of crime' minimises any division between victim and offender and maximises the sense that crime involves a relationship in which the impact of criminal victimisation depends upon, among other things, the response by agencies such as care agencies, the police and the courts. A consequence of inappropriate or unsympathetic responses from such agencies, for instance, where a victim-blaming response is evident, can result in further stigmatisation of the victim, often referred to as 'secondary victimisation' (Young, 1991: 153). Unlike the reactive approach of right realists, left realists argue for political policies which return to a concern for the causes of crime as well as an investment of resources in youth to enhance employability and provide leisure facilities:

> Present government policy has over-focused on the victim: it seeks, through target-hardening and the increasing privatisation of security, to make the public responsible for their own safety, while dealing with offenders only after the offence has been committed through the courts and a strong police force. (Young, 1991: 153)

Left realism developed an applied dimension as it promoted crime prevention policies and, in doing so, became 'more and more an administrative criminology of the left' (Downes and Rock, 2003: 290). Left realists 'embarked on a programme of policy-making as vigorous as that of any government department'. However, 'much of what is recommended is little different from the ideas of secondary crime prevention developed by the Home Office Crime Prevention Unit' (Downes and Rock, 2003: 289).

For instance, as Downes and Rock go on to note, a situational approach was taken by left realists whose solution to street crime and the fear of street crime was improved street lighting. It is not difficult to see how such a situational response might be linked to the idea that victims may be partly responsible for the crimes that are committed against them. The woman who walks along an unlit street alone, for example, might be seen to be inviting trouble.

Positivist victimology, then, can be seen to have forged a significant place in criminology through the amount of empirically generated research data which has been used to inform political agendas and policies. This has led to establishing criminal victimisation firmly at the centre of debates around crime and has provided support for the emergent victims' movement and an applied victimology. Yet, as has been identified, positivist victimology has sustained perspectives which seek to shift the responsibility for criminal victimisation on to the victim. Positivist victimology continues to provide a setting within which one of its central themes – victim-blaming – can be sustained. A key criticism of a positivist perspective is based upon its failure to treat the term 'victim' as problematic, so that it has failed to provide any analysis of the role of the state in defining that term or in distinguishing the victim from the criminal, the victim from the non-victim or the worthy from the unworthy victim.

THE CASE OF DOMESTIC VIOLENCE

We will now examine the particular issue of domestic violence in order to explore some of the issues that we have raised so far. In the 1970s, the women's movement began to draw attention to the suffering of women in the private sphere. However, at that time, the problem was understood largely in terms of the victims' own inadequate personalities, because the male psychologists who were explaining the phenomenon perceived the problem to lie in the inadequate personalities of the victims. This was a positivist approach that assumed that the causes of victimisation lay within the victim. As Mooney (2000) has pointed out, male psychologists construed abusers as sick, and victims were thought to be particular 'types' – 'masochistic', 'paranoid', 'mentally ill', 'sexually inadequate'. This demonstrates that their so called neutral science was underpinned by male assumptions about women. This can be demonstrated by the fact that these psychiatrists asked why women did not leave their violent partners and implied that it was not only irrational for women to stay, but that they were responsible for their own victimisation – see Walklate (1998).

Feminist researchers, on the other hand, began to point to the *rational* reasons why women stayed in violent relationships. They did this by shifting from a positivist approach to an interpretivist approach through which knowledge about what it is like to be an abused woman could be revealed. Women's personal accounts revealed that their reasons for staying were far from irrational. A common finding was that women who were economically dependent on men were often faced with a choice of coping with violence or destitution. Mooney (2000) found the following reasons why women stayed: economic dependence (27 per cent); hope that their partner would change (27 per cent); nowhere to go/lack of affordable accommodation (26 per cent); effect of break-up of family home on the children (20 per cent). Chigwada-Bailey (2003) also identified the specific difficulties encountered by black victims of domestic violence.

Black women are often torn between bringing their abusers to account and bringing the whole of their community into disrepute by confirming racial stereotypes. The shift from a positivist theory of knowledge, concerned with causes, to an interpretivist theory of knowledge, concerned with meaning, therefore demonstrated how women worked out, on the basis of their knowledge of their partners and of their social circumstances, the best ways in which they and their children could survive.

Once we begin to see the conditions of existence of the lives of abused women, it is possible to understand the importance of acknowledging inequalities between victims. The private sphere can often be seen to be structured and controlled by men. Women in violent relationships know that home is a risky place to be, but they have to find ways of coping with and surviving the violence – especially if they are also poor.

In recent years, feminists and anti-sexist male researchers have moved into a more obviously critical framework through which they have tried to make links between oppressive social structures and people's interpretations of the issue of domestic violence. There has also been a particular focus on *men* and *masculinity*. This has involved examining wider data on the differences between men and women's behaviour and attitudes. An array of evidence of both a quantitative and qualitative nature has been amassed to demonstrate how male violence towards women is endemic in society (see, for example, Facade et al, 1996; Hanmer and Itzin, 2000; Kelly, 1987).

This approach is important because it attempts to understand the mechanisms through which both victims and victimisers are produced. It has been argued, however, that the trend towards increasing investment in victim support is likely to have the effect of increasing state control as well as a likely redefinition of the problem of male violence as one of individual pathology. This can be explained by the failure to move beyond an outmoded positivist view of science. There are concerns that this may marginalise feminist refuges and rape crisis centres (Charles, 2000). Charles also states that evidence from the USA suggests that the separation of service provision from the feminist analysis of domestic violence has depoliticised the issue and robbed the feminist movements of their ability to define their own goals by stifling their theoretical arguments.

To summarise, domestic violence is a relatively new term, which has now entered common parlance; most people therefore have a basic understanding of what is meant by the term. We now accept the need for women's refuges and, on the whole, local authorities and the police take the issue more seriously and try to respond appropriately – but this has not always been so. At the beginning of the last century, the law protected men's rights to beat women (provided the stick they used was no bigger than their thumb!). The fact that violence was normalised in society and the term 'domestic violence' was unheard of did not mean that suffering did not exist. Theorists concerned with this issue therefore had to think in terms of uncovering a reality that was hidden from view. It was important to feminists that the issue of female victims (or, as they prefer, survivors) of domestic violence should be raised. This in turn led to questions being asked about the ways in which the law has been developed in the interests of men. This demonstrates how the suffering caused to women provided good reason for feminists to be unconstrained by the limits of the law, that is, their concern reflected the concerns of critical criminology in general to ask questions about who has the power to define what is criminal. This is an important question to ask; otherwise we are left with the inadequate conclusion that people can only be described as victims if the law proscribes the act that causes the suffering. This was a point that Sutherland (1945) made in relation to white collar crime. He was criticised by Tappan (1947) precisely because he went beyond legal definitions, yet it is only by pushing such boundaries that the law can be changed in order to offer more protection and redress to those who have the least power in society.

A critical approach to victimology is inextricably linked to a critical approach to criminology in general because it forces us to examine the relationship between agency and structure – becoming a victim or indeed committing a criminal act is not simply something that happens to, or is enacted by, some individuals. Critical criminologists ask questions like, 'Who comes to be defined as a criminal?' and 'Who decides?'. Similarly, we need to ask, 'Who comes to be defined as a victim?' and 'Are all victims equally placed to seek redress?'. Such questions point to the need to examine the inequalities that exist in society, how these come about, how they are sustained and how they can be reduced. They question the supposed 'naturalness' of our social organisation by forcing us to acknowledge the relationship between our actions (and the meanings we give to those actions) and the social order. Most importantly, they challenge the assumption of neutrality that underpins positivist approaches to research.

Whereas, as we noted earlier in this chapter, the labelling of individuals as 'criminal' has attracted much debate and criticism, there has been little critical consideration of the meanings attached to or associated with the label 'victim'. Fattah (1997: 148) has pointed out that 'its real criminological meaning remains unclear and its utility remains in doubt'. The danger is that, although the word 'victim' is the very basis of the term 'victimology' and is a status or label demanded by the criminal law and the criminal justice system (Christie, 1977), it is a pejorative, value-laden and problematic designation. Fattah criticises the use of the normative labels because, he argues, they inhibit objective investigation into crime events. A critical approach, while challenging that assumed objectivity, should support a redesignation, because the normative labels perpetuate a false dichotomy based on divisive and arbitrary distinctions which ignore the interchangeability of the roles of the criminal and victim. 'The indiscriminate use of these labels is to perpetuate the popular stereotypes of the crime protagonists and to reinforce the notion that criminals and victims are as different as night and day' (Fattah, 1997: 148). The use of labels such as 'participants' or 'parties' may be more appropriate for a critical approach which avoids a reliance on stereotyping and understands conflicts as interactions (Walklate, 1990). Fattah acknowledges that any attempt to change such firmly entrenched labels will 'encounter fierce resistance and will even require changing the name of the discipline "victimology" itself' (1997: 149). In this chapter, for the sake of academic convention, we have employed the traditional labels, but we are aware that in doing so we have engaged in reproducing the same representations that we seek to challenge.

THE ROLE OF POLITICS

As we have seen, in the study of victims of domestic violence, there have been debates about the way in which the victim support movement can depoliticise some issues. The limitations of victim support in relation to domestic violence are illustrative of the general and important point made by Elias (1996) that, whilst victimologists typically take the side of victims, they may simultaneously countenance policies that are not in the interests of victims. As he has pointed out, the main tendency is to polarise victim and offender when it might well be the case that the well-being of victims is far more dependent upon the willingness of states to question their priorities. This point is linked to an earlier point, which Elias makes in the same article, that politics is inevitable; irrespective of the stance of a researcher, those with power will promote only the aspects of research that suit their political ends. Indeed, he states that it is only by not being neutral that inappropriate use of research can be avoided. It is for this reason that we would identify Elias with a critical theory of knowledge.

Jones (2000), in the same vein, has pointed to the ways in which work with victims has provided the justification required by the political right to introduce harsher sentences for perpetrators. The unstated, but important deduction here is that the state should look to the social contexts in which crimes are committed. As Elias (1996) has suggested, the micro focus of victimological research has served to obscure the bigger picture. His suggested solution to this problem is that victimologists and victim advocates should work together to find 'a politics that works'. In short, a critical approach shifts the focus from a rights-based victimology to a justice-based victimology.

CRITICAL VICTIMOLOGY AND JUSTICE FOR VICTIMS

In this section, we will examine how a critical approach to the study of victims can help us to raise questions about justice. It is all too easy to assume that justice for victims is predicated upon harsher punishments for perpetrators and the development of crime prevention technologies, since both of these strategies are perceived to demonstrate that the law is taking victims seriously. However, we need to ask whether such 'get tough' responses will provide a solution to victimisation in the long term. The short answer to this question is that they will not. We need only to look at the increasing numbers of incarcerations to realise that victims continue to be created. Furthermore, Hughes (1998), in a critique of situational crime prevention, refers to the pioneering research of Norris and Armstrong (1997), who have suggested that technological approaches to crime prevention might produce new forms of victimisation because developments such as CCTV, for example, are focused upon certain sections of society only and involve processes of selectivity which are likely to be discriminatory. The point is that the use of technology is never neutral (see Winner, 1986). Put simply, harsher punishments and increasing controls do not appear to achieve justice for either victims or criminals. This suggests that alternatives such as restitution and reconciliation should be given more prominence in debates.

The longer answer to the question is that there is a need to take a critical view of the law and processes of criminal justice in order to question the extent to which it can be said that *all* victims are taken seriously by agencies of the state. Whilst in the example of domestic violence, we have seen that the state has made some attempt to take the issue seriously, albeit by depoliticising and limiting debates, if we now turn to the issue of corporate crime, we can see that it is much less likely that victims will receive any kind of justice. Indeed, as Mawby and Walklate (1994) have suggested, victims of corporate crime are lucky if they are recognised as such. Indeed, corporate crimes have often been perceived as 'victimless crimes' (Croall, 2001 and see Chapter 10).

Whilst the effects of all crimes upon victims will vary according to class, age, 'race' and gender, it could be argued that for the victims of corporate crimes, wider social inequalities can have the most dramatic consequences. For example, environmental risk on a global scale is highly unequally distributed, and the poorest people in the world are most likely to become victims of the malpractices of large multi-national companies. The effects of the Bhopal disaster in 1984, for example, continue to adversely affect the lives of survivors who have never received adequate compensation. Greenpeace (www.greenpeaceusa.org/bhopal) persists in its campaign to put pressure on Dow chemicals to clear up the toxic waste, but so far it continues to blight the lives of people in Bhopal.

Women have suffered more than men at the hands of the pharmaceutical industry, and many poor women, by virtue of their part-time occupational status, are excluded from occupational health research because standards are set on the basis of male experiences. It is only when certain cases come to light that the extent of women's victimisation becomes more apparent. Imperial Foods, an American company, for example, operated with locked fire doors, few fire extinguishers and no smoke alarms. As a result of these practices 25, mostly black, women were killed. Employees knew of the risks but felt unable to complain because they knew that there were plenty more unemployed, poor women waiting to take their jobs (Szockyj and Fox, 1996).

As Slapper and Tombs (1999) point out, not only are the poorest members of our society the most likely to be victims of corporate crimes, they are also the least able to mobilise the necessary resources to act upon their victimisation. A critical approach to the issue of corporate crime looks to the structure of society in which those crimes take place and asks uncomfortable questions about the adequacy of the response by the state for the victims. They argue that a society that embraces competition and the increasing commodification of all human relationships can be said to be one that is likely to engender corporate crime. Further, they point to the low levels of policing and prosecution relating to corporate crimes, which suggest that the criminal justice system itself is complicit in the achievement of business goals. This is an important point since it challenges the ideological view that the 'get tough' approach can be justified on the grounds that it demonstrates the willingness of the state to take the needs of victims seriously.

CONCLUSION

This chapter has pointed to the need to understand the different ways in which victims are constructed in our society. This has drawn attention to the ways in which discourses about crime have not only polarised criminals and victims, but have also produced polarised discourses about the extent to which victims are deserving of redress. The chapter has also pointed to the different ways of gaining knowledge about victimisation. This led to a discussion about the ways in which different knowledge claims can be appropriated by politicians, policy-makers and agents of social control. It has been suggested that the reassertion of a positivist theory of knowledge has often served the purpose of depoliticising debates because of the rather outmoded assumption that it is possible to separate fact from value.

Whilst the discussion of the specific issue of domestic violence has identified the benefits of interpretivist research in revealing the meanings that victims give to their experiences, the chapter has also sought to demonstrate that a shift to a critical research framework has the advantage of challenging the science/anti-science polarisation. Critical approaches to the study of victims will use the insights of positivism and interpretivism, but will go beyond these two theories of knowledge through a commitment to the reflective uses of values in research. This commitment has facilitated an understanding of the ways in which values influence the judgments that are made with regards to the desirable ends of research.

Finally, the chapter has identified the ways in which a critical approach to the study of crime and victims in general can facilitate a wider discussion of the issue of justice.

SEMINAR DISCUSSION TOPICS

• Is a girl hitch-hiking late at night guilty of a 'great deal of contributory negligence' in relation to her rape?

• Since certain victims are identified as 'worthy' while others are blamed for their victimisation, consider the significance of attaching different meanings to the label 'victim'.

• What are the key features of critical approaches to victimology?

• In the context of (a) domestic violence, and (b) white collar crime, consider the role of politics in both identifying victims and in developing responses to victimisation.

• Should the labels 'criminal' and 'victim' be redesignated?

KEY READINGS

Sandra Walklate's *Understanding Criminology* (Open University Press, 1998) provides a brief but accessible outline to victimology frameworks. These frameworks are analysed in detail in Mawby and Walklate's *Critical Victimology* (Sage, 1994), which also critically considers the policy issues around the provision of victim services. The use of the 'Victims' Charter' as a case study is a particularly valuable way to illustrate differing conceptual approaches in victimology. A global perspective on victimology is addressed by the specific comparative consideration of developments in Eastern Europe. Further conceptual analysis can be found in Fattah's *From Crime Policy to Victim Policy* (Macmillan, 1986) or the relevant chapters in his more recent *Criminology: Past, Present and Future* (Macmillan, 1997). More specific critical readings might include *Corporate Victimisation of Women* by Szockyj and Fox (Northeastern University Press, 1996) and *Gender, Violence and the Social Order* by Mooney (Palgrave, 2000).

REFERENCES

Amir, M (1971) *Patterns in Forcible Rape*, Chicago: Chicago UP.

Bottoms, AE (1983) 'Neglected features of the contemporary penal system' in Garland, D and Young, P (eds), *The Power to Punish*, London: Heinemann.

Brogden, M and Nijhar, P (2000) *Crime, Abuse and the Elderly*, Cullompton: Willan.

Brown, S (1998) *Understanding Youth and Crime: Listening to Youth*, Buckingham: Open University Press.

Brunskell, H (1998) 'Feminist methodology' in Seale, C (ed), *Researching Society and Culture*, London: Sage.

Charles, N (2000) *Feminism, the State and Social Policy*, London: Macmillan.

Chigwada-Bailey, R (2003) *Black Women's Experiences of Criminal Justice: Race, Gender and Class: A Discourse on Disadvantage*, Winchester: Waterside Press.

Christie, N (1977) 'Conflicts as property', *British Journal of Criminology*, vol 17(1), pp 1–19.

Christie, N (1986) 'The ideal victim' in Fattah, E (ed), *From Crime Policy to Victim Policy*, London: Macmillan.

Clark, LMG and Lewis, DJ (1977) *Rape: The Price of Coercive Sexuality*, Toronto: Women's Press.

Cohen, L and Felson, M (1979) 'Social change and crime rate trends: a routine activities approach', *American Sociological Review*, vol 44, pp 588–608.

Cornish, D and Clarke, RV (1986) *The Reasoning Criminal: Rational Choice Perspectives on Offending*, New York: Springer.

Croall, H (2001) *Understanding White Collar Crime*, Buckingham: Open University Press.

Dobash, R and Dobash, R (1980) *Violence Against Wives: A Case Against Patriarchy*, New York: Open Books.

Downes, D and Rock, P (2003) *Understanding Deviance*, Oxford: OUP.

Elias, R (1996) 'Paradigms and paradoxes' in Sumner, C, Israel, M, O'Connell, M and Sarre, R (eds), *International Victimology*, selected papers from the 8th International Symposium, 21–26 August 1994, Canberra: Australian Institute of Criminology.

Facade, B, Featherstone, B, Hearn, J and Toft, C (eds) (1996) *Violence and Gender Relations: Theories and Interventions*, Thousand Oaks, CA: Sage, pp 7–21.

Fattah, EA (1997) *Criminology: Past, Present and Future*, London: Macmillan.

Garofalo, J (1986) 'The ideal victim' in Fattah, EA (ed), *From Crime Policy to Victim Policy*, London: Macmillan.

Gayford, JJ (1978) 'Battered wives: a study of the aetiology and psychological effects among one hundred women', thesis (MD), University of London.

Hall, R (1985) *Ask Any Woman*, London: Falling Wall Press.

Hanmer, J and Itzin, C (eds) (2000) *Home Truths About Domestic Violence: Feminist Influences on Policy and Practice – A Reader*, London: Routledge.

Harvey, L (1990) *Critical Social Research*, London: Unwin Hyman.

Heidensohn, F (1989) *Crime and Society*, London: Macmillan Education Ltd.

Hindelang, MJ, Gottfredson, MR and Garofalo, J (1978) *Victims of Personal Crime: An Empirical Foundation for a Theory of Personal Victimization*, Cambridge, MA: Ballinger.

Hough, M and Mayhew, P (1983) *The British Crime Survey: First Report*, London: HMSO.

Hudson, B (2002) 'Punishment and control' in Maguire, M, Morgan, R and Reiner, R (eds), *The Oxford Handbook of Criminology*, Oxford: Clarendon.

Hughes, G (1998) *Understanding Crime Prevention*, Buckingham: Open University Press.

Jeffreys, S and Radford, J (1984) 'Contributory negligence or being a woman? The car rapist case' in Scraton, P and Gordon, P (eds), *Causes for Concern*, Harmondsworth: Penguin.

Jones, S (2000) *Understanding Violent Crime*, Buckingham: Open University Press.

Jones, T, Maclean, B and Young, J (1986) *The Islington Crime Survey*, Aldershot: Gower.

Kelly, L (1987) 'Sexual violence as a continuum' in Hanmer, J and Maynard, M (eds), *Women, Violence and Social Control*, London: Macmillan.

Kinsey, R (1985) *Merseyside Crime and Police Surveys: Final Report*, Liverpool: Merseyside County Council.

Kitsuse, J and Cicourel, A (1963) 'A note on the uses of official statistics', *Social Problems*, vol 11, pp 131–39.

Mawby, RI and Firkins, V (1986) 'The victim/offender relationship and its implications for policies: evidence from the British Crime Survey', paper presented to the World Congress of Victimology, July, Orlando.

Mawby, RI and Gill, ML (1987) *Crime Victims: Needs, Services and the Voluntary Sector*, London: Tavistock.

Mawby, RI and Walklate, S (1994) *Critical Victimology*, London: Sage.

Mendelsohn, B (1947) 'New bio-psychosocial horizons: victimology', *American Law Review*, vol 13, p 649.

Miers, D (1989) 'Positivist criminology: a critique', *International Review of Victimology*, vol 1, pp 3–22.

Mooney, J (2000) *Gender, Violence and the Social Order*, London: Palgrave.

Morgan, J and Zedner, L (1991) 'Child victims in the criminal justice system', paper presented at British Criminology Conference, York.

Norris, C and Armstrong, S (1997) 'Categories of control: the social construction of suspicion and intervention in CCTV systems' in Norris, C and Armstrong, S (eds), *Images of Control: CCTV and the Rise of Surveillance Societies*, Berg.

Pain, R (1999) 'Theorising age in criminology: the case of home abuse', www.britsoccrim.org/bccsp/vol02/06PAIN.htm.

Painter, K and Farrington, D (1998) 'Marital violence in Great Britain and its relationship to marital and non-marital rape', *International Review of Victimology*, vol 5, pp 257–76.

Painter, K, Lea, J, Woodhouse, T and Young, J (1989) *The Hammersmith Crime Survey*, Middlesex Polytechnic: Centre for Criminology.

Quinney, R (1972) 'Who is the victim?' *Criminology*, vol 10, pp 314–23.

Russell, DEH (1990) *Rape in Marriage*, Bloomington, IN: Indiana UP.

Slapper, G and Tombs, S (1999) *Corporate Crime*, Harlow: Longman.

Sparks, RF, Genn, H and Dodd, D (1977) *Surveying Victims*, London: John Wiley.

Sutherland, E (1945) 'Is "white collar crime" crime?', *American Sociological Review*, vol 10, pp 132–39.

Szockyj, ER and Fox, JG (1996) *Corporate Victimisation of Women*, Boston, MA: Northeastern UP.

Tappan, P (1947) 'Who is the criminal?' *American Sociological Review*, vol 12, pp 96–102.

von Hentig, H (1948) *The Criminal and his Victim*, New Haven, CT: Yale UP.

Walklate, S (1990) *Victimology*, London: Unwin Hyam.

Walklate, S (1998) *Understanding Criminology*, Buckingham: Open University Press.

Walklate, S (2000) 'Researching victims' in King, RD and Wincup, E (eds), *Doing Research on Crime and Justice*, Oxford: OUP.

Wertham, F (1949) *The Show of Violence*, New York: Vintage.

Wilson, JQ (1975) *Thinking About Crime*, New York: Basic Books.

Wilson, JQ and Herrnstein, R (1985) *Crime and Human Nature*, New York: Simon & Schuster.

Wilson, JQ and Kelling, G (1982) 'Broken windows', *The Atlantic Monthly*, March, pp 29–38.

Winner, L (1986) *The Whale and the Reactor: A Search for Limits in an Age of High Technology*, Chicago: Chicago UP.

Wolfgang, M (1958) *Patterns in Criminal Homicide*, Philadelphia, PA: Pennsylvania UP.

Young, J (1986) 'The failure of criminology: the need for a radical realism' in Matthews, R and Young, J (eds), *Confronting Crime*, London: Sage.

Young, J (1988) 'Risk of crime and the fear of crime: a realist critique of survey based assumptions' in Maguire M and Pointing, J (eds), *Victims of Crime: A New Deal?*, Milton Keynes: Open University Press.

Young, J (1991) 'Ten principles of realism', paper presented to British Criminology Conference, York.

Young, J (2002) 'Crime and social exclusion' in Maguire, M, Morgan R and Reiner, R (eds), *The Oxford Handbook of Criminology*, Oxford: Clarendon.

CHAPTER 9

ISLAM AND CRIMINAL JUSTICE

Basia Spalek

SUMMARY

In criminological research studies, individuals have traditionally been classified in terms of gender, age, class and/or race, with the issue of religious identity often being almost completely ignored. It seems that the modern roots of criminological discourse, in which 'rationality' and 'scientific analysis' have occupied a privileged position (Morrison, 1995), have contributed to the omission of any consideration of the spiritual underpinnings to people's lives. Nonetheless, recent events, such as the Bradford disturbances that took place in 1995 and then in 2001, and the terrorist attacks in the USA on 11 September 2001 (and the subsequent backlash against Muslim communities), together with the most recent terrorist atrocities in Bali, have brought into sharp focus the significance of faith in people's experiences of crime and victimisation. The following chapter seeks to focus upon the Islamic faith in terms of highlighting and addressing those aspects of criminal justice and victimisation that need to be considered when exploring British Muslims' lives.

KEY TERMS

Islam; Islamophobia; hate crime.

MUSLIM COMMUNITIES IN BRITAIN

When referring to the term 'Islam', it is important to note that, although this word suggests that there is one community of Muslim people who have very similar beliefs and practices, individuals classified as being Muslim in the UK are heterogeneous, as they originally came from different countries, speak different languages and follow different schools of Islamic thought (Joly, 1995). Approximately one-third of the British Muslim population is considered to be of Pakistani origin, with a significant number coming from East Africa, India and Bangladesh. The rest have Arabic, Iranian, Turkish, Malaysian and Nigerian origins (Joly, 1995: xii). Islam is not only a culturally and ethnically diverse religion; it is also spiritually diverse. There are three main strands to Islam – Shi'a, Sunni and Sufi. Ninety per cent of Muslims worldwide are Sunni Muslims, and this percentage is even greater for South Asian Muslims in Britain. Within the Sunni tradition, there are a number of different movements, including Barelwis, Deobandis, Tablighi Jamat and Jama'at-I-Islami (Conway, 1997).

Until very recently, all of the available statistics on the number of Muslims living in Britain were estimates, since the National Census (which is carried out every 10 years) has not traditionally included questions about religious affiliation; rather, ethnic identity categories have been used. For the first time in Britain, the National Census 2001 collected data about religious identity, according to the following categories:

Christian, Buddhist, Hindu, Jewish, Muslim, Sikh or None, thereby enabling policy-makers to have the most accurate picture to date of the religious affiliations of the population of England and Wales.[1] According to the Census, 72 per cent of the population of England and Wales say that their religion is Christianity. After Christianity, Islam is the most common faith recorded, with 3.1 per cent of the population describing their religion as Muslim, totalling 1.6 million people (The Census Dissemination Unit, 2001, http://census.ac.uk/cdu). It can be argued that, to a significant proportion of these persons, religion occupies a central role in their lives, since the 1994 National Survey of Ethnic Minorities revealed that 90 per cent of Muslims surveyed considered religion to be important to the way that they lead their lives, with a substantial majority attending mosque at least once a week (although nearly a third of women do not attend mosque or prayer meetings as this is not an important requirement for them) (Modood et al, 1997: 302). These figures illustrate the necessity of considering those aspects of crime, victimisation and criminal justice policy that impact upon and influence British Muslims' everyday lives.

MUSLIM OFFENDERS: SOCIAL EXCLUSION, ISLAMOPHOBIA AND INTERPRETATIONS OF ISLAM

Prison statistics reveal that there is an over-representation of Muslims in British jails. According to the Prison Statistics, England and Wales (2001), there were 4,933 Muslims, 433 Sikh, 295 Hindu male and female prisoners on 1 September 2001. Clearly, Muslims outnumber Sikhs and Hindus, since, whilst there are approximately 1.6 million Muslims in England and Wales, there are approximately 559,000 Hindus and 336,000 Sikhs (National Census, 2001). Furthermore, Islam is one of the fastest-growing religions in prison (Beckford and Gilliat, 1998). Whilst the population of all Christians shows an increase of 23 per cent between 1993 and 2001, the number of Muslims has risen by 132 per cent over the same period (Home Office, 2003: 121). Muslims comprise 8 per cent of the total prison population, the largest group of prisoners from religions other than Christians (Home Office, 2003: 122). But, before examining the British penal system and how well it caters to religious minority groups' needs, it is important to consider the possible reasons why there are so many Muslims, particularly so many young Muslim men, in prison.

Age is likely to be a factor, because around 70 per cent of all British Muslims are under the age of 25 (Conway, 1997), and research studies show that the age at which offending most commonly starts is 14, whilst the age at which it most commonly stops is 23 (Farrington, 1997). Discrimination and social exclusion are also important. The link between social deprivation and offending is now well-established (Farrington, 1997) and would appear to be a factor in offending amongst some young Muslim men. Racial inequality is evident in the labour market. The rate of unemployment of ethnic minority people is at least double the rate of unemployment of white people (Bloch, 1997: 112). People from ethnic minority groups are also more likely than white people to work in low paid jobs with poor conditions of employment (Bloch, 1997: 113). It is clear that social exclusion and inequality is high amongst Muslim

---

1   The statistics provide only an approximation since the census question on religion was voluntary.

communities. According to the Labour Force Survey 1994, Pakistani and Bangladeshi communities (the majority of whom are Muslim) tend to be the least well-paid (Bloch, 1997: 114). In the city of Bradford, unemployment is high in Muslim communities and around half of Pakistani and Bangladeshi households have no full-time workers (Ratcliffe, 1996). It is in these areas that public disturbances and riots took place between April and July 2001, which were identified by the media as the worst cases of urban rioting on the British mainland for 20 years. The disturbances are estimated to have cost the city between £7.5 million and £10 million (Denham, 2001) and the police £10 million. It seems that material deprivation, unemployment, police mistreatment, racism, the 'far right' and also Islamophobia played some role in the disturbances (see Macey, 2002).

Islamophobia has deep cultural and historical roots in Western society. The negative stereotyping of Muslims and gross misunderstandings and representations of Islam have been long-standing features of many Western countries. Islam has often been interpreted as 'the other', as the antithesis of Western society. The West has often defined itself against Islam, with Islam being portrayed as barbaric, inhumane and evil. Islam has often been viewed in monolithic ways, as an unchanging religion which lacks cultural diversity (Said, 1978). Islamophobia is endemic to British society (Conway, 1997) and so is an important factor to consider when looking at the social and economic marginalisation of Muslim communities. Indeed, the Commission on the Future of Multi-Ethnic Britain (2000) suggests that, in some cases, disaffected Muslim youth may join extremist Islamist organisations as a reaction against high rates of unemployment and the lack of educational opportunities.

The use of religion for violence and terror has featured in both Christian and Muslim religions. With respect to Islam, whilst there are many passages in the Qur'an teaching love and forgiveness towards others, there are nonetheless some which might be interpreted by individuals as justifications for violence (Sullivan, 2001). Cultural and personal interpretations of the Qur'an may be implicated in some criminal offences. These may sometimes, by a minority of individuals, be used as a way of justifying acts of physical violence against women, gay men, lesbians and prostitutes. In some communities, some men have policed women's behaviour and inflicted psychological and physical violence on women who transgress cultural norms and dress codes (Mama, 1996; Macey, 1999). Mama's (1996) work on domestic violence against black women shows that there is often a specific cultural context to the violence, as in the case, for example, where some men use religion to assert their control over women. In order to develop an understanding of criminality amongst some individuals in some Muslim communities, it might therefore be argued that it is important to take into account personal and cultural interpretations of Islam.

In prison, Muslim offenders are disadvantaged in comparison to Christian offenders. In most penal institutions in Britain, Church of England chaplains have overall responsibility for chaplaincy matters, although they might work with Roman Catholic and Methodist chaplains (Beckford and Gilliat, 1998). Instances of religious and racial discrimination occur, and in many prisons the providers of non-Christian religions continue to be marginalised from key decision-making processes. A study by Spalek and Wilson (2001) reveals that anti-Muslim sentiment, direct and indirect racism and inadequate facilities for Muslims are common features of British prisons. A Directory and Guide on Religious Practices in HM Prison Service has been issued (HM Prison Service, 1996) to enable staff to cater to the religious needs of prisoners more adequately. The directory describes matters related to worship, sacred writings, diet, dress, ministry and 'aspects of social functioning', such as the role of families, personal hygiene and race (Wilson and Sharp, 1998: 19). However, Muslim prisoners have criticised the absence or dearth of Halal meat, and concerns have been raised about the place and times of worship and the provision of a suitable minister. Imams argue that, in order for them to engage in the public life of the prison to a greater degree, it is necessary for prison authorities to increase their working hours and pay. This would benefit the prisoners both in terms if having more quality time with the Imams for their spiritual and practical needs, and also in terms of the Imams becoming more actively involved in managerial decisions that ultimately have an impact on the lives of prisoners. Spalek and Wilson's study (2001) also shows that, although many obstacles lie in the way of Imams when attempting to provide religious care, the Imams have quite clearly employed extraordinary methods to gain greater acceptance by prison authorities. This is an example of how Muslim communities in Britain have been engaged in struggles to influence criminal justice policy-making so that it takes into account their experiences and needs.

MUSLIM COMMUNITIES, HATE CRIME AND VICTIM SERVICES

Violence against minority ethnic and religious groups is an ever-present feature of British society (Bowling, 1998). Unfortunately, national and local crime surveys, which measure the nature and extent of victimisation, tend to classify people according to their ethnic rather than their religious identity. This means that, when exploring the crime experiences of particular religious communities, the researcher has to find other sources of information. Reports produced by the Islamic Human Rights Commission are particularly informative with respect to the specific experiences of Muslim communities. A recent report published by the Home Office in 2001, entitled *Religious Discrimination in England and Wales*, would suggest that policy-makers are becoming increasingly aware of faith community issues. Some of the participants in this study believed that they had been the targets of discrimination and violence as a result of their religious beliefs and practices.

   Muslim communities have experienced racial and religious, verbal and physical, harassment and abuse (Smiljanic, 2002), the frequency and severity of such experiences having been heightened in the wake of the terror attacks in the USA and Bali. Muslim men, women and children, as well as places of worship, have become the targets of hate crime in many countries, including Britain, the USA and Australia. Muslim women in particular have been the targets of hate crime, since the practice of veiling stands as a symbol of Islam and acts as a physical signifier of difference. In the aftermath of 11 September, women have been verbally and physically attacked, and there have been reports of them having their veils being pulled off their heads. A study by Spalek (2002) reveals how Muslim women felt more vulnerable in the immediate aftermath of the terrorist atrocities. Women often changed their routines, avoiding certain places that previously they would have gone to but which they now perceived to constitute an increased threat to their personal security. Women were also issued with safety tips in order to try to reduce the likelihood of them being attacked, advised to travel in groups and to be aware of their surroundings at all times (Siddiqui, 2001).

Governmental responses to the terrorist attacks across the Western world have been to implement repressive and punitive laws which target Muslim communities in particular, where they are deemed to be a threat to national security. In Britain, in 2001, Parliament passed the Anti-terrorism, Crime and Security Act, which banned 21 predominantly Arab or Islamic organisations (Karmi, 2001). Furthermore, according to the Islamic Human Rights Commission, post-11 September, Muslim charities that have donated money to Palestinian organisations for humanitarian reasons have been investigated by the Charity Commission. Recently, a leading Muslim charity, Interpal, was found innocent of assisting Palestinian terrorists. Anti-terror laws have also been used to imprison individuals suspected of terrorism. Under the Anti-terrorism, Crime and Security Act 2001, 'foreign nationals' suspected of engaging in terrorist activity can be held indefinitely without charges being brought against them. Such 'suspects' are currently being detained in high security prison, HMP Belmarsh, whose regime was found, by a recent report by the Chief Inspector of Prisons, to be significantly worse than other prisons. For example, according to this report, only 15 per cent of prisoners claim to be out of their cells for more than six hours a day, compared to the 40 per cent average in other institutions, and nearly twice as many prisoners claim difficulties in accessing a telephone in Belmarsh than in other local prisons (HM Chief Inspector of Prisons, 2003: 3). The case of Lotfi Raissi, an Algerian pilot residing near Heathrow Airport, further illustrates the potential for the authorities to target Muslims. Lotfi Raissi was the first person to be arrested following the 11 September attacks, and he subsequently spent five months in HMP Belmarsh. Investigating officers accused him of training the terrorist hijackers to fly, but offered no evidence to substantiate their claims. As a result, a British judge refused to permit Lotfi's extradition to the USA in 2002. Lotfi claims that whilst he was in prison he was assaulted and verbally abused, and that since his release he has been unable to fly as no airline will consider giving him a job.

Religious identity not only influences the ways in which particular people are targeted and victimised by state officials, agencies and individuals, but it also influences how the process of victimisation itself is experienced. Many studies indicate that having a helpful social support network can help victimised persons to cope better with the detrimental impact of crime (Cobb, 1976; Kutash, 1978; Kelly, 1988). The Islamic faith can act as an effective support mechanism, enabling an easier transition from 'victim' to 'survivor' status. Following Islam places a person within a wider community, and that wider community can provide emotional, practical and spiritual support and guidance. At the same time, Islam emphasises the transitory nature of a crime or an injustice. Passages in the Qur'an provide views on the trials that people can experience in their lives and how these trials are an opportunity for learning and growth. This kind of spiritual guidance can provide comfort to victims (Sheriff, 2001). Voluntary and statutory support services for victims have been criticised for their lack of an appreciation of the centrality of faith in many Muslims' lives (Sheriff, 2001). For example, many Muslim women choose not to go to women's refuges due to their secular nature. In 1990, the Muslim Women's helpline was established in order to provide specific support to Muslim women over a range of issues including divorce, domestic violence and sexual abuse. However, the helpline does not receive any government funding and therefore relies heavily on private donations.

RESEARCHING ISLAM: ETHICAL DILEMMAS IN RESEARCH

The analyses above illustrate the importance of including religious identity and practices when examining aspects of social life. In this way, greater diversity can be included in theoretical debates and empirical analyses about the social world. The issue arises, however, of who should carry out this kind of work and whether or not it is appropriate for non-Muslims to do this. It is clear that a researcher's values influence how a particular study is carried out and its subsequent findings (Harding, 1987). It can be argued that many research studies are Eurocentric, underpinned by a 'white' perspective, and yet the nature of such a perspective and its influence over the research process is rarely articulated. Afshar and Maynard (1995 and 2000) argue that the colour 'white' is relatively invisible in relation to literature about gender and ethnicity, yet white is a racial category, one which is privileged although taken for granted and under-analysed. Frankenberg has argued that whiteness is an 'unmarked, unnamed status that is itself an effect of its dominance' (1993: 6). Whiteness is rarely seen as a particular lens through which the world is viewed and experienced but, rather, is considered to be what is 'normal', 'neutral' or 'common sense'. This means that, where a 'white' 'Western' researcher engages in work on black[2] Muslims, it is important to reflect upon and make explicit the ways in which their identity may have affected the research results. It is important to acknowledge that being 'white' can mean occupying a privileged racial position over the interviewees, where being white is 'constituted in opposition to its subordinate other, the not-white, the not-privileged' (Lewis and Ramazanoglu, 1999: 23). As a result, the nature and extent of racial violence carried out against research participants may never be revealed to the researcher. At the same time, Western terminologies and frameworks of understanding may be inappropriate when trying to reflect and examine the experiences of people from different cultures (Afshar and Maynard, 2000). It is all too easy to assume that concepts readily in use in our own everyday lives also apply to other people. In particular, secularised, sociological perspectives are problematic if used to interpret Muslims' lives. This is because, although religious ideas and practices are influenced by societal and cultural traditions, this does not mean that researchers should solely focus upon the transmission of such traditions, because in doing so they marginalise the centrality of many Muslims' religious beliefs in their daily lives. For many followers of Islam, the Qur'an is the actual word of God that was recorded by Muhammad during the early part of the 7th century (Watson, 1994). For many followers of Islam, there is thus a legitimate, moral authority upon which the lives of men and women are based, so that, by referring solely to societal traditions and expectations, the authority of the Qur'an, and the importance of faith for many Muslims, can be undermined. There is thus a need for Western researchers to adopt a greater sensitivity to any work carried out in this area. This is both time-consuming and demanding work. One of the most challenging aspects of any study carried out with Muslim communities is attempting to understand Islamic beliefs. Active involvement with Muslim organisations and individuals is required in order to try to understand and try to portray their worldviews and lifestyles. It also requires the researcher to question his or her own understandings of Islam and the bases of these (mis)understandings. Meeting the research participants on more than one occasion in

---

2   The term 'black' is used here 'to share a common structural location, a racial location' (Mirza, 1997: 3), thereby referring to a variety of non-white ethnic groups.

order to discuss religious doctrines and practices can be particularly helpful. The heterogeneity of the Muslim population means that the researcher should try to avoid making knowledge claims about Muslims in general. Nonetheless, adopting such a relativistic stance can be problematic as it might be argued that certain oppressive structures (such as Islamophobia, for example) frame many Muslims' lives, and so these kind of generalisations can be used as a tool politically to gain adequate responses to their experiences. There is also a need for more research to be carried out by British Muslims on aspects of crime and criminal justice. This is an area that has been largely neglected, and so more work here can only be encouraged.

CONCLUSION

This chapter has highlighted some of the important issues facing British Muslims when looking at aspects of crime, criminal justice and victimisation. The analyses above illustrate the need for a greater focus upon the multi-faceted dimensions of identity, and how religious identity in particular can influence the ways in which crime and victimhood are experienced. The terrorist attacks in the USA and Bali have led to a wide range of repercussions, and it can be argued that Muslim communities have been significantly and detrimentally affected by these. Further research, therefore, needs to be carried out, looking at the specific experiences of crime and victimisation of individuals following Islam.

SEMINAR DISCUSSION TOPICS

- This chapter highlights some aspects of criminal justice that disadvantage Muslim communities. Can you think of any other religious groups that might also experience injustices as a result of a lack of sensitivity to their needs?
- How, and in what ways, have Muslim communities been victimised by the recent acts of terrorism in the USA and Bali?
- What do you think a 'white perspective' consists of in relation to carrying out research?

KEY READINGS

This is a relatively under-developed area within criminology, and thus there is comparatively little to guide those interested in pursuing this territory further. However, for an introductory read, see Spalek (ed), *Islam, Crime and Criminal Justice* (Willan, 2002).

REFERENCES

Afshar, H and Maynard, M (1995) 'The dynamics of "race" and gender' in Afshar, H and Maynard, M (eds), *The Dynamics of 'Race' and Gender*, London: Taylor & Francis.

Afshar, H and Maynard, M (2000) 'Gender and ethnicity of the millennium: from margin to centre', *Ethnic and Racial Studies*, vol 23(5), pp 805–19.

Ammar, N (2002) 'Islam' in Levinson, D (ed), *The Encyclopedia of Crime and Punishment*, Volume 2, London: Sage, pp 931–38.

Beckford, J and Gilliat, S (1998) *Religion in Prison: Equal Rites in a Multi-Faith Society*, Cambridge: CUP.

Bloch, A (1997) 'Ethnic inequality and social security policy' in Walker, A and Walker, C (eds), *Britain Divided: The Growth of Social Exclusion in the 1980s and 1990s*, London: CPAG.

Bowling, B (1998) *Violent Racism, Victimisation, Policing and Social Context*, Oxford: OUP.

Census Dissemination Unit, The (2001) http://census.ac.uk/cdu.

Cobb, S (1976) 'Social support as a moderator of life stress', *Psychosomatic Medicine*, vol 38, pp 300–14.

Commission on the Future of Multi-Ethnic Britain (2000) *The Parekh Report*, London: Profile Books.

Conway, G (1997) *Islamophobia: A Challenge For Us All*, London: The Runnymede Trust.

Crime and Disorder Act 1998, available at www.hmso.gov.uk/acts/acts1998/19980037.htm.

Denham, J (2001) *Building Cohesive Communities: A Report of the Ministerial Group on Public Disorder and Community Cohesion*, London: HMSO, available at www.homeoffice.gov.uk.

Farrington, D (1997) 'Human development and criminal careers' in Maguire, M, Morgan, R and Reiner, R (eds) *The Oxford Handbook of Criminology*, 2nd edn, Oxford: OUP, pp 361–408.

Frankenberg, R (1993) *The Social Construction of White Women, Whiteness Race Matters*, London: Routledge.

Harding, S (1987) *Feminism and Methodology*, Milton Keynes: Open University Press.

HM Chief Inspector of Prisons (2003) *Report on an Inspection of HMP Belmarsh*, London: HMSO.

HM Prison Service (1996) *Directory and Guide on Religious Practices in HM Prison Service*, London: HM Prison Service.

Home Office (2003) *Prison Statistics England and Wales 2001*, Cm 5743, London: HMSO.

Islamic Human Rights Commission (2001), www.ihrc.org/Islamophobia/fact-fiction.htm.

Joly, D (1995) *Britannia's Crescent: Making a Place for Muslims in British Society*, Aldershot: Avebury.

Karmi, G (2001) 'The new British anti-terrorist legislation', The Council for the Advancement of Arab-British Understanding *Focus*, vol 7(2), May 2001.

Kelly, L (1988) *Surviving Sexual Violence*, Cambridge: Polity.

Kutash, I (1978) 'Treating the victims of aggression' in Kutash, I and Schlesinger, L (eds), *Violence: Perspectives on Murder and Aggression*, San Francisco: Jossey-Bass, pp 25–40.

Levin, J and McDevitt, J (2002) 'Hate crimes' in Levinson, D (ed), *The Encyclopedia of Crime and Punishment*, vol 2, London: Sage, pp 822–26.

Lewis, B and Ramazanoglu, C (1999) 'Not guilty, not proud, just white: women's accounts of their whiteness' in Brown, H, Gilkes, M and Kaloski-Naylor, A (eds), *White? Women*, York: Raw Nerve Books.

Macey, M (1999) 'Class, gender and religious influences on changing patterns of Pakistani Muslim male violence in Bradford', *Ethnic and Racial Studies*, vol 22(5), September, pp 845–66.

Macey, M (2002) 'Interpreting Islam: young Muslim men's involvement in criminal activity in Bradford' in Spalek, B (ed), *Islam, Crime and Criminal Justice*, Cullompton: Willan.

Mama, A (1996) *The Hidden Struggle: Statutory and Voluntary Responses to Violence against Black Women in the Home*, London: Whiting & Birch Ltd.

Mirza, H (1997) 'Introduction: mapping a genealogy of Black British feminism' in Mirza, H (ed), *Black British Feminism: A Reader*, London: Routledge.

Modood, T, Berthoud, R, Lakey, J, Nazroo, J, Smith, P, Virdee, S and Beishon, S (1997) *Ethnic Minorities in Britain: Diversity and Disadvantage*, London: Policy Studies Institute.

Morrison, W (1995) *Theoretical Criminology: From Modernity to Post-Modernism*, London: Cavendish Publishing.

Ratcliffe, P (1996) *Race and Housing in Bradford*, Bradford: Bradford Housing Forum; Cambridge: CUP.

Said, E (1978) *Orientalism*, Harmondsworth: Penguin.

Sheriff, S (2001) 'Presentation to the Victim Support Annual Conference', 3 July, University of Warwick.

Siddiqui, S (2001) 'The Islamic Human Rights Commission', www.ihrc.org/file7.htm.

Smiljanic, N (2002) 'Human rights and Muslims in Britain' in Spalek, B (ed), *Islam, Crime and Criminal Justice*, Cullompton: Willan.

Spalek, B (2002) 'Muslim women's safety talk and their experiences of victimisation: a study exploring specificity and difference' in Spalek, B (ed), *Islam, Crime and Criminal Justice*, Cullompton: Willan.

Spalek, B and Wilson, D (2001) 'Not just visitors to prisons: the experiences of Imams who work inside the penal system', *The Howard Journal of Criminal Justice*, vol 40(1), pp 3–13.

Sullivan, A (2001) 'This is a religious war', *The New York Times Magazine*, 7 October 2001.

Watson, H (1994) 'Women and the veil: personal responses to global processes' in Ahmed, A and Donnan, H (eds), *Islam, Globalisation and Postmodernity*, London: Routledge.

Wilson, D and Sharp, D (1998) *Visiting Prisons: A Handbook for Imams*, London: IQRA Trust.

CHAPTER 10

REGULATION AND CORPORATE CRIME[1]

Dave Whyte

SUMMARY

We can learn as much about the criminal justice system by studying the types of crimes and offenders that it ignores as we can by studying the types of crimes and offenders that constitute the principal targets of criminal justice intervention and criminalisation. Corporate crimes – offences committed by legitimate business organisations – remain largely beyond the reach of the criminal justice system. Those crimes are subject to very different processes of surveillance and investigation in comparison to the crimes committed by relatively powerless, lower status individuals. Corporate offending continues to produce injury, death and financial loss on a much larger scale than 'conventional' crimes. Yet it is these forms of offending that yield comparatively low prosecution rates and attract the lightest of court sanctions. This chapter considers regulatory *under-enforcement* with reference to the work of UK regulatory agencies, before discussing the following key perspectives that provide the philosophical basis for the theory and practice of corporate crime control:

- The consensus perspective, which promotes a pragmatic approach to regulation and requires that strict enforcement and prosecution are minimised in order to encourage the active participation of business in 'self-regulation'.

- The neo-liberal perspective, which advocates regulatory under-enforcement as the desirable outcome of a shift from regulation by the state to regulation by the market.

- Capture theory, which posits that in capitalist economies, under-enforcement is the natural outcome of the vulnerability of the state to colonisation by private interest.

- The critical perspective, which views regulation as the site of ongoing struggles between opposing social forces and emphasises the dynamism of conflicts between dominant and subordinate interests in shaping strategies of enforcement.

KEY TERMS

Regulation; corporate crime; regulatory agencies; capitalism; social order maintenance; under-enforcement; consensus; public interest; compliance; capture; neo-liberalism; deregulation; neo-Marxism; social conflict; pro-regulatory forces; critical criminology.

---

1   For their invaluable observations and insights during the writing of this chapter, a big thanks to Courtney Davis, Rob MacKenzie and Steve Tombs.

INTRODUCTION

This chapter is about how the criminal justice system deals with the crimes produced by corporations engaging in industrial and market activity. Perhaps the most high profile corporate crimes have been those produced in workplace and transport 'disasters', and in the consumer and food safety 'scandals' that occasionally receive sustained media coverage (for a series of case studies, see Punch, 1996; and Ruggiero, 1996).

One of the first problems when thinking about the criminal justice system and corporate crimes is that it is only rarely that we are encouraged to think about those illegalities as *real* crimes. They are described in an anaesthetising language that talks of 'scandals' rather than crimes, of 'misselling' rather than theft or fraud, and of 'accidents' rather than murder or GBH, no matter the degree of complicity or the extent of injury involved (Wells, 2001: 10; Fooks, 2003a). Corporate crimes are dealt with by specialist agencies that are not generally recognised as part of the criminal justice system. Business offenders tend to be funnelled through separate (often administrative or civil) spheres of law (Gobert and Punch, 2002). A series of deficiencies in the criminal justice system ensure that 'companies and directors gain immunity from prosecution for violent crimes – including the offences of murder, manslaughter and causing grievous bodily harm' (Bergman, 2000: 11).

The term 'regulation' suggests the control of something other than real crime. Indeed, it is possible to find established texts on regulation that hardly mention the role of the criminal law at all, or seek to establish regulation as an entirely separate sphere of legal control (for example, Prosser, 1997: 4–6). This view endures, despite the fact that the key regulatory laws (for example, the Health and Safety at Work etc Act 1974 and the Environmental Protection Act 1990) are criminal law statutes.

The word 'regulate', according to its standard dictionary meaning, means to control or maintain the speed or the rate of a machine to enable it to continue to function properly. However, in criminology and criminal justice studies, to 'regulate' is generally held to mean the control of business activity within the framework of a set of rules, by an agency or by dedicated personnel assigned to ensure compliance with those rules (see also McLaughlin and Muncie, 2001; Picciotto, 2002). However, it will useful to bear in mind both definitions of the word 'regulate' when reading this chapter.

CORPORATE CRIME

Corporate violence

Despite the recognition by the criminal justice system of a growing public concern with such crimes (for example, the Magistrates' Association, 2001), corporate offences are not recorded systematically in recorded crime statistics. There have, however, been a number of studies that indicate in piecemeal form the scale of victimisation caused by corporate crime.

Box (1983) famously estimated that seven times as many people are injured and suffer disease as a result of work as those injured in indictable crimes of violence.

More recently, Tombs (1999) has established that only one-fifth of deaths resulting from injuries sustained in work-related incidents are recorded. Thus, we can estimate a total of between 1,200 and 1,500 annual workplace fatalities. When we factor in the figure for occupational illnesses, the total figure for corporate killing at work rises almost exponentially. Current estimates put asbestos related deaths alone at over 5,000 (TUC, 2002; see also Tweedale, 2000). Our total of those two categories of deaths caused by work comes to around 6,500.

According to official figures, the toll of deaths caused by pollution is of a similar magnitude. The UK Government estimates that there are a bare minimum of 24,000 'deaths brought forward'[2] by pollution every year. Although it is virtually impossible to estimate precisely how much pollution is caused by corporate activity, as opposed to private car or fuel use, we can make a start. At least 3,500 of those deaths are thought to be due to sulphur dioxide (SO_2) exposure (personal contact, Air and Noise Pollution Unit, Department of Health, 26 March 2004). According to government figures, 96 per cent of SO_2 is commercially produced (Department of the Environment, Food and Rural Affairs, 2001). In addition, at least 8,100 deaths are estimated to result from exposure to PM10 (particle matter pollution) and 72 per cent of PM10 is reckoned to be produced as a result of industrial and commercial activity (Greater Manchester Air Quality Steering Group, 2002). There are no official estimates of deaths related to carbon monoxide, ozone, NO_2, 1,3 Butadiene and lead pollution, yet all of those pollutants are known to have deadly effects and most are known to be caused by industrial and commercial sources. Although those totals are also likely to amount to an annual total of thousands, existing government data is deemed not reliable enough to produce estimates (Department of Health, 1998). Our existing figures on the effects of SO_2 and PM10, however, allow us to estimate that 3,360 SO_2 and 5,832 PM10 pollution-related deaths (a combined total of 9,192) are caused by corporate activity every year.

Corporate activity can also be held responsible for large numbers of food related illnesses and deaths. Salmonella alone killed at least 119 people in 2000 (Food Standards Agency, 2000; *The Observer*, 10 August 2003; UK Parliament, 2003). The full scale of food poisoning fatalities remains unknown, but it is likely to be vast. Those infected by bacteria such as salmonella or campylobacter are three times as likely to die within a year of infection compared with people who have not been infected (Helms et al, 2003). It is significant for this discussion that most of those cases of food poisoning are likely to be the responsibility of profit-making corporations. For example, around half of all food poisoning cases can be attributed to food consumed outside the home (UK Parliament, 2003), most of this food sold by large commercial firms – not least in fast food outlets – and most infected chicken consumed in the home is likely to have been bought in a chain supermarket.

Although we cannot be absolutely precise about how many deaths are caused by work, environmental pollution and infected food, we can say with some degree of certainty that those corporate killings in the UK alone can be counted in their tens of thousands and amount to a total that is many times greater than the 858 recorded homicides in the UK in 2001/02 (Flood-Page and Taylor, 2003). But the extent to which we can describe those corporate killings as 'crimes' is quite another issue. After all, not

---

2   I am grateful to Paddy Hillyard for bringing this phrase used in government definitions to
     my attention.

only are many of the activities referred to here unregulated by the criminal law, but few will ever be punished by the criminal justice system. There is a long-standing debate on the most appropriate definition of corporate crime (see Tappan, 1947; Sutherland, 1945; both reproduced in Nelken, 1994). Without revisiting this debate, the definition that this chapter follows is 'crimes committed by "for profit" business organisations that are punishable by the state'.[3] We will now apply this definition to the examples of corporate killing outlined above.

Not all deaths at work are the result of criminal breaches of health and safety law, but around 70 per cent are likely to be (see Pearce and Tombs, 1998: 129–31). Using our previous calculations, the total number of deaths at work that result from health and safety *crimes* are therefore likely to exceed 4,500 each year, and this is before we factor in the largely unknown total of deaths caused by other occupational diseases.

Many, if not most food poisoning cases are likely to be a direct result of criminal breaches of food hygiene and food safety legislation. A Food Standards Agency (2001a) report found that 45 per cent of all inspections of premises used for food preparation and sale uncovered breaches of food safety law that led to formal enforcement action.

It is perhaps even more difficult to establish the amount of pollution that can be described as environmental *crime*, not least because most pollution is permitted by government licence. However, there is evidence to suggest that some of the most harmful pollution is criminally produced. In the two years between 1999 and 2001, the Environment Agency recorded a total of 533 pollution offences committed by waste incinerator operators. Only one of those breaches led to a prosecution (*The Guardian*, 22 May 2001). Many of those breaches are likely to have involved the release of illegal levels of dioxins, amongst the most toxic and carcinogenic substances known.

Although the overwhelming majority of deaths caused by corporate offending remain unaccounted for in official data sources, our selective exploration here tells us enough to say beyond any doubt that corporations are, by a very long stretch, our most prolific and dangerous killers.

Corporate fraud

In addition to this rather fragmented data on corporate violence, we also have some selective indicators of the extent of corporate theft and fraud (see, for example, Levi, 1995; 2001). One the most prolific and well-known series of consumer thefts in recent years, the personal pensions frauds, led to as many as 2.4 million victims being defrauded of their pensions by high street firms between 1988 and 1994 (Financial Services Authority, 1999; Slapper and Tombs, 1999). To this we can add the endowment mortgage frauds of the 1990s, which allowed firms such as Abbey National, Halifax and Nationwide to accrue hundreds of millions of pounds in profits (*Hansard*, col 46WH, 16 July 2002) in perhaps as many as five million cases (Consumer Association; Fooks, 2003a). It is estimated that losses due to endowment mortgage 'misselling' could total £130 billion (www.ft.com, 3 October 2003). If we accept government estimates that around 60 per cent of endowment mortgages may have been fraudulently sold (Fooks, 2003a), we can estimate a total loss of £93 billion for

---

3   The term 'corporate crime' is not to be confused with the much more inclusive term 'white collar crime' (see Croall, 2001; and McLaughlin and Muncie, 2001 for definitions).

this set of crimes. Major financial frauds committed by respected household names and involving thousands of victims appear with a predictable regularity. The most recent financial product scandal in the UK, involving Lloyds TSB, resulted in the Financial Services Authority fining the company £1.9 million and ordering a £98 million pay-out to 22,500 victims (Financial Services Authority, 2003). Also at the time of writing this chapter, UK regulators look set to make a renewed attempt to investigate accounting fraud. Of a preliminary targeted sample of 20 city firms by the Financial Reporting Review Panel, eight were found to have committed breaches of reporting rules, some with exactly the same *modus operandi* used in the Enron, and other, frauds (*Financial Times*, 10 November 2003; Fooks, 2003b).[4] Also at the time of writing, the oil company Shell are being investigated for accounting fraud offences. It is alleged that the company's directors knowingly over-estimated their projected oil reserves in order to boost share prices and inflate executive bonuses.

Corporate price fixing (for example, in the electrical goods and car trade) and weights and measures offences have become routine activity for many of the largest and most respected corporations (Slapper and Tombs, 1999; Croall, 2001). In one UK-based study, 19% of respondents reported having been deliberately over-charged for goods or services they had purchased over a 12-month period (Pearce, 1990). A more recent study in the USA estimated a 37 per cent annual victimisation rate for consumer theft (Rebovich and Kane, 2002). Since victims are often unaware of their own victimisation, it is safe to assume that self-report studies produce under-estimates of the true extent of victimisation.

In the USA, there has been some more systematic work that estimates the total economic cost of corporate crime at up to 20 times the cost of 'traditional' crimes (Albanese, 1995; Friedrichs, 1996). Other calculations show that the losses incurred as a result of two isolated forms of corporate crime ('corporate tax fraud' and 'corporate financial crime') (Sundra, 1997) amount to between $207 billion and $615 billion. If we compare this figure to the $13 billion estimate of losses incurred due to robbery, burglary, larceny, car theft and arson for the same year (Barkan, 1997), those two categories of corporate fraud alone are found to cost between 16 and 47 times the corresponding cost of street crimes.

Although our knowledge of corporate offending is poorly documented and far from complete, we know enough from this selection of data to indicate the unrivalled scale and impact of some forms of corporate offending. But if this scale is mind-boggling, we should not lose sight of the *routine* nature of much of this crime. The primary goal of corporations is to make profits for their shareholders. In order to achieve this goal, corporations habitually engage in anti-social, illegal and criminal conduct (Clinard and Yeagar, 1980; Pearce, 1993; Sutherland, 1983/1949). In this context, it should be no surprise to us that the types of crime produced by corporations not only vastly outweigh the corresponding impact of 'street' or 'traditional' crimes, but also that they are much more pervasive.

---

4   Enron alone is now estimated to have involved total losses of around $150 billion (*The Times*, 3 December 2003).

REGULATING CORPORATIONS

The regulation of corporate crime is normally the responsibility of quasi-autonomous, publicly-funded agencies. The agencies may be responsible for regulating particular types of offending (for example, the Health and Safety Executive and the Environment Agency are responsible for safety and pollution/waste offences respectively), particular industries (the Financial Services Authority is responsible for regulating the banking and finance industry), or even enforcing regulations in self-contained aspects of that industry (regulators such as Ofwat and Ofgas are responsible for monitoring price and quality of service in electricity and gas supply).

Regulatory agencies are notoriously underfunded when compared to the mainstream apparatuses of criminal justice. This is a point noted even by commentators who are relatively hostile to regulation (Wilson, 1980: 392–93). The following examples give some indication of the gulf between the magnitude of the duties that agencies are charged with and the level of resources they are allocated to discharge those duties:

- The Health and Safety Executive employs a total of 1,651 inspectors (Health and Safety Commission, 2003) who are responsible for inspections and investigations at over 736,000 registered premises. On average, a workplace will receive a Health and Safety Executive inspection once every 20 years (Centre for Corporate Accountability, 2002).

- The Environment Agency employs 1,100 front line inspectors (Enforcement Officers).

- The relatively new minimum wage regulatory regime is enforced by 115 dedicated Inland Revenue inspectors responsible for two million workplaces. Those workplaces can expect an inspection once every 30 years (Pemberton, 2004).

To put these figures in perspective, we might also note that there are currently more police-employed traffic wardens (2,097) in the UK than Health and Safety Executive inspectors. There are also almost double the number of British Transport Police officers (2,179) than there are Environment Agency front line inspectors. Whilst we should be careful about drawing conclusions from those snapshot comparisons, at the very least they tell us something about how particular political priorities become institutionalised in the criminal justice system. After all, there are now more police officers in England and Wales than ever before (a total of 133,336 officers at 1 March 2003) (Cotton and Smith, 2003). At the same time as the number of police officers rises, there may be a creeping pressure to downsize regulatory agencies. At the time of writing, the Health and Safety Executive is facing the loss of up to 5 per cent of its total number of inspectors due to government cuts (Prospect, 2003).

Regulatory under-enforcement is, as the discussion is this section illustrates, a symptom of under-funding. But there is more to the story of under-enforcement than simply a lack of enforcement officers or legal support. We have to explain, for instance, why regulators are so reluctant to prosecute even when detected offences are deemed serious and sufficient evidence of those offences has been gathered (Hawkins, 2002). Both the Health and Safety Executive and the Environment Agency deal with the vast majority of serious offences they detect with informal advice or administrative notices that request compliance with the law. Only 33 per cent of deaths at work, 11 per cent of major injuries to workers and 1 per cent of occupational diseases are prosecuted (Centre for Corporate Accountability, 2002); the rate of Environment Agency prosecutions is similarly low, with 795 prosecutions in 2002 (*Hansard*, col 1198, 26 June 2003). In the same year, the Environment Agency issued a total of 366 enforcement notices for pollution offences (personal contact, Environment Agency, 19 December 2003). In the case of food safety crimes, around half of all local authorities failed to lay one single prosecution for breaches of food law in 2000/01 (Food Standards Agency, 2001a). In this context, it is perhaps unsurprising that regulatory under-enforcement has been a consistent theme in public campaigns run by organisations such as Hazards and the Simon Jones Campaign and in public inquiries and parliamentary committee reports (Cullen, 2001; Select Committee on Environment, Transport and Regional Affairs, 1999/2000a; 1999/2000b; see also Rossington, 1999).

As the introduction to this volume notes, criminal justice policy is a complex and often contradictory field of activity. We have to be careful when analysing rates of enforcement, since regulatory strategies can change dramatically over time, and may vary between agencies. As the introduction also notes, most criminal justice policies are justified by and grounded in particular theoretical formulations. In order to understand regulatory under-enforcement, we therefore need to understand the various perspectives and theories of regulation that compete for political influence. It is to a consideration of the most influential of those perspectives on regulation that the chapter now turns.

EXPLAINING REGULATION

Consensus theories of regulation

The 'public interest' approach looks at regulation as a process that occurs as a protective or paternalistic state response to socially damaging economic activity (for discussions of this position, see Campbell and Lee, 2003; French and Phillips, 2000; Baldwin and Cave 1999; Ogus, 1994). In this distinctly pluralist vision, systems of regulation are conceived of as a 'public good', the outcome of dialogue between a range of diffuse competing interests. Regulation is conceived of as the outcome of an open and ultimately benevolent decision-making process involving relevant stakeholders (generally understood as workers, employers and government). A different body of work produced largely in the Oxford School of Socio-legal Studies supports a consensus perspective on regulation (Baldwin, 1995; 1997; Black, 1997; Hawkins, 1984; 1997; 2002; Hawkins and Thomas, 1984; Hutter, 1988; 1997; 2001). According to this 'compliance school of regulation', the most successful regulatory strategies are likely to be those involving persuasion, bargaining and compromise between regulator and regulated. 'Self-regulation' – a model of regulation where corporations are trusted to monitor and observe their own legal compliance as part of a minimalist regulatory framework – is to be encouraged. Corporations do not respond particularly well to – indeed they are more likely to be alienated by – prosecution (see also Simpson, 2002). Corporations have the capacity to act as good corporate citizens, capable of responsible and moral decision-making. Therefore, regulators must appeal to the better nature of corporations by nurturing co-operative relationships with management. Compliance writers argue that a precondition of effective regulation is the construction of a consensus around appropriate forms of corporate crime control. Regulatory flexibility and the use of discretion (as opposed to the rigid enforcement of the law) is appropriate for determining which rules to apply (Bardach and Kagan, 1984; Black, 1996; Hawkins, 1996a; Lange, 1999). The influential work of John Braithwaite and colleagues, whilst it recognises that there are a range of options along the regulatory continuum (often represented as a pyramid of enforcement) (Ayres and Braithwaite, 1992; see also Grabosky, 1997), argues that 'monitored' or 'enforced' self-regulation is the most pragmatic regulatory outcome (Braithwaite, 1982; Braithwaite and Fisse, 1987). Braithwaite is in favour of compliance strategies, but only when they are backed up by tough sanctions: 'regulators will be able to speak softly when they carry big sticks' (Braithwaite, 2000: 99).

The following criticisms can be made about the consensus perspective:

*   There is little empirical evidence for consensus theory's claims about the desirability of self-regulation (Dalton, 2000; Dawson et al, 1988; Smith and Tombs, 1995). The case against strict enforcement regulation is always made hypothetically, since it has never been tried and tested over a sustained period (although see Alvesalo, 2003a and 2003b).

*   Consensus models see conflict over regulation as a peripheral rather than central feature of regulation (Davis, 2000). Workers' movements and popular campaigns against corporate crime rarely warrant more than a passing mention. Moreover, where *corporate* resistance to regulation is recognised in this literature, it tends to be characterised as the vice of a few malicious deviants or 'bolshie types' (Hawkins, 1996b: 312).

*   The assumption that corporations can be made into responsible, moral decision-makers underplays both the routine and pervasive nature of corporate offending. Moreover, this assumption obscures the techniques of 'creative compliance' and 'law avoidance' that corporations use systematically to undermine the letter or spirit of the law (McBarnet and Whelan, 1991; McBarnet, 1988; Marx, 1954/1887: 271–72).

*   Critics of consensus theories also note that this perspective obscures the social and legal foundations upon which corporations are built. Company directors are bound by law to pursue maximum levels of profit for shareholders and, in the final instance, corporations as presently constituted must make a profit to survive (Glasbeek, 2003). It is those features of capitalist businesses that make it unlikely that they will voluntarily consider workers, consumers or the environment before they consider the bottom line.

Neo-liberal theories of regulation

Neo-liberal theorists argue that we are over-regulated, and that government-imposed rules on markets and on corporations obstruct economic efficiency and individual freedoms (Friedman, 1982/1962; and Hayek, 1944). Market mechanisms more efficiently allocate resources and exert control over participants in markets. Deaths and injuries at work, for example, can be adequately regulated by the balance of market forces. Neo-liberal market logic holds that workers only enter employment after freely agreeing contractual terms with employers. The risks that workers are exposed to will have a nominal value in this agreement, and employers will find an optimum level of safety provision that is necessary to attract workers on competitive wages (for a critical discussion, see Moore, 1991). Whenever possible, then, the market should be used to distribute the harmful effects of capitalist markets. Thus, for example, the World Bank has argued secretly for the expansion of markets in toxic waste to ensure that pollution produced in the USA can be exported to relatively poor, less polluted developing countries, since 'their air quality is vastly inefficiently low compared to Los Angeles' (cited in Pearce and Tombs, 2002: 189).

A key element of the neo-liberal ideology that took hold in Western political systems in the 1970s and 1980s and post-Soviet societies in the 1990s was the institutionalisation of 'deregulation' as a centrepiece of economic policy. For the Reagan and Thatcher Governments, regulatory protections (particularly in the realm of 'social regulation') often created unnecessary 'red tape' or imposed 'burdens on business'. In the UK, a Deregulation Unit was established at Cabinet level, with the remit to spark a 'bonfire of controls' in concert with a mass privatisation of publicly-owned industries. What followed in the USA, the UK and in other prominent OECD countries was a twin-pronged attack upon the legislative safeguards governing some forms of anti-social business activity, perhaps most notably worker safety (Tombs, 1996), the environment (Blowers, 1987; Monbiot, 2000) and some forms of consumer protection (Palast, 2003: 215–31). Central to this strategy was the withdrawal of political support for, if not resources from, some regulatory agencies (Tolchin and Tolchin, 1983; Woolfson, 1994). Neo-liberalism remains the model of capitalism that underpins economic policy in the UK, the USA and indeed most of the largest economies of the world, and is embedded in the policies of the international economic and trade institutions (the International Monetary Fund, the World Bank and the World Trade Organisation).

Three criticisms of neo-liberalism have particular importance here:

- First, neo-liberal economic models encourage intensive production and consumption regimes (that some commentators call 'turbo-capitalism') without taking account of what economists describe as 'externalities' (the external costs to the environment or to human health that corporate accountants are not required to include in profit/loss balance sheets).

- Secondly, the neo-liberal model of the market accelerates the concentration of power and resources in the hands of a small elite and by doing so redistributes the greatest risk of victimisation to the least well off (Chomsky, 1999; see also the regular contributions posted at www.zmag.org).

- Thirdly, even the 'freest' of markets do not and cannot operate without the active intervention of states (Jessop, 2002; Moran and Wright, 1991; Polanyi 1957/1944: 139; Soros, 1998: 36–42). States establish the market conditions, rules and infrastructures within which businesses operate. Corporations themselves often recognise that regulation is in their long-term interest, and large firms in particular are generally unwilling to subordinate themselves to the vagaries of the market (Pearce, 1976: 82–84).

Some neo-liberal theorists argue that government regulation, especially in monopoly industries, has a tendency to produce a corrupting influence between large companies and state regulators (Peltzman, 1976; Stigler, 1971). The argument here is that state regulation will only ever produce unequal and unfair competition in the marketplace, because it encourages a mutually reinforcing relationship between governments and big business. In this sense, this group of theorists, sometimes known as the 'law and economics' movement, has similarities to another perspective on regulation: 'capture theory'.

Capture theories of regulation

Capture theory characterises governments and state regulatory agencies as vulnerable to 'capture' by big business. Regulatory capture theory's most well-known exponent is Marver Bernstein, who conceptualised the regulatory process as a 'life cycle' where regulatory agencies tend to go through various stages of maturity (Bernstein, 1955). His argument was that regulatory agencies are born out of a general concern about a regulatory problem, and in their early stages of development, although they tend to be outmanoeuvred by business, retain a certain regulatory zeal (or a strong political will in favour of regulatory control). This zeal ebbs away as the agency reaches maturity, and the agency is, in 'old age', debilitated by its final 'capture' by industry. Capture is achieved by a mixture of intense corporate lobbying, the consolidation of elite interests in public and private sectors, and a 'revolving door' of personnel between regulator and regulated. Other advocates of 'capture' depart from life cycle theory and simply argue that the state and its administrative apparatuses have, in advanced stages of capitalism, become colonised and ultimately controlled by large corporations. This perspective has been used widely to explain the corporate manipulation of government in a so called 'globalised' world order (for example, Sklair, 2001). Thus, Noreena Hertz's widely acclaimed book, *The Silent Takeover*, argues that corporate power has become unassailable since 'Governments are now like flies caught in the intricate web of the market' (2001: 140).

The value of the capture theories is that they are able to bring to light systematic bias in regulatory agencies (Tombs, 2002: 122). Moreover, they can explain how regulatory regimes can facilitate corporate crime production by establishing the framework for collusion between industry and government officials (Snider, 2003). However, the degree to which the government-industry relationship in any capitalist social order is best described as capture can be criticised for the following reasons:

- It cannot explain why, at particular moments, stricter regulation that harms the immediate interests of corporations – but is in the long-term interests of capital as a whole – can be introduced (Alvesalo and Tombs, 2001; Carson; 1979; Fooks, forthcoming, 2004; Marx, 1954/1887; Virta, 2000).
- It cannot explain why, over time, states and regulatory agencies can revert to more punitive strategies, even after the point that they appear to have been captured (for example, Calavita and Pontell, 1995), or that there may be conflicting policies inside 'captured agencies' (Manning, 1987; Hutter, 2001).

Critical perspectives on regulation

All of this is not to say that the capture thesis does not have any conceptual value, or that 'capture' does not happen to government agencies at particular moments (for example, Carson, 1980; 1982). Moreover, few would disagree that in capitalist societies state agencies tend to act in ways that promote organised business interests. Indeed, this point is recognised to some extent by each of the perspectives that we have reviewed so far. But what is missing from all of the perspectives considered in this chapter is a way of thinking about regulation that reconciles regulatory bias with some of the shifting and often contradictory dynamics in the politics of regulation. If capitalist states are inherently biased towards organised business interests, then how do we explain the expansion of regulatory regimes under political conditions that are generally hostile to regulation? How can the current UK Government's neo-liberal, pro-business and anti-regulation agenda (see, for example, Better Regulation Task Force, 2000) be reconciled with its creation of a Financial Services Authority with an arsenal of tough enforcement powers? Moreover, how do we explain the same Government's willingness to support the criminalisation of corporate killing (even if this remains rhetorical at the moment) (Tombs and Whyte, 2003b)?

A body of research produced by critical criminologists and neo-Marxist theorists emphasises the importance of *conflict* over corporate regulation to the formation of, and in the implementation of, regulatory regimes. This literature notes that regulatory controls have often been established only after long and bitter struggles by organised groups of workers and other social movements (Kramer, 1989; Snider, 1991; Tucker, 1990). At the same time, historically, businesses and their representatives have fought bitterly in opposition to regulation when it is not in their clear interest. They obfuscate, lie, cheat and make threats to disinvest, often fighting fierce public relations campaigns and behind-the-scenes political manoeuvres to avoid or to influence regulatory reform (Monbiot, 2000; Tombs and Whyte, 1998; Woolfson et al, 1996; Tweedale, 2000; Palast, 2003). Critical criminologists and neo-Marxist commentators therefore argue that conflicts between pro- and anti-regulatory forces from outside the state are crucial to understanding the origins of regulation and its subsequent enforcement (for example, Carson, 1979; Davis, 2000: 14–18; Harris and Milkis, 1989; Navarro, 1983; Pearce and Tombs, 1998).

Looking at the world from this perspective also means recognising that struggles and conflicts around the definition and enforcement of the law are not always visible (Grigg-Spall and Ireland, 1992; Lukes, 1974). Indeed, conflict may only become visible when people are seriously injured, when there is a court case, or when campaigns and protests are brought out into public view. So, for example, although it is not always apparent, it is possible to argue that conflict over safety in the workplace, or conflict over the production of pollution, is ever-present in capitalist social orders (on the former, see Nichols and Armstrong, 1973). Given that improving safety conditions or reducing pollution tends to incur some level of cost, either in time or in money, the very act of working always involves the juxtaposing of conflicting interests between those who suffer from injuries sustained at work, or those who suffer from pollution related illness, and those who profit from industrial production regimes. Understanding social conflict from this perspective is therefore based upon a class analysis of power. However, this is not to imply that conflicts around corporate crime are not mediated by other social cleavages of power, in particular those drawn across race and gender divisions. Women's structured vulnerability as consumers and as workers is central to understanding the unequal distribution of corporate crime victimisation along lines of class and gender (Croall, 1995; Haantz, 2000; Szockyj and Fox, 1996; Wonders and Danner, 2002). Although there is a shameful absence of work on the connections between structural racism and corporate crime victimisation, there is enough evidence to suggest that those relatively hidden forms of social conflict are also central to understanding the unequal distribution of corporate crime. Bullard's classic (1994) study demonstrated how black people in the southern states of the USA are much more likely to be exposed to environmental hazards and toxic waste than whites. No matter how 'hidden' they remain, conflicts of interest, coalescing along lines of social class, race and gender, are therefore endemic in capitalist social orders.

Regulatory agencies tend to emerge after periods of crisis and after sustained periods where conflicts over corporate activity are highly visible. They are formed by states in order to absorb and dissipate struggles between conflicting social groups and do this by claiming to represent the interests of pro-regulatory groups at the same time as protecting the general interests of society. This does not mean that regulatory agencies are neutral or balanced in the way that they deal with corporate crime; rather they are 'unequal structures of representation' (Mahon, 1979: 154). Regulatory bodies tend to subordinate the interests of non-hegemonic groups to the interests of business, but, since their purpose is a stabilising one for capitalist social orders, they may subordinate the immediate interests of particular businesses to the long-term interests of capital as a whole. In turn, the likelihood that they may regulate in order to placate or dissipate movements of opposition makes regulatory agencies vulnerable to pressure (Shapiro, 1984; Snider, 1991). From this perspective, the shape of regulatory regimes and strategies of enforcement also depend upon a range of external factors that shape the confidence and the capacity of sub-dominant groups to fight back (Tombs, 1996). In this conflict, the consensus perspective becomes less convincing. It is more accurate to think about *dissensus* rather than *consensus* as the driving force behind the politics of regulation (Snider, 1991: 211).

It is this notion of dissensus that helps us to grasp the complex and seemingly contradictory politics of regulatory reform that contour the trajectories of regulatory regimes. For example, the period of criminalisation of financial fraud in the UK in the 1980s and early 1990s coincided with a period in which, for example, health and safety at work was decriminalised (Fooks, 2003a). This apparent inconsistency can, from a critical perspective, be understood as an attempt by the UK state to secure the long-term stability of capital. In the UK during the 1970s and early 1980s, there was considerable public dissatisfaction with the system for investigating and prosecuting serious fraud, leading to the establishment of the Serious Fraud Office by the Criminal Justice Act 1987. Confidence in markets had latterly been undermined by a series of high profile frauds, some involving household names such as Robert Maxwell and Guinness, and regulation was essential to stabilise public confidence in, and the legitimacy of, the City of London. On the other hand, pro-regulatory forces concerned with safety at work had been substantially weakened by the Thatcher Governments, thus creating the conditions for the ideological reconstruction of health and safety regulation as a burden on the economy.

Regulation, then, is about much more than simply controlling corporate harms (Baldwin et al, 1998; MacKenzie and Martinez Lucio, 2003). Regulation in capitalist societies is as much about social order maintenance as it is about control efforts *per se*. Regulation maintains the steady rate and function of the machinery of industry and commerce. The official aim of the Financial Services Authority, 'to maintain efficient, orderly and clean financial markets and help retail consumers achieve a fair deal', is instructive in this respect (Financial Services Authority, 2000). This social order maintenance role also perhaps gets us closer to explaining why rates of enforcement and prosecution are so low. As Manning (1987: 297) notes: 'Prosecution is seldom invoked. Because the primary aim of activity is to maintain the current state of affairs.'

CONCLUSION: THE LIMITS OF CRIMINOLOGY

Both the under-enforcement of regulation and the absence of controls for serious corporate harm provides us with a perfect illustration of Lacey's (1994) insistence that we cannot take 'crime' for granted. Neither can we take its enforcement for granted. The criminal justice system remains preoccupied with a relatively limited number of interpersonal crimes, and criminology by and large obediently falls into line behind the 'official' version of the crime problem (Hillyard et al, forthcoming, 2004; Walters, 2003). The mass criminalisation of young people (see Chapter 15) and the rapid growth of the prison population is directed overwhelmingly at relatively powerless offenders (see Chapter 17). The punitive gaze of criminal justice looks the other way when it comes to the crimes of the powerful.

Without the ongoing battles waged by pro-regulatory social movements, we might wonder if the corporate crime epidemic is beyond any form of control. The law's embedded bias (Norrie, 2001) therefore forces us to think about a much more profound question in relation to regulation: in capitalist social orders, can state regulation ever adequately guarantee our protection? In addition to recognising regulatory under-enforcement as a major barrier to criminalisation, we have to recognise that some of the most destructive and deadly harms committed by corporations are not crimes at all but are activities sanctioned and legitimated by states (Reiman, 1995: 49–99). Moreover, as an emerging literature on state-corporate crime highlights, many corporate crimes are only made possible by the opportunity structures provided by states (Friedrichs, 2002; Whyte, 2003). To this observation we might add that there is evidence of a trend in some states to decriminalise some of the most harmful of corporate crimes (Snider, 2000).

A bigger question for criminology is therefore to think about how we change a system that encourages both corporate *crime* and corporate *harm* (Gordon et al, forthcoming, 2004). It is a question that suggests that controlling corporate harms requires much more than a mere tinkering with policy or reforming criminal justice institutions. As Kramer has urged: 'The social movement against corporate crime must be part of a broader movement to transform the institutional structure of corporate capitalism' (1989: 160). The burning issue that is likely to remain at the heart of the study of corporate crime is therefore how we secure an alternative means of organising production, consumption and investment regimes that will neither encourage nor sustain the routine killings and thefts committed by corporations, whether they are defined as crimes or not.

SEMINAR DISCUSSION TOPICS

- What are the central problems with neo-liberal approaches to corporate crime control?

- Is the 'capture thesis' appropriate for describing the regulation of business under Blair's Labour Government?

- Read the current Home Office proposals for the creation of a new law of 'corporate killing', and the commentary available at www.corporate accountability.org. To what extent do these proposals indicate that the current Government is taking corporate crime seriously?

- Thinking about the example of food safety crimes, propose a range of new measures that will improve the effective control of those crimes.

KEY READINGS

Comprehensive introductions to the key debates in corporate crime can be found in Croall (2001); Slapper and Tombs (1999); Gobert and Punch (2002); and, to debates in regulation, Baldwin and Cave (1999). Selections of readings on corporate crime can be found in Pearce and Snider (1995); Potter (2002); and Shover and Wright (2001). Invaluable in-depth studies of corporate crime have been published by Braithwaite (1984), Pearce and Tombs (1998) and Snider (1993). The classic studies of corporate crime are to be found in Sutherland (1983/1949), Pearce (1976) and Box's *Power, Crime and Mystification* (1983), Chapter 2.

REFERENCES

Albanese, J (1995) *White Collar Crime in America*, Englewood Cliffs, NJ: Prentice Hall.

Alvesalo, A (2003a) *The Dynamics of Economic Crime Control*, vol 14, Espoo, Finland: Poliisiammattikorkeakoulun tutkimuksia.

Alvesalo, A (2003b) 'Economic crime investigators at work', *Policing and Society*, vol 13(2), pp 115–38.

Alvesalo, A and Tombs, S (2001) 'The emergence of a "war" on economic crime: the case of Finland', *Business and Politics* vol 3(3), pp 239–67.

Ayres, I and Braithwaite, J (1982) *Responsive Regulation: Transcending the Deregulation Debate*, Oxford: OUP.

Baldwin, R (1995) *Rules and Government*, Oxford: Clarendon.

Baldwin, R (1997) 'Regulation: after "command and control"' in Hawkins, K (ed), *The Human Face of Law*, Oxford: Clarendon.

Baldwin, R and Cave, M (1999) *Understanding Regulation: Theory, Strategy and Practice*, Oxford: OUP.

Baldwin, R, Scott, C and Hood, C (1998) *A Reader on Regulation*, Oxford: OUP.

Bardach, E and Kagan, (1984) *Going By the Book: The Problem of Regulatory Unreasonableness*, Philadelphia, PA: Temple UP.

Barkan, S (1997) *Criminology: A Sociological Understanding*, Englewood Cliffs, NJ: Prentice Hall.

Bergman, D (2000) *The Case for Corporate Responsibility: Corporate Violence and the Criminal Justice System*, London: Disaster Action.

Bernstein, M (1955) *Regulating Business by Independent Commission*, Princeton, NJ: Princeton UP.

Better Regulation Task Force (2000) *Alternatives to State Regulation*, London: Cabinet Office.

Black, J (1996) '"Which arrow?": rule type and regulatory policy' in Galligan, D (ed), *A Reader on Administrative Law*, Oxford: OUP.

Black, J (1997) *Rules and Regulators*, Oxford: Clarendon.

Blowers, A (1987) 'Transition or transformation? Environmental policy under Thatcher', *Public Administration*, vol 65, pp 277–94.

Box, S (1983) *Power, Crime and Mystification*, London: Routledge.

Braithwaite, J (1982) 'Enforced self-regulation: a new strategy for corporate crime control', *Michigan Law Review*, vol 80, pp 1466–507.

Braithwaite, J (1984) *Corporate Crime in the Pharmaceutical Industry*, London: Routledge.

Braithwaite, J (2000) *Regulation, Crime, Freedom*, Aldershot: Ashgate.

Braithwaite, J and Fisse, B (1987) 'Self-regulation and the control of corporate crime' in Shearing, C and Stenning, P (eds), *Private Policing*, Beverly Hills: Sage

Bullard, R (1994) *Dumping in Dixie: Race, Class, and Environmental Quality*, Boulder, CO: Westview.

Calavita, K and Pontell, H (1995) 'Saving the savings and loans? US Government response to financial crime' in Pearce, F and Snider, L (eds), *Corporate Crime: Contemporary Debates*, Toronto: Toronto UP.

Campbell, D and Lee, R (2003) '"Carnage by computer": the blackboard economics of the 2001 foot and mouth epidemic', *Social and Legal Studies*, vol 12, pp 425–59.

Carson, W (1979) 'The conventionalisation of early factory crime', *International Journal of the Sociology of Law*, vol 7, pp 37–60.

Carson, W (1980) 'The other price of Britain's oil: regulating safety on offshore oil installations in the British sector of the North Sea', *Contemporary Crises*, vol 4, pp 239–66.

Carson, W (1982) *The Other Price of Britain's Oil: Safety and Control in the North Sea*, Oxford: Martin Robertson.

Centre for Corporate Accountability (2002) *Safety Last: The Under-Enforcement of Health and Safety Law*, London: CCA and Unison.

Chomsky, N (1999) *Profit Over People: Neo-liberalism and Global Order*, New York: Seven Stories Press.

Clinard, M and Yeagar, P (1980) *Corporate Crime*, New York: Free Press.

Consumer Association, *Which? Consumer Factsheet: Endowment Action*, London: Consumer Association.

Cotton, J and Smith, C (2003) *Police Service Strength, England and Wales, 31 March 2003*, London: National Statistics.

Croall, H (1992) *White Collar Crime*, Buckingham: Open University Press.

Croall, H (1995) 'Target women: women's victimisation from white collar crime' in Dobash, R and Noakes, L (eds), *Gender and Crime*, Cardiff: Cardiff UP.

Croall, H (2001) *Understanding White Collar Crime*, Buckingham: Open University Press.

Cullen, Rt Hon Lord (2001) *The Ladbroke Grove Inquiry: Part 1 Report*, Norwich: HMSO.

Curry, T and Shibut, L (2000) 'The cost of the savings and loan crisis: truth and consequences', *FDIC Banking Review*, Fall, vol 13(2), pp 26–35.

Dalton, A (2000) *Consensus Kills: Health and Safety Tripartism a Hazard to Workers' Health?*, London: AJP Dalton.

Davis, C (2000) 'Corporate violence, regulatory agencies and the management and deflection of censure', unpublished doctoral thesis, University of Southampton.

Dawson, S, Willman, P, Bamford, M and Clinton, A (1988) *Safety at Work: the Limits of Self-Regulation*, Cambridge: CUP

Department of the Environment, Food and Rural Affairs (2001) *e-Digest Statistics about: Air Quality: Sulphur Dioxide (SO2)*, available at www.defra.gov.uk/environment/statistics/airqual/download/pdf/aqtb08.pdf.

Department of Health Committee on the Medical Effects of Air Pollutants (1998) *Quantification of the Effects of Air Pollution on Health in the United Kingdom*, London: The Stationery Office.

Financial Services Authority (1999) 'FSA launches publicity campaign to ask consumers, "were you mis-sold?"', Press Release, 5 January.

Financial Services Authority (2000) *A New Regulator for the New Millennium*, London: FSA.

Financial Services Authority (2003) *Final Notice to Lloyds TSB Bank Plc*, 24 September.

Fisse, B and Braithwaite, J (1993) *Corporations, Crime and Accountability*, Cambridge: CUP.

Flood-Page, C and Taylor, J (2003) *Crime in England and Wales 2001–2002*, London: Home Office.

Food Standards Agency (2000) *A Report of the Study of Infectious Intestinal Diseases in England*, London: The Stationery Office.

Food Standards Agency (2001a) *Draft Report on Local Authority Food Enforcement in the UK*, September, London: FSA.

Food Standards Agency (2001b) 'Water added to restaurant and take-away chicken, survey finds', FSA Press Release, 11 December.

Food Standards Agency, *The Food Safety Act and You: Advice from Her Majesty's Government*, London: FSA.

Fooks, G (2003a) 'In the Valley of the Blind the One Eye Man is King: corporate crime and the myopia of financial regulation' in Tombs, S and Whyte, D (eds), *Unmasking the Crimes of the Powerful: Scrutinising States and Corporations*, New York: Peter Lang.

Fooks, G (2003b) 'Auditors and the permissive society: market failure, globalisation and financial regulation in the US', *Risk Management*, vol 5(2), pp 17–27.

Fooks, G (forthcoming, 2004) 'The Serious Fraud Office: a police force of the City or a police force for the City?' *British Journal of Criminology*.

French, M and Phillips, J (2000) *Cheated Not Poisoned? Food Regulation in the United Kingdom, 1875–1938*, Manchester: Manchester UP.

Friedman, M (1982/1962) *Capitalism and Freedom*, Chicago: Chicago UP.

Friedrichs, D (1996) *Trusted Criminals: White Collar Crime in Contemporary Society*, Belmont, CA: Wadsworth.

Friedrichs, D (2002) 'State-corporate crime in a globalised world: myth or major challenge?' in Potter, G (ed), *Controversies in White Collar Crime*, Cincinnati, OH: Anderson.

Glasbeek, H (2003) *Wealth by Stealth: Corporate Crime, Corporate Law and the Perversion of Democracy*, Toronto: Between the Lines.

Gobert, J and Punch, M (2002) *Rethinking Corporate Crime*, London: Butterworths.

Gordon, D, Hillyard, P, Pantazis, C and Tombs, S (eds) (forthcoming, 2004) *Beyond Criminology*, London: Pluto.

Grabosky, P (1997) 'Discussion paper: inside the pyramid: towards a conceptual framework for the analysis of regulatory systems', *International Journal of the Sociology of Law*, vol 25, pp 195–201.

Greater Manchester Air Quality Steering Group (2002) *Greater Manchester Air Quality Action Plan (Draft)*, Manchester: Association of Greater Manchester Authorities.

Grigg-Spall, I and Ireland, P (eds) (1992) *The Critical Lawyers' Handbook*, London: Pluto.

Haantz, S (2000) *Women and White Collar Crime*, National White Collar Crime Centre, available from webteam@nw3c.org.

Harris, R and Milkis, S (1989) *The Politics of Regulatory Change: A Tale of Two Agencies*, Oxford: OUP.

Hayek, F (1944) *The Road to Serfdom*, London: Routledge.

Hawkins, K (1984) *Environment and Enforcement: Regulation and the Social Definition of Pollution*, Oxford: Clarendon.

Hawkins, K (1996a) 'Compliance strategy' in Galligan, D (ed), *A Reader on Administrative Law*, Oxford: OUP.

Hawkins, K (1996b) 'Using legal discretion' in Galligan, D (ed), *A Reader on Administrative Law*, Oxford: OUP.

Hawkins, K (ed) (1997) *The Human Face of Law*, Oxford: Clarendon.

Hawkins, K (2002) *Law as Last Resort: Prosecution Decision Making in a Regulatory Agency*, Oxford: OUP.

Hawkins, K and Thomas, J (eds) (1984) *Enforcing Regulation*, Boston, MA: Kluwer.

Health and Safety Commission (2003) *Delivering Health and Safety in Great Britain, Health and Safety Commission Annual Report and the Health and Safety Commission/Executive Accounts 2002/03*, London: The Stationery Office.

Helms, M, Vastrup, P, Gerner-Smidt, P and Molbak, K (2003) 'Short and long term mortality associated with foodborne bacterial gastrointestinal infections: registry based study', *British Medical Journal*, 15 February, No 326, pp 357–60.

Hertz, N (2001) *The Silent Takeover: Global Capitalism and the Death of Democracy*, London: Arrow.

Hillyard, P, Sim, J, Tombs, S and Whyte, D (forthcoming, 2004) 'Leaving a "stain on the silence": contemporary criminology and the politics of dissent', *British Journal of Criminology*, vol 44(3).

Hutter, B (1988) *The Reasonable Arm of the Law? The Law Enforcement Procedures of Environmental Health Officers*, Oxford: Clarendon.

Hutter, B (1997) *Compliance, Regulation and Environment*, Oxford: Clarendon.

Hutter, B (2001) *Regulation and Risk: Occupational Health and Safety on the Railways*, Oxford: OUP.

Jessop, B (2002) *The Future of the Capitalist State*, Cambridge: Polity.

Kramer, R (1989) 'Criminologists and the social movement against corporate crime', *Social Justice*, vol 16, pp 146–64.

Lacey, N (1994) 'Introduction: making sense of criminal justice' in Lacey, N (ed), *A Reader on Criminal Justice*, Oxford: OUP.

Lange, B (1999) 'Compliance construction in the context of environmental regulation', *Social and Legal Studies*, vol 8(4), pp 549–67.

Levi, M (1995) 'Serious fraud in Britain: criminal justice versus regulation' in Pearce, F and Snider, L (eds), *Corporate Crime: Contemporary Debates*, Toronto: Toronto UP.

Levi, M (2001) 'Risky money: regulating financial crime' in Gray, N, Laing, J and Noakes, L (eds), *Criminal Justice, Mental Health and the Politics of Risk*, London: Cavendish Publishing.

Lukes, S (1974) *Power: A Radical View*, London: Macmillan.

MacKenzie, R and Martinez Lucio, M (2003) 'Accommodation, negotiation or colonisation? The realities of regulatory change', paper to the Sixth European Sociological Association Conference, September, Murcia, Spain.

McBarnet, D (1988) 'Law, policy and legal avoidance: can law effectively implement egalitarian policies?', *Journal of Law and Society*, vol 15(1), pp 113–21.

McBarnet, D and Whelan, C (1991) 'The elusive spirit of the law: formalism and the struggle for legal control', *Modern Law Review*, vol 54(6), pp 848–73.

McLaughlin, E and Muncie, J (2001) (eds) *The Sage Dictionary of Criminology*, London: Sage.

Magistrates' Association, The (2001) *Fining of Companies for Environmental and Health and Safety Offences (Magistrates' Court Guidelines)*, London: Magistrates' Association.

Mahon, R (1979) 'Regulatory agencies: captive agents or hegemonic apparatuses?' *Studies in Political Economy*, vol 1(1), pp 162–200.

Manning, P (1987) 'The ironies of compliance' in Shearing, C and Stenning, P (eds), *Private Policing*, Beverly Hills: Sage.

Marx, K (1954/1887) *Capital: Volume 1*, London: Lawrence and Wishart.

Monbiot, G (2000) *Captive State: The Corporate Takeover of Britain*, London: Macmillan.

Moore, R (1991) *The Price of Safety: The Market, Workers' Rights and the Law*, London: Institute of Employment Rights.

Moran, M and Wright, M (eds) (1991) *The Market and the State: Studies in Interdependence*, London: Macmillan.

Navarro, V (1983) 'The determinants of social policy, a case study: regulating health and safety at the workplace in Sweden', *International Journal of Health Services*, vol 13(4), pp 517–61.

Nelken, D (1994) *White Collar Crime*, Aldershot: Dartmouth.

Nichols, T and Armstrong, P (1973) *Safety or Profit: Industrial Accidents and the Conventional Wisdom*, Bristol: Falling Wall Press.

Norrie, A (2001) *Crime, Reason and History: A Critical Introduction to Criminal Law*, 2nd edn, London: Butterworths.

Ogus, A (1994) *Regulation: Legal Form and Economic Theory*, Oxford: OUP.

Palast, G (2003) *The Best Democracy Money Can Buy*, London: Robinson.

Pearce, F (1976) *Crimes of the Powerful: Marxism, Crime and Deviance*, London: Pluto.

Pearce, F (1990) *Second Islington Crime Survey: Commercial and Conventional Crime in Islington*, Middlesex: Middlesex Polytechnic.

Pearce, F (1993) 'Corporate rationality as corporate crime', *Studies in Political Economy*, vol 40, pp 135–62.

Pearce, F and Snider, L (eds) (1995) *Corporate Crime: Contemporary Debates*, Toronto: Toronto UP.

Pearce, F and Tombs, S (1990) 'Hazards, law and class: contextualising the regulation of corporate crime', *Social and Legal Studies*, vol 6(1), pp 79–107.

Pearce, F and Tombs, S (1998) *Toxic Capitalism: Corporate Crime in the Chemical Industry*, Aldershot: Ashgate.

Pearce, F and Tombs, S (2002) 'States, corporations and the New World Order' in Potter, G (ed), *Controversies in White Collar Crime*, Cincinnati, OH: Anderson.

Peltzman, S (1976) 'Towards a more general theory of regulation', *Journal of Law and Economics*, vol 19(2), pp 211–40.

Pemberton, S (2004) 'The production of harm in the United Kingdom: a social harm perspective', unpublished PhD thesis, University of Bristol.

Picciotto, S (2002) 'Introduction: reconceptualising regulation in the era of globalisation', *Journal of Law and Society*, vol 29(1), pp 1–11.

Polanyi, K (1957/1944) *The Great Transformation: The Political and Economic Origins of Our Time*, Boston, MA: Beacon.

Potter, G (ed) (2002) *Controversies in White Collar Crime*, Cincinnati, OH: Anderson.

Prospect (2003) 'Prospect campaigns: cut risks, not safety workers', 21 October, available at www.prospect.org.uk.

Prosser, T (1997) *Law and the Regulators*, Oxford: Clarendon.

Punch, M (1996) *Dirty Business: Exploring Corporate Misconduct*, London: Sage.

Rebovich, D and Kane, J (2002) 'An eye for an eye in the electronic age: gauging public attitude toward white collar crime and punishment', *Journal of Economic Crime Management*, vol 1(2).

Reiman, J (1995) *The Rich Get Richer and the Poor Get Prison*, 4th edn, Needham Heights, MA: Allyn and Bacon.

Rossington, P (1999) *Memorandum Relating to the Environment Agency*, submitted to the Select Committee on Environment, Transport and Rural Affairs, 8 November, HC 829, London: The Stationery Office.

Ruggiero, V (1996) *Organised and Corporate Crime in Europe: Offers That Can't Be Refused*, Aldershot: Ashgate.

Select Committee on Environment, Transport and Regional Affairs (1999/2000a) Fourth Report, *The Work of the Health and Safety Executive*, HC 31.

Select Committee on Environment, Transport and Regional Affairs (1999/2000b) Sixth Report, *The Environment Agency*, HC34-I.

Select Committee on Environment, Transport and Regional Affairs (2000/01) Fifth Report, *Delivering Sustainable Waste Management*, HC 36-I.

Shapiro, S (1984) *Wayward Capitalists*, New Haven, CT: Yale UP.

Shover, N and Wright, JP (eds) (2001) *Crimes of Privilege: Readings in White Collar Crime*, Oxford: OUP.

Simpson, S (2002) *Corporate Crime, Law and Social Control*, Oxford: OUP.

Sklair, L (2001) *The Transnational Capitalist Class*, Oxford: Blackwell.

Slapper, G and Tombs, S (1999) *Corporate Crime*, Harlow, Essex: Longman.

Smith, D and Tombs, S (1995) 'Beyond self-regulation: towards a critique of self-regulation as a control strategy for hazardous activities', *Journal of Management Studies*, vol 35(5), pp 619–36.

Snider, L (1991) 'The regulatory dance: understanding reform processes in corporate crime, *International Journal of the Sociology of Law*, vol 19, pp 209–36.

Snider, L (1993) *Bad Business: Corporate Crime in Canada*, Toronto: Nelson.

Snider, L (2000) 'The sociology of corporate crime: an obituary (or: whose knowledge claims have legs?)' *Theoretical Criminology*, vol 4(2), pp 169–206.

Snider, L (2003) 'Captured by neo-liberalism: regulation and risk in Walkerton, Ontario', *Risk Management*, vol 5(2), pp 17–27.

Soros, G (1998) *The Crisis of Global Capitalism: Open Society Endangered*, London: Little, Brown and Co.

Stigler, G (1971) 'The theory of economic regulation', *Bell Journal of Economics and Managerial Science*, vol 2(3), pp 3–21.

Sundra, J (1997) 'How much does white collar crime cost?', paper to American Society of Criminology Annual Meeting, 19 November 1997.

Sutherland, E (1945) 'Is "white-collar crime" crime?' *American Sociological Review*, vol 10, pp 132–39.

Sutherland, E (1983/1949) *White Collar Crime: The Uncut Version*, New Haven: Yale UP.

Szockyj, E and Fox, J (1996) *The Corporate Victimisation of Women*, Boston: Northeastern UP.

Tappan, P (1947) 'Who is the criminal?' *American Sociological Review*, vol 12, pp 96–102.

Tolchin, S and Tolchin, M (1983) *Dismantling America: The Rush to Deregulate*, Boston, MA: Houghton Mifflin.

Tombs, S (1996) 'Injury, death and the deregulation fetish: the politics of occupational safety regulation in UK manufacturing industries', *International Journal of Health Services*, vol 26(2), pp 309–26.

Tombs, S (1999) 'Deaths and work in Britain', *Sociological Review*, vol 47(2), pp 345–67.

Tombs, S (2002) 'Understanding regulation?', *Social and Legal Studies*, vol 11, pp 113–33.

Tombs, S and Whyte, D (1998) 'Capital fights back: risk, regulation and profit in the UK offshore oil industry', *Studies in Political Economy*, vol 57, pp 73–102.

Tombs, S and Whyte, D (eds) (2003a) *Unmasking the Crimes of the Powerful: Scrutinising States and Corporations*, New York/London: Peter Lang.

Tombs, S and Whyte, D (2003b) 'Two steps forward, one step back: towards accountability for workplace deaths?', *Policy and Practice in Health and Safety*, vol 1(1), pp 9–30.

Trades Union Congress (TUC) (2002) *Asbestos: No Hiding Place*, London: TUC and Hazards.

Tucker, E (1990) *Administering Danger in the Workplace: The Law and Politics of Occupational Health and Safety Regulation in Ontario, 1850–1914*, Toronto: Toronto UP.

Tweedale, G (2000) *Magic Mineral to Killer Dust: Turner and Newall and the Asbestos Hazard*, Oxford: OUP.

UK Parliament (2003) *Postnote: Food Poisoning*, London: Parliamentary Office of Science and Technology.

Virta, E (2000) 'Do penniless white-collar offenders steal, batter others and drink-drive?', *Turku Law Journal*, vol 2(1), pp 59–101.

Walters, R (2003) *Deviant Knowledge: Criminology, Politics and Policy*, Cullompton: Willan.

Wells, C (2001) *Corporations and Criminal Responsibility*, 2nd edn, Oxford: OUP.

Which? (2001) 'Tesco is best in contaminate tests', *Consumer Association Press Release*, 28 February.

Whyte, D (2003) 'Lethal regulation: state-corporate crime and the UK Government's new mercenaries', *Journal of Law and Society*, vol 30(4), pp 575–630.

Wilson, J (1980) 'The politics of regulation' in Wilson, J (ed), *The Politics of Regulation*, New York: Basic Books.

Wonders, N and Danner, M (2002) 'Globalisation, state-corporate crime and women: the strategic role of women's NGOs in the New World Order' in Potter, G (ed), *Controversies in White Collar Crime*, Cincinnati, OH: Anderson.

Woolfson, C (1994) *Deregulation: The Politics of Health and Safety*, Glasgow: University of Glasgow.

Woolfson, C, Beck, M and Foster, J (1996) *Paying for the Piper: Capital and Labour in Britain's Offshore Oil Industry*, London: Mansell.

CHAPTER 11

GLOBALISATION, HUMAN RIGHTS AND INTERNATIONAL CRIMINAL COURTS

Wayne Morrison

SUMMARY

This chapter provides an introduction to several of the interacting themes involved in the concept of globalisation, the rise of human rights discourse and the setting up of an International Criminal Court. This is an unusual chapter for a criminology text because criminology historically has been separate from international relations and has only studied actions and processes internal to the nation-state. It is no longer possible to defend this separation in a world of global communication networks and where all activities are interconnected. Globalisation is not, however, a recent event, for it can be traced back at least to the voyages of Columbus and the grand explorations and imperialisms that ensued. The subsequent colonising of the globe usually involved genocidal consequences for the inhabitants whose technological and military power could not withstand the onslaught of European military capability. Both the global slave trade and colonisation involved images of the 'other' as inferior, savage and uncivilised. Such images culminated in the Holocaust, the great crime of the 20th century, which occurred in the heart of 'civilised' Europe. Responding to state-sponsored atrocities and genocidal massacres is at the centre of the arguments for international criminal courts. Such courts encounter a conflict between desires for accountability for the political elites and the structure of international law, which since the 1640s has placed the notion of state sovereignty as fundamental to its scheme. In effect, the doctrine of state sovereignty gave a right to the rulers of a territory to behave with immunity, safe from interference (at least theoretically) from outside the state. It also meant that criminology as a discipline was located within the gaze of sovereign power and was unable to effectually critique such actions. Criminology normally recognised its basic subject matter – crime – as that which was prohibited and punished by the state, but many atrocities and almost all genocidal actions have been conducted by state-sponsored persons and have never been punished. While much current discourse holds up the ideas of human rights as a reference point to judge state action by, the reality is much more ambiguous. Human rights that are not linked with corresponding duties may become mere rhetoric; correspondingly, trying to make human rights enforceable may lower their appeal and destroy their utopian and critical heritage.

KEY TERMS

The dependent nature of traditional criminology; globalisation; imperialism; genocidal massacres; the absence of punishment; practical immunity of state actors under doctrine of state sovereignty; Nuremberg and Tokyo trials after World War II; International Criminal Court; definition of crimes; meta-narratives of progress; human rights; international governance.

INTRODUCTION: SHOULD THE SEPARATION BETWEEN CRIMINOLOGY AND INTERNATIONAL RELATIONS BE ABANDONED?

To find a chapter with the title 'Globalisation, human rights and international criminal courts' in a criminology text is highly unusual. Normally, criminology is seen as distinct from issues of international relations and the power plays of nation-states. Why is this? Part of the answer is the context in which criminology, as an academic enterprise, has evolved. The development of criminology is frequently portrayed through contrasting the legacies of the 'classical' and 'positive' approaches (see Chapter 1). However, both worked with an assumption that the activities to be explained were located within the territory of the nation-state. The writers who are drawn upon loosely as making up a classical school – for example, Beccaria (whose text was published in 1765) and Bentham (who wrote in the later 18th and early 19th centuries) – assumed a context of the nation-state and strove to make its forms of administration more rational and acceptable to the people who lived within it. The contrasting tradition of positive criminology covers a vast array of projects that claim they are 'scientific' and that seek to identify the characteristics of something rather vaguely called 'criminality', which was often presupposed as a propensity of individuals that makes them more likely to commit crime. But what were the crimes investigated? Positive criminology worked within the space allowed by the state's defining processes and assumptions as to the superiority of Western civilisation. For both traditions, criminology largely assumed that crime was behaviour, activity or omission as defined by the political process dominant in a particular territory; in other words, crime was what the nation-state defined it as. Criminology was thus an academic discipline that did not control its own terms of reference; it was an intellectual enterprise dependent upon the legitimacy and 'justice' of the nation-state. In some writings concerning international relations, this is presented as simply reflecting two different domains:

> Domestic society and the international system are demonstrably different. The latter is a competitive anarchy where formally similar states rely upon self-help and power bargaining to resolve conflict. Domestic society (not system) is, by contrast, rule based. (Caporaso, 1997: 564)

There is an in-built problem with this distinction. The language and concepts developed by criminology seemed to be universal, but in practice they were limited by the state. Robert Walker, a professor of international relations theory, sees this as a fundamental contradiction in many social scientific accounts:

> Inside the particular state, concepts of obligation, freedom, and justice could be articulated within the context of universalist accounts ... Yet these claims to universal values and processes presumed ... a boundary beyond which such universals could not be guaranteed. (1990: 165)

Today, there is widespread acceptance that global communication networks, the free flow of economic capital, the prevalence of international agreements and events such as the terrorist attacks of 11 September 2001 (shown live on television and the Internet throughout the world) show that such boundaries are very loose and permeable. The contradiction – where criminology seemed to deal with universal human concerns but in practice was limited by the defining powers and processes of the nation-state –

should be overcome. A global criminology should be established. This may sound easy, but there is a huge legacy against this which must be overcome. How are we to proceed? Here, reflection is important: we must understand aspects of the past to locate ourselves in the present and orientate ourselves for the future.

HOW RECENT IS GLOBALISATION?

Globalisation is a current buzzword. It expresses a range of experiences, such as the contemporary Western person's immersion in communication networks, the ability to travel and consume the products of world trade, as well as large-scale migration and international criminal activity such as the drug trade or terrorism. However, we should not think of globalisation as a distinctly 'modern' phenomenon. Consider the voyages of Christopher Columbus in the 1480s, which opened up the Americas and the Caribbean for colonisation and exploitation, and which created the demand for labour that fuelled the Atlantic slave trade.

The image of Columbus as a brave and intrepid explorer is well-known; less well-known is the fact that Columbus became 'viceroy and governor of [the Caribbean islands] and the mainland' of Spanish-claimed America, a position he held until 1500. He located his headquarters on the large island he called Espanola (today Haiti and the Dominican Republic) and immediately instituted policies of slavery (*encomiendo*) and exploitation of the native populace. The effect of Columbus' programmes was genocidal, reducing the Taino numbers from possibly several million at his arrival to a little over 100,000 when he left in 1500. By 1514, the Spanish census of the island showed barely 22,000 Indians still alive and, in 1542, only 200 were recorded. Subsequently, they were considered extinct, as were Indians throughout the Caribbean Basin, an aggregate population which totaled well over 10 million at the point the Columbian adventure began. This was only a part of the decimation; possibly more than 100 million native people were 'eliminated' throughout the Americas. Many of these were killed as a result of the diseases the Europeans introduced rather than by direct killing or conscious policy. However, the actions of the Europeans affected the food supply, disrupted the social structure and living conditions, thus weakening the ability of the native population to resist the new diseases. Whether intentionally, which was surely the case for many deaths, or indirectly, the grand project of European globalisation, called at the time the spread of civilisation, was lethal to the indigenous populations.

How were these native populations viewed? Consider the following passage from the *True History of New-Spain*, written in 1575 by Bernal Diaz del Castillo, one of Cortez's companions in the conquest and decimation of Mexico:

> I must say that most of the Indians were shamefully ridden with vice: ... they were almost all given over to sodomy. As far as the eating of human flesh is concerned, it may be said that they make use of it exactly as we do with butcher's meat. In every village, their custom is to construct cubes of huge wooden beams, in the form of cages, in order to enclose men, women, and children in them, to fatten them up and dispatch them to be sacrificed when they are ready and then to delect in their flesh. In addition, they are constantly at war, province against province, village against village, and the prisoners they succeed in taking are eaten after first being sacrificed. We observed the frequency of the shameful practice of incest between sons and mothers,

brother and sisters, uncles and nieces. Drunks are numerous, and it is beyond me to depict the filthiness of which they are capable. (quoted in Vidal-Naquet, 1992: 4–5)

How much of this account is factual and how much is ideology operating to justify the Spanish conquest? Certainly, anthropologists now say that there was no widespread incest and believe that the human ritual sacrifice was a complex practice, one bound by specific rules and taboos. But then del Castillo should have known this, since he knew that when the inhabitants of what is now Mexico City were besieged and starved by Cortez's men in 1521, they did indeed sacrifice their prisoners, but they only consumed the body parts ritually permitted and as a result largely died from hunger.

Del Castillo was not the only imperialist to offer a distorted account. Imperialist globalisation required that the 'other', whose lands were taken, the 'other', who was the object of the slave trade, the 'other', who was massacred when resisting, be seen as less than fully human and as uncivilised (you may note how much this idea was part of the constitution of 'positivist' criminology, for, in the hands of Lombroso and his followers, criminals were throwbacks to an earlier stage of evolution, displaying many of the characteristics of savages. Lombroso's positivist criminology was in part an ideology that explained away the political and cultural resistance to Italy's own internal colonisation of its southern regions; see Pick, 1989). Historically, the spread of European domination was the first precondition for what we now call globalisation. It destroyed many of the populations and ways of life subjected to it, but this was dressed up in narratives of the spread of civilisation and progress, not usually those of crime, theft or large-scale exploitation.

INTERNATIONAL LAW AS 'A TYRANTS' CHARTER'

Since the Thirty Years War ended with the Treaty of Westphalia in 1648, a certain 'deal' has provided the foundation for international law; this is the doctrine of absolute state sovereignty and non-intervention in the domestic affairs of a sovereign state. Theoretically, a nation-state was recognised as a bounded space in which a sovereign government provided security and allowed its citizens to engage in a variety of practices with the aim of advancing economic growth and facilitating the 'good life'. Shortly after the Treaty, the English political writer Thomas Hobbes tried to articulate a new understanding in a text he entitled *Leviathan* (1651), perhaps the most famous work of political theory written in English. He accompanied his text with a pictorial representation, the frontispiece. In this page, Hobbes allows a series of images to interact, giving his readers visual demonstrations of the benefits of his theory of sovereignty through representations of security and stability. Hobbes postulated the basis of the social bond – in place of dynasties, religious tradition or feudal ties – as rational self-interest exercised by calculating individuals. As bearers of subjective rationality, individuals were depicted as forming the social order and giving their allegiance to a government, a sovereign, because it was in their rational self-interest to do so, and the metaphor for the social bond was contractual, not traditional. The sovereign was now to have a particular *territory*, wherein he was the representative of a people and ultimately composed of the people who occupied that territory. To ensure security and maintain peace, Hobbes presented the sovereign as well-armed. The armaments he gave him were dual – the public sword and the weapons of the military – but there are also the weapons of metaphysical awe, the emblems of the church. The protected realm of the sovereign is the town and the countryside. The rolling hills of the countryside are dotted with small villages, each with its church, while the town has neat rows of substantial houses and a large cathedral, the spire of which is the highest building in the land. We have therein a representation of habitable space, an ordered territory. This has proved a foundational image for much of modernist political theory, the 'key assumption [of which] is that political community requires enclosure – that politics proper is impossible without a protected space where ideals can be realized and interests ideally adjudicated' (Magnusson, 1990: 49). But what happens when the sovereign power turns against a section of the populace? Then the space may turn into a living hell, a concentration camp and, in the case of the Nazi Holocaust of the Jews of occupied Europe in the early 1940s, a place of organised, methodological and, in part, industrial extermination. Was the Holocaust illegal? The question on the face of it seems horrific; surely there can be no doubt that the deliberate extermination of the vast majority of European Jews by the Nazis was the ultimate crime. But Rubenstein argues 'that National Socialist Germany probably committed no crime at Auschwitz'. What does he mean? It was not, he says, his intention 'to mitigate the inhumanity and the obscenity of what the Germans did, but to point out one of the most urgent dilemmas involved in the notion of political sovereignty in our era':

> Crime is a violation of behavioural norms defined by political authority. Homicide, for example, is only a crime when the victim is protected by the state's laws. Even in Nationalist Socialist Germany, there were actually a very small number of SS officers who were punished for the *unauthorized* murder of Jews during World War II. The state determined when homicide was an offence against its law and when it constituted the implementation of those same laws ... As long as the leaders of National Socialist Germany were free to exercise sovereignty, no superordinate system of norms constituted any kind of restraint in their behaviour ... *In reality there are no human rights there are only political rights*. That is why the question 'Who is to have a voice in the political community?' is the ultimate human question ... Genocide is the ultimate expression of absolute rightlessness. (Rubenstein, 2000: 298–99)

The Holocaust may seem too extreme for some to accept as the symbol of the 20th century, but theorists of genocide who have tried to count the victims of state atrocity in the century just passed arrive at a figure between 160 and 190 million persons (Runnel, 1992 and 1995; Smith, 2000). These great 'crimes' are largely ignored by criminology, a discipline that constructs its imaginary figures of crime, criminals and criminality without reference to these events, in part, simply because so few people are prosecuted in relation to them (see Morrison, 2004a).

Thus, some call Westphalian sovereignty a tyrants' charter. The historical reality is that states have been reluctant to interfere in what occurs in a sovereign state, no matter how bad the atrocities. If the political elites managed to define the activities as civil war, or claimed they were fighting insurgency or combating crime or terrorists or threats to the state, then this was seen as an internal matter. Outside commentators may cry out in sympathy, but few other nation-states would take action to intervene

But what of the international bodies, in particular the United Nations, which was formed out of the experience of the collapse of the League of Nations and World War II? In his 1981 text, Leo Kuper highlighted the difficulty for a body composed of sovereign states policing the activities of other sovereign states usually within their territorial boundaries. Indeed, he went so far as to propose a 'thesis' that:

> ... the sovereign territorial state claims, as an integral part of its sovereignty, the right to commit genocide, or engage in genocidal massacres, against peoples under its rule, and that the United Nations, for all practical purposes, defends this right. To be sure no state explicitly claims the right to commit genocide – this would not be morally acceptable even in international circles – but the right is exercised under other more acceptable rubrics, notably the duty to maintain law and order, or the seemingly sacred mission to preserve the territorial integrity of the state. And though the norm for the United Nations is to sit by, and watch, like a grandstand spectator, the unfolding of the genocidal conflict in the domestic arena right through to the final massacres, there would generally be concern, and action to provide humanitarian relief for the refugees, and direct intercession by the Secretary General. (1981: 161)

In later writings, Kuper charged the United Nations with having a negative approach to genocide and charges of political mass murder, saying that there were constant evasions of responsibility and protection of offending governments and the same overriding concern for state interests and preoccupation with the ideological and regional alliances. Yet, in the minds of the Secretary Generals of the 1990s, at least the situation was changing: active military intervention was now being conceived.[1] The talk was of a new 'international community' that would create rules of civilised conduct and insist that states that breached them were not invulnerable to active intervention from outside.

But what, if any, are the rules of such intervention? Critics argue that the interventions that have occurred, and which continue as in the case of Iraq, are not governed by any consistent normative framework.[2] For supporters of a new moral right to intervene and create a normative world order, the claim, and the hope, is that human rights provide a standard by which to judge the behaviour of states, a standard that is, in other words, becoming a global structure and source of norms superior to the positive law of individual states. Others, conversely, argue that they may be imperilling the only international organisation – the United Nations – that can offer an institution toward world governance (such as Chandler, 2002). Sceptics ask if, in reality, there is a progressive and empowering impulse at the heart of the human rights agenda, or if the language being used by the powerful Western nations is a cover for their own geopolitical interests and thus actually against the movement to a new world governance based on democratic principles.[3]

---

1   Note the words of the three Secretary Generals. Javier Perez de Cuellar (1991: 6): 'We are clearly witnessing what is probably an irresistible shift in public attitudes toward the belief that the defense of the oppressed in the name of morality should prevail over frontiers and legal documents.' Boutros Boutros-Ghali (1992: 9): 'The time of absolute and exclusive sovereignty has passed.' Kofi Annan (1998: 2): 'Even national sovereignty can be set aside if it stands in the way of the [UN] Security Council's overriding duty to preserve international peace and security.'

2   For example: '... it turns out in practice that the new universal dispensation [for humanitarian intervention] can only apply to Serbia and a mere handful of other states that meet very exacting requirements; they must be sufficiently weak to be easily defeated, yet sufficiently advanced to present worthwhile targets for no-casualty bombardment. It can hardly be argued that Serbia was attacked [by NATO in 1999 for the violations of human rights in Kosovo] because it was the world's foremost violator of human rights. In that competition, Serbia is far down the list' (Luttwak, 2000).

3   For a sophisticated history of the critical potential of human rights discourse, and ambiguous usage, see Douzinas, 2000.

HUMAN RIGHTS AS A MOVEMENT TOWARDS INTERNATIONAL JUSTICE

It is, undoubtedly, easy to be swept up into a romantic mythology concerning the rise of human rights discourse. But the reality is that claims to such rights exist alongside an absence of effective enforcement processes or corresponding duties. Today, an array of NGOs campaign for human rights and counter various forms of exploitation and abuse. These organisations are not short of work, and there are many examples of abuse and atrocities that could be drawn upon to provide material for this chapter, but one example will suffice. The oldest international human rights organisation is *Anti-Slavery International*, based in London (www.antislavery.org). In its library, it holds many of the records of the Congo Reform Association, a small campaigning association set up by ED Morel in the 1890s to expose the horrors of the brutal exploitation of the Congo by the agents of King Leopold II, the King of the Belgians. Leopold had acquired the 'Kongo' (as it was then spelt), what is now the Democratic Republic of Congo, a huge territory under the Berlin Act in 1884, where the European powers in the presence of a delegation of the USA carved up Africa. As a young man, Leopold had visited many of the colonies of European powers and was particularly impressed by the policies of the Dutch East India Company and the profits that the Netherlands had reaped from the Dutch West Indies (what is now Indonesia). He was determined to establish a colony and show the Belgians that great profits and international prestige would result. Having acquired the Congo as his personal domain, Leopold instituted a system of neo-slavery to gain profits from the emerging rubber trade as well as from ivory. The result is seen in an array of beautiful buildings that contribute to the splendour of contemporary Brussels, but which is calculated to have cost the lives of 10 million inhabitants of the Congo through killings, starvation and illness after being forced to leave their villages and towns. The abuses were covered up by Leopold but exposed by the campaign of ED Morel and the Congo Reform Association. Morel was a clerk of a Liverpool shipping line used by Leopold to ship out Congo's wealth, who discovered on his several journeys to the Belgian port of Antwerp in the 1890s that, while rubber and ivory were shipped from Congo to Antwerp, only guns and soldiers were going from Antwerp to Congo. This marked the beginning of his newspaper and lobbying campaign to expose the atrocities. He was to make a struggle for justice his lifelong mission.[4] As a result, the British Administration asked one of its consuls, Roger Casement, later to be knighted but finally executed for his activities on behalf of Irish nationalism, to make an investigative trip through the Congo. Casement contrasted what he saw and was told with his knowledge of the area before Leopold's administration had taken control. His

---

4   The English philosopher and social activist Bertrand Russell summarized the life of Morel: 'From that day to the moment of his death, Morel was engaged in ceaseless battle – first against inhumanity in the Congo, then against secret diplomacy in Morocco, then against a one-sided view of the origin of the War [WWI], and last against the injustice of the Treaty of Versailles. His first fight, after incredible difficulties, was successful, and won him general respect; his second and greater fight, for justice to Germany, brought him obloquy, prison, ill health, and death, with no success except in the encouragement of those who loved him for his passionate disinterestedness. No other man known to me has had the same heroic simplicity in pursuing and proclaiming political truth' (Russell, 1934). Morel actually became an MP after his six months' imprisonment but was broken in health terms. His fate, that of ultimately becoming one of the state's victims for not sharing its definition of the order of things, is also indicative of what befalls many that oppose the state – broken either by the state's punitive actions or the sheer human cost in fighting the imbalance of power.

report indicted the whole system (Casement, 1904). Even the simplest request for labour had coercion behind it; many died as a result of deliberate action but many more died from starvation or as refugees who fell prey to various diseases, in particular sleeping sickness. Casement noted the benefits of 'energetic European intervention', namely that 'admirably built and admirably kept stations greet the traveller at many points'; 'a fleet of river steamers' offered a means of transport 'to many of the most inaccessible parts of Central Africa'; and a railway now linked the ocean ports with a central region. However, he stated, the cost was a dramatic decrease in the Congo's population. Casement's report linked in with Morel's campaign, and the cause was taken up by writers such as Mark Twain and Arthur Conan Doyle who wrote short books and helped publish photographs of victims brought out of the Congo by missionaries. In the end, Leopold was forced to set up an inquiry that also highlighted some of the abuses the system gave rise to, and the Belgian government annexed the Congo as a colony of the Belgium nation. Hochschild (1998) relates this as the first great human rights campaign and uses this as an example of what can be achieved by determined action. However, the message is not so clear. Certainly, the Belgian government was forced to step in, but it actually bought the Congo from Leopold in 1908. Leopold's complex revenue streams and profits were not properly investigated. Under the 1908 deal, 'The Belgian government first of all agreed to assume [The Congo Free State's] 110 million francs worth of debt, much of it in the form of bonds Leopold had freely dispensed over the years to [his] favourites'. Nearly 32 million francs of the debt were owed to the Belgian government itself through loans it had given years earlier to Leopold. The government also agreed to pay 45.5 million francs towards completing Leopold's then-unfinished building projects in Belgium. On top of all this, Leopold received another 50 million francs (to be paid in instalments) 'as a mark of gratitude for his great sacrifices made for the Congo'. Furthermore, the funds were not expected to come from the Belgian taxpayer; they were to be extracted from the Congo itself! What could we call this? Theft, pillage, plunder …? We do not find these events and these expressions used in this way in any criminological text. The persons who contributed to the intellectual discipline of criminology were too busy measuring skulls in an effort to find distinguishing characteristics of delinquency to bother to count the skulls killed by the agents of the state. Nor has criminology as a discipline been concerned to trace the complex webs whereby the exploitation of the globe has resulted in massive distortions and human rights abuses. Hochschild finishes his book with a chapter he calls 'The great forgetting', reminding us how little people in Belgium know of their horrific ties to the Congo.[5] Instead, messages of 'development' and the spread of 'civilisation' still resound:

> From the colonial era, the major legacy Europe left for Africa was not democracy as it is practised today in countries like England, France and Belgium; it was authoritarian rule and plunder. On the whole continent, perhaps no nation has had a harder time than the Congo in emerging from the shadow of its past. When independence came, the country fared badly … Some Africans were being trained for that distant day; but when pressure grew and independence came in 1960, in the entire territory there were fewer than 30 African university graduates. There were no Congolese army officers, engineers, agronomists or physicians. The colony's administration had made few other steps toward a Congo run by its own people; of some 5,000 management-level

---

5   For a fuller treatment, see Morrison, 2004b, Chapters 5 and 6.

positions in the civil service, only three were filled by Africans. Yet on the day of independence, King Baudouin, the then monarch of Belgium, had the gall to tell the Congolese in his speech in Kinshasa: 'It is now up to you, gentlemen, to show that you are worthy of our Confidence.' (1998: 301)

Today, the Congo is the site of a bloody mélange (I deliberately use this term rather than that of war, because looting is very much the aim of the participants) that one United Nations organisation calculates has claimed the lives of three and a half million people. It is a conflict that involves military forces from seven neighbouring countries and up to 17 paramilitary forces. It is largely unknown in the West, and, while the West is prepared to intervene in Kosovo and more controversy in Iraq, it has largely ignored the Congo. Reading the limited accounts of the mutilations, rapes, kidnappings and mass killings that are published in Western news media, it is easy to recall Joseph Conrad's *Heart of Darkness* and believe that it is simply the lack of civilisation of the native Africans. However, to repeat one of Roger Casement's findings from his report in 1904:

> Of acts of persistent mutilation by Government soldiers ... Of the fact of this mutilation and the causes inducing it there can be no shadow of doubt. It was not a native custom prior to the coming of the white man; it was not the outcome of the primitive instinct of savages in their fights between village and village; it was the deliberate act of the soldiers of a European administration, and these men themselves never made any concealment that in committing these acts they were but obeying the positive orders of their superiors.

Today, it appears the example was well-learnt, for mutilation is common in the current conflict to intimidate villagers to co-operate and give up their possessions. This is another aspect of globalisation: the spread of the technologies of killing and depredation.

THE ADVENT OF INTERNATIONAL CRIMINAL COURTS

The 20th century was one of huge paradoxes: a time of incredible technological advances and increases in life opportunities for many, a time of desperate starvation and destitution for many others, and a time of genocide. The fall of the Berlin Wall in 1989 seemed to end an era of modernity and usher in a time where the duplicity and double dealing of the Cold War could be renounced and human rights actively respected. In 1998, a Treaty was signed creating what is intended as the world's first independent and permanent international criminal court. The International Criminal Court (ICC) is designed to investigate and prosecute those individuals accused of crimes against humanity, genocide and crimes of war. The ICC is to complement existing national judicial systems and will step in only if national courts are unwilling or unable to investigate or prosecute such crimes. It is hoped that the ICC will also help defend the rights of those, such as women and children, who have often had little recourse to justice.

Following World War II, a series of criminal trials took place in defeated Germany and Japan, the most famous being by ad hoc international military tribunals at Nuremberg and Tokyo. Both set of trials had their critics. In Tokyo, for example, there was little doubt that the defendants had been responsible for appalling atrocities, but the Indian judge on the tribunal argued in a dissenting judgment that the Allies had themselves committed grave crimes, calling the USA atomic bombings of Hiroshima and Nagasaki the most drastic war crimes of the Pacific War. But only the atrocities committed by the Japanese were punished. However, while the war crimes trial could be called 'victors' justice', they were still procedurally fair and open.[6]

The Nuremberg trials appear at first instance to be liable for criticism: they were trials by the military victors, who could also be reproached for war crimes. The statutes adopted in the inter-Allied agreement of 1945 present certain ambiguities, to the extent that the court was placed partially under the authority of the controlling council of the four occupying powers. Article 21 required the court to consider 'as authentic evidence the documents and official reports of governments of the United Nations'. Article 19 not only affirmed that 'the Tribunal will not be bound by technical rules relative to the administration of evidence', but specified that it would adopt and apply, insofar as possible, an accelerated and non-formalist procedure and would allow all means which it will judge to have probative value; in other words, it was up to the court to determine what constituted admissible evidence and what did not. However, the statutes were of little importance: in practice, the tribunal followed a liberal (and primarily Anglo-Saxon) model of due process and access to defence lawyers, rather than the Soviet model that demanded a show trial. The Soviets tried unsuccessfully to include the massacre of Polish army officers at Katyn among those attributed to the Nazis (it later transpired that the Soviets had done the killing) and they could not prevent a German lawyer (despite censorship of his arguments) from shedding some light on their 1939 pact with Germany, nor could they prevent the acquittal of three defendants. The prosecution was far from always triumphant over the defence, and the principle of *tu quo que*, which was officially forbidden, occasionally triumphed in practice, as when the German admirals were able to show that the American fleet under Admiral Nimitz had done exactly what they were being reproached for. Whilst the principle of collective guilt was officially in effect, it was not retained in practice, and the tribunal abandoned the notion of a conspiracy and did not make use of the concept of 'crimes against humanity' as a free-standing category, but treated these as a species of war crimes. The defendants were largely able to contest point by point the charges against them and frequently pleaded ignorance or innocence; you may note that they also did not deny what was undeniable.

It is important to note that the central charges at Tokyo and Nuremberg concerned the waging of aggressive war, and all events investigated were seen as war crimes. Since Nuremberg, international law has come to recognise that genocide and crimes against humanity are free-standing and can be charged independently of war crimes. The 1946 Genocide Convention gave the first recognition that gross human rights violations committed in the absence of an armed conflict can be punished. However, there were not been until recently any prosecutions until the United Nations played a lead role in the establishment of the international criminal tribunals designed to determine criminal responsibility in respect of actions in the former Yugoslavia (ICTY) and Rwanda (ICTR) during the Yugoslavia conflict and the Rwanda genocide of the 1990s respectively. The United Nations also administers the domestic criminal justice system of Kosovo and has recently concluded an agreement with Sierra Leone to establish a Special Court to prosecute violations of both international and domestic

---

6   This argument does not actually undercut the legality of the trials. The fact that the Allies were not tried does not detract from the legality of the trials conducted, provided that constraints of due process and impartiality of judgment were followed. That these criteria were met, see Maya, 2001.

crimes committed during the recent conflict there. A similar tribunal for prosecution of Khmer Rouge era crimes in Cambodia is currently under negotiation.

The newly-established International Criminal Court (ICC) was created outside of the United Nations system. The purpose is to have a body that can prosecute serious crimes against humanity no matter who committed them and that can try people for gross violations of human rights, such as those committed during military conflicts (such as Khmer Rouge-style genocide).

The Statute outlining the creation of the court was adopted at an international conference in Rome on 17 July 1998. After five weeks of intense negotiations, 120 countries voted for adoption. Only seven countries voted against it (including China, Israel, Iraq and the United States) and 21 abstained. One hundred and thirty-nine states signed the Treaty by the 31 December 2000 deadline. Sixty-six countries – six more than the threshold needed to establish the court – ratified the treaty on 11 April 2002, and the number of ratifying countries now stands at around 100. The ICC's jurisdiction commenced on 1 July 2002, the court's first 18 judges were elected in early 2002 and, in 2003, the Assembly of State Parties elected the chief prosecutor, Luis Moreno Ocampo, best known for his role as deputy prosecutor in the trials of Argentina's former military junta. He has declared that his priority is to investigate the current situation in the Congo.

Does this mean then a new era of justice? Many are wary. The ICC is the product of a treaty and cannot have the same effective authority as a legal institution that is the product of long historical process. In effect, it is the first criminal court for a world government. But there is no world government. The world's only superpower, the United States, has waged a campaign against the Court and has required many nations to declare that they would never give up USA servicemen for trial at the Court (a move that experts think is entirely unnecessary considering that the Court would only intervene if the USA were not prepared to prosecute its citizens). Conversely, there is talk of a new imperialism at a time where the USA is the only country in a position to determine the rules of a new international order. There are a variety of dangers, including the fact that, if the discourse of human rights becomes a smokescreen for cynical power plays, it may lose any critical and protective potential. This is a changing domain with many uncertainties and obstacles in the way of the moral ambition to create a just global legal order. But it is certain that criminology must change its boundaries and imaginative domain, for a global criminology must be constituted to meet this new order. Furthermore, it must be a critical and reflective one, otherwise it may just become the servant of a new and duplicitous complex of global power networks.

SEMINAR DISCUSSION TOPICS

- Reconsider the writings of Lombroso: what difference does it make to our understanding of their meaning to place these in the context of imperialism and colonialism?

- Was the Holocaust a crime? Why then is there no mention of it in criminology texts? What are the consequences of avoiding genocide as part of the subject matter for building criminological theories?

- Research the history of the Congo and the rule of King Leopold (see www.boondocksnet.com, 'Reforming the Heart of Darkness'; Hochschild, 1998; and Morrison, 2004b). Is this really a story of the triumph of human rights? How can the low profile given to the situation in the Congo from 1996 until today, compared to Kosovo and Iraq, be accounted for?

- How are the choices for intervention currently justified?

- Research the origins of the ICC (do a web search and read the various web pages devoted to it). Is this proof of the emerging paradigm of human rights that will provide a normative framework above state law?

KEY READINGS

This is a neglected area in criminology. For a book length discussion of the new role of human rights as justifying international intervention see Chandler, *From Kosovo to Kabul* (Pluto, 2002). For a book length treatment of how criminology has been constructed in a global context that is largely unacknowledged, see Morrison, *Criminology, Civilisation and the New World Order* (Glasshouse Press, 2004b).

As an introduction to the ICC, see Schabas, W, *An Introduction to the International Criminal Court* (2004, Cambridge: CUP).

REFERENCES

Annan, K (1998) *Thirty-Fifty Annual Ditchley Foundation Lecture*, UN Press Release SG/SM 6613, 26 June 1988.

Boutros-Ghali, B (1992) *An Agenda for Peace: Preventive Diplomacy, Peace-making, and Peace-keeping*, United Nations, New York.

Caporaso, J (1997) 'Across the great divide: integrating comparative and international politics', *International Studies Quarterly*, vol 41(4), pp 563–92.

Casement, R (1904) 'The Congo Report', British Parliamentary Papers, LXII, Cmd 1933.

Chandler, D (2002) *From Kosovo to Kabul*, London: Pluto.

Douzinas, C (2000) *The End of Human Rights*, Oxford: Hart.

Hochschild, A (1998) *King Leopold's Ghost: A Story of Greed, Terror and Heroism in Colonial Africa*, Basingstoke and Oxford: Pan.

Kuper, L (1981) *Genocide: Its Political Use in the Twentieth Century*, New Haven, CT: Yale UP.

Luttwak, E (2000) 'No-score war', *TLS*, 14 July 2000.

Magnusson, W (1990) 'The reification of political community' in Walker, RBJ and Mendlovitz, SH (eds), *Contending Sovereignties: Redefining Political Community*, Boulder, CO: GAM Publications.

Maya, T (2001) *Judgment at Tokyo: The Japanese War Crimes Trial*, Lexington, KY: Kentucky UP.

Morrison, W (2004a) 'Criminology, genocide, and modernity: remarks on the companion that criminology ignored' in Sumner, C (ed), *The Blackwell Companion to Criminology*, Malden: Blackwell.

Morrison, W (forthcoming, 2004b) *Criminology, Civilisation and the New World Order*, London: Glasshouse Press.

Perez de Cuellar, J (1991) 'Secretary-General's address at the University of Bordeaux', Bordeaux, France, 24 April, United Nations Press Release SG/SM 4560.

Pick, D (1989) *Faces of Degeneration: A European Disorder*, Cambridge: CUP.

Rubenstein, R (2000) 'Afterword: genocide and civilisation' in Wallimann, I and Dobkowski, M (eds), *Genocide and the Modern Age*, Syracuse, NY: Syracuse UP.

Runnel, R (1992) *Democide*, New Brunswick, NJ: Transaction Press.

Runnel, R (1995) *Death by Government*, New Brunswick, NJ: Transaction Press.

Russell, B (1934) *Freedom and Organization 1814–1914*, London: George Allen and Unwin.

Smith, R (2000) 'Human destructiveness and politics: the twentieth century as an age of genocide' in Wallimann, I and Dobkowski, M (eds), *Genocide and the Modern Age*, Syracuse, NY: Syracuse UP.

Vidal-Naquet, P (1992) *Assassins of Memory: Essays on the Denial of the Holocaust*, New York: Columbia UP.

Walker, RBJ (1990) 'Sovereignty, identity, community: reflections on the horizons of contemporary political practice' in Walker, RBJ and Mendlovitz, SH (eds), *Contending Sovereignties: Redefining Political Community*, Boulder, CO: GAM Publications.

PART 3
DELIVERING
CRIMINAL
JUSTICE

CHAPTER 12

CRIME PREVENTION, COMMUNITY SAFETY, AND CRIME AND DISORDER REDUCTION

Gordon Hughes

SUMMARY

This chapter will provide a sociological overview of recent developments in the fast changing and growing field of crime prevention and public safety. The sector of 'prevention' now complements – and at times competes with – the older fields of 'policing' and 'penality' in the late modern crime control complex (Garland, 2001). The chapter begins by plotting the emergence of the new preventive logics in the governance and control of crime and insecurity in recent decades across late modern societies like the UK.[1] Here, particular attention will be paid to the 'solution' offered by 'social' and 'situational' crime preventive measures and strategies to the crisis of both traditional criminal justice and welfare state responses to crime. These 'techniques' are now embedded in most late modern states' policies of prevention and reduction. Next, the chapter looks at the reductive, self-proclaimed, modernising 'experiment' of the New Labour Government in the UK in the first decade of the new century as a case-study of the late modern state's attempts to manage crime control and social exclusion. This discussion focuses on the inter-connected development of a national and centralised 'what works', 'evidence-based' paradigm, and the institutionalisation of statutory local crime *and disorder* reduction partnerships through which responsibility for the production of community safety is seemingly handed over to a plurality of local actors. Finally, the chapter considers in brief comparative trends in community safety and crime control and the possible futures of crime prevention and the politics of safety.

Throughout this chapter, it is argued that the changing nomenclature of preventive and safety policies (from 'crime prevention' to 'community safety' and, most recently, 'crime and disorder reduction') does not reflect a neat linear history of progressive improvement and greater scientific sophistication and enlightenment in the alleviation and discovery of 'what works' in preventing crime and disorder. Instead, the central argument here is that such shifts in strategies and techniques, as well as thinking and theorising, on the problems of crime and safety reflect wider social and political transformations affecting contemporary states and communities across the world. In conclusion, it is suggested that what is undeniable is the political centrality of the new 'third sector' of adaptive prevention and safety strategies in the contemporary crime control complex. These developments are also helping to reshape the conceptual boundaries and key questions facing criminologists today.

---

1   This chapter will focus primarily on the developments in UK. However, the analysis offered is explicitly sociologically comparative in its scope and intent. It is argued that the recent British experiences – and not least the experiences in different localities (Hughes and Edwards, 2002) – are complex expressions and context-specific reworkings of broader late modern and globalising trends in crime control and public safety.

KEY TERMS

Prevention; reduction; safety; community; situational and social crime prevention; late modernity; risk society; left realism; (multi-agency) partnership; managerialism; 'what works'; evidence-based policy; crime science; communitarianism; community governance.

UNPACKING THE POLICY FIELD OF PREVENTION, REDUCTION AND SAFETY

Definitional issues

Questions of crime prevention and control, public and private notions of safety and security, levels of personal and communal victimisation and such like are of pressing social and political importance to every citizen in a country such as the UK. Crime-evoked suffering is a social fact of living today, albeit fed and nurtured by often lurid media coverage. It is also important to note that concerns over the grim realities of criminal victimisation chime with the broader desire for security and the absence of fear, conjured up by the term 'community safety' and the not so secular crusades against the 'anti-social' elements in our midst. Such concerns may be symptomatic of a deeper sense of insecurity in contemporary culture. The American criminologist Jonathan Simon captures this Zeitgeist in the following passage:

> We live in a time of deep social anxiety when questions of what to eat, where to live, and with whom to have sex are all answered with the question of risk. It does not take long, in a society where the largest supermarket chain is named 'Safeways', to recognize that security is something that people demand, not just in general, but in each and everything we do, experience or consume. (1997: 2–3)

In other words, 'welcome to the risk society'! (Hughes, 2000).

Definitions of crime prevention and community safety will always remain the subject of intense debate, not least given that crime is a socially and historically contingent category. Few academic commentators would dissent from the starting point that there is no universally-accepted definition of crime prevention. However, for the purposes of government and governance, it tends to be associated with public or private actions aimed at preventing crimes in given contexts. Prevention, security and safety all necessarily involve political and normative, and not just technological and administrative, questions, despite the pretensions of the new so called 'crime sciences' (Sherman et al, 1997; Laycock, 2001). In accord with the famous distinction of Charles Wright Mills (1959), questions of prevention and safety are both 'private troubles' for many individuals and 'public issues' related to the very structure and dominant processes at work in specific social structures. The potency – instrumental and symbolic – of debates about crime and safety, and policies designed respectively to reduce and increase their prevalence, is difficult to ignore (see Sutton and Cherney, 2003: 345–46). In this context, it is crucial to emphasise that both crime prevention and community safety often become metaphors for much wider moral and political questions about justice, social order and the 'good society'.

You may have noticed that this chapter has three different terms contained within its title. This is not necessarily born out of sloppy thinking on behalf of the author or the editors! Instead, the different terms used to depict the policies, practices, politics and theories geared towards the 'prevention', or failing that the 'reduction', of crime and those strategies aimed at the promotion of 'community safety' are indicative of the changing and hybrid nature of the policy field under scrutiny here. In part, these different preventive logics arise out of criticisms of traditional 'reactive' criminal justice responses to crime such as punishment and individualistic treatment approaches. Both situational and social prevention approaches which came to the fore in the 1980s share a preoccupation with preventing 'criminality' *before* the event. Meanwhile, targeted crime 'reduction' approaches, based on the pragmatic evaluation of what can be measured and counted in terms of 'what works', have come to prominence since the late 1990s. The latter appear to be less concerned with 'prevention' and more focused on the manageable and seemingly 'rational', 'scientific' reduction of unacceptably high levels of crime and disorder. Finally, 'community safety' strategies appear to call for multi-agency partnership and community-based approaches in which a more expansive and broader project of social regeneration, social inclusion and communal 'responsibilisation' is sought.

Such strategies should not be read as linear steps towards greater 'success' by the state, private corporations and communities in alleviating the problems of crime, disorder and insecurity. As with the wider debate on the positions of punishment, treatment and prevention opened up in Chapter 1, it is vital to note the co-existence of these logics and their hybridisation in specific policy and political contexts. Current practices in the UK and other late modern societies in this field, for example, are simultaneously predicated on the some of the following (often contradictory) techniques and strategies:

- Techniques of 'rational' risk management.
- Responsibilising strategies towards private citizens, corporations and communities.
- Targeted projects focused on 'evidence-based policy' and 'evaluation'.
- Emotive and symbolically reassuring 'zero tolerance' policing of the 'anti-social' and 'disorderly', often drawing on popular, mass media-'mediated' fears of the dangerous and predatory 'outsiders'.
- Multi-agency, 'joined up' partnerships aiming to counter social and economic degeneration and exclusion and to promote social regeneration and inclusion.

As noted in Chapter 1, the two dominant strategies of crime prevention (and I would add, of *crime and disorder reduction* and *community safety*) remain those which emerged in the 1980s, namely *situational* and *social* logics of prevention and safety. How might the emergence of these strategies be explained?

Crisis of the 'old' criminal justice settlement

For much of the 20th century, the criminal justice system in the UK was largely insulated from overt political criticism and public scrutiny, being celebrated for its 'difference', being 'above politics', 'unique' in character, and best left to 'the experts'. Much of this was related to the hegemony and symbolic presence of the legal discourse surrounding criminal justice. As Eugene McLaughlin (1998: 162–64) notes, historically, the discourse of criminal justice 'difference' (from other areas of public policy and state agencies), and the cluster of storylines about the 'uniqueness' of the criminal justice system in the UK, constituted the overarching ideological settlement on criminal justice. It meant that all governments had to tread very warily because the criminal justice system deals with fundamental symbolic issues of principle – rights, duties, order, equity, justice and punishment – that lie at the heart of a social order that is governed by the rule of law.

However, alongside this privileged presence for criminal justice, the post-war social democratic state was also committed to state-sponsored social reform, and thus the eradication of the causes of criminality, by means of both social and individualised programmes of rehabilitation, inside and beyond the correctional system. Such *preventive* programmes in turn were experiments devised by social scientific experts. There was much optimism about the potential capacity and desirability of the state to 'engineer' social change at the local, communal level and to usher in an end to poverty, deprivation and discrimination by direct state intervention. Looking back, the mid-20th century regimes of prevention via treatment and rehabilitation and community development now appear as part of an age of criminological optimism. By the post-World War II period and the rise of the social democratic welfare state, positivist thinking, both psychological and sociological, on crime and its prevention was an integral part of the institutions of government and of the state's programme of national reconstruction. There was a widespread belief that the political will and scientific means now existed to remould and improve virtually all aspects of society. The new professionals and bureaucrats of the social democratic welfare state were given the responsibility to intervene proactively in society's whole range of social ills, not least in treating crime 'scientifically'. Positivist crime prevention strategies, particularly those targeted at juvenile delinquency and the 'problem family', were thus a small but important element in the post-war welfare settlement in the UK and across many Western societies (Hughes, 1998).

However, the last decades of the 20th century witnessed a growing strain on the criminal justice system, and the allied correctional and rehabilitative regimes of the 'welfare-penal complex' (Garland, 2001), in part as a consequence of the broader crisis tendencies affecting capitalist societies and their states. The crisis of criminal justice system and welfare state responses was manifested by, *inter alia*:

- the increasing rate of recorded crime and the numbers of people passing through the different parts of the system;
- overload combined with a crisis of efficiency (eg the declining clear-up rates of the police, overloaded courts and the overcrowding of prisons);
- a growing awareness of extensive social and economic costs of crime;
- the increasing recognition that formal processes of criminal justice (ie detection, apprehension, prosecution, sentencing and punishment of offenders) have only a limited effect on controlling crime.

This pessimism has also been connected with a crisis of confidence, most notably across the USA and UK, in the effectiveness of the social democratic 'rehabilitative ideal', captured in Martinson's phrase, 'nothing works'. Criminologists, of both the right (Wilson, 1974) and the left (Young, 1991), were amongst the most forthright voices criticising the 'old' social democratic criminal justice settlement.

Plotting the 'new' logics of crime control

In response to the widespread acknowledgement of this crisis of the criminal justice system, two preventive logics have come to the fore internationally since the 1980s (see Chapter 1), namely:

- primary situational crime prevention; and
- social crime prevention and community safety.

These logics capture 'the essential problematic which remains at the heart of crime prevention theory today: namely the tension between reducing opportunities through situational measures and social modes of intervention' (Crawford, 1998: 140). Situational or 'environmental' crime prevention chiefly concerns 'designing out' crime and opportunity reduction, such as the installation of preventive technologies in both private and public spaces. Social crime prevention, on the other hand, is focused chiefly on changing social environments and the motivations of offenders, and on 'community development' initiatives. Social crime prevention measures thus tend to focus on the development of schemes, such as youth clubs and activity-based projects, to deter potential or actual offenders from future offending. Both situational and social crime prevention approaches tend to be what is termed multi-agency in orientation, rather than being driven by one agency alone, such as the police. Common to both elements of situational and social crime prevention is their claim to be both less damaging and more effective than traditional (reactive and 'law and order') justice approaches.

Both approaches have long 'submerged' histories, but the last three decades have witnessed the key shift in terms of their combined policy and political prominence in the field of crime control. As Crawford notes (1998: 35):

> ... the 'nothing works' pessimism has precipitated a criminological shift away from the offender as the object of knowledge towards the offence – its situational and spatial characteristics – as well as the place and role of the victim ... As a consequence, a new prominence began to be accorded to crime prevention and community safety, with appeals to informal control and wider responsibility.

Appeals to the combined techniques of situational and social crime prevention are now commonplace in governmental discourses and policies, both public and private, across the world. They represent the taken-for-granted starting-point of crime prevention as policy and technology. See, for example, the following policy statement on the principles of crime prevention from the State of Victoria, Australia in its document, *Safer Streets and Homes: A Crime and Violence Prevention Strategy for Victoria 2002–2005*:

> The practical implementation of specific crime and violence prevention approaches varies greatly, but two broad approaches inform the overall **Safer Streets and Homes** strategy:
>
> - **Situational crime prevention** – involves reducing the opportunities for crime through the systematic management, design and manipulation of the immediate physical environment in which crime occurs or is likely to occur. This approach aims primarily to reduce the risk of, and opportunities for, crime to occur in particular contexts.

- **Social crime and violence prevention** – deals with the complex, underlying motivational causes of criminal and anti-social behaviour and focuses on promoting social inclusion through the measures designed to reduce social marginalisation and, at the same time, enhance opportunities for law abiding behaviour. Social crime prevention models promote multi-agency collaboration between government and non-governmental agencies and 'community-building' to generate inclusive and supportive community environments.

This type of criminologically-infused thinking is increasingly typical of modern state approaches to fostering crime prevention initiatives. It may be read as a vindication that criminological theory and research 'matter'. It is indicative of what has been termed the 'governmental project' that lies at the heart of modern criminology (Garland, 2001). Viewed optimistically, the penetration of crime prevention theory and practice into governmental discourses highlights the possibility of criminologists offering alternative policy agendas to the still dominant reactive, 'law and order' framing of problems and solutions. At the same time, it is clear from the influential 'global' policy entrepreneurs of 'crime science' and administrative criminologists (see Sherman et al, 1997; Goldblatt and Lewis, 1998) which technique always wins out in the technicist 'what works' paradigm: situational crime prevention.

THE 'WHAT WORKS' PARADIGM OF CRIME REDUCTION AND THE LOCAL PARTNERSHIP APPROACH IN THE UK

In this section, the reductive, modernising 'experiment' of the New Labour Government in the UK in the first decade of the 21st century is discussed. This ambitious national political project and programme of policy implementation is structured by two interconnected governmental imperatives, namely:

- the development and implementation of a national and centralised 'what works', 'evidence-based' paradigm for crime reduction policy and practice; and
- the institutionalisation of local crime *and disorder* reduction partnerships through which responsibility for the production of community safety against crime, disorder and the anti-social is seemingly handed over to a plurality of local actors.

Modernisation, managerialisation and the 'what works' paradigm

If we accept that there is a new organisational settlement in criminal justice in the UK, then it is vital to recognise that much of its character and form was prefigured in the reforms and multi-agency initiatives sponsored and undertaken by the neo-liberal Conservative Governments of the 1980s and 1990s. This backdrop of reforms and intensified managerialisation across all sectors of the public sector since the 1980s (Clarke et al, 2000) alerts us to the danger of assuming that all is 'new' and distinct in the New Labour policy agenda. Nonetheless, the intensity of New Labour's mission to modernise public agencies, chiefly by the logic of managerialisation and the promotion of an 'audit culture' (Power, 1997), is striking.

The Crime and Disorder Act (CDA) 1998 built directly on this thinking by stressing that, for successful outcomes to be achieved, statutory responsibility for crime and disorder reduction and community safety should be devolved ('at a distance', if not 'hands-off') from the central state to a series of local partnerships, made up of statutory and independent agencies and privatised bodies. The CDA 1998 gave both the local authority and the police new duties and powers to develop strategic partnerships to help prevent and reduce crime and disorder in their locality. There now exists a statutory duty on local authorities and police forces, in co-operation with probation services, health authorities and police authorities, to formulate and implement strategies for the reduction of crime and disorder in their area. The most striking contrast with the previous models of partnership working which influenced New Labour reforms (Hughes and McLaughlin, 2002) is that post-CDA 1998 partnerships have a statutory footing in England and Wales. Since 1998, all 376 statutory crime and disorder partnerships in England and Wales have had to:

- carry out audits of local crime and disorder problems;
- consult with all sections of the local community;
- publish three year crime and disorder reduction strategies based on the findings of the audits;
- identify targets and performance indicators for each part of the strategy, with specified timescales;
- publish the audit, strategy and the targets;
- report annually on progress against the targets.

There is as yet limited research evidence with regard to the workings and outcomes of these partnerships, but initial findings from local case studies suggest that tensions and conflicts, and political struggles between 'partners', remain, alongside the pressure to be seen publicly as 'happy' and united partners working with 'communities' (Hughes and Edwards, 2002). Furthermore, most partnerships adopted a narrow crime reduction agenda rather than promoting a broader 'community safety' approach in the first three-year phase of local implementation (1999–2002). Local strategies are largely determined by a centrally-driven performance management agenda in which cost-effective measures for the realisation of specific outcomes and reduction targets are prioritised.

Closely related to the audit culture and the cult of performance management is the Government's commitment to funding 'evidence-based' projects and programmes. The routine operation of local crime and disorder reduction partnerships in the 2000s remains massively affected by this technicist paradigm of 'success' in policy and practice. The three-year Crime Reduction Programme based at the Home Office, which was financed through £250 million made available following the 1999 Comprehensive Spending Review, was intended to build on the CDA 1998 and 'harness' the activities of local crime reduction partnerships. It was premised on the conclusions of *Reducing Offending*, a Home Office report which highlighted the 'scientifically proven' interventions most likely to provide the basis for a cost-effective, sustained reduction in the long-term rise in crime (Goldblatt and Lewis, 1998). Questions considered by the authors included: how effective is an intervention and can the benefits be quantified?; what evidence is available on the likely costs of implementation?; what is the likely timescale for the costs and benefits?; and how strong is the available evidence on effects, costs and timescales? The Crime Reduction Programme was extended in April 1999 with the announcement of an extra £153 million for CCTV initiatives and other interventions aimed at reducing vehicle crime. This ambitious, nationally-directed 'evidence-led' programme was also to be applied to interrelated programmes across the criminal justice system that received funding under the Comprehensive Spending Review, for example, the £211 million allocated to drug use and related crime and the £226 million provided for 'constructive' prison regimes (Hughes and McLaughlin, 2002).

The Crime Reduction Programme was intended to make a significant contribution by ensuring that the Home Office was achieving maximum impact for money spent and that the impact is progressively improved. The Programme hoped to promote innovation, generate a significant improvement in knowledge about effectiveness and cost-effectiveness and encourage the mainstreaming of emerging knowledge about 'best practice'. The Crime Reduction Programme thus emphasised the need for local policy-makers and practitioners to act primarily on evidence-based 'scientific' research that establishes 'what works' and to ignore alternative approaches considered uneconomic and inefficient in preventing crime and disorder. As Stenson and Edwards (2003: 225) note, 'At worst this may pressure local policy makers towards a naïve emulation of measures that in very different settings have, it is claimed, been shown to have "worked"'.

Taken together, such developments have resulted in an ever more penetrative performance management regime to which crime and disorder reduction partnerships must respond accordingly.

Local partnerships: towards a new community governance of crime, disorder and safety?

The centrally propelled development of creating Crime and Disorder Reduction Partnerships (CDRPs) is strikingly apparent across every local government authority in England and Wales in the first decade of the 21st century. This decade has seen an ever-increasing number of multi-agency community safety teams – of managers, officers, project workers, police secondees, 'drug action teams', anti-social behaviour units, etc – which form part, however uneasily, of local governmental structures and processes. In any overview of the changing landscape of crime control in the UK, it is difficult to ignore the growing salience of the developing local and, increasingly, the regional institutional architecture and the allied institution-building associated with the new governance of crime *and disorder* and the promotion of *safer communities* through the partnership approach. Partnership has become both a key technique of the new local and regional governance and, more specifically, a vital rhetorical principle of 'prevention' and 'safety' policies, involving, on the surface, the rearrangement of responsibilities between central government, public services and local government as well as the 'sharing' of responsibilities between the police and local government, alongside a dispersal of responsibilities between public and voluntary agencies and private interests in local communities.

What then are the strengths and limitations of the multi-agency partnership approach to crime reduction and community safety?

According to Crawford and Matassa (2000: 89), for example, there are strong arguments in favour of the multi-agency partnership approach to crime and disorder reduction and community safety. They note that there is now a growing consensus in UK policy circles and beyond that the most effective form of crime prevention and community safety requires structures which:

- are local, in that local problems require local solutions;
- encompass a broad focus upon wider social problems than crime;
- need to be delivered through a partnership approach, drawing together a variety of organisations and stakeholders;
- deliver holistic solutions which are problem-oriented rather than defined according to the means most readily available for their solution (and thus disrupt 'closed' bureaucratic and professional cultures).

On the other hand, despite the attractions of partnership work, the role of all such partnerships in crime and disorder reduction might be particularly onerous given:

- the mandate to act as 'agents of transformation';
- the ambitious timescales;
- the disappointing and chaotic outcomes of previous multi-agency partnerships;
- the inequalities of power, influence and knowledge between the different agencies;
- the problem of coping with the multitude of organisational reforms flowing through the different partner agencies.

Implementation of the CDA 1998 across community safety and crime reduction requires extensive changes in the working practices and thinking of all the criminal justice and partner social policy agencies (McLaughlin et al, 2001). Because the partnerships are expected to work across a series of institutional barriers and further blur and mix the boundaries between private, public, voluntary and community spaces, they have the potential to produce entirely new organisational networks within a managerialised framework.

The processes associated with the rise of local preventive partnerships and the increasingly strident appeals to 'community' as the site, agency and effect of governance across many 'neo-liberal' states has been termed the new 'community governance of crime control' (Edwards and Hughes, 2002). As already noted, this political experiment is heavily influenced by 'managerialist' policy ideas. However, an equally significant source of ideological inspiration is that of moral authoritarian communitarianism (Hughes, 1996). The British state in the first decade of the 21st century is at the forefront of contemporary attempts to both 'modernise' and 'remoralise' the nation, not least by appeals to governing through communities.

Such developments raise major questions about where the new institutional expertise and its division of labour may be heading (Gilling and Hughes, 2002). Central to the argument here is the contention that the debate on the future of these new forms of expertise is not one that can be treated as a purely technical exercise despite the ascendancy of the pseudo-technicist and pragmatic 'what works' governmental discourse. Rather, the governmental projects associated with CDRPs, embedded in 'arm's length' relations and requiring new assemblages of agencies and agents ('partnerships'), are both structurally unstable and morally and politically volatile: about the very definition of the field, about the forms of power and professional domination within the field; about which communities get to be 'safe' and suchlike (Clarke, 2002: 12). For example, as a result of the recognition that effective crime control strategies must be rooted in the dynamics of local communities, and New Labour's 'fixation' with clamping down on disorder and the 'anti-social', we appear to be witnessing in the current decade an intensive re-territorialisation and re-moralisation of highly localised crime control strategies (see Edwards and Hughes, 2002).

Lesson-drawing from the UK

What is happening here? The discussion has shown that:

- a managerialist and auditing culture is pronounced across most agencies and sites in which discourses of evaluation, audit, monitoring, target setting and performance measurement have a pervasive presence and influence;
- a partnership approach is widely promoted as the most effective and 'economic' means of both promoting crime reduction and alleviating the consequences of social exclusion;
- there is a renewed enthusiasm for the state, both centrally and locally, having a communitarian mission to reconstruct and remoralise the nation, and especially those perceived as 'anti-social' and 'socially excluded'.

Less certainly, it may also be argued that these developments are connected to the following broader trends in late modernity:

- There is a broad consensus across politicians, policy-makers and practitioners with regard to the importance of informal, 'community-based' social control mechanisms as well as formal criminal justice measures.
- Crime prevention is increasingly pluralised and dispersed throughout the social fabric.
- The logic of 'managing' crime and disorder co-exists alongside the persistent 'punishing' vision.

TOWARDS A COMPARATIVE UNDERSTANDING OF PREVENTION AND SAFETY

Much recent criminological literature confirms that crime prevention and the new local politics of public safety appear to be achieving a global, if uneven, pre-eminence as a master pattern of crime control in part as a reaction to the growing doubts about the capacity of the 'sovereign' nation-state to guarantee and supply order and security to citizens in their everyday lives (Hughes, 1998; Garland, 2001). Much is also made in contemporary social and political theory of the emergence of a new world order following the collapse of the Soviet Bloc and the rise of a global economy (Giddens, 1998). Whatever the merits and limitations of these grand narratives, what is widely accepted in the social sciences is that important transformations in the ordering of societies are both clearly evident and significant. In particular, it has been widely argued that there has been a shift across 'late modern' societies in the way in which crime and disorder is governed, and how we govern crime and disorder is of course related to how we govern ourselves. We now look at some of these comparative trends in this policy field in Europe.

Convergences and divergences in the politics and practices of preventive and safety governance in Europe

Comparative criminological research suggests that there are convergent and divergent processes at play as a result of which there is a redefinition of the governance of security and crime control occurring across Europe and, in particular, at the local (urban) level. Institutionally, there is now a growing number of new actors in, and emergent occupations involving new methods and technologies – not least through the technique of partnership – of 'policing' and 'security' (Hughes, 2004). Alongside these institutional developments, there is the parallel articulation of new 'problems', ranging from the control of local disorders and incivilities and minor but persistent street crimes to the management of the volatile mobilities of migrant peoples and finally in response to the 'global' threats to security, post-11 September. And, in turn, we see the rise of 'locality'-based policies which attempt to get the public authorities closer to local populations and their 'fears'.

Among some of the key points of policy and political convergence then are the pluralisation of local policing and the rise of multi-agency partnerships, the growth of crime prevention and reduction strategies alongside historically dominant criminal justice policies. We are also seeing the common recognition of wider social harms and problems in addition to crime *per se* in tandem with technical approaches to the management of risks. More worryingly for liberals and human rights supporters alike, these developments co-exist alongside more populist and 'primitive' communitarian appeals for order, etc, in the wake of the new 'global' mobilities, with the populist 'law and order' conflation of 'immigrant'/'migrant'/'terrorist'. Perhaps the latter is the most striking of all shared European 'nightmares', matched only by the crusading demonisation of local and 'anti-social' outcast within.

However, the story is not a simple one of policy convergence. There remain, for example, significant differences in the degree to which the rhetoric and practice of evidence-based policy-making, the 'whole of government' mantra and the technicist 'what works' paradigm of policy evaluation has crossed the Channel from the UK, despite current attempts by the European Union's Crime Prevention Network to disseminate this naïve brand of policy transfer thinking and practice. Another key divergence is over the very vocabulary used to translate problems of 'crime reduction', 'community safety', 'social harm', 'public security', etc, employed in different European societies and regions. Perhaps the concept of 'public safety' – rather than the UK notion of *community* safety – may provide us with as inclusive a term as possible to signify the range of social ills and difficulties encompassed by strategies of control and social inclusion in different European countries and localities (see Hughes and Edwards, 2004).

There is currently a lively 'export and import' trade in ideas across academic advisers, policy-makers and practitioners in this field, and the 'policy transfer' debate on the question of 'how does crime prevention *and safety* policy travel?' has now entered the critical academy (see Hughes, McLaughlin and Muncie, 2002). Such debates open up the investigation of the *intra-* and *trans-*national, as well as *inter-*national developments in the governance of public safety as one of the most exciting and challenging fields for criminological research. It is clear that we may learn as much from diversity as from uniformity, both within the UK, across Europe and globally. Furthermore, future work and lesson-drawing may need to address the linguistically ugly but sociologically important processes of 'glocalisation' in which communities are thinking globally but acting locally. To pull off this coup, the relationship of traditional 'expert' (researcher and policy maker?) and 'local' (practitioner and community activist?) knowledge will need to be transformed.

CONCLUSION

The discussion in this chapter should confirm that crime policies in general and crime-preventive and safety-promotive policies specifically are as much about politics and the normative and the ideological as about rational debates about 'what works' according to evidence-based evaluation, currently promulgated by the so called 'crime sciences'. Perhaps in accord with the political and normative goals of critical and progressive scholarship, we need to follow the advice of the Australian criminologist, Adam Sutton (Sutton, forthcoming, 2004), in arguing that advocates of crime prevention as a viable political alternative to 'law and order' need to recognise that crime prevention and community safety must 'work' at the symbolic and normative levels, associated with the advocacy of social inclusion, social justice and non-punitive and restorative principles. Accordingly, the challenge for a critical criminology of crime prevention and public safety may be to aspire to satisfy these goals rather than the currently fashionable 'pragmatic', 'instrumental' and 'technical' goals of managing the processes of the state's strategies of crime reduction management.

SEMINAR DISCUSSION TOPICS

- Do crime prevention and community safety strategies represent an alternative to reactive law and order policies?
- What advantages does a situational crime prevention strategy hold over social and community-based approaches?
- To what extent do local crime and disorder reduction/community safety strategies reflect, or challenge and depart from, the priorities of New Labour's national crime and disorder reduction strategy?
- We have discussed the nature of local crime and disorder partnerships and their strategies at great length. However, you may have been struck by the absence of any specific examples of the published reports which are now legally required from all local authorities in England and Wales (and increasingly evident in Scotland and Northern Ireland). To correct this absence, we would like you to try and get hold of one or more example of local crime and disorder (or community safety) strategies. You can get these by post from your local authority (where applicable) or you can access a number of these documents on local authority websites.
- What are the seductions as well as pitfalls of appeals to community in crime prevention and safety politics?

KEY READINGS

Crime Prevention: Theory, Politics and Practice by Daniel Gilling (UCL Press, 1997) and *Understanding Crime Prevention: Social Control, Risk and Late Modernity* by Gordon Hughes (Open University Press, 1998) probably remain the most comprehensive critical and sociologically informed attempts, respectively, to plot the development of the field in the UK and internationally. *Crime Prevention and Community Safety: New Directions* by Hughes, McLaughlin and Muncie is the most thorough edited collection of work on both UK and international analyses of the policy and politics of crime prevention and community safety. Those wishing to engage more fully with the debate on the new local governance of crime and safety should consult *The Local Governance of Crime* by Adam Crawford (Clarendon, 1997) and *Crime Control and Community*, edited by Gordon Hughes and Adam Edwards (Willan, 2002).

REFERENCES

Clarke, J (2002) 'The instabilities of community governance', conference paper, Bielefeld.

Clarke, J, Gewirtz, S, Hughes, G and Humphrey, J (2000) 'Guarding the public interest? Auditing public services' in Clarke, J, Gewirtz, S and McLaughlin, E (eds), *New Managerialism, New Welfare*, London: Sage.

Crawford, A (1997) *The Local Governance of Crime*, Oxford: Clarendon.

Crawford, A (1998) *Crime Prevention and Community Safety*, London: Longman.

Crawford, A and Matassa, M (2000) *Community Safety Structures: Review of the International Literature*, Belfast: NIO.

Edwards, A and Hughes, G (2002) 'Introduction: the new community governance of crime control' in Hughes, G and Edwards, A (eds), *Crime Control and Community*, Cullompton: Willan.

Garland, D (2001) *The Culture of Control*, Oxford: OUP.

Giddens, A (1998) *The Third Way*, Cambridge: Polity.

Gilling, D (1997) *Crime Prevention: Theory, Policy and Politics*, London: UCL Press.

Gilling, D and Hughes, G (2002) 'The community safety "profession"' *Community Safety Journal*, vol 1(1), pp 3–12.

Goldblatt, P and Lewis, C (eds) (1998) *Reducing Offending: An Assessment of Research Evidence on Ways of Dealing with Offending Behaviour*, London, Home Office Research Study 187, London: HMSO.

Hughes, G (1996) 'Communitarianism and law and order' *Critical Social Policy*, vol 16(4), pp 17–41.

Hughes, G (1998) *Understanding Crime Prevention: Social Control, Risk and Late Modernity*, Buckingham: Open University Press.

Hughes, G (2000) 'Community safety in the era of the risk society' in Ballantyne, S et al (eds), *Secure Foundations: Issues in Crime Prevention, Crime Reduction and Community Safety*, London: IPPR.

Hughes, G (2002) 'Auditing crime reduction and disorder partnerships: exorcising the wicked issue of community safety?', *Crime Prevention and Community Safety: An International Journal*, vol 3(3), pp 2–25.

Hughes, G (2004) 'The politics of public safety in Europe', *Community Safety Journal*, Special Edition, vol 3(1).

Hughes, G and Edwards, A (2002) (eds) *Crime Control and Community: The New Politics of Public Safety*, Cullompton: Willan.

Hughes, G and Edwards, A (2004) 'Beyond community safety?', *Community Safety Journal*, Special Edition, vol 3(1).

Hughes, G and McLaughlin, E (2002) 'Together we'll crack it: partnership and the governance of crime prevention' in Glendinning, C et al (eds), *Partnership, New Labour and Governance of Welfare*, Bristol: Policy Press.

Hughes, G, McLaughlin, E and Muncie, J (2002) 'Teetering on the edge: the futures of crime control and community safety' in Hughes, G, McLaughlin, E and Muncie, J (eds), *Crime Prevention and Community Safety: New Directions*, London: Sage.

Laycock, G (2001) 'The future of crime science', Inaugural Lecture, London, Jill Dando Institute.

McLaughlin, E (1998) 'Probation work: social work or social control?' in Hughes, G and Lewis, G (eds), *Unsettling Welfare: The Reconstruction of Social Policy*, London: Sage.

McLaughlin, E, Muncie, J and Hughes, G (2001) 'The permanent revolution', *Criminal Justice*, vol 1(3), pp 301–19.

Matthews, R and Pitts, J (2002) *Crime Reduction and Community Safety*, London: Routledge.

Matthews, R and Young, J (2003) *New Labour and the Politics of Crime*, Cullompton: Willan.

Power, M (1997) *The Audit Explosion*, London: Demos.

Sherman, L et al (1997) *What Works, What Doesn't and What's Promising in Crime Prevention*, Washington, DC: NIJ.

Simon, J (1997) 'Governing through crime' in Friedman, L and Fisher, G (eds), *The Crime Conundrum*, Boulder, CO: Westview Press.

Stenson, K (1998) 'Displacing social policy through crime control' in Hanninen, S (ed) *The Displacement of Social Policies*, University of Jyvasyla: SoPhi Publications.

Stenson, K and Edwards, A (2003) 'Policy transfer in local crime control: beyond naïve emulation' in Newburn, T and Sparks, R (eds), *Criminal Justice and Political Cultures*, Cullompton: Willan.

Sutton, A and Cherney, A (2003) 'Crime prevention and reduction' in Goldsmith, A et al (eds), *Crime and Justice*, Pyrmont, NSW: Thomson Legal.

Sutton, A (forthcoming, 2004) *Understanding Crime Policy: The Honest Criminologist's Guide*, mimeograph.

Wilson, JQ (1974) *Thinking about Crime*, New York: Basic Books.

Wright Mills, C (1959) *The Sociological Imagination*, New York: OUP.

Young, J (1991) 'Left realism and the priorities of crime control' in Cowell, D and Stenson, K (eds), *The Politics of Crime Control*, London: Sage.

Young, J (1994) 'Incessant chatter: recent paradigms in criminology' in Maguire, M et al (eds), *The Oxford Handbook of Criminology*, Oxford: OUP.

CHAPTER 13

POLICE AND POLICING

Douglas Sharp

SUMMARY

This chapter will present a narrative overview of the development of policing, from the first signs that an organised and professional system was necessary to the present day. It places policing within the context of the social and economic conditions of the times and seeks to identify the theoretical underpinnings of police development. As a guiding structure for the chapter, the notion of there being seven ages of policing has been used to link historical developments to current realities. The chapter concludes with some thoughts about policing in the future.

KEY TERMS

Local versus centralised control; professional policing; preventative patrol; policing by consent; unit beat policing; politicians; the performance culture – policing by objectives; community policing.

NEW BEGINNINGS

Any narrative account of the 'origins' of the police – by which is meant those bodies employed by the state to maintain order and to prevent and detect crime (Emsley, 1991: 1) – has to be conscious of two competing historiographical traditions. These can be described as 'Whig' and 'Revisionist'. Whig histories, for example, tend to see the origin and development of the police from 1829 onwards as progressive and rational, based on a desire to improve the old parochial policing structures which could no longer cope with sustained increases in crime, whilst Revisionist interpretations begin to see the police as an instrument to be used by those with power to discipline the growing, urban working class (for a general introduction to these competing traditions, see Wilson, Ashton and Sharp, 2001: 10–27). This chapter has been informed by the best of both these traditions, although it is clearly more sympathetic to the Revisionist approach. Nonetheless, it also attempts to root its historical account in the practical concerns of policing and how these concerns affect the police.

As the 19th century dawned, Britain was a country ill at ease. The upheavals caused by land enclosure and the mechanisation of farming, which later became known as the Agricultural Revolution, had resulted in rural unemployment, poverty and hardship. As a direct result, people had begun to desert the countryside and move to the towns and cities in search of work. Following hard on the heels of the Agricultural Revolution, the Industrial Revolution changed patterns of employment from cottage industries based around the family unit to large-scale industrial production. As a consequence, communities changed in character as the workers moved to the factories, and both the nature of their work and their social relationships were altered forever.

These were times of growing prosperity for some, but for the vast majority of the population the conditions of life and work deteriorated and became increasingly difficult, dangerous and uncertain. Many people worked long hours, often in hazardous and unhealthy conditions, for low pay and with no security of tenure. It was an age of growing political dissent, and new levels of violence, drunkenness and crime began to challenge the traditional systems of law and order that had sustained the country for centuries. Nowhere was this more apparent than in London.

The population of London had grown steadily during the 17th and 18th centuries as its importance as a commercial and trading centre had developed. By the 19th century, this massive increase in the population was creating problems of crime and social disorder of such a scale and nature that the ancient systems of watchmen and parish constables were unable to cope. The need to modernise the system of policing had in fact been recognised for some years, and there were a number of attempts to create a more professional policing service during the 18th century. For the most part, these initiatives centred around a better organised and managed system of watchmen operating within parish boundaries. In some cases, parishes began to work together to establish more effective systems and in the 1750s the Bow Street magistrates, John and Henry Fielding, established uniformed patrols in the main roads that led into London. These patrols operated first at night but were eventually extended and developed into an organised body of both foot and mounted patrols operating around the clock.

This form of piecemeal development was never going to provide a satisfactory solution to the problem of crime and disorder on the streets of the capital, and the first serious attempt to establish organised policing was in 1785 after the Gordon Riots of 1780. Emsley notes that in fact it was not the riots that prompted this first Police Bill, but rising crime (1991: 80). However, in the event, rising crime did not prove to be of sufficient concern to persuade Parliament of the need for organised policing, and the Police Bill failed. It took a series of piecemeal Acts of Parliament and a further 43 years before a proper system of policing was established.

Those who lobbied for police reform at the time would have preferred some form of national co-ordination and control, but there was little prospect of that being achieved. Opposition to the establishment of an organised, professional system of policing was deep-seated in Britain and was based around two major issues. First, the only system of organised policing that people were familiar with was that in France. The French, quasi-military, disciplined, centralised organisation with its system of paid informers and police spies was seen to run counter to the traditions of freedom and liberty in Britain. Secondly, and probably equally important, was cost. The system of parish constables and watchmen was paid for partly by local rates, which were never popular but which could be varied according to need, and partly from a system of rewards paid for the capture of certain categories of criminal. It was clearly understood that the any widescale reform of policing would require substantial resources that could only be raised through significant rises in local rates or through general taxation. Neither was desirable, but a rise in taxes was particularly unwelcome. The hated income tax that had been introduced as a temporary measure to finance the Napoleonic Wars had been abolished in 1816 and no one wanted to see it return.

By the 1820s, and despite all of the changes that had taken place in policing London, it was clear that more substantial reform was necessary. The tinkering of the previous years had not succeeded in bringing either crime or disorder under control, and it was obvious that a new and different system was required. Robert Peel was made Home Secretary in 1822 and immediately set about reforming the criminal law and arguing for a more rational and organised policing system. Political dissent in the country as a whole remained a serious problem that clearly exercised the Government, and indeed both Peel and Disraeli made reference to disorder during the debate on the Metropolitan Police Bill. It was the rising crime figures in the capital, skilfully presented by Peel both in his arguments to Parliament and in private correspondence to the prime minister (Parker 1899), which proved to be the deciding factor in getting the legislation passed in 1829.

Whilst the Metropolitan Police Act was and remains a significant milestone in the evolution of modern policing, it did not sweep away everything that had existed before, nor did it find unqualified support with the population or some influential politicians. In fact, the first Metropolitan Police officers took their place alongside those other law enforcement bodies that had developed over the previous years, and 'much of the discussion by parliamentary committees during the 1830s focussed on the need to sort out the different tasks of the various organisations' (Emsley, 1991: 28).

Peel had been very aware of the public's hostility to his new police and had deliberately set out to counter the suspicion that they were a quasi-military organisation. His search for the first Commissioner reflects a desire to appoint someone with a non-military background, and he looked first amongst the magistrates who had experience of policing in Ireland. The uniform of those first police officers was deliberately designed not to resemble those of the military, and they were only lightly armed with truncheons that were carried concealed while on normal patrol. In addition, considerable efforts were made to attract recruits from the agricultural working class rather than former soldiers. Furthermore, it was clear from the instructions given to the new police by the first commissioners, Rowan and Maine, that their main purpose was to be the prevention of crime. This was to be achieved by a regular system of patrolling in uniform intended to act simultaneously as a deterrent and a reassurance to law-abiding members of the community.

Nevertheless, the size of the force, its organisation, rigid discipline and the vigour with which it exercised its duties did not immediately dispel lingering doubts among the population of the capital. Indeed, opponents were influential in delaying the creation of a detective branch until 1842 and restricting its size and activities for a further 10 years.

FROM PERSUASION TO COMPULSION

Although the problems of London were more acute than elsewhere in the country, the effect of increasing urbanisation and poverty were creating similar tensions in other places. Crime was rising out of control, political protest was developing and local magistrates were finding that they were having to rely more and more on the local yeomanry to restore order. The use of these poorly trained and ill-disciplined, part-time soldiers could never have been completely satisfactory, and their heavy-handed tactics generated great hostility within the population. Nevertheless, outside the capital, there was no real appetite to develop a more professional approach to law and order at this time.

There were of course worries about rising crime, but, as a general rule, local feeling was that crime could be dealt with effectively by better organisation, rather than by wholesale restructuring. There was particular resistance to any interference in local affairs by a police force centrally organised from Westminster. The Government seems to have taken a rather pragmatic approach, and, as a result, the problem was not addressed directly. It came about as a consequence of the restructuring of local government as the country changed from an essentially medieval and agrarian society to a modern industrial nation.

Development was accordingly unco-ordinated: in some cases, local authorities took advantage of the Lighting and Watching Act of 1833 to create or improve street patrols, while others sought authority through private Acts of Parliament to establish police forces. Outside of the towns, the Rural Constabulary Act of 1839 gave authority to local magistrates to establish police forces, but did not require them to do so.

The notable exception to this *laissez-faire* approach was the Municipal Corporations Act 1835. The Act applied to the 178 incorporated boroughs in the country and was mainly about local government, but it did require that a police force should be established. However, it was never fully enforced and a number of corporations failed to implement the relevant sections. Those corporations that did comply found little specific guidance in the legislation, and as a consequence the police forces that were established lacked any common focus or structure.

Parliament was, however, concerned about the scale and frequency of civil disorder in some of the larger industrial towns and cities in the Midlands and the North. The issue that prompted these concerns was Chartism, a largely working class movement that campaigned for electoral reform. Chartist meetings were attended by very large numbers of people and were inevitably rowdy and disorderly affairs that threatened to break out into open rioting. In the absence of organised police forces, the only recourse that the authorities had to control the situation was to call out the military. This only served to enrage the crowds, and disorder was invariably put down with considerable ferocity that resulted in serious injuries and deaths.

Chartist protest reached its peak in 1839 and was centred particularly on Birmingham, Manchester and Bolton, none of which had established police forces. The events which led to the creation of organised policing in each of these towns is detailed by Critchley (1978: 80–88). The forces that were established were not local in character with a local system of accountability, but they were directly accountable to the Home Secretary who appointed the first Commissioners. In the light of the circumstances surrounding the creation of professional policing in these three towns, there seems to be little doubt that concern about the state of crime was not uppermost in the minds of the Government at the time; it was disorder and revolution that they feared.

Over the next 17 years, a similar pattern emerges with the development of policing continuing in the disorganised and piecemeal fashion that had characterised the earlier decades of the century. In London, the New Police gradually established themselves and replaced or absorbed the other policing agencies that remained from the earlier reforms. Outside London, the situation was rather more complex and could be characterised as a combination of dogged resistance to change and unco-ordinated development to meet emerging situations.

There seems to have been little appetite for further significant change until the middle of the century, but by 1853 it had become clear that major reform was necessary. Disorder in industrial towns and cities was increasing, and the Government found itself facing increasing requests to dispatch detachments of Metropolitan Police to assist inadequate local forces. The outbreak of the Crimean War in 1854 meant that troops were no longer available to assist the local magistrates in times of disorder, and the end of transportation of convicted criminals to Australia was placing increased demands on inadequate local policing (Emsley, 1991: 53). After an exhaustive Select Committee inquiry into the state of policing, a new Police Bill was presented to Parliament in 1854. That Bill was withdrawn following concerted opposition, as was a second Bill some months later. It was not until 1856 that legislation was finally passed.

CONSOLIDATION AND CONTROL

The County and Borough Police Act 1856 marks an important step forward. It required the establishment of police forces. In addition, it provided that the Government would contribute 25 per cent of the cost of establishing and maintaining the force and created, in the Inspectorate of Constabulary, an organisation specifically set up to ensure standardisation and efficiency. The Government now had financial leverage on the direction and style of policing and the mechanism to ensure that forces were efficient. The Act did not, however, define clearly what the police were for or what 'efficiency' in this context meant.

From this point on, we can see a prolonged period of development into the middle of the 20th century as modern police forces evolved. This was a time of great social and economic change, and the Police Service was not immune from its effects. The two World Wars, the development of trades unions, and unemployment and hardship during the Depression all had an impact on the way that the police operated. In addition, the lack of clear lines of operational and managerial accountability led to allegations of corruption by senior officers and unwarranted interference by local politicians. It remains a matter of dispute amongst historians whether the police found easy acceptance as they went about their duties. Some historians, for example, Reith (1956), place the police within a society that shares a concern about crime and where disorder is interpreted as a form of criminal behaviour. He argues that the police quickly became accepted as they began to exert control over crime and criminality. On the other hand, Hirst, in a radical Marxist interpretation, places emphasis on the police role in controlling and disciplining the population, imposing order as a means of guaranteeing a compliant workforce (1975: 225).

In fact, a great deal of reform and modernisation took place during this period, although it attracted little attention. This is probably a reflection of the fact that policing was not politically contentious and attracted little in the way of media attention. What is clear, however, is that the police eventually became embedded at the centre of communities, and by the 1950s there are ample references to the central role that the police were playing. What seems to have happened is that, gradually, the police became central to good government and the maintenance of order. It is less clear whether this came about as a result of a deliberate strategic plan or as an indirect consequence of the reforms of local government that were taking place at the time. Modernising local government required a degree of regulation and enforcement, and the police were the obvious organisation to take on the responsibility because they were disciplined, they had a ubiquitous presence and, most importantly, they were not expensive. While many of their duties and responsibilities related to control and enforcement, there were others that provided direct and tangible benefits to the community. Robert Mark in his autobiography, for example, refers to the police emergency ambulance, for in the early part of the century, there was no independent ambulance service (Mark, 1978: 24).

The end of the Second World War in 1945 marks the beginning of the welfare state and a profound change in the nature of British society. The economy had been devastated by the War, and it took 10 years to establish a basis for future prosperity. However, during this time, the country did not stand still, and the reforms to education, health and social services created a different climate in the population. The old deferential society of the 19th and early 20th centuries quickly disappeared. Improved education taught people to question rather than to passively accept what they were told, and people began to expect that their conditions would continue to improve. Then, when manufacturing industry was re-established on a peacetime footing, Britain entered a period of prosperity and full employment.

All of this might have been good for the country, but it created problems for the police. Law is essentially conservative, that is to say to break the law is to challenge established order and is therefore to be discouraged. It is natural, therefore, that the police and the other agencies of criminal justice tend to resist change rather than embrace it. The change that took place in the country, when all authority was questioned, presented an enormous challenge to the service.

As the 1960s wore on, it was therefore obvious that policing needed to change. The War years had demonstrated the need for greater collaboration and some rationalisation of policing had taken place, but the service had in fact changed little since Victorian times. A series of corruption scandals involving Chief Constables in the late 1950s and a general dissatisfaction with the mechanisms for police accountability led to calls for radical reform. Accordingly, in 1959, the Government appointed a Royal Commission on the Police that reported in 1962. During its deliberations, the Commission had considered the establishment of a national police force for England and Wales, but in the end it opted for a more conservative approach and recommended that many of the smaller forces that then existed should be amalgamated to form larger, more efficient organisations.

The Government accepted most of the recommendations of the Royal Commission, and the subsequent 1964 Police Act effectively gave birth to the modern Police Service. It created the tripartite system of police accountability that, despite substantial modification in subsequent legislation, remains in place today. It required for the first time that Chief Constables establish a system of recording complaints against the police, and it provided the Home Secretary with the authority to make regulations relating to pay, conditions of service and discipline and to order the amalgamation of forces on the grounds of efficiency

It is difficult to say which of those reforms has been the most influential as all in their way played a part in shaping the Police Service of today, but it is hard to over-estimate the significance of the 1964 Act. The years since 1856 had seen a gradual move towards centralisation of power in the hands of the Home Secretary, but the 1964 Act marks a step change in that process. The establishment of the tripartite relationship for the governance of the police, setting out, as it does, the roles of the

Police Authority, the Chief Constable and the Home Secretary, creates the appearance of a shared and equal relationship. However, Oliver notes that it would have been difficult for any Police Authority to act contrary to the views of the Home Secretary (1987: 19), and there is a vagueness and imprecision in the wording of the Act which conceals the very real power which is conferred on the Home Secretary (Wilson, Ashton and Sharp, 2001: 69–72), who 'exercises a very powerful centralising force' (Oliver, 1987).

The establishment of complaints procedures was a positive reform and brought about a measure of democratic accountability, but was only a first step. Subsequent reforms moved gradually towards a completely independent system that was only established in 2002. While these reforms have succeeded in addressing misconduct and inefficiency in the police, and have driven improvements in transparency and accountability, they have also underlined a gradual loss of confidence in the Service.

One of the more significant reforms was to give the Home Secretary the power to order the amalgamation of police forces on the grounds of efficiency. Amalgamations were not new but had previously required a specific Act of Parliament; for example, the 1888 Local Government Act and the 1946 Police Act had required the amalgamation of small borough forces with the county forces, yet the police had remained resolutely local in character. In 1964, there were a total of 120 police forces outside London ranging in size from little more than 100 officers in the smallest forces to, in the largest forces, around 3,000.

In 1966, the Home Secretary began to exercise his powers, and by 1968 the number of forces had been reduced to 49. It could be argued that there were good practical reasons for many of those amalgamations: the very small forces did not have the resources or the pool of experienced officers to enable them to respond effectively to the demands that were being placed upon them and there were considerable cost savings to be made from the creation of larger units. However, in 1974, a further round of amalgamations created the present 43 forces, but unlike those of 1966, the principal reason for these amalgamations had little to do with policing; it was mainly about the restructuring of local government. Not for the first time, effective policing was a secondary consideration in a wider reform programme.

Whatever the motivation behind the amalgamations, they had one very significant effect, in that they broke the link between the police and their communities and thus played a part in creating distance between police and the public.

There were other pressures on the police at this time, created by the booming economy and increased prosperity. Crime was rising steadily, and the rise in car ownership resulted in traffic accidents and congestion. More people than ever were being brought into contact with the police, some as victims of crime and road accidents and others as defendants having been caught speeding or parking inappropriately.

PROFESSIONAL POLICING

Up until this point in police history, the principal function of the police could be characterised as one of *preventative patrol*. The presence of uniformed police officers patrolling on foot established a model of policing that was to become known as *policing by consent*, a style of policing that is still held up as one of the defining characteristics of policing in England and Wales, although it is not without its critics. Waddington (1999a), for example, examines the notion of consent in the policing context and prefers to refer to policing by authority. Whatever the merits of the debate, policing was about to change.

By the middle of the 1960s, the police were facing additional problems that were associated with a booming economy. Police officers were not well-paid and, while conditions of service had improved over the years, had not kept pace with changes in society. It was proving difficult to recruit and retain suitable officers and the service needed to find a way of making policing more interesting, attractive to recruits and responsive to rising crime. The solution that was adopted was known as *unit beat policing*.

Unit beat policing was developed originally in Kirkby in Lancashire as a means of improving policing in a new town development. It involved police officers patrolling in cars to enable them to respond quickly to calls from the public and on foot to provide visible presence. The scheme received enthusiastic support and soon led to the establishment of a further pilot scheme in Accrington. However, the Home Office, encouraged by early positive reports and eager to see improved policing, began to encourage Chief Constables to adopt the scheme before the pilot had been fully evaluated. By the mid-1970s, every force in the country had introduced a form of unit beat policing.

The challenges faced by the Police Service in the years immediately following the 1964 Act necessitated far greater co-operation and co-ordination than at any time in the past. Demands on the police had been increasing steadily since the 1950s and, by the 1970s, rising and increasingly violent crime, large-scale industrial disputes, political demonstrations and the threat of terrorism resulting from the political situation in Northern Ireland had created a need for a more professional service. Unit beat policing had put police officers in cars, but, as crime, traffic and other demands increased, the police response was to create more mobile teams of officers who often operated in plain clothes. The introduction of computerised command and control systems and improved personal radios meant that forces could concentrate their resources more effectively and close small outlying police stations that were expensive to maintain.

It is difficult to assess which of these factors was the more influential, but there is no doubt that the public began to lose faith in the police. Some writers place the blame squarely at the door of unit beat policing, arguing that by putting police officers in cars they became distant, remote and unapproachable, but that is too simplistic an account. Butler (1992) and Weatheritt (1986) point out that a combination of poor management, inadequate training and over-optimistic predictions combined to ensure that the scheme could never have fulfilled its expectations, while rising crime rates and increased demand from the public for police response to incidents created a pressure on resources that could not have been met without a substantial increase in establishments.

What is clear, however, is that changes were also taking place within the police itself. Whittaker (1979) notes that, in evidence to the Royal Commission on the Police in 1959, the Police Federation commented that for the police to be regarded as a profession would be disastrous for their relationship with the public, yet by 1974, Robert Mark was confident to note that the police had truly become a profession. But in his report into the Brixton disorders in 1981, Lord Scarman was critical of the professional model of policing.

It is probable that the professional status was at least as damaging to police-public relations as any other factor because it implied an exclusivity of specialised knowledge and expertise. The police began to believe that they alone understood the problems of crime and disorder and that they could apply the solution without reference to the public. In its original form, policing had been undertaken on behalf of the public, but, once the police had styled themselves as professionals, the public became the subject of policing.

It is probably equally important that, just as the police were aspiring to professional status, academic research was beginning to examine the principles and practice of policing. Banton (1964), Skolnick (1966) and others demonstrated that policing was more about the maintenance of public tranquillity than law enforcement, and Reiss (1971) and Punch and Naylor (1973) highlighted the relatively minor role that crime played in policing activities. In England, Cain (1973) began to illuminate the unpleasant face of racism in policing that was eventually to be revealed at the Macpherson Inquiry (1999) into the murder of Stephen Lawrence, while Reiner (2000), Waddington (1999b) and others have investigated the concept of a 'cop culture', which informs and guides the behaviour of police officers both on and off duty. This scrutiny of policing was to continue, but policing was also to enter the political arena.

POLITICISATION

There is a common theme that runs through the literature on British policing, a theme that distinguishes Britain from the United States and most other countries, and that is political independence. It was always a principal in the English common law and confirmed in case law (see, for example, *R v The Commissioner of Police for the Metropolis ex p Blackburn* [1968] 1 All ER 763) that Chief Constables were operationally independent of politics. That principal was to be brought into question by the events of the 1970s and 1980s.

The 1970s were a period of turmoil in the political and industrial life of the country and a time of rising crime. The quality of life for large sections of the population was being affected for the first time by crime and disorder, and confidence in the police was beginning to fall. In addition, a series of major corruption scandals in the Metropolitan Police in the early 1970s contributed to growing public dissatisfaction.

Confrontation and conflict had increased during the late 1960s. Protest against the Vietnam War had radicalised sections of society, the need to modernise industrial practices, to adopt new technology and to create a flexible workforce generated conflict with an increasingly powerful and militant trades union movement, and violent confrontations between militant left- and right-wing political movements all combined to highlight deficiencies in the Police Service.

In 1968, the Metropolitan Police nearly lost control of an anti-war demonstration outside the American Embassy in Grosvenor Square. In 1972, a mass picket in Saltley, Birmingham, during a miners' strike defeated police attempts to keep a fuel depot open. Other industrial disputes, including a national docks strike in 1972 and the now infamous dispute at the Grunwick plant in 1977, contributed to a feeling that the police were unable to cope.

In fact, the police were ill-prepared to respond to these challenges. They were neither trained nor equipped to deal with large-scale disorder, and the modest improvements in pay and conditions of earlier years had failed to solve the problems of under-recruitment. The Police Service of the 1970s was undermanned and demoralised, unit beat policing had failed to deliver its promise of a better service to the public and was actually blamed for creating barriers between police and the public. Holdaway (1977) even goes as far as suggesting that the scheme resulted in the politicisation of the relationship. In addition, there was a growing feeling that the rules of criminal procedure that had developed to safeguard the rights of suspects were being abused to the advantage of the guilty.

In the mid-1970s, the Police Federation, which represented the majority of police officers in the country, supported by the Association of Chief Police Officers, began a major publicity campaign to highlight the problems faced by the service. The well-organised and high profile campaign succeeded in bringing their concerns to the fore and, for the first time in British history, the problems of crime and of policing became major issues during the General Election of 1979. Both major political parties vied with each other with promises to improve the conditions of the police service, but in the end it was the pledge by the Conservative Party to reform the law on industrial relations and criminal procedure that won the day.

The implication behind the law and order campaign of the Police Federation and the Association of Chief Police Officers was that, if the Government provided reforms to the law and the financial resources to modernise the police, then the crime problem could be solved. It placed the police firmly in the centre of the political map and contributed to the politicisation of criminal justice, but it was to take a further five years, serious civil disorder and a major industrial dispute before the allegation that the police had lost their traditional political independence was to gain real currency.

The industrial conflicts of the 1970s had fostered a determination in the minds of Conservative politicians to reform industrial relations and break the power of the trades unions. On returning to power in 1979, they set about an ambitious programme of reform and began a process of repealing earlier legislation and putting new, more restrictive laws in place.

One of the first actions of the Government in 1980 was to honour a pledge made during the election campaign and finance in full the pay increases that had been recommended by the Edmund Davies Review, which had been set up by the previous Labour Government. For the first time in many years, police pay was competitive with other occupations and police morale quickly improved; the leaders of the Police Service began to believe that they would receive the support that they considered necessary to defeat the twin problems of crime and disorder.

They were soon to be tested, for in 1980 and 1981, serious rioting broke out first in Bristol and then in Brixton, Manchester, Liverpool and Birmingham. The subsequent report by Lord Scarman (1982) catalogued a series of failures of public policy and policing that lay at the heart of those disturbances. One of his more serious criticisms of the police related to what he described as their failure to consult effectively with their communities. In effect, he was casting doubt on the claim that the British police model was underpinned by the consent of the public. The inner city riots also highlighted tensions between some Police Authorities and their Chief Constables, tensions that were to be raised further during the Miners' Strike of 1984/85.

The planned closure of large sections of the coal industry in the early 1980s lay at the heart of the strike, but there can be little doubt that the Government was determined to defeat the National Union of Mineworkers and that the leadership of the Union in turn was determined to see the downfall of the Government. Policing of the strike was a complex and controversial operation. Large numbers of officers from forces all over England and Wales were sent to assist those forces at the centre of the dispute. Miners taking part in pickets were prevented from travelling, and police tactics were criticised as being confrontational and unnecessarily violent. The bitter and sometimes violent strike lasted for 12 months and divided the country and the mining community. It further highlighted tensions between some Chief Constables and Police Authorities and created a lasting impression that the police had colluded with the Government in its political ambition.

Whatever the truth of that allegation, the Miners' Strike had highlighted other problems that had been facing the police for a number of years, and which had to be addressed if they were to deal effectively with the challenges of disorder and complex crime. Operational demands were driving the Service towards a greater degree of collaboration and standardisation than had been previously envisaged. Deficiencies in equipment and training that had first been identified during the riots of 1980/81 became increasingly clear during the policing of the strike. Radio systems were incompatible, and the use of differing tactics and words of command made co-ordination difficult. The need for national standards became quickly apparent, but it was not only disorder that troubled the police. Terrorist bombing campaigns and increasingly complex criminal investigations highlighted the need for co-operation between police forces on a scale that had never previously been necessary. Computers were beginning to be used in criminal investigations, but systems were often incompatible and the sharing of information was difficult. One particular case, known as the Yorkshire Ripper inquiry, highlighted all of the deficiencies in the existing arrangements and procedures and created a demand for a national standard for computerised systems to be used in major investigations.

CENTRALISATION AND THE PERFORMANCE CULTURE

In 1980, the Government had other priorities in addition to the changes envisaged in criminal justice and industrial relations: it was determined to introduce the disciplines of market capitalism as part of an ambitious programme of reform of the public services. The Health Service, Education and the Civil Service soon found themselves faced with demands for improved efficiency and value for money that were to transform the way in which they worked. The police, on the other hand, managed to avoid the most rigorous of those demands. By the mid-1980s, they did face some pressure to demonstrate efficiency and cost-effectiveness, but overall the operational challenges faced by the police enabled them to call upon government support for most of the decade.

That should not be taken to imply that the police stood still during this time; in fact, some enlightened leaders of the service saw clearly that there was need to reform the way in which the police were managed, and they looked to the United States for inspiration. What they found was an approach that had its basis in the business system known as 'managing by objectives' that had been adapted and developed for the police. The system was known as *policing by objectives*.

The principles of policing by objectives had been developed in the United States by Lubans and Edgar and first published in 1979. In fact, their work was never published in this country, but it did attract the attention of some influential senior officers, including Sir Kenneth Newman, who was the Commandant of the Police Staff College. This high profile support ensured that the principles soon became established, and in 1980 the publication of *Police Management* by AJP Butler set out the principles of the system and provided a guide to establishing 'Policing by Objectives in a Police Force'. The scheme was given a further impetus in 1983 when the Home Office published Circular 114 that required that all Chief Constables should set objectives for their forces. Although it is doubtful if any force truly adopted an objective-setting approach to policing, Circular 114/83 and subsequent circulars, together with advice and guidance to Chief Constables from Her Majesty's Inspectorate of Constabulary, set in train a process that has led directly to the development of policing dominated by the demands of performance targets and league tables.

Despite a more managerial approach to policing and the additional resources allocated by the Government, crime rates continued to increase. In 1990, the Audit Commission published a report that highlighted 'serious shortcomings in police management style, vision and leadership', and, according to Kenneth Baker (1993), a former senior Cabinet Minister, many senior Conservative politicians had lost faith in the Service. The tolerance that the Government had previously shown to the police was to give way to a renewed emphasis on efficiency and value for money.

The strategy of setting demanding performance targets had already begun to transform the Health Service and Education, and in 1990 the Home Office, the Inspectorate of Constabulary and the Audit Commission began to impose the same discipline on the Police Service. At first, the Association of Chief Police Officers and the Police Federation were successful in arguing that quality of service, rather than strict target setting, was a more appropriate way for police performance to be judged, and a series of indirect measures or performance indicators linked to local conditions were established. This was to prove only a temporary respite for the Service and the performance indicators were gradually hardened and eventually used to compile the comparative league tables that had become the norm by the end of the century.

The Government's strategy was not limited to setting targets; it was determined to reform the police and to bring a more business-like approach to the Service through a streamlining of management and operational practices. In 1992, two working parties were established that were to have a profound effect.

The Report of the Sheehy Inquiry (1993) recommended sweeping changes to police management and the pay and conditions of police officers. It was fiercely opposed by the Police Federation, and many of its recommendations were subsequently modified or shelved, but it did mark the beginnings of a more business-like approach to policing.

The Inquiry into Police Core and Ancillary Tasks (1995) raised important questions about the role of the police that have still not been fully answered, but it continued the debate about the police role and what is expected of the police.

In 1993, after the publication of what was to prove to be the first in a series of police reform White Papers, the Government published the Police and Magistrates Courts Bill, which proposed major changes in the structure of policing. Central to the proposals was a significant centralisation of power in the hands of the Home Secretary. In the event, the Bill was received with hostility in the House of Lords and was seriously amended before becoming law in 1994. Nevertheless, it did consolidate the power of the Home Secretary and marked an important step in the centralisation of responsibility for policing by empowering the Home Secretary to set key performance objectives and requiring that Police Authorities should publish an annual policing plan that had to take account of those objectives. The production of the plan was envisaged to be a consultative process involving the Chief Constable and the general public, but in practice the process tended to be dominated by the need to meet the key performance objectives specified by the Home Secretary.

The 1994 Act marked a further step in the centralising of policing by establishing the National Crime Squad, in effect a 44th police force, with its own Police Authority and its own terms of reference. The Squad is targeted specifically at the international drugs trade, money laundering, international terrorism and illegal immigration, and, while it normally operates in conjunction with local police forces, it can function entirely separately and does not even have to inform a local Chief Constable that it is operating in the area.

The Police and Magistrates Courts Act 1994 was in effect the last significant piece of police legislation of the Conservative Government, although it was subsequently slightly amended and consolidated into the Police Act 1996. When New Labour came to power in 1997, one might have expected a change of direction in policing policy. The election campaign had been dominated by criminal justice, and the slogan 'tough on crime, tough on the causes of crime' could have been interpreted to herald an approach that owed more to communitarian values than that of the previous administration.

As it transpired, the first and in fact the only significant piece of criminal justice legislation of that Labour Government, the Crime and Disorder Act 1998, did go some way to returning police planning and priority setting to the community. However, following the 2001 General Election, the direction of police reform seemed to move inexorably in the direction of even greater centralisation of power.

For a number of years, successive governments have been obsessed with the notion that improvement in performance in the public services can only be achieved by setting increasingly challenging performance targets. The police have not escaped this process, and performance management has dominated policing for over 10 years. During that time, the Police Service, influenced by Audit Commission Reports on Criminal Investigation (1993; 1996b; 1996c), changed its operational practices and adopted a more targeted, intelligence-led approach to crime with some success, but in 2001, the climate changed. The Home Secretary had become increasingly frustrated at the inability of the Home Office to directly influence police policy and by the ability of some independently-minded Chief Constables to subvert the performance agenda. In order to reinforce his determination to improve police performance, the Home Secretary established a new body, the Police Standards Unit, as an advisory body to assist the Home Office to drive forward a process of standard setting and improvements in crime detection. This was followed by another police reform White Paper and the Police Reform Act 2002, an Act that continued to consolidate the power of the Home Secretary. It contained two very important provisions: it enabled the Home Secretary to make a National Policing Plan that must be at the centre of local policing plans and it gave him power to instruct a Police Authority to dismiss a Chief Constable on grounds of efficiency. Policing policy was now firmly in the hands of the Home Secretary, who was enabled to set priorities and monitor performance through the Police Standards Unit. The Police Authority's role is very much the minor party in the tripartite relationship, and in many respects the constitutional position of the Chief Constable has been reduced to that of a subordinate.

At the same time, there was a realisation that the general public did not wholeheartedly subscribe to this national agenda. No amount of publicity about the reduction in crime rates and headline grabbing soundbites about performance targets could persuade the public that things were getting better. Despite falling crime rates, fear of crime continues to rise, the public continue to demand more 'bobbies on the beat', and minor crime and disorder on the streets of our towns and cities is identified as a significant contribution to public dissatisfaction.

We are faced with a problem of balancing demands. While serious crime must always remain a priority for the police, and the problem of drugs and terrorism must be a focus for the activities of all law enforcement agencies, local issues involving volume crime and anti-social behaviour are an equally important factor in quality of life and must therefore be given careful consideration in planning the future shape and direction of policing.

POLICING THE FUTURE

In fact, the future of policing began to be shaped in 1998 when the Crime and Disorder Act received royal assent. It began then, not because the Act had any significant impact on police powers and responsibilities, but because it required the police and local authorities to plan strategies for dealing with minor crime and disorder, and in so doing it ran counter to much of the centralising legislation that had been the cornerstone of policing policy since 1964.

As early as the 1980s, it was apparent to police and policy-makers alike that the police alone could not control the growing crime rates, and the search began for effective strategies to engage the general public. The first initiative in this quest was the introduction of Neighbourhood Watch. This idea had originated in the United States and derived from the situational approach to crime prevention based on the work of Jacobs (1962) and Newman (1972). The idea was that new building developments should be designed in a way that encouraged residents to take responsibility for their environment and to look out for each other's property. Neighbourhood Watch schemes were initially popular with both police and public: they offered the promise of assistance to the police in defeating burglars and other criminals at little cost to the service, while at the same time providing a degree of reassurance to the public.

In fact, neither Neighbourhood Watch nor any of its derivatives had any significant impact on crime rates or on detection rates, but there was evidence that they contributed to a reduction in the fear of crime. Whatever success they may have had in residential areas, they could not work in town centres with transitory populations and where crime and anti-social behaviour was rife. The solution seemed to be offered by closed circuit television (CCTV) and, very soon, CCTV schemes were being installed in car parks and on the streets of our towns and cities in an effort to both deter crime and detect offenders. Again, there is little evidence of their success in either case, although there are indications that they have raised public confidence.

At the same time, the police were beginning to respond to the demands for more local accountability by adopting a range of *community policing* strategies. The ideas behind community policing had originated in 1979 in a book entitled *Policing Freedom* (Alderson, 1979) but had not found favour in Britain. They had, however, been influential in informing police policy in the United States and were reintroduced into this country in the 1980s in a bid to improve police community relations and police performance. While there is no doubt that community policing is a political success in that it gives all of the right messages, in most cases it is such a vague concept that it has universally popular appeal and suffers from what Weatheritt terms the 'foregone conclusion syndrome', in that it is assumed that the outcomes will always be positive (1986: 18–19). In fact, there is little evidence that community policing provides any tangible benefits in the form of improved detections or increased crime prevention (Bennett, 1996).

It was clear that a new focus was required for crime prevention, and in 1990, the Government commissioned an investigation into crime prevention measures, entitled *Safer Communities: The Local Delivery of Crime Prevention through the Partnership Approach*, better known as the Morgan Report (1991). The Report examined progress in crime prevention and concluded that it was unrealistic to place responsibility for crime prevention solely in the hands of the police. The solution was to recognise that crime was a complex phenomenon and that crime prevention needed to recognise that complexity. All statutory agencies and the general public had a part to play and mechanisms had to be found that harnessed the collective resources to deal with the problem. The solution the Report suggested was to require local authorities to work with the police to devise effective strategies. This was not a popular message with the Conservative Government, as it had spent most of the previous decade reducing the power of local authorities, and the Report was effectively shelved. Some of the ideas were, however, incorporated in subsequent attempts to create a partnership approach to crime prevention.

New Labour's approach, when it came to power in 1997, was very different. It accepted most of the philosophy behind the Morgan Report and its principles were built into the Crime and Disorder Act 1998. What this Act does is to require the police and local authorities to work together, first to conduct a Crime and Disorder Audit of the locality and then to produce an action plan to deal with the problems identified. In doing so, it seems to address some of the problems that were manifest in the centralist agenda of the recent past, where targets were being set against a national rather than a local agenda. In fact, it highlights the very real tensions that exist between local and national priorities in policing. One of the main problems with the Act is that it does not allocate any additional resources to crime prevention partnerships, and they have to be financed from existing sources.

The other problem with the Crime and Disorder Act 1998 is that the local authorities which have to work with the police are not the same areas that are covered by the Police Authority. Take the case of the West Midlands, for example. There is now no such entity as the West Midlands Council, which only existed between 1974 and

1986. There is, however, a West Midlands Police and a West Midlands Police Authority that covers the area that was the West Midlands Metropolitan County, which comprises seven separate local authorities. The budget for policing the West Midlands lies in the hands of the Police Authority and is calculated on the basis of the annual policing plan, which itself is developed against the background of the national policing plan. Whilst there may be a desire to incorporate local priorities into that plan, there is bound to be tension, and national priorities, backed by the threat of sanctions, are inevitably going to take precedence. It should therefore be no surprise that there are calls for greater local accountability for policing.

So, at the beginning of the 21st century, we are faced with a problem. The present structure of policing cannot cope with the competing demands of national and local priorities. The scale and nature of international crime and terrorism demands a police response that is sufficiently focused and resourced to deal with problems wherever they arise, yet this is incompatible with local autonomy. The current political agenda requires police forces to respond quickly and effectively to identified crime problems, and the Home Secretary now has the powers to direct policing strategy. At the same time, demands are growing for more local accountability and a police service that is more responsive to local needs. These dilemmas have both a practical and a political dimension, for they affect the future structure and purpose of policing, and they also contain elements of discussion about the future of local democracy.

Some of the possible solutions are set out in the recently published Consultation Paper, *Building Safer Communities Together* (2003), which suggests that a combination of national, regional and local police forces could be established, each with its own remit and resourced to deal effectively with the problems that they confront. Such a solution would be a radical departure, and we would see for the first time a system of policing that was designed with specific purposes in mind and with a clearly defined remit. It would only then be truly possible to measure and ascertain whether the police were efficient and effective in undertaking their role.

CONCLUSION

This chapter has attempted to set out some of the key milestones in the development of modern policing. The early years were characterised by conflict between those who saw the need for radical reform and a professional police service and those who were content to see the old systems modified and brought up to date. What resulted was a compromise that produced a policing system that was not designed but developed over time. It is a system that has never had an official *raison d'être* or a clear and unambiguous mission statement. It was a resilient system, but it was a system that could not adapt easily to rapid social and economic change, and it was also an inefficient system ill-prepared to meet the demands of the 21st century.

The transformation of policing over the past 40 years has produced a Service that is subject to more central direction and more accountability for the way in which resources are utilised than at any previous time. It is also a service that is more focused on crime detection than on crime prevention, a complete reversal of the principles that informed the Metropolitan Police in 1829. There are currently 43 separate forces (plus the National Crime Squad), all of which have individual characteristics that have evolved in response to economic, geographic and cultural factors. There are of course problems that are manifest at a national level that all police forces need to address, but they are not necessarily the problems that concern ordinary people. Fear of crime is driven as much by minor disorder and anti-social behaviour as it is by the high profile serious crime that receives so much attention in the media and in television drama. People, especially the elderly and the vulnerable, want to feel safe in their homes and on the streets, and they want to feel confident that their homes and their cars are safe from thieves and vandals. Patrolling police officers may not be an efficient and effective means of crime control, but they do give that reassurance and policing needs to recognise that.

It is clear that, in the past, proposals for radical change have been met with controversy and opposition, and most of the changes that have taken place have been as a result of a rather pragmatic, gradual and piecemeal response to circumstances. What we find is that change has sometimes been driven by disorder or fear of disorder. Sometimes crime has been the prime concern; on other occasions, policing has been a secondary consideration in a wider agenda involving the reform of local government. More recently, the threats of global terrorism, drug trafficking and illegal immigration have created the need for police collaboration on an international scale. And sometimes change has been driven by political dogma. What is much more difficult to discern is any theoretical underpinning for policing practice or any evidence base for different styles of policing. There are commonly used terms like 'policing by consent' or 'community policing', but they are difficult to define in practice. They are, however, politically popular and often seem to be used only to reassure the public rather than to illuminate the principles which inform everyday policing activities.

There is no doubt that the police must continue to change to meet different circumstances. Today's police may be more focused than at any time in the past, but there is also a danger that officers have lost some of the interpersonal skills and the ability to build relationships within the community that were the hallmark of traditional policing. If policing is to be reorganised, it must maintain its links with the community and find ways to re-engage with the public at large, who have always been and remain their principal source of information and evidence.

SEMINAR DISCUSSION TOPICS

- Is there any underlying theoretical basis for policing practice?
- Are there any grounds for believing that the police in England and Wales are accountable in any meaningful way to the general public?
- What impact has the history of police and policing had on modern policing developments?

KEY READINGS

What Everyone in Britain Should Know about the Police by David Wilson, John Ashton and Douglas Sharp (Blackstone, 2001) offers a general introduction to the subject. Those readers with a deeper interest should consult *The Politics of the Police*, 3rd edn, by Robert Reiner (OUP, 2001), *Policing Citizens* by PAJ Waddington (UCL Press, 1999) or *Core Issues in Policing*, 2nd edn, edited by Frank Leishman, Barry Loveday and Steven Savage (Longman, 2000).

Anyone who is interested in police history is directed to *The English Police*, 2nd edn, by Clive Emsley (Longman, 1996) or the more recent *Policing, A Short History* by Philip Rawlings (Willan, 2001).

The constitutional position of the police and arrangements for the governance and accountability of the service can be found in *The Governance of the Police* by Laurence Lustgarten (Sweet and Maxwell, 1986), *Police, Government and Accountability* by Ian Oliver (Macmillan, 1987) or *Policing After the Act* by Trevor Jones and Tim Newburn (Policy Studies Institute, 1997).

There is a comprehensive literature on crime prevention, but for those with an interest in this area, *Understanding Crime Prevention: Social Control, Risk and Late Modernity* by Gordon Hughes (Open University Press, 1998) is a readable and authoritative introductory text.

Detailed reports on police performance are available from the Audit Commission, 1 Vincent Square, London SW1P 2PN or at www.audit-commission.gov.uk and Her Majesty's Inspectorate of Constabulary, The Home Office, 50 Queen Anne's Gate, London SW1H 9AT or at www.homeoffice.gov.uk. The Government's Consultation Paper, *Policing: Building Safer Communities Together*, can be obtained from HMSO or from the Police Reform website: www.policereform.gov.uk/docs/consultation2003.html.

REFERENCES

Alderson, J (1979) *Policing Freedom: A Commentary on the Dilemmas of Policing in Western Democracies*, Plymouth: Macdonalds & Evans.

Audit Commission (1990) *Effective Policing: Performance Review in Police Forces*, London: HMSO.

Audit Commission (1993) *Helping with Enquiries; Tackling Crime Effectively*, London: HMSO.

Audit Commission (1996a) *Streetwise: Effective Police Patrol*, London HMSO.

Audit Commission (1996b) *Tackling Crime Effectively*, London: HMSO.

Audit Commission (1996c) *Detecting Change; Progress in Tackling Crime*, London: HMSO.

Baker, K (1993) *The Turbulent Years; My Life in Politics*, London: Faber and Faber.

Banton, M (1964) *The Policeman in the Community*, London: Tavistock.

Bennett, T (1996) 'What's new in evaluation research?', *British Journal of Criminology*, vol 36(4), pp 567–73.

Butler, AJP (1992) *Police Management*, 2nd edn, Ashgate.

Cain, M (1973) *Society and the Policeman's Role*, London: Routledge and Kegan Paul.

Critchley, TA (1978) *A History of Police in England and Wales*, London: Constable.

Emsley, C (1991) *The English Police*, Harlow: Addison Wesley Longman.

Hirst, PQ (1975) 'Marx and Engels on law, crime and morality' in Taylor I, Walton, P and Young, J (eds), *Critical Criminology*, London: Routledge, pp 203–32.

Holdaway, S (1977) 'Changes in urban policing', *British Journal of Sociology*, vol 28(2), pp 119–37.

Home Office (1962) *Final Report of the Royal Commission on the Police*, Cmnd 1728, London: Home Office.

Home Office (1983) *Manpower, Effectiveness and Efficiency in the Police Service*, Circular 114/83, London: Home Office.

Home Office (1993) *Police Reform: A Police Service for the Twenty-First Century*, Cm 2281, London: HMSO.

Home Office (1995) *Review of Police Core and Ancillary Tasks, Final Report*, London: HMSO.

Home Office (2001) *Policing a New Century, A Blueprint for Reform*, Cm 5326, London: HMSO.

Home Office (2003) *Policing: Building Safer Communities Together*, London: HMSO.

Jacobs, J (1962) *The Life and Death of Great American Cities*, New York: Vintage Books.

Lubans, VA and Edgar, JM (1979) *Policing by Objectives*, Hartford, CT: Social Development Corporation.

Macpherson of Cluny, Sir William (1999) *The Stephen Lawrence Inquiry: Report of an Inquiry by Sir William Macpherson of Cluny*, Cm 4626, London: HMSO.

Mark, R (1978) *In the Office of Constable*, London: Collins.

Newman, O (1972) *Defensible Space; People and Design in the Violent City*, London: Architectural Press.

Oliver, I (1987) *Police, Government and Accountability*, London: Macmillan.

Parker, CS (1899) *Robert Peel Vol II*, London: John Murray.

Punch, M and Naylor, T (1973) 'The police: a social service', *New Society*, vol 24, pp 358–61.

Reiner, R (2000) *The Politics of the Police*, 3rd edn, Oxford: OUP.

Reiss, AJ (1971) *The Police and the Public*, New Haven, CT: Yale UP.

Reith, C (1956) *A New Study of Police History*, London: Oliver and Boyd.

Scarman, Lord (1982) *The Brixton Disorders*, Cmnd 8427, London: Home Office.

Sheehy, P (1993) *Report of the Inquiry into Police Responsibilities and Rewards*, Cm 2280, London: HMSO.

Skolnick, J (1966) *Justice Without Trial*, New York: Wiley.

Waddington, PAJ (1999a) *Policing Citizens*, London: UCL Press.

Waddington, PAJ (1999b) 'Police (canteen) sub-culture: an appreciation', *British Journal of Criminology*, vol 39(2), pp 286–308.

Weatheritt, M (1986) *Innovations in Policing*, London: Croom Helm.

Whittaker, B (1979) *The Police in Society*, London: Eyre Methuen.

Wilson, D, Ashton J and Sharp, D (2001) *What Everyone in Britain Should Know about the Police*, London: Blackstone.

CHAPTER 14

SENTENCING AND COURT PROCESSES

Anthea Hucklesby

SUMMARY

This chapter aims to introduce readers to some of the principal issues arising from the operation of the courts and, in particular, the sentencing of offenders. The process of sentencing is one of the most cohesive actions that the state can apply to individuals as, at its most extreme, it can deprive people of their liberty for very long periods of time. For sentences to be seen as legitimate, they must be imposed after the accused has been found guilty as a result of a fair trial in which the decision has been reached by those with the authority to do so. Sentencing decisions must also be consistent between individuals and geographic location. We shall see in this chapter that the fundamental principles of our criminal justice process of truth, justice and fairness are stretched by the current court and sentencing process.

Although the focus of this chapter is the sentencing process, it is important to stress that sentencing decisions are the end of a long, complex and often protracted process which begins with the arrest or summons of a person for an offence. A number of significant decisions are taken in the pre-trial process, including whether or not defendants should be remanded in custody prior to trial and in which court their case should be heard. Research suggests that the decisions taken earlier in the court process affect the final outcome of the case (Ashworth, 1998; Hucklesby, 1996; Sanders and Young, 2001). The most important decision taken prior to sentencing is, of course, the determination of guilt. The traditional image of this process, as portrayed most graphically by many television programmes and films, is one where guilt is found after a long trial with the prosecution and defence pitted against each other, usually in front of a judge and jury. This, however, is far from the reality, with the majority of defendants pleading guilty, thus avoiding the necessity of a trial (Baldwin and McConville, 1977; McConville et al, 1994; McConville, 2002; Sanders and Young, 2001). Why so many defendants plead guilty in a criminal justice process premised on the maxim that people are innocent until proven guilty is an interesting question which is explored elsewhere (Ashworth, 1998; McConville, 2002; Sanders and Young, 2001).

Another important factor is the high profile given to sentencing decisions. Crime and the operation of the criminal justice process have become daily fodder for the media, and sentencing decisions are some of the most controversial and as a result some of the most commented-upon aspects of the crime phenomenon. Recent cases which have been highlighted by the press include that of Tony Martin, jailed for killing a burglar whom he found in his isolated farmhouse. In such cases, the courts are derided for either being too lenient or too harsh. The high media profile of crime has contributed to its political importance and sensitivity and its use as a pawn in the fight between the political parties to be seen as the bastion of law and order. This has resulted in a plethora of criminal justice legislation at the end of the last and beginning of this century, most of which has included changes to the sentencing process.

KEY TERMS

Magistrates – lay magistrates and District Judges; discrimination in sentencing; justifications for sentencing; 'the cafeteria style'; discretion in sentencing; mandatory sentences.

THE COURTS AND THE SENTENCERS

There are two types of courts where sentencing decisions are made, namely magistrates' courts and Crown Courts. Nearly all cases start off in the magistrates' courts where the vast majority (about 97 per cent) of cases are also completed (Ashworth, 1998). Magistrates' courts also deal with nearly all cases involving young people. Less serious cases are completed in magistrates' courts. These include all those involving summary offences, such as minor public order offences. Sentencing powers in magistrates' courts are, at present, restricted to six months for any one offence and a maximum of 12 months' imprisonment and a £5,000 fine. Crown Courts, on the other hand, deal with indictable only offences, which are offences of a serious nature such as murder and rape. A third category of offences, either way offences, are of intermediate seriousness and can be dealt with, as the name suggests, either in the magistrates' court or the Crown Court. Either way offences cover a wide range of offences and are the subject of recent debate about the curtailment of jury trial. At present, defendants charged with either way offences may elect for Crown Court trial if the magistrates decide that the case is suitable for trial in the magistrates' court. Contrary to popular belief, the majority of either way cases dealt with in the Crown Court are sent there by magistrates rather than defendants choosing this mode of trial (for a fuller discussion, see Sanders and Young, 2001).

There are two types of sentencers in magistrates' courts, namely lay magistrates and District Judges (magistrates' courts). Lay magistrates are unpaid members of the local community. They are not legally trained, although they do receive induction and ongoing training. Lay magistrates usually sit in twos or threes and are given legal advice by court clerks. Court clerks are theoretically neutral and are supposed to offer advice on legal matters only, including law, procedure and sentencing. Their role is not to persuade magistrates on issues of guilt or innocence or on what sentences to actually impose. Only a limited amount of research has been undertaken on the role of court clerks, but this research indicates that they play a more active decision-making role than is generally supposed (Darbyshire, 1984). This is of particular concern when not all clerks are legally qualified (Darbyshire, 2002). They are also being given greater powers, particularly as case managers, which enable them to play a more active decision-making role in court proceedings (Sanders and Young, 2001; Darbyshire, 2002).

The lay magistracy has a long history and is based on ideas of local justice, with magistrates having to live within 15 miles of the court area where they sit (Parker et al, 1989; Raine, 1989). In this respect, they are supposed to reflect the make-up of the local population and be representative of it (Dignan and Whynne, 1997). In theory, anyone can be a lay magistrate, but lack of diversity is the key issue. Magistrates are predominantly drawn from the white, middle class, conservative establishment (Baldwin, 1976; Dignan and Whynne, 1997). There is an approximately 50:50 split between the sexes, but the majority of magistrates are drawn from the older age groups and minority ethnic groups are under-represented (Darbyshire, 2002; Lord Chancellor's Department, 2003). This has led to concerns about the unrepresentativeness of lay magistrates, particularly when offenders are predominantly drawn from the lower classes and much younger age groups and when minorities ethnic groups are over-represented (Darbyshire, 2002). Many commentators blame the appointments system for this unrepresentativeness as, until recently, magistrates were appointed by existing magistrates (Darbyshire, 2002). In order to tackle this problem, the Lord Chancellor's Department carried out its first national recruitment campaign in 1999 and it has introduced a shadowing scheme in an attempt to increase the number of magistrates drawn from minority ethnic groups (Lord Chancellor's Department, 2003). Yet the criteria for appointment inevitably militates against some sections of the population being appointed. Darbyshire (2002) gives the example of the criteria of local standing, which would prevent the unemployed, young or those who have recently moved into the area from being appointed.

District Judges (magistrates' courts) were until recently called stipendiary magistrates. They are professional lawyers who have been legally trained for at least seven years and sit alone. In 2003, there were 105 full-time District Judges (magistrates' courts) and 150 Deputy District Judges (magistrates' courts). District Judges are able to sit anywhere in the country (see the Department for Constitutional Affairs at www.dca.gov.uk/judicial/judapp.htm). There is some evidence that District Judges are given the more serious cases to deal with (Morgan and Russell, 2000). They are also assumed to be quicker, thus getting through more cases and reducing delays in the criminal justice process (Narey, 1997; Morgan and Russell, 2000; Seago et al, 1995; 2000). For these reasons, and for the simple fact that they are professionals, some commentators have argued that more District Judges should be appointed. In fact, it has been suggested that a system of professional magistrates should replace lay magistrates altogether. However, this is unlikely to occur, primarily because of the costs involved, but also because of concerns about one person, albeit a professional, being both judge and jury and responsible for admitting evidence, findings of guilt and sentencing.

Both lay magistrates and District Judges make decisions about guilt and the sentence which will be imposed. In Crown Courts, these responsibilities are divided between the jury, which makes decisions about guilt, and the judge, who imposes sentence. Practically anyone can be called for jury trial, and the basis of the system is trial by one's peers. Successive governments have tried to curtail the use of juries, believing them to produce adverse judgments, ie acquitting the guilty and/or convicting the innocent. These restrictions have been fiercely opposed by many commentators who believe that jury trial is a fundamental right and one of the cornerstones of a democratic society (Doran, 2002; Findley and Duff, 1988; Sanders and Young, 2001).

Judges are experienced lawyers. Judges are in charge of proceedings in Crown Courts and their role includes directing the jury on law, determining the admissibility of evidence and sentencing. According to the doctrine of judicial independence, there must be a separation of powers between the legislative (Parliament) and the judiciary. This prevents interference with individual decisions by politicians and makes judges independent. There is a constant debate about how much Parliament should be able to curtail the discretion of judges and impose its will upon them. This is exemplified by recent debates about the introduction of automatic life sentences and the proposal to introduce criteria for setting the time offenders sentenced to life imprisonment can normally expect to serve (known as their tariff).

The main criticism of judges is that they are highly unrepresentative of the population as a whole and are therefore perceived to be out of touch. They are predominantly a white, male, Oxbridge-educated elite (Sanders and Young, 2001). The Lord Chancellor's Department is trying to redress this imbalance, but this will take some years as the issue is not so much with the people appointed but the criteria for, and method of, appointment.

SENTENCING

Sentencing is the method used by the state to impose punishment on an offender who has been found guilty of a criminal offence. Ultimately, sentencing is the process by which the state responds to those who are known to have broken the law. As Ashworth (2002: 1077) points out, 'When a court passes sentence, it authorises the use of state coercion against a person for committing an offence'. The form of punishment varies from country to country. In certain states in the United States, for example, the range of punishments still includes capital punishment. In the UK, however, punishments generally fall into three categories, namely deprivation, restriction or positive obligation (Ashworth, 2002). Deprivation can take the form of imprisonment, which deprives the offender of their liberty, or a fine, which deprives offenders of money. Restrictions may involve curfew orders and the use of electronic tags, and obligations may mean that offenders have to perform unpaid work in the community. Whatever form the punishment takes, it involves an element of condemnation, labelling and censure (Ashworth, 2002).

Only a small proportion (about 2 per cent) of criminal acts actually result in a sentence being imposed (Ashworth, 2002). The high attrition rate within the criminal justice process is a result of the range of decisions and decision-makers involved in the lengthy process between an act being committed and an offender being sentenced. The mechanics of the criminal justice process means that there is a material difference between the social reality of crime and the cases which are completed with a sentence. Completed cases are shaped not simply by the offence or offenders but by the working practices and priorities of criminal justice personnel (Ashworth, 2002; Bottomley and Pease, 1986; Maguire, 2002). As Ashworth (2002) notes, this throws considerable doubt upon the efficiency with which crime can be tackled by changes in sentencing. In short, changes in sentences have little, if any, effect on the crime rate. Despite this, the sentencing process has an important social and symbolic function. It is a public display of the behaviour which society will and will not tolerate. It also enables the label 'offender' to be attached to people who are perceived to deserve it.

Sentencing can have severe and far-reaching effects on offenders. The consequences of punishment may be direct, such as the loss of liberty, money or time, or indirect. The indirect consequences of punishment may be wide-ranging and last long after the infliction of official punishment has ended. For example, prisoners may lose their job and home as a result of their sentence and often do not find employment when they return to the community. As a result, the infliction of punishment requires justification, which is the subject of the next section.

JUSTIFICATIONS FOR SENTENCING

There are two basic perspectives which are used to justify punishment, namely utilitarian and retributive. According to the utilitarian perspective, punishment is justified on the basis that it reduces the incidence of crime. Punishment is therefore useful. Its aim is to reduce the level of crime and is forward looking, as it takes note of possible future consequences. Conversely, the retributive perspective is primarily backward looking, concentrating solely on the criminal act which has been committed. According to this perspective, it is morally right to punish offenders. Offenders deserve to be punished and no other justification is necessary. Offenders have gained an unfair advantage over other members of society, and this has to be addressed through the imposition of punishment (see Chapter 1).

Utilitarian justifications

The utilitarian perspective encompasses a number of justifications, namely deterrence, incapacitation and rehabilitation, which will now be discussed in turn.

Deterrence

Deterrence is a common sense notion that people can be deterred from committing an offence because of the consequences. As Walker (1991: 13) notes, 'People are deterred from action when they refrain from them because they dislike what they believe to be the possible consequences of those actions'. People can be deterred for a number of reasons, including moral commitment and social disapproval, but in the context of sentencing we are particularly interested in the power of punishment to deter offending. According to deterrence, offenders are rational calculating individuals who weight up the costs and benefits of offending. If the costs (punishment) outweigh the benefits (rewards), then the offence will not be committed. It follows then that, in order to cut the incidence of a particular offence, the punishment would need to be increased. There is some debate about whether or not offenders undertake a rational calculation about whether or not to commit an offence. Certainly, the evidence that at least some offences are opportunistic or unplanned offences presents questions for deterrence theories (Bennett and Wright, 1984; Gill, 2000).

In order for deterrence to work effectively, there needs to be a hierarchy of punishment so that the more serious the offence, the more severe the punishment imposed. If this was not the case, then there would be nothing to deter offenders committing the most serious offences. For example, if the punishment for possessing a firearm was the same as for killing a person, there would be nothing to stop the offender from killing someone during an armed robbery as the punishment would be the same whatever the outcome. A hierarchy of punishment therefore offsets the potential gain to potential offenders of more serious criminal acts and as a consequence will deter them while protecting victims from more serious harm.

There are two types of deterrence: specific and general. Specific, also sometimes referred to as individual, deterrence occurs when individuals who have committed an offence are prevented from committing another offence by the punishment they have received. In other words, the experience of punishment has resulted in the individual deciding that the costs outweigh the benefits of offending. General deterrence is when the general population is prevented from offending due to an awareness of both the threat of punishment and the knowledge that particular individuals have been punished. So general deterrence involves calculating penalties on the basis of what might be expected to deter others from committing similar offences.

It is difficult to prove or disprove the existence of deterrence owing to a number of factors. The most important are the high level of hidden crime, which means that most offenders are not apprehended and punished, and the fact that it is hard to distinguish between the deterrent effects of punishment and other factors, such as situational factors, lifestyle and relationships with significant others. The high reconviction rates for offenders, which reaches over to 70 per cent for young offenders released from custody, also suggests that punishment is not a very efficient deterrent (Home Office, 2002a; 2003). Yet, there is some evidence that the total absence of a policing structure, such as during riots or wars, results in increased lawlessness, as we have recently seen in Iraq during the invasion (Beylevald, 1980; Christiansen, 1975).

Research has concentrated on the effect of the nature, severity or certainty of punishment on deterrence. In terms of the first two of these, important questions are whether or not community sentences deter offenders as much as imprisonment and whether or not increasing the level of punishment will decrease the incidence of particular offences. There is little methodologically sound work which answers these types of questions, but what evidence there is suggests that sentences would have to be increased dramatically in order to have a very small and insignificant effect on the crime rate (Brody and Tarling, 1980; Tarling, 1993) and that community sentences are as effective as imprisonment, at least in terms of reconviction rates (Lloyd et al, 1994). Evidence also suggests that offenders and the general public are poorly informed about the level of punishments and changes which are made to them (Hough and Roberts, 1998; Roberts, 2002). In terms of the certainty of punishment, research has been more fruitful. It suggests that the likelihood of detection is an important deterrent, but that it is the *perceived* likelihood rather than the actual likelihood of being caught which is most significant (Beylevald, 1978; 1980; von Hirsch et al, 1999).

Incapacitation

Incapacitation is also about preventing future offending. This is done by simple restraint which renders the offender incapable of offending. The most common form of incapacitation in the UK is custodial sentencing, although treatment centres and curfews enforced by electronic monitoring can also incapacitate offenders. Incapacitation is the least philosophically sound justification for punishment, but it is probably the most important to the public as it is perceived to be a way of protecting them from dangerous individuals. As Dunbar and Langdon (1998: 19) note, 'its simplicity and clarity of aim ... gives it great political potency'. Incapacitation is viewed as a cynical approach which fits squarely in the 'nothing works' camp, as there is no expectation that offenders can or will be reformed or rehabilitated through punishment. They are simply prevented from offending.

Selective incapacitation is what is usually meant when incapacitation is referred to. This means that only offenders who are identified as the most likely to reoffend or as the most dangerous are identified as requiring special incapacitative measures. In this way, incapacitation protects society from the most prolific and dangerous offenders. In order for this to be operationalised, offenders who are likely to cause serious harm in the future need to be identified. Consequently, incapacitation is very much linked to the prediction of dangerousness and risk to the public. According to von Hirsch (1984), three things are necessary for incapacitation to be effective: a definition of dangerousness, valid prediction methods and a known link between dangerousness and violence. In terms of the first of these, there is no agreed definition of dangerousness. The Floud Report (Floud and Young, 1981: 213) concluded that 'there was no such psychological or medical entity as a dangerous person. It is not an objective concept. Dangers are unacceptable risks ... Risk is, in principle, a matter of fact; but danger is a matter of judgement or opinion'.

There are similar problems in terms of valid prediction methods. Incapacitation involves predicting future behaviour. The usual technique for doing this is to study offenders' past offending history and their social and economic circumstances. Various studies (Greenwood, 1984; Tarling, 1993) have suggested that there is limited capacity to predict future offending. Evidence suggests that forecasts tend to over-predict. For example, the Floud Report (Floud and Young, 1981) concluded that predictions are more likely to be wrong than right. In addition, predictions tend to become self-fulfilling prophecies which result in more and more offenders being confined (von Hirsch, 1984). This occurs because erroneous confinements are concealed as those offenders wrongly identified as dangerous have no chance of demonstrating their trustworthiness, while a proportion of those released will go on to reoffend.

The direct link between violence and dangerousness which is often made has been criticised. Walker (1980), for example, notes that violence is often associated with specific situations, actions or activities rather than people. He cites the very low reconviction rate for murder in support of his arguments. Walker (1991) also states that incapacitation of serious offenders is only likely to make a small contribution to the prevention of crime because most serious offences are committed by one-off offenders. Again, he uses the example of murderers. Another important point to make about utilising a policy of incapacitation is that it may cause increasing practical problems. By locking more and more offenders up for long periods of time, prisons become costly warehouses. It is also true that most offenders have to be released at some point, and their successful reintegration into society becomes less likely the longer they are in prison because of the deterioration of their mental health, loss of community ties and general institutionalisation.

Rehabilitation

Rehabilitation aims to prevent further offending by reforming offenders' characters, thus 'curing' them of their criminal tendencies. Offenders are rehabilitated to return to society as law-abiding citizens. In essence, it is about changing offenders' personalities, outlook and habits so that they no longer commit crime. Rehabilitation is based on determinism. Individuals are not seen as rational, and crime is caused by something outside of their control. As a result, it is the individual rather than the offence which is the focus of attention for the criminal justice process. Ideas of rehabilitation are analogous to a medical model. In order to prevent crime, individuals must be treated. Experts from a range of disciplines, such as psychiatry and sociology, classify and diagnose the cause of offending behaviour and recommend the appropriate type and level of treatment required to 'cure' offenders. So sentences are tailored to individuals and the treatment deemed necessary for them, rather than to the nature or seriousness of the offence. There are no limits on the extent of intervention in offenders' lives.

The main tenets of rehabilitation are as follows. First, sentences should be individualised so that the type and level of punishment is tailored to the individual, not the offence. Secondly, sentences should be indeterminate so that release depends upon an individual's progress towards a cure. This means that release decisions are made by penal administrators and experts who have daily contact with prisoners, rather than by the judiciary. Thirdly, treatment programmes, which include group therapy, counselling and training, are available to all offenders. Fourthly, the most appropriate way of dealing with offenders is by using diagnosis, classification and treatment.

Rehabilitation was the predominant justification for punishment during most of the 20th century. It reached its height during the 1960s before falling into disrepute in the 1970s. Its popularity in the 1960s coincided with an optimism that the state could spend its way out of problems such as crime. At this time, rehabilitation was seen as humanitarian. However, this approach was increasing criticised and, by the middle of the 1970s, the rehabilitative ideal was in decline. A number of criticisms undermined its popularity and authority. First, and probably most importantly, Martinson (1974) published research which purported to show that 'nothing works'. Despite this being an exaggeration, the label stuck (Brody, 1976). Secondly, crime rates continued to rapidly increase despite the money being spent so that people started to question the state's ability to tackle crime. Rehabilitation started to be seen as a 'soft option', letting offenders off rather than punishing them. Thirdly, the use of indeterminate sentences was seen as unfair and mitigated against offenders' rights (Hudson, 1987; 1993). For example, offenders could play the system by presenting themselves as model prisoners simply to secure their release, so it was those who conformed, rather than the reformed, who were released. Indeterminate sentences also resulted in unjust disparities in sentencing and gave the authorities unfettered power over the release of individuals which could be abused. Prisoners felt obliged to take part in any treatment they were offered, including the taking of drugs, and the fear that their release would be prevented or delayed reduced their propensity to complain. Fourthly, it was felt that the criminal justice process was being brought into disrepute because of the discretion which it gave to professionals and experts, whose knowledge base was sometimes questionable, which resulted in disparities in sentences and possible discrimination.

Together, the criticisms of rehabilitation were persuasive and led to its demise. However, a number of points in its defence need to be made. First, it is argued that many of the main ideas of rehabilitation including the treatment programmes were never fully implemented and that evaluations of the programmes which were put in place were only partial (Cullen and Gilbert, 1982; Hudson, 1987). Secondly, Martinson's (1974) study and others which purported to demonstrate that 'nothing works' have been criticised due to the methodologies that were used (see Brody, 1976). There is now a consensus of opinion that some forms of treatment do work for certain offenders (Crow, 2001; Raynor, 2002). This has spawned a large body of research into 'what works' (McGuire and Priestley, 1995; Raynor, 2002). This research basically shows that treatment can be effective if it is properly targeted and delivered as intended (Crow, 2001).

Retributive justifications

The other main justification for punishment is retributive. This differs from utilitarian perspective in that it is backward looking. As we have seen, according to the retributive perspective, punishment is a natural and appropriate response to crime. Retribution concentrates solely on the offence. This justification replaced the vacuum left by the decline of rehabilitation and, in essence, can be seen as the antithesis to rehabilitation. Retribution has been dominant rationale for sentencing in recent years under the guise of 'just deserts'.

According to just deserts theory, the punishment an offender receives is linked to the offence, not the offender. The central tenet of just deserts is proportionality, where the sentence received is proportional to the seriousness of the offence. Thus, the more serious the offence, the more severe the punishment. Sentences are, fundamentally, statements of the gravity of the offence. It is argued that this produces consistent sentencing and means that punishment is fixed by events, rather than personalities, and by known past events, not the anticipated future. The seriousness of the offence is measured in two ways – by the harm done by the act and the offender's blameworthiness or culpability. Although this approach deals with many of the criticisms of a system based on rehabilitation, it does raise its own problems. First, it treats everyone the same, which itself can result in injustice and discrimination as all offenders are clearly not the same (Ashworth and Player, 1998). Differences in individual offenders arising from sex, age, income and so on mean that the same penalties inflict different levels of severity. For example, a £100 fine would mean very different levels of deprivation to someone on income support than to someone earning £40,000 per year. Secondly, it is practically impossible to measure the harm caused by offences, and the level of harm will depend on who the victim is. For example, the theft of £100 from the two people above will have very different consequences for them. Finally, just deserts theory ignores the unintended consequences of sentences such as the loss of employment or accommodation and the effect on the offenders' family. According to Walker (1991), this means that the totality of the sentence and the suffering involved may exceed that which is intended. In short, the incidental punishment involved in sentences varies from one offender to another and therefore defeats the ideal of proportionality.

REPARATION

Another increasingly important principle in sentencing is reparation. This involves the offender repairing the damage caused by the offender. The idea behind reparation is not only to redress the balance between the offender and society, but also to make offenders aware of the harm they have caused and, therefore, to acknowledge their law-breaking behaviour (Cavadino and Dignan, 2002). It is believed that, if offenders are forced to come face to face with the consequences of their actions, they will see the error of their ways.

Reparation may be made to the actual victim of the offence or to society as a whole. Reparation is an important component of community punishment orders (formerly community service orders) where punishment in the form of unpaid work in the community is designed to pay back the community. Reparation also forms an integral part of restorative justice. Restorative justice has become an important element in criminal justice in recent years, especially for young offenders (Crawford and Newburn, 2003). As Crawford and Newburn (2003) note, restorative justice means different things to different people, which makes it difficult to define. However, Cavadino and Dignan (2002: 45) provide a useful starting point when they write that restorative justice aims 'to restore and repair damaged relations between offenders, victims and the community as a whole' (Cavadino and Dignan, 2002: 45).

SENTENCING POLICY

We have seen in the last section that there are a number of different ways in which the imposition of sentences may be justified. We have also seen that different justifications predominate at different times. However, one of the features of sentencing policy is that it draws on more than one justification at any one time. In other words, sentencing policy does not have one coherent goal. It has also been noted that sentencing legislation in England and Wales has developed in a piecemeal fashion without an overall plan (Ashworth, 2002; Thomas, 2003). As a consequence, legislation relating to sentencing has no coherence. Sentences for particular offences are fixed at different times and circumstances without reference to other sentences.

Legislative changes relating to sentencing are constantly taking place, partly because of its high profile and political sensitivity. Every session of Parliament has at least one crime-related bill to enact and nearly all of these contain changes to the sentencing process. A detailed outline of such changes will not be attempted here, but the following section will give a general flavour of the trends in sentencing policy in recent years.

An overriding concern of sentencing policy over the last two decades or so has been to mediate between two contradictory pressures. On the one hand, the prison population has exploded, and successive governments have attempted to stabilise or reduce it, mainly due to the lack of space in the prison estate and the cost of housing high numbers of prisoners. Consequently, new provisions have been introduced in an attempt to reduce the prison population. These have included new community penalties, such as electronically monitored curfew orders, the toughening up of community sentences in an attempt to increase their use and changes to schemes which allow prisoners to be released early from prison, such as the introduction of the home detention curfews. On the other hand, because of high crime rates, public concerns about crime and the requirement for governments to be seen to be tackling the problem of crime, governments have needed to ensure that they are not open to the accusation of being 'soft on crime' by punishing offenders in the community rather than prison. Any explicit move to reduce the numbers of offenders being sent to prison or enabling them to be released early could, and often does, leave them open to this allegation. Managing these competing objectives has resulted in two sentencing policies running alongside each other which deal with different groups of offenders. This is called 'bifurcation' (Bottoms, 1983). In the context of sentencing, this means that serious and persistent offenders are sentenced to longer terms of imprisonment enabling governments to be seen to protect the public from dangerous and persistent offenders, while 'run of the mill', less serious offenders are diverted from prison and subjected to financial or community penalties.

The Criminal Justice Act 1991 attempted for the first time to provide a coherent sentencing framework and epitomises a bifurcatory approach. The ethos of the Act was to reduce the use of custody so that a larger proportion of offenders would be punished in the community. To this end, the main parts of the Act were based on the just deserts principles. Accordingly, the sentence imposed was to be proportional to the seriousness of the offence. However, this overall rationale was undermined by the inclusion of a section which allowed longer sentences, based on deterrence and incapacitative principles, to be imposed for certain serious offenders who committed violent and sexual offences. The Act was heralded as a landmark piece of legislation by some, but sentencers were very unhappy with some of the provisions and with the restrictions on their discretion which the Act imposed. Consequently, many of its provisions were repealed by the Criminal Justice Act 1993, which dismantled the coherent sentencing policy, albeit with exceptions, of the 1991 Act.

1993 also saw the murder of James Bulger by two 10-year-old boys. The shock and outrage which followed contributed to a radical change in the direction of criminal justice policy, generally, and sentencing policy, in particular. The then Home Secretary, Michael Howard, gave his infamous 'prison works' speech, which signalled an end to explicit attempts to divert offenders away from prison and the consensus which underpinned the Criminal Justice Act 1991 that prison only 'makes bad people worse'. This was replaced by a general assumption that prison was the only and correct way to deal with offenders, particularly those who committed serious offences or who persistently offended. Public protection became the primary rationale for sentencing, making incapacitation the principal justification for punishment. Since this time, sentencing policy has focused on longer and tougher sentences for offenders who pose a threat to the public either because of the seriousness or persistency of their offending and is epitomised by the 'two strikes and you're out' provisions of the Crime (Sentences) Act 1997. Alongside this policy, the Government has also been toughening up community sentences. This has not only made them more palatable to sentencers so that they might use them more often, but also increases the deterrence and incapacitative effects of the sentences by ensuring that they are more restrictive and that compliance is monitored more closely. At the time of writing, these policies have resulted in the highest prison population ever, which is predicted to rise still further (Home Office, 2002a).

SENTENCING PRACTICE

Different sentences prioritise different justifications so that sentencers may use different justifications for individual offenders. This results in what Ashworth (2002) terms a 'cafeteria style' of sentencing, where the sentencing process has no one aim and sentencers can pick and mix whichever sentence they believe is most appropriate for the individual case. The lack of coherent sentencing principles gives sentencers wide discretionary powers. Initiatives which aim to curtail sentencers' discretion flounder as they are able to argue that sentencing is an 'art not a science' which cannot conform to guidelines and rules and regulations about what they should do in individual cases (Walker and Padfield, 1996: 15).

The wide discretionary powers of sentencers are enhanced by a number of other factors which will now be discussed. Firstly, the UK has a tradition of only laying down maximum sentences in legislation. So, for example, the only legislative guidance for the offence of theft is that it carries a maximum sentence of seven years, yet theft covers a wide range of offences in terms of seriousness, from theft of a Mars bar to millions of pounds. Secondly, sentencers have a wide range of sentences to use below the maximum set out in the legislation, which is usually quoted in terms of imprisonment and/or a fine. Available sentences can be grouped into three main categories, namely imprisonment, community sentences (community punishment orders, community rehabilitation orders, and community punishment and rehabilitation orders) and fines and discharges. Sentencers in magistrates' courts have restrictions on their sentencing powers (currently a maximum of six months' imprisonment for each offence up to a total of 12 months and/or a £5,000 fine), but no such restrictions exist in the Crown Court, enabling judges to select sentences from a very broad range. Finally, the UK has a strong tradition of judicial independence (Cavadino and Dignan, 2002). It is important for any democratic society to have a separation of powers between the judiciary and the legislative, but it has meant that successive government plans to change sentencing policy have been undermined by judicial opposition. Battles between governments and the judiciary about sentencing policy perennially occur (see Dunbar and Langdon, 1998, for example). The most notorious example of this was when the Conservative Government was forced to undertake a complete U-turn and undermine its attempt to set out a clear and coherent sentencing policy in the Criminal Justice Act 1991. Sentencers opposed the Act because they believed that it reduced their discretion (see Ashworth, 2002). In order to try and have more control over sentencing decisions, governments have recently started to impose minimum sentences for certain offences. Despite judicial opposition to these, a number have been implemented, most notably under the Crime (Sentences) Act 1997. This Act imposes mandatory minimum sentences for several groups of repeat offenders, including drug offenders and residential burglars, and also introduced an automatic life sentence for repeated grave offences such as murder and manslaughter.

Despite government attempts to harness sentencers' discretion by the introduction of minimum sentences, guidelines and so on, sentencers still have an enormous amount of discretion about which sentence to impose in each individual case. Discretion, of course, can be positive (Gelsthorpe and Padfield, 2003): for example, it enables sentences to be reduced if there are particular reasons for it and it prevents unjust sentences being imposed. Generally, however, discretion has two negative consequences which are of great concern. First is what has been termed 'justice by geography', in other words, the sentence you receive depends on which court you appear in rather than what you have done. As a result, offenders who have committed similar offences are given different sentences. Evidence for this is widespread (Cavadino and Dignan, 2002; Moxon and Hedderman, 1994). 'Justice by geography' is produced partly because of the existence of 'bench cultures'. This refers to magistrates basing their decisions not simply on their own views and opinions but on what they believe is expected of them from their fellow magistrates in their particular court (Parker et al, 1989; Rumgay, 1995; Hucklesby, 1997). Numerous studies have found evidence of the existence of 'court cultures', which refers to the informal rules and norms mediated through social relationships between court participants. Court cultures help to explain differences in practices and decisions made by courts but also why the impact of legal and policy changes in often contrary to what is expected (Church, 1982; 1985; Eisenstein and Jacob, 1977; Hucklesby, 1997; Lipetz, 1980; Rumgay, 1995).

The second consequence is discrimination on the grounds of ethnic origin, class or gender (Hudson, 1998). There is a mass of evidence that men and women are treated differently by courts, but it is not clear whether or not this differential treatment results in more or less lenient sentences for women than men (Hedderman and Gelsthorpe, 1997; Heidensohn, 1996; Morris, 1987). There is also evidence that some ethnic minority groups are treated differently during the sentencing process (Hood, 1992). Black offenders are certainly over-represented in the prison population, and this appears to be as a result of an accumulation of factors which arise as they move through the criminal justice process, which involves both direct and indirect discrimination (Bowling and Phillips, 2002; Cavadino and Dignan, 2002; Hood, 1992).

A number of initiatives have tried to reduce discretion and therefore increase consistency in sentencing. First, sentencing guidelines were issued to magistrates but these have no statutory footing and can be simply ignored. Secondly, the Court of Appeal issues guideline judgments. These give general guidance about the normal range of sentencing for a range of connotations for a particular offence. These are useful for the offence in question but do not create consistency between offences or, in general, deal with 'run of the mill' offences, which make up the majority of the business in magistrates' courts (Ashworth, 2002). Thirdly, in some states in the USA, most notably Minnesota, strict sentencing guidelines in the form of a sentencing grid have been introduced. This means that the appropriate sentence is calculated according to preset factors which reduces the discretion of sentencers to an absolute minimum. Fourthly, the Crime and Disorder Act 1998 created the Sentencing Advisory Council. This is an independent body with an advisory and consultative remit to promote consistency in sentencing. More specifically, its role is to provide guidance to the Court of Appeal on sentencing guidelines. While this is an important initiative, the Council only has an advisory role; it is up to the Court of Appeal whether or not to act upon its advice. The Council falls short of a Sentencing Council, which many believe to be the most appropriate way of dealing with inconsistencies within the sentencing process (Ashworth, 2002; Cavadino and Dignan, 2002). The creation of the Sentencing Guidelines Council by the Criminal Justice Act 2003 goes some way to meeting these concerns. The Council will be chaired by the Lord Chief Justice and will include judicial and non-judicial members. According to official sources, it will provide guidelines for particular offenders, offences and other matters related to sentencing. Its aim is to promote consistency, but it is also required to consider cost and promote public confidence.

CONCLUSION

This chapter has introduced some of the contemporary issues and controversies relating to the court and sentencing process. It has highlighted that what happens to defendants who appear in court is often less about what they have done and more to do with which court they appear in and who they are. In addition, there are fundamental issues with the composition of the magistracy and judiciary, who are mainly drawn from sections of society far removed from those of most defendants/offenders. There is a particular issue with the work of District Judges (magistrates' courts), who sit alone and make judgments about the admissibility of evidence, guilt or innocence and sentence.

Sentencing has important symbolic and political functions, but has little impact on the crime rate due to the attrition rate within the criminal justice process. Its political significance results in periodic attempts by governments to harness the independence of the judiciary by imposing restrictions on its discretion. To date, these have been largely unsuccessful, but successive governments seem focused on achieving greater control over how people are sentenced. Recently, the Government has adopted the strategy of imposing minimum sentences, but even these provide 'get out' clauses which enable sentencers to get around imposing the minimum sentence. What this does mean is that sentencers can resist government policy, whether they see it as too harsh or too lenient. The ethicality of sentencers doing this is one of the most enduring debates within criminal justice. On the one hand, sentencers' reliance on imprisonment and their lack of faith in community sentences as tough alternatives to custody have contributed to the expediential rise in the prison population so that it now stands at the highest ever figure and means that the UK imprisons more offenders per head of population than any other European country (Home Office, 2002c; 2002d). On the other, governments' attempts to control the prison population through sentencing policy have largely failed due to the ability of sentencers to impose the sentences they see fit and to ignore sentencing guidance.

The final question which this chapter has addressed is: 'what are the aims of sentencing?' Should the objective of sentences be to rehabilitate, deter, incapacitate or simply punish offenders? While incapacitation and simple punishment may seem like the best short-term solutions, as offenders are seen to be punished and may be locked away for long periods of time, the long-term benefits are limited, as the vast majority of offenders return to society. It is within this context that it would seem better for sentences to attempt to address some of the underlying problems faced by offenders, rather than simply confining them until they are released back into society in a potentially worse situation than when they entered prison, with the consequence that they may be more likely to offend.

SEMINAR DISCUSSION TOPICS

- Should all sentences be imposed by professional, legally qualified judges?
- What are the advantages and disadvantages of each justification of punishment?
- Identify the main sources and consequences of sentencers' discretion.

- Should sentencers' discretion be curtailed?
- In what ways could sentencers' discretion be decreased?

KEY READINGS

There are numerous introductory overviews of processes of criminal justice, the most accessible being Newburn's *Crime and Criminal Justice Policy* (Longman, 1995; 2nd edn 2003); Cavadino and Dignan's *The Penal System: An Introduction* (Sage, 1992; 3rd edn 2002), Ashworth's chapter in *The Oxford Handbook of Criminology* (OUP, 3rd edn, 2002) and Ashworth's *The Criminal Process: An Evaluative Study* (OUP, 2nd edn, 1998). To keep up to date with the pace of legislative reform/debate, check the Criminal Justice Weblog on www.ukcjweblog.org.uk.

For further discussion of controversies surrounding race and sentencing and gender and sentencing, see Chapters 6, 7 and 9 of this volume. For more advanced study, a comprehensive analysis of all aspects of the criminal justice process is provided by McConville and Wilson's *The Handbook of the Criminal Justice Process* (OUP, 2002) and of particular relevance is the chapter by Darbyshire on magistrates. A comprehensive introduction to discretion in the criminal justice process is provided by the Introduction in Gelsthorpe and Padfield's *Exercising Discretion: Decision-Making in the Criminal Justice System and Beyond* (Willan, 2003).

REFERENCES

Ashworth, A (1998) *The Criminal Process: An Evaluative Study*, 2nd edn, Oxford: OUP.

Ashworth, A (2002) 'Sentencing' in Maguire, M, Morgan, R and Reiner, R (eds), *The Oxford Handbook of Criminology*, Oxford: OUP.

Ashworth, A and Player, E (1998) 'Sentencing, equal treatment and the impact of sanctions' in Ashworth, A and Wasik, M (eds), *Fundamentals of Sentencing Theory*, Oxford: Clarendon.

Baldwin, J (1976) 'The social composition of the magistracy', *British Journal of Criminology*, vol 16(2), pp 171–74.

Baldwin, J and McConville, M (1977) *Negotiated Justice*, Oxford: Martin Robertson.

Bennett, T and Wright, R (1984) *Burglars on Burglary*, Aldershot: Gower.

Beylevald, D (1978) *The Effectiveness of General Deterrents Against Crime: An Annotated Bibliography of Evaluative Research*, Cambridge: Institute of Criminology.

Beylevald, D (1980) *A Bibliography of General Deterrence Research*, London: Saxon House.

Bottomley, AK and Pease, K (1986) *Crime and Punishment: Interpreting the Data*, Milton Keynes: Open University Press.

Bottoms, AE (1983) 'Neglected features of contemporary penal systems' in Garland, D and Young, P (eds), *The Power to Punish*, London: Heinemann.

Bowling, B and Phillips, C (2002) *Racism, Crime and Justice*, Harlow: Longman.

Brody, S (1976) *The Effectiveness of Sentencing*, Home Office Research Study No 35, London: HMSO.

Brody, S and Tarling, R (1980) *Taking Offenders Out of Circulation*, Home Office Research Study No 64, London: HMSO.

Cavadino, M and Dignan, J (2002) *The Penal System: An Introduction*, London: Sage.

Christiansen, KO (1975) 'On general prevention from an empirical viewpoint' in National Swedish Council for Crime Prevention, *General Deterrence: A Conference on Current Research and Standpoints*, 2–4 June, Stockholm: National Swedish Council for Crime Prevention, pp 60–74.

Church Jr, T (1982) 'The "old and the new" conventional wisdom of court delay', *The Justice System Journal*, vol 7(3), pp 395–412.

Church Jr, T (1985) 'Examining local legal cultures', *American Bar Foundation Research Journal*, Summer, No 3, pp 449–518.

Crawford, A and Newburn, T (2003) *Youth Offending and Restorative Justice*, Cullompton: Willan.

Crow, I (2001) *The Treatment and Rehabilitation of Offenders*, London: Sage.

Cullen, F and Gilbert, K (1982) *Reaffirming Rehabilitation*, Cincinnati, OH: Anderson.

Darbyshire, P (1984) *The Magistrates' Clerk*, Chichester: Barry Rose.

Darbyshire, P (2002) 'Magistrates' in McConville, M and Wilson, G (eds), *The Handbook of the Criminal Justice Process*, Oxford: OUP.

Dignan, J and Whynne, A (1997) 'A microcosm of the local community?', *British Journal of Criminology*, vol 32(2), pp 184–97.

Doran, S (2002) 'Trial by jury' in McConville, M and Wilson, G (eds), *The Handbook of the Criminal Justice Process*, Oxford: OUP.

Dunbar, I and Langdon, A (1998) *Tough Justice: Sentencing and Penal Policies in the 1990s*, London: Blackstone.

Eisenstein, J and Jacob, H (1977) *Felony Justice*, Boston, MA: Little, Brown and Co.

Findley, M and Duff, P (eds) (1988) *The Jury Under Attack*, London: Butterworths.

Floud, J and Young, W (1981) *Dangerousness and Criminal Justice*, London: Heinemann.

Gelsthorpe, L and Padfield, N (2003) *Exercising Discretion: Decision-Making in the Criminal Justice System and Beyond*, Cullompton: Willan.

Gill, M (2000) *Commercial Robbery*, London: Blackstone.

Greenwood, P (1984) 'Selective incapacitation: a method of using our prisons more effectively', *NIJ Reports*, January, pp 4–7.

Hedderman, C and Gelsthorpe, L (1997) *Understanding the Sentencing of Women*, Home Office Research Study No 170, London: Home Office.

Heidensohn, F (1996) *Women and Crime*, 2nd edn, Basingstoke: Macmillan.

Home Office (2002a) *Criminal Statistics England and Wales 2001*, Cm 5696, London: Home Office.

Home Office (2002b) *Projections in Long Term Trends in the Prison Population to 2009*, Statistical Bulletin 14/02, London: Home Office.

Home Office (2002c) *The Prison Population in 2001: A Statistical Review*, Home Office Research Findings 195, London: Home Office.

Home Office (2002d) *World Population List*, Home Office Research Findings 188, London: Home Office.

Home Office (2003) *One Year Juvenile Reconviction Rates: First Quarter of 2001 Cohort*, RDS online publications 18/03, London: Home Office.

Hood, R (1992) *Race and Sentencing*, Oxford: OUP.

Hough, M and Roberts, J (1998) *Attitudes to Punishment: Findings from the British Crime Survey*, Home Office Research Study No 179, London: Home Office.

Hucklesby, A (1996) 'Bail or jail?: the practical operation of the Bail Act 1976', *Journal of Law and Society*, vol 23, p 213.

Hucklesby, A (1997) 'Court culture: an explanation of variations in the use of bail by magistrates' courts', *Howard Journal*, vol 36(2), pp 129–45.

Hucklesby, A (2002) 'Bail in Criminal Cases' in McConville, M and Wilson, G (eds), *The Handbook of the Criminal Justice Process*, Oxford: OUP.

Hudson, B (1987) *Justice Through Punishment: A Critique of the Justice Model of Corrections*, London: Macmillan.

Hudson, B (1993) *Penal Policy and Social Justice*, London: Macmillan.

Hudson, B (1998) 'Doing justice to difference' in Ashworth, A and Wasik, M (eds), *Fundamentals of Sentencing Theory*, Oxford: Clarendon.

Lipetz, M (1980) 'Routine and deviations: the strength of the courtroom workgroups in a misdemeanour court', *International Journal of the Sociology of Law*, vol 8(1), pp 47–60.

Lloyd, C, Mair, G and Hough, M (1994) *Explaining Reconviction Rates: A Critical Analysis*, Home Office Research Study No 136, London: Home Office.

Lord Chancellor's Department (2003) *Judicial Statistics*, March, available at www.dca.gov.uk.

McConville, M, Bridges, L and Pavlovic, A (1994) *Standing Accused*, Oxford: OUP.

McConville, M (2002) 'Plea bargaining' in McConville, M and Wilson, G (eds), *The Handbook of the Criminal Justice Process*, Oxford: OUP.

McGuire, J and Priestley, P (1995) 'Reviewing "what works": past, present and future' in McGuire, J (ed), *What Works: Reducing Reoffending*, Chichester: Wiley.

Maguire, M (2002) 'Crime statistics: the "data explosion" and its implications' in Maguire, M, Morgan, R and Reiner, R (eds), *The Oxford Handbook of Criminology*, Oxford: OUP.

Martinson, R (1974) 'What works? – questions and answers about prison reform', *The Public Interest*, vol 35, Spring, pp 22–54.

Morgan, R and Russell, N (2000) *The Judiciary in the Magistrates' Courts*, London: Home Office and Lord Chancellor's Department.

Morris, A (1987) *Women, Crime and Criminal Justice*, London: Basil Blackwell.

Moxon, D and Hedderman, C (1994) 'Mode of trial decisions and sentencing between courts', *Howard Journal*, vol 33, pp 97–108.

Narey, M (1997) *Review of Delay in the Criminal Justice System*, London: Home Office.

Newburn, T (1995) *Criminal and Criminal Justice Policy*, Harlow: Longman.

Parker, H, Sumner, M and Jarvis, G (1989) *Unmasking the Magistrates*, Milton Keynes: Open University Press.

Raine, J (1989) *Local Justice*, London: T & T Clark.

Raynor, P (2002) 'Community penalties' in Maguire, M, Morgan, R and Reiner, R (eds), *The Oxford Handbook of Criminology*, Oxford: OUP.

Roberts, J (2002) 'Public opinion and sentencing policy' in Rex, S and Tonry, M (eds), *Reform and Punishment: The Future of Sentencing*, Cullompton: Willan.

Rumgay, J (1995) 'Custodial decision making in a magistrates' court', *British Journal of Criminology*, vol 35(2), pp 201–17.

Sanders, A and Young, R (2001) *Criminal Justice*, 2nd edn, London: Butterworths.

Seago, P, Walker, C and Wall, D (1995) *The Role and Appointment of Stipendiary Magistrates*, Leeds: University of Leeds.

Seago, P, Walker, C and Wall, D (2000) 'The development of the professional magistracy in England and Wales', *Criminal Law Review*, pp 631–51.

Tarling, R (1993) *Analysing Offending: Data, Models and Interpretations*, London: HMSO.

Thomas, D (2003) 'Judicial discretion in sentencing' in Gelsthorpe, L and Padfield, N (eds), *Exercising Discretion: Decision Making in the Criminal Justice System and Beyond*, Cullompton: Willan.

von Hirsch, A (1984) 'The ethics of selective incapacitation: observations on the contemporary debate', *Crime and Delinquency*, vol 30, April, pp 175–94.

von Hirsch, A, Bottoms, AE, Burney, E and Wikstrom, P (1999) *Criminal Deterrence: An Analysis of Recent Research*, Oxford: Hart.

Walker, N (1980) *Punishment, Danger and Stigma: The Morality of Criminal Justice*, Oxford: Basil Blackwell.

Walker, N (1991) *Why Punish?*, Oxford: OUP.

Walker, N and Padfield, N (1996) *Sentencing – Theory, Law and Practice*, London: Butterworths.

CHAPTER 15

YOUTH CRIME AND YOUTH JUSTICE

Barry Goldson

SUMMARY

This chapter will aim to provide a critical overview of contemporary patterns of youth crime and key developments in youth justice law, policy and practice. Although 'official' statistics do not appear to indicate that youth crime is significantly increasing in scope and/or severity, recent policy and practice responses to 'young offenders' have taken a markedly punitive turn. In order to account for this apparent anomaly, it will be argued that the politics of youth crime and youth justice, derived from constructions of 'fear' and 'panic', are once again distorting popular conceptualisations and formalised responses.

KEY TERMS

Respectable fears; moral panics; welfare; justice; informalism; rights; responsibilities; retribution and punishment; hybridity; the politics of youth justice; intervention; custodial detention; critique.

YOUTH CRIME

Youth crime is one of the great preoccupations of late modernity. It appears to attract sustained and high profile attention from politicians, the media and the public. Indeed, the notions that youth crime is a uniquely modern phenomenon, that 'it wasn't like this in our day', and that 'things are getting worse', are not uncommon. Such belief is aptly captured by the popular phrase: 'the trouble with kids today' (Muncie, 1984). In actual fact, however, youth crime, and the anxieties and fears that it might induce, has a long history. The widely-held belief that youth crime is associated with a contemporary breakdown in law and order, a modern wave of indiscipline and lawlessness, is just as erroneous therefore as the impression that it is becoming increasingly more serious and commonplace.

'RESPECTABLE FEARS' AND 'MORAL PANICS'

Geoffrey Pearson (1983) has chronicled the prevalence of what he calls 'respectable fears' in relation to delinquency, disorder and youth crime from the time of pre-industrial 17th century England. Moreover, he illustrates the way in which more recognisably 'modern' concerns about 'juvenile delinquents' and 'young offenders' emerged at the beginning of the industrial revolution, continuing to consolidate throughout the 19th century. The term 'yob', for example, derives from the late 19th century as backslang for boy, and the word 'hooligan' also appeared around the same time. Both expressions were widely used to describe young members of street gangs in the new urban centres and developing cities of industrial Britain. In charting history in this way, Pearson helps us to understand that the idea of a past 'golden age', whereby the 'British way of life' is characterised in terms of undisturbed 'law and order', is actually a 'myth'. Indeed, many other criminologists, sociologists and social historians have also observed that youth crime, and the respectable fears that it tends to elicit, far from being a distinctive hallmark of modern times, has a much longer history (see, for example, Cox and Shore, 2002; Gillis, 1974; Hendrick, 2003).

Youth crime is more accurately conceived therefore as a perennial feature of post-industrial society, rather than a present day aberration. However, it is equally true, as Stan Cohen (1972: 9) famously noted, that 'societies appear to be subject, every now and then, to periods of moral panic [when] a condition, episode, person or group of persons emerges to become defined as a threat to societal values and interests' (see Chapter 5). In recent history, young people's involvement in episodes of public disorder and/or crime have tended to comprise primary focal points for such 'moral panics'. In this way, the 'mods' and 'rockers' of the 1960s (Cohen, 1972), the 'street muggers' (Hall et al, 1978) and 'football hooligans' (Hall, 1978) of the 1970s, and the 'bail bandits' and 'persistent young offenders' of the 1990s (Goldson, 1997) have each been 'demonised' and 'folk devilled' within populist discourses of moral panic. In such cases, the processes are essentially the same: 'new social problems' are 'created' and then 'amplified' by the media; respectable fears are mobilised; and those who are held responsible – the 'demons' and 'folk devils' – are subjected to withering criticism. More significantly perhaps, public anxiety and political calculation demand that 'something must be done about it'.

We shall consider the most recent expressions of respectable fears and moral panics later in this chapter. However, for now, two points are particularly noteworthy. First, a general public ambivalence to identifiable constituencies of young people is seen to be constant throughout history. Secondly, the anxieties that are 'created' and 'amplified' specifically by moral panics, and more generally by sustained media coverage, tend to distort our understanding of the depth and scope of youth crime.

OFFENDING, OFFENCES AND OFFENDERS

Analyses of official statistics and research evidence, and the insights that can be drawn from the practice of youth justice, can provide a more accurate picture of youth crime and young offenders.

Offending

Self-report studies tend to indicate that offending is a relatively 'normal' part of growing up for the majority of young people (Graham and Bowling, 1995). In a recent study, Claire Flood-Page and her colleagues (2000) reported that 60 per cent of boys aged 16–17 admitted having committed a criminal offence. Moreover, it is widely acknowledged that the 'peak age' for known offending is 18 and 15 for males and females respectively.

Notwithstanding this, and contrary to popular belief, it is important to note that children and young people are *not* responsible for the majority of recorded and detected crimes. During 2001, for example, almost 88 per cent of detected crime was committed by adults (NACRO, 2003a). Perhaps more significantly, the incidence of youth crime appears to be in decline when measured over the last decade or so. Thus, official statistics indicate that between 1992 and 2001, the number of 10–17-year-olds cautioned or convicted of indictable offences fell by 21 per cent from 143,600 to 113,800 (Home Office, 2002). It is also clear that such decline is not simply attributable to demographic changes (that is, fewer children and young people in the overall population), as it is also expressed in proportionate terms. In other words, the number of children and young people per 100,000 of the population cautioned, reprimanded, warned or convicted of an indictable offence fell from 2,673 in 1992 to 1,927 in 2001 (Home Office, 2002). Whilst it is always necessary to exercise some care in reading and analysing official crime statistics, these figures certainly appear to challenge populist constructions of contemporary youth crime.

Offences

In the same way that the incidence of youth crime tends to be 'amplified', so too is its gravity and seriousness. The common emphasis on violent offences against the person is fundamentally misleading. Most offences committed by children and young people are directed against property. In 2001, theft, handling stolen goods, burglary, fraud or forgery and criminal damage accounted for 66 per cent of recorded youth crime. Furthermore, those offences generally regarded as the least serious, that is, theft and handling stolen goods, comprised almost half of all offences committed by children and young people (Home Office, 2002). In actual fact, violent offences against the person account for less than 14 per cent, and robbery for only 2.4 per cent, of all offences for which children and young people are responsible. Moreover, it is important to place 'robbery' in context, as a significant proportion of such offences involve taking mobile telephones from other children and young people (Harrington and Mayhew, 2001).

Indeed, this latter point is significant in terms of introducing two further qualifying observations. First, the victims of youth crime are often other children and young people, and it is not uncommon for 'offenders' to be 'victims' too. The Howard League for Penal Reform (2002) has noted that 'children have complicated lives, and involvement in largely low level crime is part of the growing up process, whether as victim, perpetrator or both'. Secondly, the risk of being a victim of youth crime is not evenly distributed, and most youth crime is situated in poor neighbourhoods and communities (Simmons, 2002), the very places where young offenders predominantly live. Conversely, middle class, middle England is a comparatively safe enclosure.

Offenders

Young offenders are normally male. Over the last 10 years, boys consistently account for almost 80 per cent of detected youth crime, and the available data does not bear out the common perception that girls are becoming significantly more inclined to offend (NACRO, 2003a). Boys are not only responsible for most youth crime, but they also tend to commit more serious offences. Turning to the question of ethnicity, black children and young people are no more likely than their white counterparts to commit offences (Graham and Bowling, 1995). Bearing these points in mind, the disproportionate increase in custodial sentencing in relation to girls over boys (NACRO, 2003b), and the massive over-representation of black children and young people at every discrete point of the youth justice system (Goldson and Chigwada-Bailey, 1999), is anomalous. Indeed, such phenomena are more indicative of the intrinsic gendered and racialised injustices of the youth 'justice' process than they are of the offending proclivities of any identifiable group of children and young people.

Alongside gender and 'race', social class comprises an important lens through which youth crime and youth justice can be examined. Youth justice systems, however they are nuanced, characteristically process working class youth. This is not to suggest that all working class children commit crime, or that only working class children offend, but the connections between class, poverty, inequality and associated forms of social adversity on the one hand, and state intervention through youth justice systems on the other, are well-established. It is no coincidence that complex and layered patterns of disadvantage (including formal child welfare and social services intervention; fractured and impoverished families who have buckled under interminable pressure; neighbourhoods beset with multiple forms of deprivation; disrupted, incomplete, unhappy and relatively unproductive school careers; unemployment, boredom and alienation; and health-related problems not infrequently related to alcohol and drug misuse) normally comprise the lived realities of children and young people in conflict with the law. Indeed, such 'young offenders' can just as readily be conceptualised as 'children in need', and in many senses the means by which state agencies and youth justice systems respond to them comprise an important touchstone of society's regard for its youngest – and often most disadvantaged – citizens, for human rights and for the wider social justice project (Goldson, 2002a).

YOUTH JUSTICE

There is significant variation in youth justice systems across the world, and formal responses to 'young offenders' fluctuate from country to country (Muncie, 2003; Muncie, 2004). In this sense, 'justice' is differentiated in accordance with cultural and jurisdictional specificities. Differential justice is not only evident within the wider global context, however; it is also present within the UK itself. Indeed, the three separate jurisdictions (England and Wales, Scotland and Northern Ireland) have produced – to a greater or lesser extent – quite distinctive approaches to the general governance of children and, more particularly, to the management of youth justice. Moreover, recent political developments in relation to devolution have meant that the potential for further differentiation has significantly increased (Goldson, 2004a). In a chapter such as this, however, it is not possible to engage with the detail of comparative analysis. The emphasis here, therefore, will lie with the youth justice system in England and Wales.

THEMATIC CONCEPTS

Since the 'invention' of 'juvenile delinquency' in the 19th century, and the subsequent inception of a specific corpus of legislation, court structures, policies, procedures and practices for the processing of 'young offenders' at the beginning of the 20th century, youth justice has been beset by tension and complexity (Goldson, 2002b). John Muncie and Gordon Hughes (2002: 1) have reflected that 'youth justice is a history of conflict, contradictions, ambiguity and compromise ... [it] tends to act on an amalgam of rationales, oscillating around and beyond the caring ethos of social services and the neo-liberal legalistic ethos of responsibility and punishment'. Furthermore, the balance that is struck between the 'caring' and the 'punitive' dimensions of the system is subject to the vagaries of political imperative and policy contingency. In short, youth justice systems are dynamic and ever-changing sites of contestation and change, the settlements of competing and/or intersecting thematic concepts. Six such concepts are particularly significant for our purposes here: 'welfare'; 'justice'; 'informalism'; 'rights'; 'responsibilities' and 'retribution/punishment'.

Welfare

The principle that children and young people should be protected from the full weight of the 'adult' criminal jurisdiction underpins the concept of welfare in youth justice, and is long-established in law. Section 44 of the Children and Young Persons Act 1933 provides that: '*every court* in dealing with a child or young person who is brought before it either as an offender or otherwise shall *have regard to* the *welfare* of the child or young person.' Similarly, s 1(1) of the Children Act 1989 states that: 'when a court determines *any question* with respect to [a child] ... the child's *welfare* shall be the court's *paramount consideration*.' Bearing in mind the point that has been made in terms of the disadvantaged circumstances of most 'young offenders', the welfare principle is particularly salient.

The 1960s and 1970s marked the 'high water mark' of welfare in youth justice in England and Wales (Blagg and Smith, 1989). The Children and Young Persons Acts 1963 and 1969 were introduced either side of two overtly welfarist White Papers: *The Child, the Family and the Young Offender* (1965) and *Children in Trouble* (1968). Taken together, such developments in law and policy introduced a range of welfare-based reforms and practices into youth justice which matured throughout the decade of the 1970s (for a more detailed discussion, see Goldson, 2002b).

Towards the end of the 1970s, and into the 1980s, the welfarist priorities of youth justice attracted critique on three principal fronts, however. First, conservative critics argued that the primary function of the youth justice system should be to *control* young offenders, rather than to *care* for them. The concept of welfare was thus regarded as evidence that the youth justice system had become too lenient and 'soft on crime'. Secondly, academic commentators and radical youth justice practitioners questioned the legitimacy of imposing wide-ranging interventions on the basis of 'need' and challenged individualised notions of 'rehabilitation' and 'treatment'. They argued that channelling ostensibly 'welfare' interventions through a youth justice system often produced 'more harm than good' (Thorpe et al, 1980). Thirdly, the same academics and radical practitioners, together with rights advocates and legal professionals, also argued that wide-ranging discretionary judgments in respect of 'welfare' undermined the child's *right* to 'justice'.

Justice

Central to the concept of justice (in respect of youth justice) is the proposal that the intensity of formal intervention should be proportionate to the severity/gravity of the offence, rather than the level of perceived 'need'. This principle derives from a classical justice formula comprising due process and proportionality. The practical application of the justice principle has three primary implications. First, it is claimed that the legal rights of children and young people must be secured and safeguarded through due legal process by professional representation and the engagement of lawyers. Secondly, formal intervention is conceived in terms of 'restrictions of liberty' that must be limited to the minimum necessary, in accordance with principles of proportionality. Thirdly, custodial sentencing should be strictly reserved for the most serious offences for which no other sentence is considered to be justified. Such justice-based priorities effectively prevailed in England and Wales from the early 1980s to the early 1990s, and they were statutorily expressed through the Criminal Justice Acts of 1982, 1988 and 1991 (for a fuller discussion, see Goldson, 2002b).

Informalism

Informalism is underpinned by a range of theoretical perspectives, practical propositions and 'destructuring impulses' (Cohen, 1985) that combine to challenge the legitimacy of *all* youth justice systems. Informalist perspectives fundamentally question formal intervention, claiming that youth justice processes essentially stigmatise children and young people by applying criminogenic 'labels'. Such 'labelling' is not evenly applied by state agencies and, as we noted earlier, girls, working class and black children and young people are particularly susceptible. Furthermore, labelling triggers negative 'social reaction' which, in turn, has enduring and spiralling consequences (Becker, 1963). In this way, it is argued that formal intervention and labelling 'creates' (or at least consolidates and confirms) criminogenic 'identities' for specific constituencies of disadvantaged children that, once established, tend to produce further offending. This led Edwin Lemert (1967) to conclude that 'social control leads to deviance' and David Matza (1969: 80) to comment on the 'irony' and self-defeating nature of formal interventions: 'the very effort to prevent, intervene, arrest and "cure" persons ... precipitate or seriously aggravate the tendency society wishes to guard against.' In short, informalism shifts the conceptual emphasis by problematising the formal legal and disciplinary apparatus of youth justice, as distinct from the 'young offender' (Goldson, 2004b). Although informalism has never been fully 'formalised' within the youth justice system in England and Wales, some of its core claims have influenced justice-based approaches as outlined above.

Rights

We have touched already on the question of formal legal rights for children and young people in the youth justice system. In addition to the rights provided by domestic statute (including the Human Rights Act 1998), there are a range of international conventions, standards, treaties and rules that inform youth justice policy and practice. Particularly notable in this respect are: the United Nations Standard Minimum Rules for the Administration of Juvenile Justice (the Beijing Rules, 1985); the United Nations Guidelines for the Prevention of Juvenile Delinquency (the Riyadh Guidelines, 1990); and the United Nations Rules for the Protection of Juveniles Deprived of their Liberty (the JDL Rules, 1990). Perhaps most important of all is the United Nations Convention on the Rights of the Child (UNCRC, 1989), which sets out principles and detailed standards for the rights of children, for the care of children, for laws, policies and practices which impact on children, and for both formal and informal relationships with children. With some exceptions – perhaps most notably the USA – the UNCRC has been accepted more quickly and more comprehensively than any other international convention in history, and the UK Government ratified it in 1991. Some commentators have argued that children's human rights should be safeguarded within youth justice systems (see, for example, Scraton and Haydon, 2002). More significantly perhaps, the United Nations Committee on the Rights of the Child, which is based in Geneva, periodically assesses the extent to which laws, policies and practices are consistent with the provisions of the UNCRC, and we shall return to this point towards the end of the chapter.

Responsibilities

Just as welfare is tempered by justice, and vice versa, so rights are mitigated by responsibilities. The concept of responsibility is most clearly expressed in youth justice with regard to the age of criminal minority, otherwise known as the age of criminal responsibility. This relates to the age at which a child is held to be fully accountable in criminal law: the point when a child's act of transgression can be formally processed as a 'crime'. We have noted already that youth justice systems vary across the world, and there are significant differences in the age at which children and young people are deemed to be criminally responsible (Muncie, 2003; Muncie, 2004). In England and Wales, the age of criminal responsibility is set at 10 years old. Many commentators have argued that it is perverse to hold a child as young as 10 to be as legally responsible as an adult, and in this sense criminal law is clearly inconsistent with civil statute (see, for example, Bandalli, 2000). The contested question of responsibility is complicated further in modern youth justice by the fact that parents can also be held to be formally responsible for their children's behaviour (Goldson and Jamieson, 2002). Notwithstanding critique, constructions of child and/or parental responsibility – moral obligation and civic duty – have made a significant impact on policy formation and practice development in contemporary youth justice.

Retribution and punishment

Throughout the history of youth justice, and despite the varying configurations that youth justice systems have taken, retribution has been ever present, and the state has always reserved the power to punish. Ultimately, retribution and punishment is expressed through the practices of institutional containment. Since the establishment of the first penal institution exclusively for children at Parkhurst Prison for Boys in 1838, an array of policy initiatives, legal developments and carceral experiments have created and sustained a panoply of institutional forms: the *reformatories* and *industrial schools* of the mid-19th century; the *borstals* of the early 20th century; the *approved schools* that were introduced in the 1930s; the *remand centres* and *detention centres* established by the Criminal Justice Act 1948; the *community homes with education* ushered in by the Children and Young Persons Act 1969; the *secure units* that have developed and expanded since the 1970s; the *youth custody centres* introduced in the early 1980s; and the *young offender institutions* that emerged in the 1990s, soon to be followed by the *secure training centres,* the first private jails for children in England and Wales. In the final analysis, the locked institution is the linchpin of the youth justice system (Goldson, 2002c; 2004c).

Hybridity

We have noted that youth justice comprises a complex 'amalgam of rationales'. It may be helpful to conceive of youth justice systems as hybrid arrangements, with core components drawn from a variety of otherwise competing and contradictory conceptual sources. In this sense, 'welfare' and 'justice', 'rights' and 'responsibilities', and 'informalism' and 'punitivism' *co-exist,* however uneasily. Clearly, there are times when certain conceptual themes are more ascendant than others, for example, the 1960s and 1970s, when 'welfare' priorities were emphasised, and the 1980s and early 1990s, when 'justice' imperatives reached a level of primacy. In the final analysis, however, youth justice is a dynamic and hybrid form. Moreover, at any one time, political exigency, as distinct from criminological rationality, exercises significant determining influence over the precise nature and shape of the youth justice system. Ultimately, this returns us to the questions of 'moral panic' and 'respectable fears'.

THE NEW YOUTH JUSTICE

In the early 1990s, and for a variety of reasons that are explored in greater detail elsewhere (see, for example, Davis and Bourhill, 1997; Goldson, 1997; Hay, 1995; Haydon and Scraton, 2000), political, professional and public attention (re)turned to the question of youth crime in England and Wales. Within a context akin to 'moral panic', 'respectable fears' were re-mobilised and youth crime was re-politicised and re-profiled. Such processes have effectively endured and, accordingly, recent years have witnessed extraordinarily energetic reform in youth justice law, policy and practice. The mood of such reform has been characterised by 'toughness', it has primarily been driven by the New Labour Government, and its depth and breadth has been so substantial that it has been described as the 'new youth justice' (Goldson, 2000a).

'No More Excuses'

Within months of first coming to power in 1997, the New Labour Government published a White Paper, the title of which – *No More Excuses: A New Approach to Tackling Youth Crime in England and Wales* – left little to the imagination in terms of its penological emphasis. The White Paper served to consolidate the newly-elected Government's policies on youth crime – which had been developing incrementally through a series of published papers and consultation documents during its latter years in Opposition (Jones, 2002) – and it signalled the far-reaching measures that were to be introduced via the provisions of subsequent legislation. Indeed, the Crime and Disorder Act 1998 and the Youth Justice and Criminal Evidence Act 1999 have provided the statutory footing for the most radical reform of youth justice policy and practice in England and Wales in the post-war period. Further and more recent developments in law and policy, including 'anti-social behaviour' legislation, have defined an approach to youth justice that is underpinned by a new correctional continuum. The 'shallow end' of the continuum is characterised by an emphasis on 'crime prevention' through intensive intervention. The 'deeper end' comprises a range of tough, punitive sanctions and the expansion of custodial detention.

Intensive intervention

The Crime and Disorder Act 1998 provides that 'the purpose of the youth justice system is to cut offending [and] action must be taken quickly to nip youth offending in the bud' (Home Office, 1998: 1). Indeed, early, and often quite intensive, intervention comprises a cornerstone of the new youth justice. The Act introduced a range of new powers and statutory orders – including parenting orders (ss 8–10), so called child safety orders (ss 11–13) and child curfews (ss 14–15) – which have served to substantially extend the reach of the youth justice system. Moreover, previous policies and practices, which were explicitly intended to *divert* children and young people from formal intervention and criminalisation, have been abandoned. Sections 65 and 66 of the Crime and Disorder Act 1998 put an end to cautioning and established instead, on a statutory basis, the system of reprimands and final warnings (Goldson, 2000b; Bateman, 2003). Formal intervention by way of 'rehabilitation programmes' attached to final warnings now applies to children as young as 10 for only their second (usually minor) offence (and in certain cases their first offence). In the event of a third (or possibly even second) transgression, such measures (together with reports relating to the child's standard of compliance with 'rehabilitation') are citable in court. In such circumstances, conditional discharges are not normally available to the courts, and children instead face further intervention by way of 'programmes of behaviour' and 'youth offender contracts' attached to the referral order, as provided by Part 1 of the Youth Justice and Criminal Evidence Act 1999 (Goldson, 2000b).

Furthermore, legislation has introduced new modes of intervention targetted at children and young people *below* the age of criminal responsibility who are considered to be 'at risk' of offending, via identification, referral and tracking initiatives and so called youth inclusion and support programmes. Interventionist imperatives are also being extended to encompass 'anti-social behaviour' and to embrace children and young people whose presence in public places is *'believed'* to be *'likely to cause* intimidation, harassment, alarm or distress' (Home Office, 2003, emphasis added).

The ideologies and domain assumptions which drive such developments are problematic. They represent the perfect exemplar of net-widening – whereby the intensity of intervention, previously determined and defined along a vertical sentencing tariff in accordance with principles of proportionality, is increasingly tilted horizontally, rooted in discretionary judgments and spurious assessments – as the youth offending system and ancillary networks extend their reach to draw in more and younger children. Even more controversially, in certain instances, guilt is no longer the founding principle of such interventions, which can now be triggered without the necessity of an offence being committed and will increasingly be justified on grounds other than the guilt of the subject. The new modes of intervention are unencumbered by such legal principles as 'the burden of proof', 'beyond reasonable doubt' and 'due legal process'. Instead, intervention is triggered by assessment, discretion and a spurious logic of prediction. Children and young people are being exposed to formal intervention, not only on the basis of what they *have done*, but also in respect of what they *might do, who they are* or who they are *thought to be*.

Custodial detention

Expanded and diversified forms of custodial detention, and the policy and practice of re-penalisation, perhaps comprise the most conspicuous expression of the punitive turn in youth justice in England and Wales over the last decade. Custodial sentences rose from approximately 4,000 per annum in 1992 to 7,600 in 2001, a 90 per cent increase. During the same period, the juvenile remand population grew by 142 per cent. Within this general expansionist pattern, four sub-patterns are especially noteworthy.

First, changes in legislation have provided for the incarceration of younger children. In 1992, approximately 100 children under the age of 15 years were sentenced to custody (under grave crimes provisions). In 2001, however, 800 children under 15 years were sent to jail, an increase of 800 per cent (NACRO, 2003b). Secondly, as we noted earlier, more girls are being detained in custody, and the rate of growth is proportionately higher than that which relates to boys. The use of custody in relation to girls over the last decade has increased by 400 per cent (compared with the overall increase of 90 per cent). Thirdly, as also noted earlier, the substantial over-representation of black children and young people continues to prevail at every discrete stage of the youth justice system, from pre-arrest to post-sentence (Goldson and Chigwada-Bailey, 1999). While the latest demographic data provides that approximately 2 per cent of the population are classified as 'black' (this figure excludes children of Asian origin), 9.3 per cent of children sentenced to custody in 2001 were classified as 'black' or 'black British'. More dramatically still, 18.2 per cent of all children and young people sentenced to long-term detention under the provisions of the Powers of the Criminal Courts (Sentencing) Act 2000 were black (NACRO, 2003b). Fourthly, within a comparative international context, rates of custodial detention in England and Wales are conspicuously high. Indeed, proportionately more children and young people are locked up in England and Wales than in almost any other country in the European Union.

Critical attention

The United Nations Committee on the Rights of the Child (2002) has formally raised a range of concerns about youth justice policy and practice in England and Wales. The House of Lords/House of Commons Joint Committee on Human Rights (2003) has raised similar disquiet. Such concern is focused on the criminalising interventions to which children and young people are being exposed at an early age and the extraordinarily high rates of child incarceration in England and Wales. The direction that the new youth justice has taken is not only inhumane in its violation of rights, it is also financially costly and almost certainly ineffective in terms of crime prevention. Indeed, for a government ostensibly wedded to financial prudence on the one hand, and 'evidence-based' policy formation (informed by 'what works' principles) on the other, such an approach is utterly paradoxical. In the final analysis, the new emphasis on wider and more intensive intervention at the 'shallow end' of the youth justice process, and expanded and diversified forms of custodial detention at the 'deeper end', is fundamentally at odds with research findings and the 'effectiveness' lessons drawn from previous practice experience (Goldson, 2000b; 2002b).

CONCLUSION

Although our analysis of youth crime and youth justice has been relatively brief, it has served to highlight a number of important criminological issues, summarised as follows:

- 'Modern' constructions of youth crime were essentially consolidated in the 19th century.
- Youth crime has always induced public anxiety and 'respectable fears', and at particular moments in history 'moral panics' have served to 'amplify' such concerns.
- Offending is a relatively 'normal' part of growing up for most children and young people.
- The 'official' evidence does not appear to suggest that youth crime is becoming substantially more widespread or serious in nature.
- Young offenders are predominantly male. Black males are no more inclined to commit offences than their white counterparts.
- Disproportionately punitive responses to girls, and the over-representation of black children and young people in the youth justice system, comprise fundamental injustices.
- The children and young people most heavily enmeshed within the youth justice system are drawn from disadvantaged backgrounds and are invariably victims of systemic welfare neglect.
- Youth justice systems vary from one country to another. In many respects, they symbolise wider values and principles in relation to human rights and social justice.
- Youth justice is a site of contestation where an 'amalgam of rationales' intersect and compete for ascendancy.
- Contemporary youth justice in England and Wales has been re-politicised, and 'toughness' imperatives currently determine the direction of law, policy and practice.
- A new correctional continuum has emerged, characterised by intensive intervention at one end and custodial detention at the other.
- The 'new' approach to youth justice has attracted critique from various quarters and, in the final analysis, it is unlikely to deliver positive results in terms of youth crime prevention.

SEMINAR DISCUSSION TOPICS

- How might media coverage of particular constituencies of children and young people perpetuate negative images and even create 'respectable fears'? In considering this question, you may wish to recall specific examples of newspaper, radio or television items.

- To what extent does the youth 'justice' system perpetuate class-based, 'racialised' and gendered injustices?

- A politics of 'toughness' has displaced criminological rationality in youth justice. Consider the legitimacy of this statement in the light of contemporary developments in law, policy and practice.

- The human rights of some of society's most disadvantaged children and young people are being systematically violated by youth justice interventions. Discuss.

KEY READINGS

Geoffrey Pearson's *Hooligan: A History of Respectable Fears* (Macmillan, 1983) and the third edition of Stan Cohen's *Folk Devils and Moral Panics* (Routledge, 2002) are definitive contextual books for any student of youth crime and youth justice. Barry Goldson's edited collection *The New Youth Justice* (Russell House, 2000) provides an accessible analytical insight into the most recent policy and practice developments, and John Muncie and his colleagues offer an excellent anthology of critical essays with their *Youth Justice: Critical Readings* (Sage, 2002). Roger Smith's textbook *Youth Justice: Ideas, Policy, Practice* (Willan, 2003) comprises a clear and well-researched recent addition to the literature, as does the second edition of John Muncie's *Youth and Crime* (Sage, 2004). Many academic journals publish articles in the area of youth criminology, although *Youth Justice*, the journal of the National Association for Youth Justice, is the only journal that exclusively specialises in the field. Other edited texts that provide a wider critical analysis of contemporary policy responses to childhood and youth include Phil Scraton's *'Childhood' in Crisis?* (UCL Press, 1997), and Barry Goldson and colleagues' *Children, Welfare and the State* (Sage, 2002).

REFERENCES

Bandalli, S (2000) 'Children, responsibility and the new youth justice' in Goldson, B (ed), *The New Youth Justice*, Dorset: Russell House.

Bateman, T (2003) 'Living with final warnings: making the best of a bad job?', *Youth Justice*, vol (3), pp 131–40.

Becker, H (1963) *Outsiders*, New York: Free Press.

Blagg, H and Smith, D (1989) *Crime, Penal Policy and Social Work*, Harlow: Longman.

Cohen, S (1972) *Folk Devils and Moral Panics: The Creation of the Mods and Rockers*, London: MacGibbon and Kee.

Cohen, S (1985) *Visions of Social Control*, Cambridge: Polity.

Cox, P and Shore, H (eds) (2002) *Becoming Delinquent: British and European Youth, 1650–1950*, Aldershot: Ashgate.

Davis, H and Bourhill, M (1997) '"Crisis": the demonization of children and young people' in Scraton, P (ed), *'Childhood' in Crisis?*, London: UCL Press.

Flood-Page, C, Campbell, S, Harrington, V and Miller, J (2000) *Youth Crime: Findings from the 1998/1999 Youth Lifestyles Survey*, Research Study 209, London: Home Office.

Gillis, JR (1974) *Youth and History: Tradition and Change in European Age Relations 1770–Present*, New York: Academic Press.

Goldson, B (1997) 'Children in trouble: state responses to juvenile crime' in Scraton, P (ed), *'Childhood' in Crisis?*, London: UCL Press.

Goldson, B (ed) (2000a) *The New Youth Justice*, Dorset: Russell House.

Goldson, B (2000b) 'Wither diversion? Interventionism and the new youth justice' in Goldson, B (ed), *The New Youth Justice*, Dorset: Russell House.

Goldson, B (2002a) 'New Labour, social justice and children: political calculation and the deserving-undeserving schism', *The British Journal of Social Work*, vol 32(6), pp 683–95.

Goldson, B (2002b) 'Children, crime and the state' in Goldson, B, Lavalatte, M and McKechnie, J (eds), *Children, Welfare and the State*, London: Sage.

Goldson, B (2002c) 'New punitiveness: the politics of child incarceration' in Muncie, J, Hughes, G and McLaughlin, E (eds), *Youth Justice: Critical Readings*, London: Sage.

Goldson, B (2004a) 'Differential justice? A critical introduction to youth justice policy in UK jurisdictions' in McGhee, J, Mellon, M and Whyte, B (eds), *Meeting Needs, Addressing Deeds: Working with Young People Who Offend*, London: NCH.

Goldson, B (2004b) 'Beyond formalism: towards "informal" approaches to youth crime and youth justice' in Bateman, T and Pitts, J (eds), *The Russell House Companion to Youth Justice*, Dorset: Russell House.

Goldson, B (2004c) 'Victims or threats? Children, care and control' in Fink, J (ed), *Care: Personal Lives and Social Policy*, Bristol: Policy Press.

Goldson, B and Chigwada-Bailey, R (1999) '(What) justice for black children and young people?' in Goldson, B (ed), *Youth Justice: Contemporary Policy and Practice*, Aldershot: Ashgate.

Goldson, B and Jamieson, J (2002a) 'Youth crime, the "parenting deficit" and state intervention: a contextual critique', *Youth Justice*, vol 2(2), pp 82–99.

Graham, J and Bowling, B (1995) *Young People and Crime*, Home Office Research Study 145, London: HMSO.

Hall, S (1978) 'The treatment of football hooliganism in the press' in Ingham, R (ed), *Football Hooliganism*, London: Inter-Action.

Hall, S, Critcher, C, Jefferson, T, Clarke, J and Roberts, B (1978) *Policing the Crisis: Mugging, the State and Law and Order*, London: Macmillan.

Harrington, V and Mayhew, P (2001) *Mobile Phone Theft*, Home Office Research Study 235, London: Home Office.

Hay, C (1995) 'Mobilisation through interpellation: James Bulger, juvenile crime and the construction of a moral panic', *Social and Legal Studies*, vol 4(2), pp 197–223.

Haydon, D and Scraton, P (2000) '"Condemn a little more, understand a little less": the political context and rights' implications of the domestic and European rulings in the Venables-Thompson case', *Journal of Law and Society*, vol 27(3), pp 416–48.

Hendrick, H (2003) *Child Welfare: Historical Dimensions, Contemporary Debate*, Bristol: Policy Press.

Home Office (1998) *Crime and Disorder Act 1998: Introductory Guide*, London: Home Office.

Home Office (2002) *Criminal Statistics England and Wales*, London: Home Office.

Home Office (2003) *Respect and Responsibility – Taking a Stand Against Anti-Social Behaviour*, London: The Stationery Office.

House of Lords/House of Commons Joint Parliamentary Committee on Human Rights (2003) *The UN Convention on the Rights of the Child*, Tenth Report of Session 2002–03, London: The Stationery Office.

Howard League for Penal Reform (2002) '96 per cent of teenagers are victims of crime according to Howard League consultation', Howard League Press Release, 11 April.

Jones, D (2002) 'Questioning New Labour's youth justice strategy: a review article', *Youth Justice*, vol 1(3), pp 14–26.

Lemert, E (1967) *Human Deviance, Social Problems and Social Control*, Englewood Cliffs, NJ: Prentice Hall.

Matza, D (1969) *Becoming Deviant*, Englewood Cliffs, NJ: Prentice Hall.

Muncie, J (1984) *The Trouble with Kids Today: Youth and Crime in Post-war Britain*, London: Hutchinson.

Muncie, J (2003) 'Juvenile justice in Europe: some conceptual, analytical and statistical comparisons', *Childright*, No 202, pp 14–17.

Muncie, J (2004) 'Youth justice: globalisation and multi-modal governance' in Newburn, T and Sparks, R (eds), *Criminal Justice and Political Cultures*, Cullompton: Willan.

Muncie, J and Hughes, G (2002) 'Modes of youth governance: political rationalities, criminalisation and resistance' in Muncie, J, Hughes, G and McLaughlin, E (eds), *Youth Justice: Critical Readings*, London: Sage.

NACRO (2003a) *Some Facts about Young People who Offend – 2001*, Youth Crime briefing, March, London: NACRO.

NACRO (2003b) *A Failure of Justice*, London: NACRO.

Pearson, G (1983) *Hooligan: A History of Respectable Fears*, London: Macmillan.

Scraton, P and Haydon, D (2002) 'Challenging the criminalisation of children and young people: securing a rights-based agenda' in Muncie, J, Hughes, G and McLaughlin, E (eds), *Youth Justice: Critical Readings*, London: Sage.

Simmons, J (2002) *Crime in England and Wales 2001/02*, Home Office Statistical Bulletin 07/02, London: Home Office.

Thorpe, DH, Smith, D, Green, CJ and Paley, JH (1980) *Out of Care: The Community Support of Juvenile Offenders*, London: George Allen and Unwin.

United Nations Committee on the Rights of the Child (2002) *Concluding Observations of the Committee on the Rights of the Child: United Kingdom of Great Britain and Northern Ireland*, Geneva: United Nations.

CHAPTER 16

PROBATION AND COMMUNITY PENALTIES

Mike Nash

SUMMARY

If a member of the public were asked to explain the term 'probation' to a visitor from another planet, he or she would as likely as not describe a process of helping offenders. If so, this would result in a considerable amount of teeth gnashing in the headquarters of the National Probation Service where, since its inception in April 2001, considerable efforts have been made to transform the public image of the service. The Probation Service came into being in 1907 as a helping organisation. It arose from an era of tolerance and a desire to reform and rehabilitate those who had fallen from the path of righteousness or at least conformity with the law. McWilliams (1983) describes the role of the early probation pioneers as engaging in 'special pleading' with the court, essentially for mercy and a second chance for offenders. With the right guidance and role models alongside work opportunities, 'deserving' offenders could be encouraged back into the community as responsible individuals. Offenders were thus regarded as unfortunates, who suffered from a variety of privations or had been led astray by the wrong sort of people. With the right advice and opportunities, they could be redeemed. It is easy therefore to understand where the popular notion of probation officers helping offenders derives from. Yet, for the past two decades at least, concerted efforts have been made to change this perception and reposition the Probation Service as an agency of law enforcement and, more recently, public protection. That so many people still regard the service as something it is striving not to be points us to the continued tension suffered by an organisation that has had to perform a number of tricks and turns to survive a period of penal populism and pessimism which had set in during the early 1970s. In an era where Victorian and Edwardian forgiveness and tolerance for the 'deserving' appears increasingly less obvious, the Probation Service has had, in many respects, to change its entire *raison d'être*. That it still survives as an organisation is testimony to its success in transforming itself, but serious questions remain about the nature of its future existence (Nash, 2001). This chapter will give an overview of this attempted transformation with a particular focus on the work of the Probation Service in supervising community penalties.

KEY TERMS

Tolerance; reform; rehabilitation; punishment; penal welfarism; corrections; multi-agency; inter-agency; public protection.

INTRODUCTION

Readers wishing to understand the history of the Probation Service would do well to study McWilliams' series of articles from the 1980s (1983, 1985, 1986 and 1987). In essence, he charts the changes in an organisation from its philanthropic roots to its position in the late 1980s as the agency destined to take on the role as 'punisher in the community' (see endnote for a description of the major court orders supervised by the Probation Service). If he were alive today, it would be fascinating to hear McWilliams' view on the developments since then, not least those under Labour Governments. For, undoubtedly, the Probation Service at the beginning of the 21st century is beyond recognition in its aims and philosophy from the position held by the early pioneers. Yet, as it transforms and remodels itself into a punishing organisation, it appears as if there is always another change on the horizon. An example of this might be the change in terms of a scheme whereby offenders perform unpaid work in the community. The initial scheme was known as community service (and still is in many people's minds), then, in 2001, it became a community punishment order and the latest manifestation is an 'enhanced' community punishment order. What lies beyond enhancement? The changing words and terms represent a continued effort to build confidence both in the courts and in the public's mind that probation is no longer a soft option. The example just given is perhaps a bad one, however. The enhanced elements of the order are related to improving the learning experience for offenders performing their work obligations by a combination of pro-social modelling (leading by example) and offering problem-solving and employment-related skills opportunities. Those involved in the beginnings of the community service scheme sought to achieve these objectives by matching offender and placement/supervisor in a careful selection process. The more bullish 1980s saw community service drift towards a greater degree of supervised group work with leanings towards public shaming (Pratt, 2000). The latest developments therefore see something of a return to the past with the addition of a New Labour package based on 'what works' principles (see below). Although numbers on community punishment orders may prevent the detailed matching of two decades ago, the enhanced element of the 2003 scheme does suggest that we can learn from the past rather than ditch it all, as many Labour Government modernisers would argue.

ON THE OFFENDER'S 'SIDE'?

The Probation Service performs a range of tasks within the community that have, over the years and still today, reflected the central philosophy of criminal justice in the UK. What this suggests of course is that, as penal philosophies change, then so must the Probation Service. It might be argued that this is the case for all criminal justice agencies, but the small Probation Service, performing tasks traditionally regarded as 'on the offender's side', and largely secret and unaccountable, would be more susceptible to the winds of change. Garland (1996) describes the decline of 'penal welfarism' (or a therapeutic, treatment-based approach to offending) in the late 20th century, a decline that directly challenged the future of the Probation Service. For much of that century, the 19th century notion that crime for many offenders resulted from a range of factors outside of their control fed directly into the emerging expertise of probation officers. Those once deemed worthy of redemption became those for whom professional intervention might bring about the degree of change necessary to reduce future offending. As this philosophy suffered a crisis of confidence in an era of penal pessimism (Martinson, 1974; Brody, 1975), so the Probation Service began a phase of both changing from within and being changed from without. Failure was on the criminal justice agenda, and those regarded as experts found their status challenged. It would be important for the Probation Service to hoist its colours to a more successful mast.

A series of reports and legislative developments began to significantly shift the Probation Service from the 'advise, assist and befriend' ethos established by the 1907 Probation of Offenders Act to a more mainstream criminal justice organisation. The early stage in this process was to focus on increasing the number of more serious offenders on the caseload, ostensibly by increasing the responsibility of the Service for the supervision of those released from custody. A major aspect of this was the development of parole supervision for those prisoners released from custody under licence conditions (consolidated in the 1967 Criminal Justice Act) and life licence supervision in 1968. Not only were these offenders' crimes generally more serious than those on the traditional probation caseload, but the requirement of the offenders' supervision was more stringent and controlling. The work of probation officers had taken on a new element, one less inclined to befriending or social casework and more inclined towards regulation and control. The secondment of probation staff to work inside of prisons by 1966 further sent out a message that the old divide between these organisations was reducing. The introduction of community service orders in 1973, branded as a strict alternative to custody initially, also provided a new aspect to probation practice. This new development did not require social work skills, and this part of the job increasingly became staffed by those not holding the professional qualification in social work. At this point, two discernible trends can be identified: the emergence of a more controlling and intrusive form of supervision increasingly linked to post-custodial work, and the development of practice no longer seen as requiring professional social work training. These two trends have considerably increased in the two decades or so since their inception and have in many respects completely re-shaped the service.

However, we need to remain in the past for a little longer to really understand the Probation Service of the present. Many in the Probation Service saw the election of Margaret Thatcher as Conservative Prime Minister in 1979 as an immediate threat to its future. The electorate had been wooed with talk of more police officers and prison places, tougher sentences and a generally less forgiving attitude to offenders (Dunbar and Langdon, 1998; Nash and Savage, 1994; Downes and Morgan, 2002). Pushing a 'new right' attitude to offenders, the Government declared that people chose to offend and were not driven to it. A penal philosophy based on such simplistic assertions held great threat for the Probation Service, with its tradition of working with the supposed 'causes' of crime. It was evident, from the early 1980s, that the Probation Service of old, already undergoing changes as we have seen, would have to change a whole lot more. A strong sign of the shape of the things to come came with the introduction of the Statement of National Objectives and Priorities for the Probation Service (SNOP) (Home Office, 1984). A list of priorities for the Service was developed which began to steer it away from its welfare roots towards a more corrections-based future, aimed at providing credible alternatives to custody. Tasks such as those requiring work in the civil courts with families in dispute over children were relegated towards the bottom of the priority list. The culmination of this particular process saw the complete removal of this work in 2001 and the creation of a new agency, the Children and Family Courts Advisory and Support Service (CAFCASS). Perhaps more important than the actual list of priorities was the signal that central government would be taking a much stronger interest in the direction of the Probation Service. A long history as a local organisation with accountability through local committees and local government funding would be shifted towards the centre, another process easily tracked through to the present. The Home Office took on a greater percentage of the funding of local services (from 50 per cent to 80 per cent in 1971) and eventually abolished the mechanism whereby they had to match on a pro-rata basis whatever the local authority decided to budget for probation services. This would inevitably mean that local services would have to do more of what the centre demanded – and of course would become 100% centrally funded in 2001, with all that this would entail. Local chief officers had to respond to SNOP by producing their own local response, a Statement of Local Objectives and Priorities (SLOP), and were thus increasingly held to account.

A CHANGING ETHOS

The growth in central control was to accelerate rapidly in the late 1980s and early 1990s. A Green Paper, *Punishment, Custody and the Community* (Home Office, 1988), signalled the direction in which criminal justice policy would unfold. The view that offenders were more culpable for their actions than proponents of penal welfarism would have would find its way into legislation. In crude terms, people choosing to offend would have to face the consequences of their actions and they would have a much clearer idea of what might happen to them in court. With this notion of choice (watered down a little in the subsequent White Paper – see below) came a recasting of the notion of supervision in the community. The Probation Service would see one its major areas of work, probation supervision, transformed into a sentence, with one of its principal aims being to restrict the liberty of offenders. The White Paper, *Crime, Justice and Protecting the Public* (Home Office, 1990), aimed to rationalise sentencing arrangements around 'just deserts' or proportionality criteria. It would achieve this by creating clear criteria by which certain sentences could be passed. These criteria, however, were not as clear as the Government might have wished. For example, three sentencing bands were developed in an attempt to target offences against certain sentences. At the lower end would be fines and discharges, in the middle, offences would be 'serious enough' for community punishment and, at the top end, 'so serious' that only custody would suffice. Probation disposals would therefore fall into that middle band of 'serious enough' but not 'so serious'. For an agency that for a decade or so had been developing alternatives to custody as a priority, the future again appeared uncertain. The enactment of the proposals in the Criminal Justice Act 1991 softened the boundaries of the sentencing bands, enabling the Probation Service to offer alternatives where there were mitigating factors that would lessen the seriousness of the offence. Essentially, the Act embraced a 'just deserts' or proportionality rule, the seriousness of the offence would determine sentence severity. However, the Probation Service's traditional role in analysing the social, personal and economic factors that might contribute to crime was allowed to continue, but only if clear links could be made to offending behaviour. A threat had therefore become an opportunity.

The price for survival did mean, however, a significant change in ethos for the Probation Service. As noted above, community penalties were to be recast as restrictions on liberty, the amount determined by offence seriousness. With its new place in the sentencing structure came a determined attempt to increase sentencer confidence. A significant aspect of this process was the introduction of national standards (Home Office, 1992), whereby minimum standards for all aspects of probation practice were established. This made expectations of the Service much more public and accountable and, indeed, was to set in process a train of revisions that have massively increased central control of operational probation practice. The watering-down noted above concerned the importance of deterrence as a sentencing aim. The White Paper claimed that offenders were unlikely to be deterred from criminal behaviour by increasingly severe sentences because many did not think far enough ahead. Responsibility would not be learned in prison; indeed, the White Paper contained the immortal phrase for a Conservative Government, 'custody is a good way of making bad people worse'. More offenders would therefore be kept in the community and face up to their responsibilities by strengthened community supervision. The Probation Service would therefore become centre stage in delivering the new policy, but the price for this enhanced status would be adopting a style of working increasingly distant from its roots and subject to ever-greater central scrutiny.

Although many of the developments experienced by the Probation Service at this time can be regarded as centrally and externally driven, there was a considerable internal impetus for change. A good example of this can be found in the title of the 1988 Association of Chief Officers of Probation (ACOP) document entitled *More Demanding than Prison*. Here we find chief officers attempting to almost outmanoeuvre the Government by anticipating the direction of future policy and jumping before they are pushed. The changes wrought into the Probation Service were not universally welcomed, and certainly the rank and file members of the National Association of Probation Officers (NAPO) alongside the central council of probation committees appeared to regret the direction in which ACOP was taking the service (Nash, 2001; Nash and Ryan, 2003). The politicisation of law and order issues throughout the 1990s ensured that the role of the Probation Service remained firmly on the Government's agenda. The Criminal Justice Act 1991 had undoubtedly achieved one of its central, if somewhat underplayed, aims: to reduce the use of custody. Although adopting a more overtly correctionalist mode of operating, the Probation Service was certainly central to the delivery of the Government's strategy. Yet by 1993, the murder of the toddler James Bulger and the elevation of Tony Blair, first as shadow Home Secretary, then as leader of the Labour Party, signalled a major change in policy (Dunbar and Langdon, 1998; Ryan, 2003). In 1993, the new Home Secretary, Michael Howard, responded to a deteriorating electoral position (even on the usually strong law and order ticket) by declaring a new policy of 'prison works'.

At a stroke, much of the reductionist good generated by the Criminal Justice Act 1991 disappeared, and once again it is not difficult to see the potential harm in this statement for the Probation Service. If its new central position as the deliverer of community punishment were threatened, then where was there to go? During the mid-1990s, the law and order debate was certainly ratcheted up by the Conservatives, with the importation of many American policies on serious and dangerous offenders.

Disaffection from the country's most senior judges did little to dissuade Howard; indeed, he regarded this as a sign that he was meeting public expectations. The general trend of an upwardly punitive drift continued unabated, as did central control of the Probation Service by the revisions to national standards. However, in 1995, one of the most unambiguous messages yet was sent out to the Probation Service. Following a review by Eileen Dews (Home Office, 1995), a report recommended the ending of the formal requirement for probation officers to hold a professional diploma in social work. Here at last was the change that had been incremental for some time but was now to be revolutionary in nature. A formal casting-off of the probation pioneers' philanthropic origins took place, despite some opposition in both Houses of Parliament. A new corrections future was dawning for the Probation Service, and, certainly in public, the Labour Party offered little hope of an alternative vision whilst in Opposition. They had matched and at times exceeded Michael Howard's excesses, policies that Lord Ackner had described as playing politics with justice (*The Guardian*, 2 December 1996). The mid-1990s fears about predatory paedophiles had led to the introduction of new policies that placed public protection at the centre of the criminal justice process. This had knock-on effects not only for legislation but also daily practice (Nash, 1999a; 2003) and opened a new chapter in the history of the Probation Service, where it would work more closely with other agencies, notably the police, and have a more upfront and public role. The election of the Labour Government in 1997 held promise for many. Would the training decision be reversed? Would the punitive drift be halted? Would reform and rehabilitation re-enter the agenda? After all, had not Tony Blair promised to be as tough on the causes of crime as on crime itself? However, the early signs were not promising for those who harkened after a golden probation past.

PRISON AND PROBATION

One of the first tasks of the new administration was the establishment a review body (Home Office, 1998) to consider the amalgamation of the Prison and Probation Services. Discussions on the future of probation training saw the reintroduction of a higher education qualification alongside a national vocational award, but the scheme remained firmly outside of the social work departments. The merger of Prison and Probation Services did not take place, but much closer working between them was envisaged and epitomised by the phrase, 'seamless sentences'.[1] The public protection agenda was pushing the Probation Service towards closer working with the police and other services, and the flagship Labour legislation, the 1998 Crime and Disorder Act, enshrined multi-agency working as a fundamental principle of daily criminal justice practice. The Probation Service appeared as if it was again facing an uncertain future when, as so often in its recent past, something came along to offer salvation. This time it came in the form of a new policy in which the new Home Secretary, Jack Straw, boldly announced that 'prison doesn't work'. The basis of this bold claim was the publication of Home Office research that suggested that, for some types of offenders, focused programmes of intervention could reduce reoffending rates

---

1   In January 2004, following a Whitehall review by Patrick Carter, the Government announced the imminent establishment of the National Offender Management Service (NOMS), a fusion of prison and probation services.

(Goldblatt and Lewis, 1998). The New Labour Government was committed to evidence-based practice, and this new finding was like manna from heaven. It meant that it could appease at least some of its traditional supporters by returning to a policy that aimed to see more offenders in the community. This was the beginning of the 'what works' programme (Home Office, 1999). Here, methods of intervention with offenders would in future be based upon practice, where success had been evidenced through research and evaluation. The generally punitive drift had not been halted, however, as mandatory life sentences for second time sexual and violent offenders, and fixed minimum periods for drug offenders and (later) burglars were implemented in the Crime (Sentences Act) 1997. 'What works' itself would be framed in the new tougher language of the Probation Service, and it is to the most recent phase in Probation Service history that we now turn.

In April 2001, the National Probation Service (NPS) was created with a national director, Eithne Wallis, in place for the first time. It was intended that this new post would give the Probation Service access to the centre of criminal justice policy-making, much as senior police and prison staff had enjoyed. Opportunities were seen for the director to influence policy, although the direction of that influence might have been more towards rather than away from the Service (Nash 2001; Nash and Ryan, 2003). Many people were relieved that the new Service retained the word 'probation' in its title. The Home Secretary had been keen on 'public or community protection service', reflecting the enhanced public protection role, whilst ACOP had favoured 'community justice service'. We have already noted that civil work had been moved to a new agency – although perhaps this separation came home to roost in the deficiencies revealed in child protection work by a joint inspectors' report (Department of Health, 2002). The move to a more correctionalist stance was reflected in the renaming of the major probation-supervised orders. The probation order became a community rehabilitation order and the community service order, as we have seen, became a community punishment order. A combination of both, introduced in the Criminal Justice Act 1991, became a community punishment and rehabilitation order. We have noted the importance of national standards in reshaping the Probation Service and building public and sentencer confidence. The new standards (Home Office, 2000) for community-based sentences give a flavour of how these measures are now viewed, perhaps compared with the early ethos of advise, assist and befriend. Standard C7 states the purpose of a community sentence as follows:

- to provide a rigorous and effective punishment;
- to reduce the likelihood of reoffending;
- to rehabilitate the offender, where possible;
- to enable reparation to be made to the community; and
- to minimise risk of harm to the public.

Supervision in the community shall include the following elements (Standard C8):

- to address and reduce offending behaviour;
- to challenge the offender to accept responsibility for the crimes committed and their consequences;
- to contribute to the protection of the public;
- to motivate and assist the offender towards a greater sense of personal responsibility and discipline; and

- to be arranged so as not to interfere with offenders' ability to seek or take up work or educational opportunities.

In this standard, it is still possible to detect some of the earlier history of the Probation Service, but it is now couched in much stronger terms. The context in which probation officers would practice would be more concerned with controlling or managing the problem of crime than really getting at its causes. The basic elements of the orders remain unchanged, but their execution has been transformed. The trends identified in this chapter have continued unabated, and those hoping for a return to a less correctionalist probation service under a Labour Government have been disappointed.

Change has been the byword of the Labour administration to date and those resistant to change have been branded as dinosaurs. The Probation Service itself have been caught up in the Government's desire to 'join-up' justice. Working ever more closely with other departments is regarded as the most efficient and effective way to tackle the problem of crime. At the same time, the Service is exhorted to work with increasingly serious and potentially dangerous offenders with a view to offering greater protection to the public. The management of risk has begun to dominate daily practice, and increasingly sophisticated assessment and prediction tools eat into probation officers' time on a daily basis. The inherent unpredictability of these offenders, however, makes this a fraught professional experience (Nash, 1999b). In working more closely with other organisations, we can detect greater evidence of what Crawford (1998) describes as 'inter' rather than 'multi' agency working. By this he means a way of working that impacts to such an extent on the component agencies that they alter their way of working – a new working culture emerges out of the component elements. Recent developments are likely to accelerate this process. For example, a new sentence is to be launched across the country, and it brings probation and police officers together in a way unforeseen in the past. In April 2003, a new community measure was launched, the *Intensive Control and Change Programme* (ICCP), aimed at 18–20 year old offenders (accounting for 42 per cent of all first time offenders and 20 per cent of all reconvictions). This new programme, piloted in five probation areas from April 2003, aims to include the following elements:

- *Control*

  The Probation Service and the police working closely together to provide public protection through close monitoring and restriction of liberty through:

  (a) daily curfew to home address backed by electronic tagging;

  (b) direct police involvement and surveillance;

  (c) rapid reaction to breach.

The order will also encourage:

- *Change*

  The Probation Service working with Jobcentre Plus and other partners to rehabilitate offenders through 25 hours a week of demanding and intensive activity consisting of:

  (a) 18 hours a week of an offending behaviour programme, education, employment and training;

  (b) seven hours a week of unpaid work as reparation to the community;

(c) working with a mentor; and

(d) a compensation order requiring the offender to pay damages to the victim or a fine as appropriate.

In launching the scheme, Hilary Benn, the then Home Office Minister, said that, 'this [is] a tough and demanding community penalty [that] aims to provide a credible alternative to custody', not only a tough alternative to custody but a completely new way of working. Joint home visits by police and probation officers to prolific offenders will undoubtedly change significantly the way in which probation intervention is viewed by offenders. Evidence from the evaluation of similar projects involving prolific offenders suggest that probation 'success' can be transformed into rapid breach action and a return to custody – almost an inversion of earlier probation ambition (Worrall and Walton, 2002).

Much is therefore happening with the Probation Service and its community penalties. Stringent targets of a 5 per cent reduction over three years (2001–04) have been set by the National Probation Service (NPS) in reoffending rates. To achieve this, probation staff (many of whom are increasingly not trained as probation officers) work to programmes of intervention built upon 'what works' principles, and these programmes are themselves 'accredited' by a Joint Prisons and Probation Accreditation Panel (JPPAP), established in 1999 (renamed the Correctional Services Accreditation Panel (CSAP)), before they can be used with offenders. It has been argued by Ledger (2001) that this stifles the creativity and innovation for which the Probation Service was once noted. Effectiveness targets are increasingly tied in with other agencies, and these targets inexorably relate to higher risk offenders (see the overall three-year strategy for the NPS as outlined in the 'New Choreography' (NPS, 2001)). Because of this targeting of high-risk cases, the Probation Service finds itself increasingly stretched in terms of resources and time. This scenario has led the former Chief Inspector of Probation, Professor Rod Morgan, to request that the Service sheds its responsibility for the lower risk offenders that he believes are 'clogging up the system' (Morgan, 2003). Yet, in many respects, it is the lower risk offenders who clog up the prison system itself, who constantly return to prison and who commit the type of low level but persistent offending that fuels anxiety and fear of crime. It is these offenders for whom the courts seek advice as to disposal, the very cases that saw the Probation Service established in the first place. If the present pattern continues, we are likely to see these types of cases returned to the voluntary sector, from where they originally came, or even, according to Morgan, to the private sector.

CONCLUSION

The Probation Service has then come a long way from its voluntary and philanthropic roots. Its history spans almost a century and, for a large part of that period, it almost exactly mirrored a consensus approach to crime and offenders. If there ever is such a thing as a 'golden age' in any organisation, then it was the post-war era (the 1940s and 1950s) for the Probation Service. Penal welfarism, supported by the expansion of the new welfare state, witnessed a closeness of fit between probation leaders (often the head of NAPO) and the Home Office, which has not been seen since (King and Jarvis, 1976). The Probation Service reflected the modern approach to crime, and probation officers became the 'experts' trusted to deal with the problem in the community. Yet, as we have seen, that trust was transitory. By the 1960s and 1970s, it appeared as if the crime problem had not only not been 'solved', but was actually worsening. Those experts trained to deal with the problem had failed and their status declined. An increasingly intolerant attitude to offenders had developed, and probation staff began to doubt their role as agents of social control (Walker and Beaumont, 1981). All of these developments led to incremental change, but the election of four successive hardline Conservative Governments sparked a much more significant acceleration of this process. The Probation Service needed to change significantly if it was to survive. The fact that it has survived and is now a national service is testimony not only to its chameleon-like character, but also to the continued need for governments to have cheap alternatives to custody.

This survival has, however, resulted in nothing short of a transformation of the service (Nash and Ryan, 2003). Its whole ethos has been shifted and even its professional training base revolutionised – in many ways, a case of 'organisational cleansing'. Its success in surviving is due in part to the way in which its major orders have changed to reflect the prevailing penal philosophy. Its primary client base is, at the same time, becoming ever more focused on the top end of offenders and in that it works more closely with the police and prison services. As a Home Office minister, Lord Faulkner, was moved to say recently, the Police and Probation Services must work together to become a more effective crime-fighting force. The appointment of Martin Narey as the Commissioner for Correctional Services (and new chief executive of NOMS), overseeing prison and probation work, sent out more signals about the future direction of the Probation Service. Yet, at the same time, worrying messages are beginning to leak out of government. *The Guardian* newspaper carried a report on 8 August 2003, saying that the new cognitive behaviour groups (based on 'what works' principles) were in fact not working – a leak from the Carter Review of Downing Street, Home Office and Treasury. The leak also suggested that the NPS targets for group completions had been revised downwards from 30,000 to 15,000 over a three-year period ending in 2004. Newspapers carried reports from offenders stating that they would sooner go into prison than sit in groups with others (*The Observer*, 21 September 2003). The Probation Service is nailing its colours to a very specific mast at the present time. It is seeking success with the most difficult of offender groups. This may well be a double-edged sword. In working closely with the Police Service under a public protection banner, the Probation Service gains credibility and assures its place at the centre of criminal justice policy. However, success with this group of offenders is far from guaranteed and, in a world obsessed by results, this may yet prove fatal. The group of offenders that Professor Morgan wishes to lose often gravitate to more serious offending and remain ensconced in the ranks of domestic violence and child abuse offenders. Prevention is said to be better than a cure. It appears as if we as a society cannot cure, but who will we get to do the prevention?

ENDNOTE

The major court orders administered by the Probation Service:

* *Community rehabilitation order* – supervision by a probation officer (and/or agents, with or without additional conditions) for a period from six months to three years.

- *Community punishment order* – unpaid work in the community for a period between 40 and 240 hours (see *enhanced community punishment order* above).

- *Community punishment and rehabilitation order* – a combination of the above; one to three years' probation with 40 to 100 hours of community punishment.

- *Drug treatment and testing order* – a demanding course of treatment to get offenders off drugs. Offenders are routinely tested to ensure that they are responding to the treatment. Especially valuable for defendants committing crimes to raise money for drugs. Duration is six months to three years.

- *Curfew orders with electronic monitoring (or tagging)* – a form of 'house arrest' where offenders are monitored via an electronic tag on the ankle, which sends a signal through the phone line to a control centre. If the signal is broken, the control centre is immediately alerted. The court specifies which hours the offender has to be at home – between two and 12 hours a day. Duration is up to six months.

SEMINAR DISCUSSION TOPICS

- Is there a continued role for an agency committed to reform and rehabilitation at the heart of the criminal justice process?

- Will the Probation Service be more effective as a part of a corrections complex?

- Is an increasingly confrontational approach the best way to deal with the complex social problems that may lead to criminal behaviour?

- Can probation survive New Labour?

KEY READINGS

The early history and development of the Probation Service can be found in the series of articles by Bill McWilliams published in the *Howard Journal of Criminal Justice* in 1983, 1985, 1986 and 1987. Those interested in more recent accounts should consult Nash, *Police, Probation and Protecting the Public* (Blackstone, 1999) and Ryan, *Penal Policy and Control in England and Wales* (Waterside, 2003).

REFERENCES

Brody, S (1975) *The Effectiveness of Sentencing*, Home Office Research Study No 64, London: HMSO.

Crawford, A (1998) 'Community safety and the quest for security: holding back the dynamics of social exclusion', *Policy Studies*, vol 19, pp 237–53.

Department of Health (2002) *Safeguarding Children: A Joint Chief Inspectors' Report on Arrangements to Safeguard Children*, October 2002, London: Department of Health.

Downes, D and Morgan, R (2002), 'The skeletons in the cupboard: the politics of law and order at the turn of the millennium' in Maguire, M, Morgan, R and Reiner, R (eds), *The Oxford Handbook of Criminology*, 3rd edn, Oxford: OUP.

Dunbar, I and Langdon, A (1998) *Tough Justice: Sentencing and Penal Policies in the 1990s*, London: Blackstone.

Garland, D (1996) 'The limits of the sovereign state: strategies of crime control in contemporary society', *British Journal of Criminology*, vol 36, pp 445–71.

Goldblatt, P and Lewis, C (eds) (1998) *Reducing Offending: An Assessment of Research Evidence on Ways of Dealing with Offending Behaviour*, Home Office Research Study No 181, London: Home Office.

Home Office (1984) *Probation Service in England and Wales: Statement of National Objectives and Priorities*, London: Home Office.

Home Office (1988) *Punishment, Custody and the Community*, Cm 424, London: HMSO.

Home Office (1990) *Crime, Justice and Protecting the Public*, Cm 965 London: HMSO.

Home Office (1992) *National Standards for the Supervision of Offenders in the Community*, London: Home Office.

Home Office (1995) *Review of Probation Officers Recruitment and Qualifying Training: Discussion Paper by the Home Office*, London: Home Office.

Home Office (1998) *Joining Forces to Protect the Public. Prisons-Probation: A Consultation Document*, London: Home Office.

Home Office (1999) *The Correctional Policy Framework: Effective Execution of the Sentences of the Courts so as to Reduce Re-offending and Protect the Public*, London: Home Office.

Home Office (2000) *National Standards for Supervision of Offenders in the Community*, London: Home Office.

King, JFS and Jarvis, FV (1976) 'The influence of the probation and after-care service' in Walker, N and Giller, H, *Policy-making in England*, papers presented to the Cropwood Round-Table Conference, December, Cambridge: Institute of Criminology.

Ledger, J (2001) 'The National Probation Service dancing to its own tune?', *Probation Journal*, vol 48(3), pp 211–13.

McWilliams, W (1983) 'The mission to the English police courts: 1876–1936', *Howard Journal of Criminal Justice*, vol 22, pp 129–47.

McWilliams, W (1985) 'The mission transformed: professionalisation of probation between the wars', *Howard Journal of Criminal Justice*, vol 24(4), pp 257–74.

McWilliams, W (1986) 'The English probation system and the diagnostic ideal', *Howard Journal of Criminal Justice*, vol 25(4), pp 241–60.

McWilliams, W (1987) 'Probation, pragmatism and policy', *Howard Journal of Criminal Justice*, vol 26(2), pp 97–121.

Martinson, R (1974) 'What works? – questions and answers about prison reform', *The Public Interest*, vol 35, pp 22–54.

Morgan, R (2003) Speech at *Offenders and Punishment: Options for the 21st Century*, a seminar organised by the Correctional Services Standards Unit, Home Office and NACRO, 5 March, Church House, London.

Nash, M (1999a) 'Enter the Polibation Officer', *International Journal of Police Science and Management*, March, vol 1(4), pp 360–68.

Nash, M (1999b) *Police, Probation and Protecting the Public*, London: Blackstone.

Nash, M (2001) 'Influencing or influenced? – the Probation Service and its policy networks' in Savage, S, Ryan, M and Wall, D (eds), *Policy Networks in Criminal Justice*, Basingstoke: Palgrave.

Nash, M and Ryan, M (2003) 'Modernising and joining-up government; the case of the prison and probation services', *Contemporary Politics*, vol 9(2), pp 157–69.

Nash, M and Savage, S (1994) 'Law and order: the Conservative agenda' in Atkinson, R, Robins, L and Savage, S (eds), *Public Policy in Britain*, London: Macmillan.

National Probation Service (August 2001) *A New Choreography*, London: Home Office.

Pratt, J (2000) 'The return of the Wheelbarrow Men; or, the arrival of postmodern penality', *British Journal of Criminology*, vol 40, pp 127–45.

Ryan, M (2003) *Penal Policy and Culture in England and Wales*, Winchester: Waterside.

Walker, H and Beaumont, B (1981) *Probation Work: Critical Socialist Practice*, Oxford: Blackwell.

Worrall, A and Walton, D (2002) 'Prolific offender projects, and the reduction of volume property crime: targeted policing and case management', *Vista*, vol 7(2), pp 34–37.

CHAPTER 17

THINKING ABOUT IMPRISONMENT[1]

Joe Sim

SUMMARY

This chapter considers a question of central concern to criminologists, politicians and policy-makers, namely: 'what are prisons for?' In order to answer this question, the chapter focuses on a number of key debates concerning the *role* of the prison in England and Wales and the USA. As in the other substantive areas in criminology, this is a *contested* terrain, in that there are hotly debated theoretical positions articulated by different writers. These positions compete with each other, not only for domination in the academic world, but also, perhaps more crucially, they seek to influence the world of policy and politics.

In thinking about these issues, it is important to recall a point made in Chapters 1 and 2 concerning the complex nature of the criminal justice system. This point also applies to prisons. They are immensely complicated, hybrid institutions which respond to a range of different, often overlapping pressures. Some of these pressures are internal: for example, overcrowding, prisoner protests or staff culture. Some are generated by external events: for example, a hardening in sentencing policies, media controversies over serious crimes, or law and order campaigns. Often it is difficult to pinpoint exactly the direct influence of specific pressures at particular moments. On other occasions, these pressures are more overt and direct and thus easier to detect.

The chapter is organised into three parts. First, it focuses on recent debates concerning prisons in England and Wales through comparing and contrasting penal policy under successive Conservative Governments with that of the New Labour Government. Secondly, it considers how writers from different theoretical traditions have explained policy changes in England, Wales and the USA. Finally, it focuses on the debate between reformers and abolitionists, a debate which is central to thinking about the future of a system which, in England and Wales in the financial year 2002–03, cost over £2.2 *billion* to operate.

KEY TERMS

Rehabilitation; deterrence; incapacitation; 'prison works'; the working prison; continuities and discontinuities; liberalism; reform; partnerships and 'joined-up government'; social divisions; prisons and social order; gender and punishment; negative reform; abolitionism.

---

1   This chapter is dedicated to John Doogan.

FROM REHABILITATION TO PUNISHMENT

Since its emergence in the late 18th century, the modern prison has fulfilled a number of publicly-specified, overt roles including incapacitation, punishment, deterrence, reform and rehabilitation. These often contradictory goals have sat uneasily together for the last 200 years. Alternatively, at different moments during this period, one or more of these goals has taken precedence over the others. Thus, during the 1950s and 1960s, rehabilitation (at least in theory) was emphasised. This goal was built on the idea that the prison could change the behaviour of the offender through a series of professional and policy interventions designed, in the words of the 1964 Prison Rules, 'to establish in [offenders] the will to lead a good and useful life on discharge, and to fit them to do so' (cited in Fitzgerald and Sim, 1982: 25).

From the mid-1970s, critics from the left and the right attacked the rehabilitative ideal. For the former group, the rhetoric of rehabilitation justified unacceptable interventions into the lives of prisoners, often by non-accountable professionals. For those on the political right, rehabilitation represented no more than an exercise in the pampering of prisoners (Hudson, 1987). Finally, for prisoners, rehabilitation was merely ideological rhetoric. In practice, the grim reality of prison life was built on punishment and humiliation. This, in turn, led directly to individual recidivism and collective alienation (Fitzgerald and Sim, 1982). In short, to paraphrase Robert Martinson, 'nothing work[ed]'.

The cynicism towards rehabilitation was intensified, in May 1979, with the election of a neo-conservative government in the UK, led by Margaret Thatcher. Thatcher's election (and that of Ronald Reagan as President of the USA a year later) challenged the social democratic consensus that had developed since 1945 and within which the discourse of rehabilitation was firmly situated. Instead, Thatcher and Reagan's neo-conservatism was built on the doctrine of free market economics and constructing social and criminal justice policies based on punishment, individual responsibility, respect for authority, minimal support for state welfare provision and maximum support for law and order institutions (Sim, 1987; Ryan and Sim, 1998).

THE CONSERVATIVES IN POWER

Ian Crow has noted that in the 1980s there were different strands in the debates around penal policy. The Thatcher Government 'extolled' the prison as a place to punish the most serious offenders. At the same time, ministers recognised that for less serious offenders, using prisons was 'expensive and ineffective ... Consequently the Home Office began to develop a policy which, by focussing more on the punitive aspects of community-based sentences, would reduce reliance on imprisonment' (Crow, 2001: 104–05).

This process was central to the debate around penal policy through the 1980s and into the early 1990s as successive Conservative Home Secretaries, such as William Whitelaw, David Waddington and Kenneth Clarke, called for alternatives to custody to be implemented and for prisons to be used more sparingly for less serious offenders. These calls, many argue, had some success, particularly in the early 1990s, when the prison population fell to the point where 'the average population in 1992 was lower than any year since 1984 (apart from 1990)'. This fall was due to changes in the parole system and 'the introduction of the Criminal Justice Act 1991 on 1 October 1992' (Home Office, 1993: 2–3).

However, within a year, this policy was to be overturned. The appointment of Michael Howard as Home Secretary in May 1993 was to see the reassertion of the prison as *the* institution for preventing crime through a penal policy based on the punitive combination of discipline, deterrence and incapacitation (Crow, 2001: 106).

THE MOMENT OF MICHAEL HOWARD

As soon as he became the sixth Conservative Home Secretary in 14 years, Michael Howard instituted a range of policies that extended the coercive capabilities of an already powerful state apparatus. As in the 1970s, the intensification in state authoritarianism was legitimated by a series of media generated moral panics which provided the Government with a populist groundswell of support for its policies. The brutal abduction and murder of two-year old James Bulger by two 10-year-old boys in Liverpool in February 1993 was a key moment in this process of intensification. For both the Conservative Party and their New Labour opponents, the child's death at the hands of two strangers, who themselves were children, symbolised the desperate state of a society in which the feral young appeared to be beyond control and therefore needed some harsh and punitive discipline in order to secure their redemption (Ryan and Sim, 1998).

For Howard, this redemption was to be achieved through retribution and revenge. In his now notorious speech to the Conservative Party conference in October 1993, he reversed many of the precepts that had underpinned the 1991 Criminal Justice Act and declared that the prison could be made to work in the fight against crime. This would be done by pursuing policies that subjected prisoners to regimes based on bleak and disciplined austerity (Sparks, 1996). Like Bentham's 19th century Panopticon, its grim, late 20th century descendant was designed to grind the consciousness of the confined between the twin millstones of retribution and revenge, out of which would come a submissive respect for order and authority.

Howard's belief in the discourse of 'prison works' had profound consequences. Numbers inside began to accelerate. By 1994, the population had climbed to 48,800. This was 4,200 more than in 1993 and represented 'the highest annual rise since 1970' (Home Office, 1995: 1). Changes were also felt on the ground:

> Education and preparation for release were scaled down to meet financial targets. Parole and home leave ceased to be a normal expectation as an essential aid to rehabilitation and resettlement and became a privilege to be awarded on criteria dominated by the possible risk to the public. 'Treatment' became a matter not of change but of compulsion and control, with its emphasis on drug treatment and incentives ... The professional cynicism which led to the belief in the '70s that 'nothing works' gave way in the '90s to the public and political conviction that 'punishment works'. (Prison Service Journal, 1998: 1)

However, there are two important qualifications to be made with respect to Howard's time at the Home Office. First, the spiraling prison population cannot solely be blamed on his interventions. Magistrates and judges (as well as the mass media) were also proactive in the tightening of the penal screw:

[In 2003] sentencers are now imposing longer prison sentences for serious crimes, and they are more likely to imprison offenders who 10 years ago [in 1993] would have received a community penalty or even a fine. Tougher sentencing practice has come about through the interplay of several factors: an increasingly punitive climate of political and media debate about punishment; legislative changes and new guideline judgments and sentencers' perceptions of changes in patterns of offending. (Hough et al, 2003: 1)

Secondly, how far Howard's policy was a departure from past policies is a matter of conjecture. For example, during the 1950s and 1960s, when the emphasis on rehabilitation was at its peak, it could be argued that the authoritarian discourses of punishment, pain and revenge remained fundamental to the operationalisation of power inside and that these discourses had simply remained invisible, hidden behind the ideological cloak of medical benevolence and reform (Sim, 1990). Therefore, according to this view, Howard's appointment in May 1993 only reasserted and made more visible the already-existing authoritarian discourses that lay at the heart of the modern prison (Sim, forthcoming(a)).

By 1997, a bitterly divided Conservative Party, mired in allegations of political sleaze, moral corruption and policy failure, lost the General Election to a rejuvenated Labour Party whose catchphrase, 'tough on crime, tough on the causes of crime', had not only seeped into the popular imagination but also sent a clear message to the wider society about its law and order credentials and intentions. The prison remained central to the new Government's strategy for crime control. The key question was: what role would the institution play in Tony Blair's modernised 'cool Britannia'?

NEW LABOUR AND THE WORKING PRISON

When New Labour came to power, there were both continuities *and* discontinuities in the Government's law and order strategy. What does this mean? Put simply, New Labour both followed the Conservative position in some areas of social policy and law and order, while deviating in other areas through carving out its own position on these vital issues. The introduction of the Human Rights Act 1998, implemented in October 2000, and heralded by Jack Straw as 'the most significant statement of human rights in domestic law since the 1698 Bill of Rights' (cited in Sim, 2000: 186), is a good example of a discontinuity between New Labour and their Conservative predecessors.

What about continuities? Like the Conservatives, New Labour's law and order gaze remained fixed on regulating and criminalising the activities of the powerless, particularly those involving young people, while simultaneously engaging in the effective non-regulation and non-criminalisation of the illegal behaviour of the powerful. Arguably, the latter's activities have as much impact on the lives of many people, and society's social fabric, as conventional crimes committed by the powerless (Sim, 2000). Nonetheless, between 1997 and 2003, 45 law and order and immigration bills were passed which created over 600 new crimes, the majority of which were concerned with the behaviour of the economically powerless and the socially marginalised (Cohen, 2003).

What about the prison system? In terms of continuity with the Conservatives, prisons remained central to New Labour's law and order strategy. Listed below are some of the more important facts concerning prisons, culled from various reports published between 2001 and 2003, a period in which New Labour consolidated its hold on power by winning a second term in office:

- In 2002, a total of 136,200 people were sent to prison either as remand or sentenced prisoners.
- In July 2003, the average daily prison population stood at just over 74,000 and was rising at 150 a week. In early 1993, the population was 41,000.
- By June 2009, the figure could be as high as 109,600.
- With an incarceration rate of 139 per 100,000 of its population, England and Wales had the highest rate of imprisonment in Western Europe.
- Black people were six times more likely to be jailed than white people. One in every 100 black adults in Britain was in prison. The incarceration rate for white people was 170 per 100,000 of the population; for South Asians it was 166; for Chinese and other groups it was 536; and for black people it was 1,140.
- In the decade up to 2001, the number of adult female receptions into prison rose by 223 per cent compared with 74 per cent for adult males.
- In June 2001, 26 per cent of the female population were ethnic minority women.
- Between 1997 and 2002, 471 prisoners committed suicide.
- In July 2003, reports leaked to *The Guardian* newspaper indicated that in a two week period there were 1,200 serious incidents, while assaults, escapes and deaths in custody had reached record levels. For many, the newspaper's headline summed up the situation: 'Britain's jails hit crisis point: leaked reports reveal prison chaos' (*The Guardian*, 16 June 2003).

Like their Conservative predecessors, an expanding prison system was a fundamental cornerstone in New Labour's response to crime. This expansion was underpinned by a number of significant changes to sentencing policy. In December 1999, the Government implemented the final part of the Crime (Sentences) Act 1997, which had been introduced initially by Michael Howard. This Act allowed mandatory sentences to be imposed by the courts, including life sentences for those convicted for a second time of a serious, violent or sexual offence and mandatory minimum sentences of three years for domestic burglars convicted for a third time.

However, there was one very important difference – a discontinuity – between New Labour and the Conservatives regarding penal policy. The Government believed that the prison could be *made* to work, not by pursuing Howard's policy of bleak austerity, but through committing staff and resources to developing a range of different programmes specifically designed to change attitudes, challenge behaviour and lower the rate of recidivism. Programme delivery was to be achieved through the construction and consolidation of a web of *partnerships* operating *between* different criminal justice and local authority agencies in order to provide a '*joined-up*' response to crime and punishment. The principles of this strategy were laid down in the Crime and Disorder Act 1998. By 2000/01, partnerships were delivering programmes at over 100 sites in the prison estate. Over 1,700 staff, including psychologists, prison officers, probation officers and education officers, were involved (Blud et al, 2003). The programmes included Reasoning and Rehabilitation, Enhanced Thinking Skills, Problem Solving, and CALM (Controlling Anger and Learning to Manage it) (Stewart, 2000).

A further key element in New Labour's strategy involved the continuous evaluation and monitoring of the programmes by different groups of researchers, including criminologists, in order to identify 'what works', so that 'best practice' could be extended across the prison system to enhance the fight against crime and recidivism. New Labour's position is best summed by Jack Straw who, in 1998, as the new Home Secretary, delivered the annual Prison Reform Trust lecture, pointedly entitled 'Making Prisons Work' (Straw, 1998).

EXPLAINING THE 21ST CENTURY PRISON

These developments bring us back to the central question that underpins this chapter: what is the role of the prison in the modern world? It is here that the chapter considers a number of *different* and *competing* theoretical explanations.

The liberal perspective

For liberals, the prison fulfils a number of different functions, including deterrence, incapacitation, punishment, reform and rehabilitation. As noted above, since its inception at the end of the 18th century, the prison has been defended by reference to one or more of these functions (Mathiesen, 2000). For liberals, reform and rehabilitation provide *the* justification for the continued existence of the prison. Thus, the changes instituted by New Labour are regarded positively, in that both Jack Straw and David Blunkett have rejected the bleak warehousing underpinning Michael Howard's discourse of 'prison works' and have resurrected the idea of rehabilitation and reform. They welcome the proactive nature of the Government's position and the direct engagement with prisoners to meet their emotional and educational needs in order to prevent the desperate slide back into recidivism when they are released. Liberals would also support New Labour's policy of 'joined-up' government.

However, they would criticise the general direction of penal policy and would identify a number of problems that need to be confronted if the prison is to perform its crime prevention role. These problems would include overcrowding. As the prison population has increased, so has overcrowding, particularly in local prisons. By June 2003, 85 out of 138 prisons were overcrowded, while nine of the 13 prisons built since 1993 were also overcrowded (Solomon, cited in NACRO, 2003: 6). The 'knock-on' effect of overcrowding is also very important for liberals as it generates often appalling, lock-down conditions for short-term prisoners in particular, to the detriment of decent and stimulating prison regimes. It also impacts on prisoners' families (particularly women's families) as prisoners will often be transferred to less overcrowded prisons some distance away from their relatives and friends, who, because of their own economic circumstances, cannot afford to travel to see them. At the end of February 2003, 40,000 prisoners were in this position (www.prisonreformtrust.org.uk/responses5.html).

Liberal campaigning groups would also criticise New Labour's sentencing policies. For the Prison Reform Trust, too many people are being sent to prison, and within this category too many of the *wrong* people are being incarcerated, for example, the mentally ill and the non-violent offender. In July 2003, the Trust published a report by Hough et al (2003). Many of the authors' recommendations chimed with the Trust's position on reforming the sentencing process by issuing guidance to the judiciary not only to send *fewer* people to prison but also to incarcerate them for *shorter* periods of time. They also advocated a 'greater use of fines, the freeing-up of "probation resources"' and deferring 'the time when the "last resort" of imprisonment has to be used' (Prison Reform Trust, 2003: flyer). This last point reinforces the liberal belief in the viability of alternatives to custody in reducing the prison population and underlines the more general liberal belief in the process of enlightened reform. Campaigning for the 'right' policy reforms and supporting their implementation is, for liberals, the key to breaking away from the bankrupt policy that continues to place an ever-increasing reliance on the prison as a response to crime. Finally, liberals would also contend that there are questions to be asked about the effectiveness of the various offending behaviour programmes discussed above, as well as questioning the Government's commitment to adequately resourcing programmes such as prison education and training (www.prisonreformtrust.org.uk/responses5.html).

Critical perspectives

In a chapter of this length, it is impossible to isolate the one, definitive, critical position regarding the role of the contemporary prison. Rather, there are a number of different critical positions, each with their own theoretical roots and substantive arguments. What *does* unite these perspectives, however, is the question of *power* and its relationship to punishment. And, while there might be differences between critical theorists with respect to the definition of power, nonetheless, it is their emphasis on how power operates both inside and outside the walls of the prison that remains a key theoretical and political difference between their accounts and more liberal accounts.

A second key difference between them concerns the scepticism within critical theory regarding liberal notions of reform. For critical theorists, reforms often simply extend the state's power to punish and do little to confront the problem of the prison itself and indeed may simply legitimate its further expansion. This issue is considered in greater depth in the conclusion to this chapter.

SOCIAL ORDER AND THE PRISON

The role of the prison in the maintenance of an inequitable and unjust social order is the focus for a number of critical writers, some of whom adopt an explicitly Marxist position on this issue, some of whom do not. However, what unites them is the shared view that the expansion in prison numbers in North America and Western Europe has *little* to do with crime control. Rather, it has *everything* to do with maintaining an unequal and unjust social order. This perspective has a long history in criminology, but became particularly significant in the 1970s, when a number of theorists argued that the institution, historically and contemporaneously, was concerned *not* with the elimination of crime but with the struggle to regulate and normalise those groups who posed problems for maintaining social order (Mathiesen, 1974; Ignatieff, 1978; Foucault, 1979: Fitzgerald and Sim, 1982). For Foucault, the 19th century prison was not designed to control crime or reduce delinquent recidivism. Rather:

> ... the creation of delinquency is useful in a strategy of political domination because it works to separate crime from politics, to divide the working classes against

themselves, to enhance the fear of prison and to guarantee the authority and powers of the police ... [In Foucault's] account then, the prison does not control the criminal so much as control the working class by creating the criminal ... (Garland, 1990: 150)

For Mathiesen, the contemporary prison fulfils a number of roles. This includes a *material* role, in that it regulates and controls groups such as the unemployed whose presence and behaviour is problematic for the ongoing functioning of the capitalist free market. It also performs an *ideological* role, in that it distracts attention away from the destructive crimes committed by the powerful through focusing on those inside who are socially constructed as the 'real' criminals within society (Mathiesen, 1974).

For more recent writers, penal developments in the USA provide a perfect illustration of the relationship between the prison and the maintenance of an unjust and inequitable social order. In 2000, the rate of imprisonment was 680 per 100,000 of the population. This was 'five times as large as it was in 1972' (Garland, 2000: 1). This process of 'mass imprisonment', which has taken the prison population to over two million, has impacted disproportionately on black Americans (Wacquant, 2001). As Garland notes, 'if current trends continue 30 per cent of black males born today [in 2000] will spend some of their lives in prison' (Garland, 2000: 2). By October 2003, black Americans made up 50 per cent of the prison population (and 30 per cent of the American army) despite only constituting 12 per cent of the general population (www.criticalresistance.org).

For Davis, this situation has profound ideological implications:

We ... think about imprisonment as a fate reserved for others, a fate reserved for the 'evildoers', to use a term recently popularized by George W Bush. Because of the persistent power of racism, 'criminals' and 'evildoers' are, in the collective imagination, fantasized as people of color. The prison therefore functions ideologically as an abstract site into which undesirables are deposited, relieving us of the responsibility of thinking about the real issues afflicting those communities from which prisoners are drawn in such disproportionate numbers. This is the ideological work that the prison performs – it relieves us of the responsibility of seriously engaging with the problems of our society, especially those produced by racism and, increasingly, global capitalism. (Davis, 2003: 16)

For women (and black women in particular), the numbers detained have been even more spectacular:

... the economic and political shifts of the 1980s – the globalization of economic markets, the deindustrialization of the US economy, the dismantling of such social service programs as Aid to Families of Dependent Children, and, of course, the prison construction boom – produced a significant acceleration in the rate of women's imprisonment both inside and outside of the United States. In fact, women remain today the fastest growing sector of the US prison population. (Davis, 2003: 65)

Beckett and Western (2001: 36) argue that these developments are built on the classic neo-conservative doctrine of rolling back the welfare state, while constructing a prison system to regulate and discipline those groups marginalised by the workings of the free market economy. Therefore, 'governments that provide more generous welfare benefits have lower incarceration rates, controlling for other relevant factors, while governments that spend less on welfare incarcerate a larger share of their residents'. For Downes (2001: 64), prisons are the end-product of a 'macho' economy built on cut-throat competition, instability, low wages, asset stripping and lack of respect for human dignity, so that 'the machismo of the powerless is a symmetrical parody of that of the powerful in a winner/loser culture'.

For Parenti, prisons, along with the other institutions of a highly militarised *and* violent American state, are central to the management of 'rising inequality and surplus populations' that have been generated as a result of neo-liberal economic restructuring. He notes that 'throughout this process of economic restructuring the poor have suffered, particularly poor people of color' (Parenti, 1999: xii). Shelden and Brown (2000: 39) have developed a similar argument and point to the role of corporate interests in the 'crime control industry' where 'profits are a major moving force ... rather than the goal of reducing crime and suffering. An important component of this industry is the "prison industrial complex", one of the fastest growing industries in the US'.

Finally, American critics would argue that instead of spending billions each year on prisons, the Government should redirect resources towards schools, welfare and health. In the view of these critics, this redirection would directly challenge the criminogenic circumstances that underpin the criminal behaviour of many of the poor (www.criticalresistance.org).

While the arguments provided by Parenti and Wacquant are persuasive, they have also been criticised by Matthews (2003a), who argues that Parenti's 'account ... is too "top down"'. In other words, he 'does not explain why so many of the poor and working class endorse, indeed demand, effective "law and order" policies, unless one is to assume that they are extremely gullible and are duped into apparent agreement by manipulative politicians' (Matthews, 2003a: 240). Matthews also maintains that Wacquant does not explain why a white powerful elite expends so much energy and spends so much money on regulating poor black people: 'from a neo-liberal vantage point it would presumably be cheaper and easier to reduce intervention to a minimum, and to leave ghetto residents to deal with their own problems, while spending their money protecting themselves' (Matthews, 2003a: 241). Ultimately, for Matthews, both writers provide 'an overly conspiratorial and functionalist account' of the modern prison in America (Matthews, 2003a: 241).

GENDER AND THE PRISON

For feminist and other critical writers, the huge rise in the number of women in prison has little to do with the impartial application of the law to the lawbreaker, as liberals would contend. Rather, it has everything to do with maintaining a social order divided not just by social class and 'race', but also by gender.

For Carlen, women's criminality is directly related to their economic marginalisation which generates grinding poverty (Carlen, 1988). The prison is part of a criminal justice apparatus which is geared, *not* towards some liberal notion of rehabilitation, but towards the disciplinary regulation *and* punishment of those who have transgressed the dominant discourses that define what is a 'normal' woman: feminine, sexually respectable, home-loving, compliant and maternal. In short, the power to punish is no more than the power to 'normalise' the deviant woman (Carlen, 1983).

Recent research has added to this critique by pointing out that the various reforms and programmes that have been introduced into women's prisons have been subverted by the prison's punitive apparatus. In a process of 'carceral clawback' (Carlen, 2002a), not only have these programmes been incorporated into the system and mobilised *against* imprisoned women to disempower them further, but also they leave untouched the complex inter-relationship between structures of domination and subordination arising out of, and embedded in, social divisions around social class, gender and 'race' (Hannah-Moffat, 2001; Hannah-Moffat and Shaw, 2001; Carlen, 2002b).

Feminist and others would also critique the cognitive behaviour programmes developed by New Labour which were discussed earlier. First, the new professional partnerships accept the prison as inevitable and fail to confront the power of the institution to inflict punishment and pain. These professionals should be conceptualised as 'prison-illiterate therapeutic experts who have failed to remember (or who have never realised) that prison is for punishment by incarceration' (Carlen, 2002c: 156). Secondly, the knowledge developed by professional groups via these programmes is used to reinforce the powerlessness of prisoners. Professionals are thus intervening as 'judges of normality' whose power and knowledge are being operationalised for the benefit of the institution and its management (Foucault, cited in Sim, forthcoming(b)). Thirdly, more women are increasingly being labelled as 'at risk' of becoming recidivists and are therefore deemed to be in need of intervention, usually of a psychiatric or medical nature. Finally, these programmes marginalise the question of social inequality. Explanations of women's deviance 'are based on a reductionist presupposition, namely that it is their mangled perspective and understanding about the world that needs to be altered' (Sim, forthcoming(b)). Or in Carlen's words, the problem is seen as 'being in [the women's] heads, not their social circumstances' (Carlen, 2002c: 169).

CONCLUSION

In 2003, more than 8.75 million people were confined in 205 countries, half of them in three countries alone: USA (1.96 million), China (1.43 million) and Russia (0.92 million). The UK had the highest rate of imprisonment in the European Union (Wamsley, 2003: 1). Globally, therefore, the prison system is a growth industry which employs hundreds of thousands of workers and generates a whole sub-strata of work for private companies who are increasingly involved in building and managing institutions, as well as providing high-tech security equipment and contracted-out services such as catering and education. (The system also generates work for criminologists to study and write about them.)

What do the theoretical perspectives discussed in this chapter suggest about the future? In many ways, this is a relatively easy question to answer as it comes down to the issue of reform versus abolition. What does this mean?

As we have seen throughout this chapter, reform is central to the liberal position if prisons are to be improved. Together with viable and well-funded alternatives to custody, and a change in the culture and attitudes of the judiciary, reforms will generate a prison system that will rehabilitate prisoners, prevent crime and benefit the society overall.

Critics would argue that this position is naïve. Foucault, for example, maintained that the prison has always been offered as a solution to its own problems. In his book, *Discipline and Punish*, he pointed to a series of critiques mounted against the prison:

- Prisons do not diminish the crime rate.
- Detention causes recidivism.
- Prison encourages the organisation of delinquents who are loyal to each other – it educates in crime.
- When freed, the conditions ex-prisoners experience, for example, unemployment, stigmatisation and surveillance, condemn them to recidivism.
- Prison produces delinquency by throwing the prisoner's family into destitution (Foucault, 1979: 265).

To contemporary ears, these critiques will sound familiar as they are continuously articulated by the mass media and different prison reform groups. And yet, for Foucault, the key point is that these critiques are *not* contemporary, but are taken from newspaper reports published between 1820 and 1845, the period that saw the dawn and consolidation of the modern prison. Therefore, reform is a pointless exercise as:

> ... word for word, from one century to the other, the same fundamental propositions are repeated ... So successful has the prison been that, after a century and a half of 'failures', the prison still exists, producing the same results ... (Foucault, 1979: 270 and 277)

Others, such as Mathiesen, have argued that reforms should only be supported if they have a subversive, 'negative' effect on the system and lead to its eventual abolition. He contrasts these reforms with 'positive' reforms which are incorporated by the system and thus support its never-ending expansion (Mathiesen, 1974). Mathiesen's abolitionist arguments have been very influential in Europe, at least among academics. However, their impact on policy remains difficult to gauge.

In the UK, the early abolitionist movement was heavily influenced by Mathiesen's ideas (Ryan, 1978). British abolitionists have supported the demand for 'negative' reforms and the abolition of the prison system in its present form. They have been involved in a number of successful campaigns around deaths in custody and prison health care. They have also supported prison regimes in the Barlinnie Special Unit and Grendon Underwood, regarding them as examples of regimes which can have an empowering and rehabilitative effect on long-term prisoners in particular. They provide a vision of prisons built on the view that offenders are sent to prison *as* punishment and not *for* punishment (Sim, 1994). For Carlen, the prison should be abolished *'as a "normal" punishment for women'* leaving *'a maximum of only 100 custodial places ... for female offenders convicted or accused of abnormally serious crimes'* (Carlen, 1990: 121, emphasis in the original).

However, abolitionists have also been criticised. Liberals would ask: 'are the prison gates simply to be opened and dangerous individuals released?' In response, abolitionists would argue that there *are* conventionally dangerous individuals who *do* need to be detained, such as men who have raped and/or murdered women. Crucially, however, they would also argue that the definition of dangerousness needs to be debated, redefined and indeed extended to other harmful acts and activities such as those engaged in by the powerful: states, corporations, organisations and individuals. These activities can have a devastating impact on the lives of others but are either not criminalised or do not generate the same punitive response as conventionally dangerous acts such as murder. So, for abolitionists, a key question is: 'who defines what is dangerous and what are dangerous crimes?'

One final critique comes from Matthews (2003b). He maintains that it is important for both liberals and radicals to move beyond their narrow focus on the prison and instead concentrate on: the *total* number of people moving in and out of the institution each year; the *total* number in the penal system overall, that is, those in prison, those on parole and those serving community sentences; and the *total* number who are recycled through the system each year. This would mean analysing 'the processes of recidivism and re-entry' in order to show 'how the continual recycling of the same individuals and groups between prisons and communities creates a damaging but self-sustaining process' (Matthews, 2003b: abstract).

Whichever side you take in this debate, it is undeniable that the modern prison has been a central component in the delivery of punishment for the last 200 years. The key question is this: will the institution still be utilised 200 years from now or will we as a society have found a different, and many would say, more humane strategy for responding to phenomena as socially complex and controversial as crime and punishment?

SEMINAR DISCUSSION TOPICS

- Paying particular attention to continuities and discontinuities between them, compare and contrast the Conservative Party's policies on law, order and prisons with that of New Labour.
- How would liberals justify the continuing use of the prison? What critiques have been made of their position by more radical writers?
- How has gender impacted on prisons and prison regimes?
- What are the main features of the American prison system? How valid is Matthew's critique of Parenti and Wacquant's arguments?
- Critically consider the strengths and weaknesses in the abolitionist position regarding the prison system.

KEY READINGS

There is no one general text that is worth recommending. This is not necessarily a bad thing, as it is very important to read around the subject and not rely on one general text. The following readings cover and elaborate on the debates discussed above, so it is worth exploring as many as possible, as well as exploring the references utilised in the body of this chapter.

Carlen, P (ed) (2003) *Women and Punishment*, Cullompton: Willan.

Crow, I (2001) *The Treatment and Rehabilitation of Offenders*, London: Sage.

Davis, AY (2003) *Are Prisons Obsolete?*, New York: Seven Stories Press.

Gordon, A (1998) 'Globalism and the prison industrial complex: an interview with Angela Davis', *Race and Class*, vol 40(2/3), pp 145–57.

Mathiesen, T (2000) *Prison on Trial*, Winchester: Waterside.

Parenti, C (1999) *Lockdown America*, London: Verso.

Ryan, M and Sim, J (1998) 'Power, politics and punishment in England and Wales 1975–1996' in Weiss, R and South, N (eds), *Comparing Prison Systems*, Amsterdam: Gordon and Breach.

REFERENCES

Beckett, K and Western, B (2001) 'Governing social marginality: welfare, incarceration and the transformation of state policy' in Garland, D (ed), *Mass Imprisonment*, London: Sage.

Blud, L, Travers, R, Nugent, F and Thornton, D (2003) 'Accreditation of offending behaviour programmes in HM Prison Service: "what works" in practice', *Legal and Criminological Psychology*, vol 8(1), pp 69–81.

Box, S (1981) *Power, Crime and Mystification*, London: Tavistock.

Carlen, P (1983) *Women's Imprisonment: A Study in Social Control*, London: Routledge.

Carlen, P (1988) *Women, Crime and Poverty*, Milton Keynes: Open University Press.

Carlen, P (1990) *Alternatives to Women's Imprisonment*, Buckingham: Open University Press.

Carlen, P (2002a) 'Carceral clawback', *Punishment and Society*, vol 4(1), pp 115–21.

Carlen, P (ed) (2002b) *Women and Punishment*, Cullompton: Willan.

Carlen, P (2002c) 'Controlling measures: the repackaging of common-sense opposition to women's imprisonment in England and Canada', *Criminal Justice*, vol 2(2), pp 155–72.

Cohen, N (2003) '661 new crimes and counting', *New Statesman*, 7 July 2003, pp 18–19.

Crow, I (2001) *The Treatment and Rehabilitation of Offenders*, London: Sage.

Davis, AY (2003) *Are Prisons Obsolete?*, New York: Seven Stories Press.

Downes, D (2001) 'The *macho* penal economy: mass incarceration in the United States – a European perspective' in Garland, D (ed), *Mass Imprisonment*, London: Sage.

Fitzgerald, M and Sim, J (1982) *British Prisons*, Oxford: Blackwell.

Foucault, M (1979) *Discipline and Punish*, Harmondsworth: Penguin.

Garland, D (1990) *Punishment and Modern Society*, Oxford: Clarendon.

Garland, D (2000) 'Introduction: the meaning of mass imprisonment' in Garland, D (ed), *Mass Imprisonment: Social Causes and Consequences*, London: Sage.

Hannah-Moffat, K (2001) *Punishment in Disguise*, Toronto: Toronto UP.

Hannah-Moffat, K and Shaw, M (eds) (2001) *An Ideal Prison?*, Halifax, NS: Fernwood.

Home Office (1993) *The Prison Population in 1992*, London: Home Office.

Home Office (1995) *The Prison Population in 1994*, London: Home Office.

Hough, M, Jacobson, J and Millie, A (2003) *The Decision To Imprison: Key Findings*, London: Prison Reform Trust.

Hudson, B (1987) *Justice Through Punishment*, Basingstoke: Macmillan.

Ignatieff, M (1978) *A Just Measure of Pain*, Basingstoke: Macmillan.

Mathiesen, T (1974) *The Politics of Abolition*, London: Martin Robertson.

Mathiesen, T (2000) *Prison on Trial*, Winchester: Waterside.

Matthews, R (2003a) 'Rethinking penal policy: towards a systems approach' in Matthews, R and Young, J (eds), *The New Politics of Crime and Punishment*, Cullompton: Willan.

Matthews, R (2003b) 'Beyond the "revolving door": the emergence of an autopoietic penal system', paper presented at the European Group for the Study of Deviance and Social Control Conference, Helsinki, Finland, September.

NACRO (2003) 'Overcrowded jails aren't working', *Safer Society Magazine*, Autumn, pp 6–7.

Parenti, C (1999) *Lockdown America*, London: Verso.

Prison Reform Trust (2003) *The Decision to Imprison: Sentencing and the Prison Population*, flyer, London: Prison Reform Trust.

Prison Service Journal (1998) 'Comment', *Prison Service Journal*, vol 120, November, p 1.

Ryan, M (1978) *The Acceptable Pressure Group*, Farnborough: Saxon House.

Ryan, M and Sim, J (1998) 'Power, punishment and prisons in England and Wales 1979–1996' in South, N and Weiss, R (eds), *Comparing Penal Systems*, Amsterdam: Gordon and Breach.

Shelden, R and Brown, W (2000) 'The crime control industry and the management of the surplus population', *Critical Criminology*, vol 9(1/2), pp 39–62.

Sim, J (1987) 'Working for the clampdown: prisons and politics in England and Wales' in Scraton, P (ed), *Law, Order and the Authoritarian State*, Milton Keynes: Open University Press.

Sim, J (1990) *Medical Power in Prisons*, Buckingham: Open University Press.

Sim, J (1994) 'The abolitionist approach: a British perspective' in Duff, A, Marshall, S, Dobash, RE and Dobash, RP (eds), *Penal Theory and Practice*, Manchester: Manchester UP.

Sim, J (2000) '"One thousand days of degradation": New Labour and old compromises at the turn of the century', *Social Justice*, vol 27(2), pp 168–92.

Sim J (forthcoming(a)) *The Carceral State: Punishment and Prisons in a Hard Land*, London: Sage.

Sim, J (forthcoming(b)) 'At the centre of the new professional gaze: women, medicine and confinement' in Chan, W, Chunn, D and Menzies, R (eds) *Women, Mental Disorder and the Law*, London: Cavendish Publishing.

Sparks, R (1996) 'Penal "austerity": the doctrine of less eligibility reborn?' in Matthews, R and Francis, P (eds), *Prisons 2000*, Basingstoke: Macmillan.

Stewart, C (2000) 'Responding to the needs of women in prison', *Prison Service Journal*, vol 132, pp 41–43.

Straw, J (1998) *Making Prisons Work*, London: Prison Reform Trust.

Wacquant, L (2001) 'Deadly symbiosis: when ghetto and prison meet and mesh' in Garland, D (ed), *Mass Imprisonment*, London: Sage.

Walmsley, R (2003) 'World Prison Population List (fourth edition)', Home Office Research, Development and Statistics Directorate Findings 188, London: Home Office.

WEBSITES

www.criticalresistance.org, downloaded 11 October 2003

www.prisonreformtrust.org.uk/responses5.html, downloaded 28 October 2003

CHAPTER 18

RESTORATIVE AND INFORMAL JUSTICE[1]

Gerry Johnstone

SUMMARY

Recent years have witnessed the emergence of an increasingly influential international campaign for restorative justice. Proponents of restorative justice suggest that criminal justice should become less focused upon the punishment of offenders and more geared towards committing lawbreakers to repair the harm they have caused. They also suggest that victims, offenders and other ordinary citizens should have the opportunity to play a more active role in the criminal justice process. A basic understanding of restorative justice is now essential for anybody who wishes to participate in the conversation about the future of criminal justice. This chapter looks at what a full-scale shift in the direction of restorative justice might involve, what its benefits might be, and at some concerns which have been expressed about the increasing use of restorative justice.

KEY TERMS

Punishment; reparation; victims; conferencing.

INTRODUCTION

Criminal justice in the modern West is built upon certain assumptions. To most people, these assumptions go without saying. They include:

- the appropriate response to criminal lawbreaking is to punish the lawbreaker;
- the punishment should fit the crime, ie the more malicious or frightful the offender's conduct, the more severe the punishment should be;
- decisions about the punishment to be inflicted in any particular case should be made in a law court by disinterested professionals.

In recent years, faith in these apparently commonsensical beliefs has been undermined. The main challenge has come from an increasingly influential group of campaigners for 'restorative justice'. They suggest that:

- the appropriate response to criminal lawbreaking is to commit the lawbreaker to repairing the damage he or she has caused;
- the principle of making punishment proportionate to a crime should give way to the idea that those injured by criminal acts should receive appropriate and adequate reparation and have other needs met;

---

1   I thank Declan Roche for his very helpful suggestions for improving this chapter.

- decisions about the type and amount of reparation required of an offender should be made outside of a law court by the parties themselves – ie the victim and offender – along with their family members and most important friends.

Many people find such ideas interesting, but cannot see them having a huge practical impact. Nevertheless, campaigners for restorative justice have succeeded in influencing the thinking of policy-makers in numerous countries. Indeed, the British Government has recently published a consultation document announcing its strategy of encouraging the use of restorative justice throughout the adult criminal justice system (Home Office, 2003).

This chapter addresses the following questions:[2]

- What is the thinking behind restorative justice?
- What would a significant shift towards it involve?
- How might society benefit from such a shift?
- Are there reasons for being concerned about the rise of restorative justice?

Before proceeding, it is important to point out that a very wide range of activity and thinking has been promoted under the rubric of restorative justice. Also, individual proponents of restorative justice often disagree among themselves about what counts as restorative justice and about other fundamental matters. In a short chapter such as this, it is necessary to focus on what I take to be some fairly core distinctive features of restorative justice. This involves neglecting many interesting features and glossing over a great deal of the 'internal debate' about the definition of restorative justice. This chapter should hence be read as a very rough guide to restorative justice, useful for somebody who wants to embark upon their own study of the phenomenon, rather than as a comprehensive summary of the topic.

THE TROUBLE WITH PUNISHMENT

Most people think it is natural to respond to criminal lawbreaking by punishing the lawbreaker. If asked why punishment is the appropriate response, they would probably reveal a number of further beliefs:

- Punishment might improve the conduct of offenders. It might drive the message home that the way in which they have behaved is wrong or at least imprudent.
- Punishment is necessary in order to deter other people tempted to break the criminal law.
- Justice requires that those who hurt others should be hurt in return.

There is a long tradition of seeking to undermine such beliefs. Critics of punishment argue that it seldom improves the behaviour of wrongdoers and, for a variety of reasons, often makes their conduct worse. The idea that punishment works as a general deterrent is also frequently dismissed as based upon poor psychology and as clearly refuted by empirical evidence. Moreover, the notion that justice requires

---

2   It draws upon, but also develops and re-articulates, some of the analysis presented in my book *Restorative Justice: Ideas, Values, Debates* (Johnstone, 2002). Given the pedagogic intent of this handbook, I will frequently refer readers to relevant sections of my book on restorative justice, rather than provide detailed reference to primary sources.

hurting those who hurt us tends to be denounced as mean-spirited, irrational or inconsistent with higher moral principles.

The problem faced by critics of punishment is that, even if they succeed in convincing people that punishment is a far from perfect solution to criminal lawbreaking, it is difficult to point to any other solution that is better. For instance, those opposed to punishment frequently suggest, as an alternative, that we should adopt a policy of treatment for offenders.[3] However, as a method of improving people's behaviour, treatment seems to be just as futile as punishment. It is difficult to see how a policy of pure treatment would function as a general deterrent or how it would satisfy those who demand *justice* in the aftermath of a crime. Moreover, treating offenders against their will seems in many ways worse – in ethical terms – than punishing them.

According to its proponents, what is so attractive about restorative justice is that it addresses the age-old problem of finding an alternative to punishment. Restorative justice, they claim, not only does most of the things we expect punishment to do – it holds offenders accountable for their behaviour, it improves their future conduct and it satisfies people's sense of justice – it does these things more effectively and is less costly in both fiscal and human terms. Moreover, it has the potential to meet needs – such as the needs of victims for restitution and healing – which conventional criminal justice neglects.

REPARATION

In the distant past, the punishment of offenders was often not possible, because there was no central authority in society strong enough to impose it. In the absence of state authorities with the power to punish, people wronged by another had to rely upon 'private justice'. This sometimes took the form of violent retaliation. For most people, however, private vengeance was risky, because it could easily escalate into a destructive cycle of tit-for-tat violence. For the same reason, it was often discouraged by the rest of the community. Instead, those who injured others through what we would now define as 'criminal' acts were encouraged and brought under pressure by the community to make things right by paying compensation or restitution to the injured party. Through restitution, many conflicts arising from 'criminal' acts were resolved without violence (Weitekamp, 1996*: 111ff).[4]

Restorative justice campaigners suggest that this system of restitutive justice had a number of advantages over the system of state punishment which eventually displaced it (Johnstone, 2002: Chapter 3). Payment of restitution can have an educative effect, as it makes offenders more aware of the actual harm that their behaviour has caused to real people. From a moral perspective, making people pay for damage they have caused seems easier to justify than inflicting harm upon them and, crucially, restitution provides crime victims with an experience of justice – indeed, its core aim

---

3   See Johnstone (1996: Chapter 1) for an account of the debate about therapeutic approaches to crime as an alternative to punishment.
4   Where an asterisk appears after the date of a publication, an excerpt from the publication is reproduced in a restorative justice reader which I have recently compiled and edited (see Johnstone, 2003). Page references are to the version in the reader.

is less to make offenders pay for their crime and more to satisfy victims by compensating them for their suffering and loss (Barnett, 1977*).

Accordingly, early proponents of restorative justice suggested that this ancient idea of culpable offenders making good the loss they have caused should be revived, as the basis for a new paradigm of criminal justice (Barnett, 1977; Zehr, 1990). Instead of punishing offenders, they suggested, the aim should be to bring them to compensate their victims for the harm sustained (Van Ness and Strong, 2002: 85–86).

However, even if it has the advantages claimed for it, there are several practical and ethical problems with the notion of restitutive justice, at least when it is conceived narrowly as taking the form of offenders replacing property, making monetary payments or performing direct services for their victims. Here I will mention just a few of these problems:

- many offenders will lack the resources required to make up for all the damage their acts caused;

- conversely, some well-off offenders will be able to break the criminal law with near-impunity;

- on its own, it is often insufficient to ease the psychological and emotional harm many victims suffer;

- it is difficult to apply the idea to conduct such as damaging public amenities which does not directly harm an individual or small group but which indirectly harms large numbers of people;

- the idea that offenders can make up for certain crimes simply by paying money to or performing services for their victims seems to trivialise serious wrongdoing.

In response to these problems, proponents of restorative justice have developed the narrow notion of restitution into the broader idea of 'symbolic reparation'.

Symbolic reparation

When a person commits a crime against another, no amount of restitution will undo the 'injury' that has occurred. However, restitution can sometimes perform two functions. First, it might alleviate some of the 'material' loss or damage suffered by the injured party. The second function of restitution is 'symbolic'. As Howard Zehr explains it:

> Restitution by offenders is often important to victims, sometimes because of the actual losses, but just as importantly, because of the symbolic recognition restitution implies. When an offender makes an effort to make right the harm, even if only partially, it is a way of saying 'I am taking responsibility, and you are not to blame'. (Zehr, 2002: 15)

Crucially, once one starts thinking in these terms, it becomes clear that symbolic reparation can be achieved in ways other than payments of money or rendering of services. For instance, some symbolic reparation can be achieved by offenders apologising to their victims and by doing things which will render them less likely to reoffend (Johnstone, 2002: Chapter 6): somebody who injures another through careless driving might, by agreeing to take part in a driver improvement course, let the injured party know that they are accepting responsibility for what happened. Accordingly, a great deal of restorative justice practice is now geared towards getting offenders to communicate – through words, gestures and deeds – that they recognise that what occurred was wrong, that they accept responsibility for the damage caused and that they genuinely repent their criminal conduct and are determined not to repeat it.

VICTIM-ORIENTED JUSTICE

So far, we have looked at some ways in which campaigners for restorative justice answer a very old question: how should we deal with criminal lawbreakers? However, one of the most significant themes of restorative justice is that it is wrong to prioritise this question over the question of what we should do for the victims of criminal lawbreaking. For many restorative justice proponents, the *key* argument for reparation rather than punishment is not that reparation is more appropriate for offenders, but that it is better for victims in that it meets their needs, such as needs for information about the processing and outcomes of their cases, for participation in their cases, and for material and emotional restoration (Strang, 2002: 2–3).

The emergence of restorative justice, then, needs to be understood as part of a broader shift away from a purely offender-focused system of criminal justice towards a more victim-focused system (cf Christie, 1977*: 63–64; Home Office, 2003: 4). However, advocates of restorative justice part company with some other promoters of victims' rights in one important respect. They insist that a criminal justice system can meet victims' needs *without making things worse for suspects and offenders*. They argue that criminal justice need not be a zero-sum game, in which gains for victims mean losses for offenders and vice versa (Strang, 2002: 155ff). Restorative justice can result in 'win-win outcomes', ie a better deal for both victims and offenders.

FROM JUDICIAL SENTENCING TO CONFERENCING

It would, of course, be quite conceivable to shift the emphasis of criminal justice, from punishing offenders to committing them to repair the harm they have caused, whilst retaining the conventional method of decision-making. 'Disinterested strangers' – such as judges or magistrates – could simply be encouraged to impose reparation orders upon offenders, instead of sentencing them to undergo punishment. However, a shift to restorative justice involves more than a shift from punishment to reparation. It also entails a shift in the process by which sentencing is carried out. A central theme of restorative justice is that, in appropriate cases, there should be a conference between the victim and offender, accompanied by family members and most important friends of each, and other people affected fairly directly by the offence, presided over by a facilitator or mediator. Those at the meeting should come to an agreement as to what the offender should do to help repair the damage they have caused.

It is important to make it clear that the proposed conference is intended to perform other functions besides being a forum for sentencing decisions. The conference itself is expected to play a role in repairing the harm done. The very fact that the offender and victim meet face-to-face, in a safe setting, can contribute to repair of the relationship between them. For instance, it can:

> ... break down preconceived and fixed notions: victims discover that offenders are almost certainly less fearsome than they imagined; and, brought face-to-face with their victims, offenders can no longer avoid responsibility by denying to themselves the harm they have caused. (Roche, 2003: 2)

Such meetings also function as forums in which victims can ask questions of offenders which only they can answer and can express their feelings about what happened to them and have these feelings validated by others; these processes are considered vital to recovery from the trauma of victimisation (Zehr, 1990: Chapter 2). Conferences can also function as a forum for 'reintegrative shaming' to take place, ie for people whose opinion matters to offenders to express strong disapproval of what the offender has done, whilst also expressing care for the offender as a person and offering practical and emotional support to them in their efforts to redeem themselves (Moore, 1993; cf Braithwaite, 1989). They also enable offenders to explain what happened in their own terms and from their perspective and to participate in the search for ways of putting things right. This can be crucial to their chances of reintegration, ie re-entering community life as contributing and respected persons.

Conferences, then, are forums in which a group of ordinary citizens, brought together because they have been involved in or affected by a criminal act, can, through respectful dialogue:

- try to ascertain the reasons why one person (or group) inflicted harm upon others;
- try to ascertain and communicate to each other how the offence has affected them – materially and psychologically – and their relationships with others;
- discuss ways of repairing all the damage the crime has caused;
- explore ways of repairing the pre-existing harm that led the offender to choose to harm others;
- explore ways by which the offender can continue to live in the community, in a relationship of mutual trust;
- learn to see and treat each other as human beings who, despite the conflict which now separates them, have a great deal in common.

Conferences could, of course, fulfil all of these functions without them having any sentencing powers. However, most advocates of restorative justice suggest that the conference itself should result in a binding resolution as to:

- what the offender should do to help repair the damage resulting from the crime; and
- what further steps should be taken to prevent reoffending and reassure victims.

We need to be quite clear then that a central proposal of the campaign for restorative justice is that *sentencing powers should be given to groups of ordinary citizens, which will include those affected by the offence, who will exercise those powers not in a public law court but in a 'private' meeting.* Restorative justice proponents hope and sometimes claim that these citizens will use these powers fairly and will exercise compassion and understanding in order to achieve restorative goals such as reparation, reintegration and reconciliation. However, it is also clear that, in the absence of safeguards, such powers can be abused and 'can provide an opportunity for people to indulge their impulses for highly punitive and stigmatizing treatment' (Roche, 2003: 3). Moreover, even if we firmly believe that restorative conferences will bring out the best human qualities of those who participate in them, it is clear that conference participants will lack the knowledge required to ensure that sentences are consistent with those for similar cases elsewhere and that the principle of proportionality is respected (Ashworth, 2002*).

I have mentioned these issues in order to underscore how *radical* this core proposal of restorative justice is. If implemented, it would amount to a fundamental break not only with established sentencing principles, but with our most basic assumptions about how justice takes place. We are accustomed to thinking that:

> Justice occurs in a somber courtroom where a robed judge, sworn jurors and informed counsel calmly and deliberately apply their highest powers of reason to reach a legal decision. (Pillsbury, 1989: 655)

Proponents of restorative justice seem to suggest that justice has a stronger chance of emerging from informal, emotionally-charged meetings of ordinary people affected by the offence, who will be guided as much by their feelings as by legal reason.

What rationale could there be for such a far-reaching shift? To answer this question, we need to look at the restorative critique of 'legal' and 'professional' justice (Johnstone, 2002: Chapter 7). The main thrust of the critique is that when the power and responsibility for dealing with criminal offences is placed in the hands of disinterested strangers (lawyers and other professionals), there are certain gains but also a number of significant losses. In particular:

- decision-makers aim to meet the requirements of universal principles of justice and the bureaucratic needs of the criminal justice system, rather than the more personal needs of ordinary people whose everyday lives are most affected by crime;
- the decision-making process is deprived of the 'local knowledge' and 'nuanced' human judgment which ordinary people can provide;
- decisions have less moral and emotional significance for those subject to them – they are perceived as reflecting the values of a distant state bureaucracy and an abstract law and morality, rather than those of family, friends and community;
- for the same reason, the decisions often fail to provide victims of crime and members of the public with a subjective *experience* of justice;
- families and communities lose their confidence, aptitude and appetite for handling misbehaviour which occurs in their sphere. They become over-dependent upon professionals. As a result, families and communities themselves become weaker.

BENEFITS OF RESTORATIVE JUSTICE

In the early days of the campaign for restorative justice, proponents often made some pretty large claims about what restorative justice can achieve:

- spectacular reductions in reoffending;
- healing of victims;
- reintegration of offenders;

- an increased feeling amongst those subjected to criminal justice that they have been dealt with fairly;
- considerable monetary savings;
- raised morale in criminal justice agencies; and
- the re-creation of strong communities.

Today, such claims are still heard. However, after around two decades of experimentation with various forms of restorative justice, and the publication of results of increasingly sophisticated evaluative studies (for example, Miers et al, 2001; Strang, 2002), statements about the benefits of restorative justice are becoming modest. Yet, the overall message remains that a shift from punitive to restorative justice will improve victim satisfaction with the justice process, reduce crime and reoffending, and deliver justice more effectively (Home Office, 2003).

The increased tendency of restorative justice campaigners towards carefulness in making claims about the advantages of restorative justice, and the seriousness with which they have engaged with 'scientific evaluations' of the approach, are signs of maturity and confidence. It strikes me, however, that there is a tendency towards thinking too narrowly about the benefits of restorative justice. When promoting restorative justice, the inclination of most proponents is to present it as a new justice process which can outperform the more conventional processes of trial and punishment at achieving a number of goals that society thinks the criminal justice system ought to achieve. However, there are other ways of thinking about what restorative justice is and what its benefits to contemporary society might be. In particular, restorative justice might be considered as an important new *perspective* for *thinking critically* about criminal justice.[5]

To explain what I mean by this in the space available here, it is necessary to present an over-simplified picture of existing perspectives on criminal justice. There is a tendency for thinking about criminal justice to fall into one of two opposed camps.

First, there is the *conservative* camp (with a small c). For members of this camp, criminal lawbreakers are – through their own choice – enemies of society who make life a misery for many law-abiding citizens. The job of criminal justice is to suppress this group. In order to carry out this function, criminal justice agencies need more powers and resources, but they should use these resources economically, concentrating on the tasks of identifying and repressing criminal and anti-social elements. Whilst they should remain within the boundaries of justice and decency, they should not waste resources by placing huge obstacles in the way of conviction or by attempting to rehabilitate offenders. The main responsibility of criminal justice agencies is to victims and potential victims of crime and anti-social behaviour.

Second, there is the *progressive* camp. For members of this camp, the harmfulness of the behaviour targeted by the police and dealt with by the criminal justice system tends to be overstated; law-abiding citizens suffer more as a result of socially approved forms of behaviour – including the activities and policies of respectable politicians and business people – than they do at the hands of 'criminals'. Moreover, many of those who break the criminal law do so in response to social conditions

5   For the benefit of students, whereas up to this point I have attempted to act as a fairly neutral guide to restorative justice, in what follows I am consciously expressing more personal opinions.

which restrict their choices and responsibility for the choices they make. Society's response to this group should be less repressive and should also include interventions designed to improve social conditions and promote the welfare of offenders. Society's treatment of suspects and offenders needs to pay much greater attention than it does to their rights and to the demands of civilised behaviour. If we are more compassionate towards offenders, we will in fact have more chance of improving their behaviour; compassion and security are not opposed in the way conservatives assume.

There can be little doubt that, in the battle to influence society's response to criminal lawbreakers, it is the penal conservative camp which currently has the upper hand (Garland, 2001; Pratt, 2002). How has the progressive camp responded to this? Their main strategy so far has been one of ironic commentary.[6] Each new 'conservative' policy or statement, and its consequence, is subjected to scathing exposure, presumably in the hope that people will be persuaded or shocked into rejecting penal conservativism. Less common has been the questioning of the adequacy of the progressive perspective. Yet, it strikes me (among many others) that the progressive perspective is increasingly unable to provide a satisfactory framework for assessing and responding to developments in the field of crime and justice. When faced with many developments – such as the emergence of policies which give victims and the public a more effective voice in the criminal justice process or of public concerns about the lack of any meaningful sanction for juvenile lawbreaking – the stock progressive responses sound increasingly dogmatic.

Is it possible, however, to respond less dogmatically to such developments, without jumping ship from the progressive to the conservative camp? One of the benefits of restorative justice is that it seems to provide a plausible third perspective.[7] This perspective not only allows 'penal progressives' to keep hold of the most important values of their perspective (such as not demonising offenders and regarding their needs as important), it also provides new ways of justifying those values. However, if we look at crime and justice from a restorative perspective, it is also possible to address public concerns which the penal conservative perspective highlights (such as the concern that offenders be held accountable for their conduct and that victims' needs be taken seriously and addressed) without buying into the conservative prescription for meeting these concerns (step up the repression of offenders). Arguably, the neglect of these (legitimate) public concerns by the penal progressive perspective is a major source of its current debilitation.

By adopting a restorative justice perspective, those troubled about the drift toward harsh justice can respond less negatively to developments such as the emergence of policies which allow victim participation in the sentencing process. Instead of dogmatically resisting such policies as dangerous for offenders, restorative justice proponents tend to argue that such policies are dangerous *within the framework of punitive justice*, but are nevertheless an attempt to meet important needs that could be met within a restorative-oriented system. The restorative justice perspective suggests, then, that the response to such policies should not be simply to resist them, but to

6   I am aware, of course, that this is a simplification. To qualify things, the books by David Garland and John Pratt, to which I have just referred, represent two of a number of major attempts to develop sophisticated analyses of and responses to the punitive turn in criminal justice.

7   See also Braithwaite (2000) and Shearing (2001).

show that – in order to be acceptable – they would have to be accompanied by a more fundamental shift in the goals and processes of the criminal justice system.

Finally, a further benefit of the restorative perspective is that it enables those who adhere to the values of penal progressivism to address some of questions which they have found awkward to handle without slipping into the language and proposals of penal conservatives: phenomena such as corporate crime,[8] racially motivated violence and other crimes for which progressives deviate from their general advocacy of compassionate treatment for offenders.

CAUSES FOR CONCERN

Nevertheless, a wide range of concerns have been raised about restorative justice, even by people who are broadly sympathetic towards the idea (see Johnstone, 2003: Part E; Cunneen, 2003). In what follows, I will touch on just a few of these, and pitch the discussion at a fairly general level.

Will the marginalisation of punishment undermine security?

Any proposal to marginalise punishment and replace it with something which seems less harsh on offenders is, of course, going to strike many people as based upon a naïve and dangerously optimistic view of human nature. A typical reaction to such proposals is that there are many people who have no moral qualms about breaking the criminal law, and it is only the fear of punishment that keeps them in check. Even if punishment were retained as an ultimate last resort, such people would regard society's reluctance to use it as a sign of weakness to be exploited. For all its simplicity, this is a fundamental and not unreasonable concern about restorative justice, and the biggest challenge facing the restorative justice movement remains that of convincing people who think like this that their security will not be endangered with a shift from punishment to restorative justice. It would be difficult to over-estimate the size of this challenge.

Mixing benevolence and control

There are other, quite different, concerns about a move away from punishment: concerns about net-widening – ie an increase rather than reduction in the number of people subjected to penal control (Johnstone, 2002: 32; Roche, 2003: 39–40) – and the unjustified interference with liberty. These concerns arise whenever interventions which are intended to promote the well-being of those subject to them are carried out coercively and are blended with a concern to control the same people (Garland, 1985). Those who raise such concerns suggest that, in some ways, we might be better off with a welfare-less system of punishment, based on a principle such as just deserts (von Hirsch, 1990). In such a system, the presupposition would be that penal intervention is harmful to those upon whom it is imposed. Concomitantly, in a liberal society, it would be taken as given that penal interventions should be used sparingly

---

8   Leading restorative justice advocate John Braithwaite (2002) argues that there are in fact strong similarities between the approaches used successfully to regulate corporate crime and those of restorative justice.

and that those threatened with it should be protected by an array of procedural safeguards.

However, once we move away from a pure punitive system, towards one in which punitive goals are combined with intentions to benefit offenders, the temptation arises to use penal intervention less sparingly and to be less concerned to provide procedural safeguards. The 'logic' becomes as follows: if it is our intention to help these people, then why should they be denied our help or be provided with legal safeguards which might prevent them from receiving it? The flaw in this logic is, of course, that it ignores the significance of the fact that coercion is being used (even if it only lurks in the background). Even the most obviously beneficial intervention can become ethically unsound when it is forced upon a person. In a liberal society, people should be protected from the coercive interventions of others, no matter how genuinely benevolent their aims are, since the recipient of benevolence may not see things in the same way. When benevolent interventions are also intended to benefit people other than those subject to them, the need for protection is even greater.

Having raised this concern, it should in fairness be pointed out that most proponents of restorative justice are very alert to this issue. As people who generally exhibit a strong interest in human rights, they have gone to some lengths to develop principles governing the use of restorative justice designed to ensure that the suspects' and offenders' rights are protected and respected (see, for example, the appendices in Johnstone, 2003). On the other hand, there remain plenty of advocates and practitioners of restorative justice who arguably have not grasped fully the nature of this cause for concern.[9]

Concerns about informal justice

We have already touched upon another major concern about restorative justice, which has to do with the dangers of giving ordinary citizens a much more direct role than they currently enjoy in the administration of justice. This may be justifiable on grounds of principle – conflicts are the property of ordinary citizens and this property should be returned to them – and in terms of its possible beneficial social consequences (Johnstone, 2000; cf Christie, 1977*). However, there are also clear risks involved. As Declan Roche bluntly puts it, restorative justice can 'provide an opportunity for people to indulge their impulses for highly punitive and stigmatizing treatment. The rhetoric of restorative justice may be reconciliatory, but the reality can be pure vengeance' (2003: 3). Roche takes many of his fellow restorative justice proponents to task for assuming that restorative justice meetings will always bring out people's better selves. What is required in place of this naïve optimism, he suggests, is some serious attention to the question of how restorative justice programmes can be made publicly accountable, whilst still holding on to the informality and citizen involvement features which are so crucial to their identity and success.

As Roche's own study shows, this issue is far from irresolvable, but a lot more work needs to be done before this and other quite proper concerns about restorative justice can be allayed.

---

9   See Morris (2002*: 462–64) for a discussion of this issue by a firm restorative justice supporter.

FROM METHOD TO GUIDING QUESTIONS

To finish on a positive note, many of these concerns might be avoided if, instead of promoting restorative justice as a new method of responding to wrongdoing, it is envisaged and promoted as a set of guiding questions. Such a suggestion emanates from one of the restorative justice movement's pioneers and most stimulating thinkers, Howard Zehr (2002: 38–40). His idea is that restorative justice be conceived as a set of guiding questions that enable us to reframe issues, thinking beyond the confines of conventional criminal justice. When a wrong occurs, Zehr suggests, in order to sort out what needs to be done, we need to ask:

(1) Who has been hurt?

(2) What are their needs?

(3) Whose obligations are these?

(4) Who has a stake in this situation?

(5) What is the appropriate process to involve stakeholders in an effort to put things right? (Zehr, 2002: 38)

A shift towards restorative justice would mean us giving priority to these neglected questions.

SEMINAR DISCUSSION TOPICS

• Discuss the ways in which restorative justice challenges 'common sense' assumptions of criminal justice.

• How does restorative justice help the victims of crime?

• Using the example provided in Chapter 2, discuss whether you would be prepared to accept a restorative justice resolution if you had experienced a theft from your accommodation by someone that you trusted.

KEY READINGS

Johnstone, G, *Restorative Justice: Ideas, Values, Debates* (Willan, 2002) provides an overview and analysis of debates and critical issues concerning the phenomenon of restorative justice.

Johnstone, G (ed), *A Restorative Justice Reader: Texts, Sources, Context* (Willan, 2003) brings together extracts from the most important and influential contributions to the restorative justice literature, accompanying these with an informative commentary.

Young, R and Hoyle, C, 'Restorative justice and punishment', in McConville, S (ed), *The Use of Punishment* (Willan, 2003), pp 199–234, provides a very useful discussion of the role which restorative justice might play within a reformed criminal justice system, followed by an invaluable bibliographical review.

Zehr, H, *Changing Lenses: A New Focus for Crime and Justice* (Herald Press, 1990) is a highly readable introduction to the principles and philosophies of restorative justice by one of the movement's pioneers.

Zehr, H, *The Little Book of Restorative Justice* (Good Books, 2002) is, as the title suggests, a short overview of the field by Zehr, with the underlying goal of ensuring that restorative justice does not become sidetracked and diverted from its core principles.

www.restorativejustice.org is an excellent website containing tutorials, resources, web tours, reading guides and much else.

www.restorativejustice.org.uk is the website of the British-based *Restorative Justice Consortium*, which brings together a range of organisations and groups with an interest in restorative justice and contain lots of useful links and resources.

REFERENCES

Ashworth, A (2002) 'Responsibilities, rights and restorative justice', *British Journal of Criminology*, vol 42(3), pp 578–95.

Barnett, R (1977) 'Restitution: a new paradigm of criminal justice', *Ethics*, vol 87, pp 279–301.

Braithwaite, J (1989) *Crime, Shame and Reintegration*, Cambridge: CUP.

Braithwaite, J (2000) 'The new regulatory state and the transformation of criminology' in Garland, D and Sparks, R (eds), *Criminology and Social Theory*, Oxford: OUP, pp 47–69.

Braithwaite, J (2002) *Restorative Justice and Responsive Regulation*, Oxford: OUP.

Christie, N (1977) 'Conflicts as property', *British Journal of Criminology*, vol 17(1), pp 1–15.

Cunneen, C (2003) 'Thinking critically about restorative justice' in McLaughlin, E, Ferguson, R, Hughes, G and Westmarland, L (eds), *Restorative Justice: Critical Issues*, London: Sage.

Garland, D (1985) *Punishment and Welfare: A History of Penal Strategies*, Aldershot: Gower.

Garland, D (2001) *The Culture of Control: Crime and Social Order in Contemporary Society*, Oxford: OUP.

Home Office (2003) *Restorative Justice: The Government's Strategy*, London: Home Office Communication Directorate.

Johnstone, G (1996) *Medical Concepts and Penal Policy*, London: Cavendish Publishing.

Johnstone, G (2000) 'Penal policy making: elitist, populist or participatory?', *Punishment and Society*, vol 2(2), pp 161–80.

Johnstone, G (2002) *Restorative Justice: Ideas, Values, Debates*, Cullompton: Willan.

Johnstone, G (ed) (2003) *A Restorative Justice Reader: Texts, Sources, Context*, Cullompton: Willan.

Miers, D, Maguire, M, Goldie, S, Sharpe, K, Hale, C, Netten, A, Uglow, S, Doolin, K, Hallam, A, Enterkin, J and Newburn, T (2001) *An Exploratory Evaluation of Restorative Justice Schemes*, London: Home Office.

Moore, D (1993) 'Shame, forgiveness and juvenile justice', *Criminal Justice Ethics*, vol 12(1), pp 3–25, also at www.lib.jjay.cuny.edu/cje/html/sample2.html.

Morris, A (2002) 'Critiquing the critics: a brief response to critics of restorative justice', *British Journal of Criminology*, vol 42(3), pp 596–615.

Pillsbury, S (1989) 'Emotional justice: moralizing the passions of criminal punishment', *Cornell Law Review,* vol 74, pp 655–710.

Pratt, J (2002) *Punishment & Civilization,* London: Sage.

Roche, D (2003) *Accountability in Restorative Justice,* Oxford: OUP.

Shearing, C (2001) 'Punishment and the changing face of governance', *Punishment and Society,* vol 3(2), pp 203–20.

Strang, H (2002) *Repair or Revenge: Victims and Restorative Justice,* Oxford: Clarendon.

Van Ness, D and Strong, K (2002) *Restoring Justice,* 2nd edn, Cincinnati, OH: Anderson.

von Hirsch, A (1990) 'Proportionality in the philosophy of punishment', *Criminal Law Forum,* vol 1(2), pp 259–90.

Weitekamp, E (1996) 'The history of restorative justice', in Bazemore, G and Walgrave, L (eds), *Restorative Juvenile Justice: Repairing the Harm of Youth Crime,* Monsey, NY: Criminal Justice Press, pp 75–102.

Zehr, H (1990) *Changing Lenses: A New Focus for Crime and Justice,* Scottdale, PA: Herald Press.

Zehr, H (2002) *The Little Book of Restorative Justice,* Intercourse, PA: Good Books.

CHAPTER 19

CRIMINAL JUSTICE IN SCOTLAND

Anne Reuss

SUMMARY

This chapter aims to provide a brief narrative introduction to the key characteristics and principles of Scottish criminal justice. Different criminal justice systems do exist in the UK (see Chapter 2), contrary to what many may think, and there are indeed English and Welsh, and Scottish criminal justice systems, each with their own history, their own laws, their own practices and their own policies for dealing with and addressing criminal behaviour. The practitioners within each system are accountable to different parliaments, but because the nature of criminal justice is ever-changing, the chapter will focus on those aspects of Scottish criminal justice that are unique to it and which give it a separate and distinct identity from other systems. The chapter will introduce three dimensions of Scottish criminal justice:

- a brief history of Scots criminal law;
- the Scottish criminal courts and personnel;
- the criminal justice process in Scotland.

It is important to reiterate the point made earlier in this book (see Chapter 1) that there is currently a '… bewildering array of public and private responses to crime'. This chapter does not seek to provide any kind of judgment on or detailed account of every aspect of Scottish criminal law and Scottish criminal justice in the response to crime. Rather, it hopes to raise awareness of 'difference' that is socially, culturally, politically and economically embedded, whilst simultaneously recognising that crime, deviance and the strategies adopted for their control have an homogeneous quality that impacts upon the lives of many people in the UK.

It is also worth pointing out that, in observing 'the territorial principle', the Scottish courts are only concerned with crimes committed in Scotland, although this can be complicated where, for example, a crime is committed in Scotland with effect beyond Scotland or, conversely, a crime is committed abroad that has an effect in Scotland. In some circumstances, therefore, criminal acts may be triable and subject to the principles of Scots law depending upon how the 'main act' or element of an offence has been performed (McCall Smith and Sheldon, 1997).

KEY TERMS

Act of Union 1707; legal personnel in Scotland – judges, Lord Advocate, advocates, solicitors; the criminal courts; children's hearings; the criminal justice process in Scotland; penalties.

A BRIEF HISTORY OF SCOTS CRIMINAL LAW

Most writers of texts on the history of the Scottish legal system will be at pains to point out the richness and diversity of that history and its inextricable links with the notion of a Scottish nation where an independent legal system with 'its own distinctive character' (Busby et al, 2000: 1) symbolises a great deal of what it is that is unique about Scotland and what differentiates it from England in particular. In a kind of 'chronological reversal' of historical events, it is as well to state at the outset that Scotland does indeed have its own parliament again, established on 1 July 1999 (the first was established in the 14th and 15th centuries, but was adjourned in 1707 under the Act of Union while retaining its own system of law).

That rich and diverse history of Scottish law, however, can be traced back to the 9th century, when matters of land rights and land ownership were 'settled' through battle (particularly prior to this time) and with recourse to Norse law, as the land that is now known as Scotland was subject to raids and attacks from Scandinavia. However, the 12th century saw the beginnings of mainstream historical developments in Scots law, characterised by local administration, and by the 13th century there was a degree of recognition both within and beyond what had become a kingdom. Mediaeval law in Scotland was itself to develop around the forms and origins of English law, although one would have to acknowledge that it was never quite the same, but these early forms of law also saw developments within what would eventually become the Scottish Sheriff Court and High Court of Justiciary which prevail today. It was around this time that Scotland developed its own parliament, which was responsible for legislation, some of which still forms part of Scots law today. Throughout the 14th and 15th centuries, the clergy, through canon law and ecclesiastical jurisdiction, also played a powerful role in the formation and development of Scots law. It was not until the 16th and 17th centuries that secularisation came to characterise the court system as, by the mid-1500s, canon law and the power of the Catholic church became somewhat lessened as a result of the Reformation. However, as long as there was a degree of 'theological neutrality' about the law, it remained as was and subsequently became part of general Scots law. Power struggles, conquests, alliances of one sort or another, absolute monarchy, canon law, Roman law, wars – all have played a significant role in the history and development of the law in Scotland, just as they have elsewhere, but it is in tandem with the development of English law and its domination through the Westminster Parliament that we can discern the maturation of the Scottish legal system, especially from the 18th century onwards.

Scotland retained its own separate laws and legal system after the Act of Union of 1707, which ensured and safeguarded the independence of Scots law. Several writers were by this time systematically bringing together the decisions of the Scots courts in an attempt to rationalise Scots law grounded in European notions of equity and natural justice, one of the most significant writers being the Viscount of Stair, James Dalrymple (1619–95). However, no great changes were made throughout the 18th century other than perhaps the Criminal Procedure Act of 1701, which safeguarded against detention without trial. By the 19th century, English law was having a profound influence on Scots law, more especially as Parliament was based in London with the House of Lords standing as the supreme court of appeal in civil matters. The Anglo-American tradition came to characterise civil law in Scotland in particular, but criminal law remained somewhat distinct from English law. Throughout the 20th century, many changes were made, particularly in the sense that society itself saw rapid social change at this time, and these changes were mirrored in developments in the law in Scotland. This has been most notable with developments relating to the jurisdiction of the European Court of Human Rights and the Human Rights Act of 1998. Finally, with the acceptance of the new devolved Scottish Parliament by referendum in 1997 and the subsequent passing of the Scotland Act 1998, it has to be acknowledged that the Scottish legal system is perhaps experiencing more changes now than at any other time in its long and complex history. Some of the old Scottish Acts of Parliament still apply today, although many have fallen into disuse or have been repealed by later legislation. However, it is worth noting that there are some differences in the application of legislation both north and south of the border. If, for example, the word 'Scotland' is in brackets in the title of an Act, the legislation applies only to Scotland, but the UK Parliament legislates for England and Scotland unless otherwise stated. The Scottish Parliament, however, has an exclusive right to legislate for Scotland in all Scottish matters, but with some 'reserved areas'. While under the Scotland Act 1998, power was devolved from Westminster, that power is still subordinate to the UK Parliament.

The new Scottish Parliament has slightly different legislative procedures from the UK Parliament, although it is beyond the scope of this chapter to examine them in any detail. Any attempts to explore criminal justice processes in Scotland will be certainly more thorough and more easily understood if the student has some idea of these historical processes, simply because criminal justice in Scotland is different from that in England and Wales. A closer examination of the 'make-up' of the legal personnel and the types of courts that exist in Scotland should be helpful in gaining an understanding of those differences.

THE LEGAL PERSONNEL AND THE SCOTTISH CRIMINAL COURTS

There are elements and characteristics of the Scottish judicial system which are independent of and distinct from the English system. This section of the chapter concerns the Scottish criminal courts and their personnel, who themselves have names and titles that are not always familiar to those who live outside Scotland.

LEGAL PERSONNEL IN SCOTLAND

The personnel of the Scottish legal system have their origins in the early history of Scotland and can be divided into the following categories:

- judges;
- public prosecutors;
- the legal profession;
- witnesses, jurors, messengers-at-arms and sheriff officers (these groups will not be described in any detail).

Judges

Unlike the rest of Europe, judges are drawn from their legal practitioners, rather than being specially trained as judges throughout their legal career. The senior judges in Scotland are called the Lord President and the Lord Justice-Clerk, appointed by the Crown as advised by the Prime Minister and recommended by the Lord Advocate, one of the law officers of the Crown. Court of Session (see below) judges and High Court judges are appointed on recommendation from the Secretary of State for Scotland. There is no mechanism for removing a judge from office.

Sheriffs and sheriffs principal are judges who preside over Sheriff Courts (see below). They are also appointed by the Crown on the advice of the Secretary of State. As part of the Scottish judiciary, they are advocates or solicitors who have at least 10 years' standing, and they can be removed from office 'by reason of inability, neglect of duty, or misbehaviour'.

Justices of the Peace appointed by the Crown preside in District Courts, other than in Glasgow, which has salaried stipendiary magistrates who are appointed by the local authority.

Public prosecutors/law officers of the Crown

The principal law officer of the Crown in Scotland is the Lord Advocate, assisted by the Solicitor General for Scotland. Appointed on the advice of the First Minister in Scotland, and with Scottish parliamentary approval, both these Crown law officers are now members of the Scottish Executive, which they represent in criminal and civil matters. The Lord Advocate, as head of the Crown Office, is ultimately responsible for the prosecution of crimes in Scotland and also for the appointment of 'advocates depute', who appear in all High Court cases except the most important, where the Lord Advocate or Solicitor General will appear. The Lord Advocate also appoints judges and sheriffs. Under the Scotland Act 1998, there is also now an Advocate General who, as a member of the UK Government, advises on legal issues which affect Scotland.

Other prosecutors are the procurators-fiscal who prosecute in the Sheriff and District Courts. It is to them that the police will report the details of a crime, and they have absolute discretion whether to prosecute. They are independent of the judiciary.

THE LEGAL PROFESSION IN SCOTLAND

There are two branches of the legal profession, which are as follows.

Advocates

Advocates are equivalent to barristers elsewhere in the UK and are members of the Faculty of Advocates. They are the 'elite of the legal profession' in Scotland with rights to practise in the superior courts. Collectively known as 'the Bar', there are two types, junior counsel and senior counsel (also known as QCs). They practise alone or work together but not in partnership, and a client cannot contact them directly in a case. This can only be done through the offices of a solicitor, who must be present at any meeting between the two. They can present opinions on issues to do with the law, which may heighten the chances of success in any court action.

Solicitors

Solicitors are the general practitioners of the law in Scotland, working in private practice or in partnership. They represent clients in criminal courts, mainly in the District and Sheriff Courts, but now have extended rights of audience in the superior courts, where they are known as solicitor-advocates. They must be members of the Law Society of Scotland, a statutory body that governs Scottish solicitors and is responsible for education, training, regulating standards, disciplining and admission to the practice of the law in Scotland.

Both advocates and solicitors undergo rigorous training in order to enter the legal profession, and all possess law degrees from a Scottish University plus diplomas in legal practice and a 'traineeship' in legal offices. For advocates, the training is known as 'devilling' and the trainee advocate a 'devil'.

THE CRIMINAL COURTS IN SCOTLAND[1]

Criminal courts '... act as a forum in which the state can punish those who have acted contrary to the criminal law' (Busby et al, 2000: 41). In Scotland, criminal matters are dealt with by three courts: the District Court, the Sheriff Court and the High Court of Justiciary. In summary, the District Court deals with minor offences, the Sheriff Court with more serious ones and the most serious crimes, such as murder and rape, are dealt with in the High Court, so there is a distinct hierarchy. There are also courts of special jurisdiction, such as 'children's hearings', which will be described as they do have a bearing on what happens to those under the age of 16 who may come into contact with the law. The European Court of Justice and the European Convention on Human Rights can also play a role in determining points of law from the domestic courts in Scotland.

The District Court

These courts were set up in 1975 in order to merge Scotland's minor criminal courts. They deal with breaches of the peace, road traffic offences and misdemeanours that might be committed within a specific local authority area. They are presided over by a lay judge or Justice of the Peace (JP) who can, for example, impose up to 60 days of imprisonment or a limited fine, so the penalties may not be too severe. Glasgow has its own salaried magistrates, known as stipendiary magistrates, who, unlike the JPs, are legally qualified and have greater sentencing powers not dissimilar from those of a sheriff under 'summary procedure', which is adopted for less serious crimes (see below).

---

1   This chapter does not describe civil courts in Scotland in any detail.

The Sheriff Court

The Sheriff Court is presided over by a sheriff appointed by the Crown. The Court may be manned by a number of sheriffs with a 'sheriff principal' responsible for the organisation of a particular Court. Scotland is divided into six 'sheriffdoms': Grampian, Highlands and Islands; Tayside, Central and Fife; Lothian and Borders; Glasgow and Strathkelvin; North Strathclyde; South Strathclyde, Dumfries and Galloway. Each of these areas is made up of 49 Sheriff Court districts and, in relation to criminal matters, the Sheriff Court can adopt one of two court procedures: the summary procedure for less serious crimes or the 'solemn procedure' for serious offences. If a sheriff feels that he or she is limited in his or her powers in any case, he or she can send a person to the High Court for sentencing. In summary procedure, the sheriff sits alone determining questions of fact and law; in solemn procedure, the sheriff will hear a case with up to 15 members of a jury. He or she will determine legal issues, whilst the jury will determine fact. An unlimited fine or sentence of up to three years can be imposed in this Court.

The High Court of Justiciary

The High Court of Justiciary is the supreme criminal court in Scotland, established in 1672. There is no right of appeal from the High Court of Justiciary to the House of Lords, and the Court travels to other parts of Scotland if required. As a trial court, it sits in other cities as well as Edinburgh, but, as an appeal court, it only sits in Edinburgh, where all appeals are heard by a panel of three judges. The most senior person in the High Court is the Lord President of the Court of Session, also known as the Lord Justice-General. The Lord Justice-Clerk is the second most senior judge; other Court of Session judges are known as Lords Commissioners of Justiciary. All serious crimes, such as treason, murder, rape and offences under the Official Secrets Act, are dealt with by this Court, and it has jurisdiction over the whole of Scotland, with no limitation other than that imposed by statute on the sentencing power of the judges. If found guilty of murder, statute imposes life imprisonment in Scotland. If sitting as a trial court, one judge may sit with a jury of 15.

In matters of appeal, there is an independent body made up of members of the legal profession. This is known as the Scottish Criminal Cases Review Commission, which can exercise powers granted under the Crime and Punishment (Scotland) Act 1997 to review cases if it is in the interests of justice. In summary appeals, the High Court may order retrial or acquittal, confirm the original verdict or reduce or increase a sentence where the appeal is only on a point of law. In solemn appeals which may be against conviction or sentence, any miscarriage of justice may be brought under review of the High Court of Justiciary.

Children's hearings

Eight is the age at which criminal responsibility is said to begin in Scots law, but no child under 16 years of age can be prosecuted in criminal courts without the approval of the Lord Advocate. This is also applicable to the District Courts, which only hear minor offences and do not prosecute children but refer them to the children's hearing system. The Children (Scotland) Act 1995 provides the basis upon which the law can act with regard to children in Scotland today following the original recommendations of the Kilbrandon Committee in 1964.

The children's hearing panel in Scotland is unique within the UK. Set up in 1971 following the Kilbrandon Committee's recommendations, these special panels deal with children under the age of 16 in cases in need of care and protection and with children who offend and are in need of control and discipline. The function of a panel is to determine the appropriate disposal, ie which measures must be taken in respect of each child who is referred. Each panel is based on principles of welfare, the Social Work (Scotland) Act 1968 stating that any distinction between children who offend and those in need of care and protection was largely 'irrelevant'. Intervention measures would therefore be assessed according to the circumstances of each case and determined by either the need for protection or the need for control and discipline, on the grounds that 'normal' processes of socialisation were probably inadequate for both groups of children.

The actual panel is a kind of tribunal made up of lay people from the local authority in which the child resides. Every local authority in Scotland has a children's panel with both male and female members present every time it sits – the chairman and two other members must be present. Decisions are made by the panel based on 'needs' not 'deeds', and the Scottish courts are only involved if:

- the facts are in dispute for both groups of children;
- there is an appeal;
- a serious offence has been committed.

The panel does not decide on questions of law or fact; only a sheriff can do this before a case can be disposed of by a panel. This type of community-based intervention is much-admired, working as it does in the best interests of the child (Busby et al, 2000).

An official called the Principal Reporter will refer a case to a panel and, under the Children (Scotland) Act 1995, appeals can be made against decisions that a panel may make. If a child under 16 allegedly commits a serious offence, he or she may be dealt with under normal criminal justice procedures in Scotland, which may involve appearing before the High Court of Justiciary, but even then the case may be referred back to the panel for disposal. It should also be noted that any case or criminal procedure involving children may now have to conform to the Human Rights Act 1998.

THE CRIMINAL JUSTICE PROCESS

According to Hudson (2001), criminal justice can be defined as 'the process through which the state responds to behaviour that it deems unacceptable'. In responding to (allegedly) criminal behaviour, a state will impose a number of specific processes upon an individual from the moment that a person is charged, through prosecution and trial to sentencing, punishment and possibly appeal.

Criminal justice systems are determined by legislation, and each nation may have differing sanctions and penalties associated with particular crimes. Discretionary penalties, for example, may be imposed by courts, but mandatory penalties, such as 'life' sentences for murder, are becoming increasingly popular. Scotland is no different in this respect than the rest of the UK, where it would seem that matters of controlling crime rather than issues of due process have come to dominate and characterise the criminal justice system. The legacy of this approach is perhaps to ignore equality and fairness and also the rights of both offender and victims at the expense of satisfying public and political demands for a 'law and order' society.

Scotland has a relatively 'uncodified' system of criminal justice – which means that the criminal law is not brought together in one single Act of Parliament – with many crimes based on the common law of custom 'embodied in the decisions of the criminal courts' – including those deemed most serious such as murder or rape. According to McCall Smith and Sheldon (1997), this is considered one of the strong points of Scots criminal law, leading the courts to be more 'flexible' and 'responsive'. Rather than amend legislation applying to the crime of rape so that husbands could be convicted, for example, the change was easy to achieve because rape was a common law crime and not defined by statute. However, this does mean that, in some cases, there may be more 'potential doubt' concerning the scope of criminal law in Scotland – 'fuzzy' borders might mean 'fuzzy' decisions. It is therefore difficult to compare Scotland's criminal justice system or its laws with any other. As we have seen, it is very similar to the English system, having developed in tandem with it, but it retains unique and distinct characteristics embedded for the most part in legal writings that date back to Mackenzie (1678), Forbes (1730) and, most significantly, David Hume (1797). However, the works of these Institutional Writers, as they are known, also have to be placed in their historical, social and political context. Apparently, the work of Hume carries great authority before the courts, but there are more modern legal writings today that are in daily use in Scottish courts that contain statements of criminal law and to which students within law and criminology can refer.

Ultimately though, it is the decisions taken by the courts, ie judgments made in the High Court and the Sheriff Court, that are the sources of the law. More often than not, decisions made in modern courts will draw on decisions made no earlier than the 19th century, and it is worth noting that there is no appeal to the House of Lords in England. Scots law has been described as 'more local in character', although, on occasion, cases from elsewhere will be referred to, most notably from other Commonwealth jurisdictions. As McCall Smith and Sheldon point out, 'the ingenuity of criminal defenders – or their counsel – means that novel points will always arise' (1997: 5). It is, however, beyond the scope of this chapter to examine all the sources of Scots criminal law; suffice it to say that of equal importance are the roles of criminal statutes and the power of the High Court to declare conduct a crime, although the value of this is questioned.

At this point, it is worth considering how crimes are classified in Scotland, and this is best done by considering which interests the law tries to protect or favour. In Scotland, this follows the Anglo-American tradition:

- crimes against the person, from minor assault to murder;
- crimes against property, from theft to wrongful destruction;
- crimes against the state, including crimes against security and good government;
- crimes of public order and public morality if a community as a whole has been harmed;
- regulatory offences that include those offences that transgress any laws involving the administering of modern society, such as health and safety

offences, road traffic offences, environmental offences and so on. Depending on their consequences and/or effects, these offences may be seen as minor or major in terms of infringement of the law, and they are not always seen as crimes.

'True' crimes in Scotland, such as murder, rape or culpable homicide, are seen as such because they contravene deeply-held notions of morality. Those who are perpetrators of these crimes are obviously going to be perceived as people unable to live as citizens in communities, so long-held notions of citizenship play an important role behind any enforcement of the criminal law in Scotland. However, the regulatory function of criminal law also has to be considered alongside the broader function of applying sanctions to those whose conduct constitutes an infringement of the moral codes of society. Acts deemed as socially unacceptable therefore have fallen increasingly under the gaze of the law on the grounds that social cohesion is always worth striving for, and so there has to be an element of flexibility within the criminal law.

THE CRIMINAL JUSTICE PROCESS IN SCOTLAND

As people encounter the various stages in any criminal justice system, they come into contact with all those institutions that respond to crime in an official capacity – police, prosecution authorities, the courts and, in some cases, the penal system. All these institutions tend to work separately from each other, but it has to be acknowledged that they are interdependent (Cavadino and Dignan, 2002), all the more so because they have in common the fact that the people who are involved with these institutions are themselves responsible for either committing crimes (if they are alleged offenders) or controlling crime (if they are practitioners or policy-makers) and are therefore accountable to many others in society. The criminal justice process is also a social process (Garland, 1990) and the Scottish institutions that aim for the goals of punishment, deterrence, reparation, rehabilitation, incapacitation and/or retribution are embedded in wider social networks whose structures and interdependencies provide a complex framework against which crime and its control must be understood.

Criminal justice has to be administered according to areas of law which vary from one jurisdiction to another. We have seen that Scots law differs from English and Welsh law for a variety of reasons and historical traditions, so the procedures to be followed and the manner in which rules are applied and how facts are proved or admitted are also different. These differences are also applicable to the way in which lawyers practise in criminal work, so this section will outline the key stages in the criminal justice process in Scotland which, according to Busby et al (2000), is embedded in a system that can be described as 'peculiar' in nature in that it 'straddles' Anglo-American common law tradition and the civil law systems of Western Europe.

Criminal apprehension and investigation

Crime in Scotland is investigated by the police on behalf of the procurator-fiscal who has the power under the 1967 Police (Scotland) Act to direct the police. Suspects and witnesses may be questioned, and those suspected of serious crimes may be detained without being arrested for up to six hours, although a person does not need to answer any questions during this time other than to provide a name and address. On arrest, a person must be charged and cautioned, or any confession may be held to be inadmissible on trial. A case is then referred to the procurator-fiscal as the police are not public prosecutors in Scotland. Investigations by the police are completed by the submitting of a report for consideration to the procurator-fiscal, who then decides independently whether the accused has to appear in court. Other non-police agencies, such as local authorities, can also submit reports to the procurators-fiscal, although they do not need to for consideration for prosecution. The procurator-fiscal has no power in such cases to direct the non-police agencies.

There are alternatives to prosecution, for example, the procurator-fiscal may simply issue a warning to someone concerning the unacceptability of his or her behaviour, or offer someone guidance from a voluntary organisation. There may also be the option of paying a fine or, in the case of road traffic offences, a fixed penalty notice.

The procurator-fiscal can decide not to prosecute if the offence is trivial or if it is not in the public interest to do so.

Public prosecution

The supreme public prosecutor in Scotland is the Lord Advocate, who is assisted by the Solicitor General and Advocates Depute (collectively known as Crown Counsel). The Crown Office is responsible for the preparation of prosecutions in the High Court and for directing and controlling the procurator-fiscal service. In Scotland, all public prosecutions are commenced in the public interest, and there must be sufficient evidence central to the decision to prosecute. Public prosecutors also decide the forum or court in which the case must proceed. This in turn is determined by solemn or summary procedure. (Private prosecutions do occur but are rare.)

The procurator-fiscal decides which procedure to use, depending upon the nature and seriousness of the crime, and also takes into consideration any previous convictions a person may have. Sheriffs try summary cases without a jury in the Sheriff Court, or these cases may be heard before a magistrate or JP in a District Court. Solemn procedure takes place before a sheriff and jury in the Sheriff Court or judge and jury in the High Court, with each side presenting evidence. The onus of proof is with the prosecution, with the accused presumed innocent, and there must be 'proof beyond reasonable doubt' as the standard.

Solemn procedure

Solemn procedure follows where a procurator-fiscal decides an offence has to be prosecuted 'on indictment'. The stages are as follows under the Criminal Procedure (Scotland) Act 1995:

- Petition – the procurator-fiscal presents a petition to a sheriff, which identifies the accused and the charge under consideration and also seeks a warrant for search and arrest and the citing of witnesses.
- First appearance/examination /pre-trial – when arrested, an accused person has certain entitlements, such as having the place of detention communicated to a solicitor or one other named person. The accused is then sent before a sheriff in private 'on the next lawful court day' after arrest for judicial examination

relating to responses to the charge. Any record made of this can be used in trial. The case is then prepared by the procurator-fiscal, with the Crown Office deciding what the charge should be and whether to proceed and under which procedure. An indictment is then served, setting out the offences to appear at a trial. Scotland has very strict laws concerning the amount of time a person spends in custody before trial. Trial must begin within 12 months of the first appearance where an accused person is on bail, otherwise the trial cannot proceed. If a person is 'committed until liberated in due course of law', the trial has to be commenced within 110 days.

- The indictment – this is prepared and signed in the name of the Lord Advocate in the High Court or on his authority in the Sheriff Court; the form is set out in law. Preliminary points are considered or evidence agreed in a first diet in the Sheriff Court or in a preliminary diet in the High Court.

- Trial – 15 members of the public make up the criminal jury in Scotland. Individual jurors can be objected to if there is good reason. The prosecution has to convince the jury, not the judge, of the guilt of the accused, beyond reasonable doubt. The majority verdict can be guilty, not guilty or not proven. For guilt to be established, at least eight jurors have to vote for this outcome. Evidence is presented by the prosecution, and the defence may test the evidence and argue that there is no case to answer due to insufficient evidence being given. The judge advises on relevant law and can instruct a jury to return a verdict of not guilty if insufficient evidence has been presented. If a guilty verdict has been reached, the judge passes sentence and, at this stage, any previous convictions are taken into account.

Summary procedure

Criminal courts in Scotland all have 'summary procedure', where a sheriff, stipendiary magistrate or others may sit without a jury in order to decide matters of fact and/or points of law. The exception to this is the High Court of Justiciary. Under this procedure, a sheriff can impose a fine not exceeding £5,000, a requirement to find money (caution) or security for good behaviour for a period not exceeding 12 months, and imprisonment for up to three months. These fairly extensive powers of sentencing can be extended further for second or subsequent offences and are embedded in the Criminal Procedure (Scotland) Act 1995. The types of offences that can be tried under this procedure are also laid down in this Act, so, for example, the Sheriff Court can try all common law offences except murder, rape, incest and wilful fire-raising, and the District Court also has specific entitlements when it comes to powers of convicting and sentencing. Ultimately, it is the Lord Advocate and procurator-fiscal who determine in which court a case proceeds.

Cases at the 'lower end of seriousness' do not find their way into the Scottish courts where alternatives to prosecution are used, such as fixed penalties or warning letters. In Scotland, the Crown 'prosecutes in the public interest and not for some narrow or vexatious purpose' (Shiels, 1999: 58).

Under summary procedure, the procurator-fiscal carries out the prosecution following a summary complaint against the accused person. If there are any previous convictions, these have to be put before the court also. An 'intermediate diet' is held before the trial to confirm whether it should proceed, to ensure the preparedness of the prosecutor and accused, to establish the plea and to ensure that evidence is not contentious. All parts of the trial must take place in the presence of the accused.

Appeals to the High Court of Justiciary can be made from summary proceedings to review any alleged miscarriage of justice or to seek the opinion of the higher court against conviction or sentence, but the High Court does not pass sentence on summary cases.

It is worth noting that, in criminal cases in Scotland, the rules of evidence are more strictly applied than in civil cases. Under both procedures, the Crown must prove a charge beyond reasonable doubt. Independent checks from other sources must be made to support and corroborate the evidence given to prove the crime was committed by the person accused of it. If a verdict of 'not guilty' or 'not proven' is given, then the accused is discharged and is immune from further criminal court action in relation to the offence.

Penalties

All societies have a 'variety of available penalties' (Sparks in McLaughlin and Muncie, 2001: 205) that can be imposed on offenders, and Scotland is no exception. Ranging from warnings through to life imprisonment, the methods of punishment or disposals that a court may impose can be perceived and interpreted by wider society in many complex ways. A penalty may be seen as far too harsh or not harsh enough, so the criminal justice system is frequently caught up in a much wider debate relating to authority and to the legitimacy of what it actually has the power to do in relation to punishing people who offend.

The most common penalties used in Scotland are:

* fine;
* warning/admonition;
* imprisonment/detention;
* community service orders;
* probation;
* compensation orders.

The Scottish Prison Service (SPS) began as an agency of what was the Scottish Office in 1993 and, in a manner similar to all criminal justice agencies, it has seen rapid changes in its development and progress over recent years. There are, at the time of writing, 16 penal establishments in Scotland, 15 of which hold adult prisoners, and there is one dedicated Young Offenders Institution at Polmont with three others incorporated into other prisons at Cornton Vale, Dumfries and Glenochil. Cornton Vale is the only all-female prison in Scotland. There is one private prison at Kilmarnock, and the current average number of prisoners in custody (at the time of writing) is approximately 6,500, of which approximately 300 are female and approximately 600 are sentenced young offenders. In 2002, ethnic minority groups made up about 2 per cent of the prison population. Currently, within the SPS, there is a focus on risk management, the provision of good healthcare and support, throughcare services, partnership working and business improvement. It is perhaps worth noting the types of crime groups that comprised the prison population in Scotland, again in 2002:

- serious crimes of violence – murder, serious assault, robbery (39 per cent);
- crimes of dishonesty – housebreaking and other theft (17 per cent);
- crimes of indecency (7 per cent);
- motor vehicle offences (6 per cent);
- miscellaneous offences (6 per cent);
- other crimes (18 per cent);
- fire-raising, vandalism (1 per cent).

Crimes of serious assault, homicide, robbery and drug-related crimes were predominantly committed by males, with the largest group of female prisoners being convicted of drugs offences. Overall in Scotland, at this time, there were 129 prisoners for every 100,000 of the general population. This compares with a rate of 137 in England and Wales at the same time and 702 in the USA. It is worth remembering that custodial sentences are only one form of punishment across the penal range in Scotland, and imprisonment must be seen as the last resort in the hierarchy of penalties that can be imposed for transgressing the law and society's norms. But it is worth noting that there are one or two examples of newer 'alternatives' that are proving relatively effective in controlling crime in Scotland.

The Drug Court – there are special courts in Glasgow and Fife – functions as a Sheriff Court to tackle drug use and related crimes. The Drug Court is multi-agency in its approach, with staff assigned from police, medical teams and Drug Court supervision and treatment teams made up of social workers and drug workers. Two sheriffs sit in this Court and work with the rest of the team, using probation orders with a condition of drug treatment and drug treatment and testing orders. Every offender on order is reviewed in Court by the sheriff at least on a monthly basis with the review taking the form of a dialogue between the offender and the same sentencer – without the mediation of a defence agent. The sentencer oversees the order, acting as motivator and sanctioner simultaneously. Prior to review, the sheriff meets with the whole team in a private pre-court meeting to discuss progress, regress or any other issues pertaining to the offender. This is unique in practice in Scotland, although compares with other drug courts in Toronto, Dublin, Sydney and the USA. The team attend training together to enhance the effectiveness of their collective approach, and the results have proved to be successful in terms of a decline in drug use and reductions in associated crime. This type of community-based supervision disposal, as it is known, is a positive step forward in the non-use of custodial sentences within the Scottish criminal justice system.

East Port House is a secure accommodation unit in the city of Dundee that offers an alternative to custodial sentences. It functions as part of the criminal justice service in Dundee and works in partnership with criminal justice agencies in Perth and Kinross and Angus. Residents are offered support and a constructive programme of activities to help in addressing their offending behaviour. If they breach the terms of their residency, then their case is reviewed and they may conceivably be returned to custody. Again, the ethos and rationale behind the approach is multi-agency, with East Port House commanding a great deal of respect within the local community and having considerable success in reintegrating its residents into the community.

CONCLUSION

Legal systems are not static, and so any attempt to pin down the essential characteristics of Scottish criminal justice is not easy, in the sense that the changes taking place within the Scottish legal system are occurring relatively quickly since devolution. In any case, an exploration of criminal justice in Scotland has to be seen as part of a wider social setting that must be understood in the context of whose interests are best served according to the specific criminal laws that are constitutive of legal power and authority. This in turn has to be viewed as a dimension of social, economic, cultural and political power and authority, reflecting the claims of those who govern. Furthermore, conceptions of justice itself have been subject to change through time, despite historical efforts to see it as something timeless and unchanging, an absolute value that can guide conduct (Garland, 1990). Criminal justice in Scotland therefore has indeed been enacted in different ways and conceived through different 'mentalities'. The 'doing' of justice is constantly open to challenge and reform on a scale that is global, and it is conceivable that contradictory goals, such as those of punishment and welfare, will continue to co-exist well into the 21st century, and even assuming that some kind of 'corrections agency', embracing the many institutions that form the criminal justice system, comes into existence. 'Talk' about crime, criminals, criminality and controlling crime is, in a sense, 'talk' about what people 'do' and how they interact with others in specific social and cultural settings. The people being spoken about are not only the alleged offenders, but those who make up and enforce the criminal justice systems that have developed through time to deal with crime. The criminal justice system in Scotland exists within and is shaped and influenced by Scottish culture and more directly by Scottish penal culture. Its distinctive practices are 'local' in character, but this is not to say that they are in any sense 'less than' or insignificant when compared with any other system. Those who 'operate' within and experience this criminal justice system are those who give it meaning, who bestow it with what Garland describes as a 'specific form of life' (1990: 210) and, as we have seen, it does indeed possess its 'own terms, categories and symbols'. Whilst wider issues of class, age, gender, ethnicity and disability have not been examined in this chapter, they do impinge upon criminal justice matters in Scotland just as they do elsewhere, but, hopefully, this brief introduction to some of those 'terms, categories and symbols' should encourage the reader to explore the specific culture of criminal justice in Scotland with some enthusiasm and some determination in order to gain an enhanced understanding of the diversity of criminal justice practice in the UK.

SEMINAR DISCUSSION TOPICS

- Consider how and to what extent the Scottish criminal justice system differs from that which exists in England and Wales.
- What makes the Scottish criminal justice system unique?
- Discuss how devolution has influenced the direction of criminal justice in Scotland.

KEY READINGS

Scots Law – A Student Guide by Busby, Clark, Mays, Paisley and Spink (Butterworths, 2000) provides the best and most comprehensive introduction to key areas of law in Scotland, covering the history of Scots law, its sources, the judicial system and a detailed breakdown of particular laws and their application. This is an invaluable student text for those wishing to gain an overall understanding of criminal justice in Scotland in the wider context of Scots law. For those seeking a more detailed account of the principles of Scots criminal law, RAA McCall Smith and David Sheldon's *Scots Criminal Law* (Butterworths, 1997) also provides details of statutes and cases covering common law and statutory offences. Gordon Hughes' chapter 'The competing logics of community sanctions' in *Controlling Crime*, 2nd edn, edited by McLaughlin and Muncie (Sage, 2001) provides a useful commentary on the links between punishment and welfare in Scotland, focusing in particular on the Scottish children's hearing system. Taking a broader approach to criminal justice matters, both Barbara Hudson's *Understanding Justice* (OUP, 1996) and Sandra Walklate's *Understanding Criminology* (OUP, 1997) provide overviews in understanding ideas, theories and perspectives on crime against which students can evaluate criminal justice practice in Scotland.

REFERENCES

Busby, N, Clark, B, Mays, R, Paisley, R and Spink, P (2000) *Scots Law*, Edinburgh: Butterworths.

Cavadino, M and Dignan, J (2002) *The Penal System*, London: Sage.

Garland, D (1990) *Punishment and Modern Society*, Oxford: Clarendon.

Hudson, B (2001) 'Criminal justice' in McLaughlin, E and Muncie, J (eds), *The Sage Dictionary of Criminology*, London: Sage.

Lynch, M (ed) (2001) *The Oxford Companion to Scottish History*, Oxford: OUP.

MacQueen, HL (1993) *Studying Scots Law*, Edinburgh: Butterworths.

McCall Smith, RAA and Sheldon, D (1997) *Scots Criminal Law*, Edinburgh: Butterworths.

McLaughlin, E and Muncie, J (2001) *Controlling Crime*, 2nd edn, London: Sage

Manson-Smith, D (1995) *The Legal System of Scotland*, Edinburgh: HMSO.

Scottish Executive National Statistics Publication, CrJ/2003/6, Prison Statistics Scotland, 2002.

Sellar, WDH (2001) 'Law and Lawyers' in Lynch, M (ed), *The Oxford Companion to Scottish History*, Oxford: OUP.

Shiels, RS (1999) *Law Basics, Scottish Legal System*, Edinburgh: W Green.

WEBSITES

Scottish Parliament: www.scottish.parliament.uk.

Scottish courts: www.scotcourts.gov.uk/index1.asp

East Port House: www.dundeecity.gov.uk

Statistics: www.scotland.gov.uk/stats

INDEX

Abbey National 136
Abolitionism 16–17
   prison abolitionists 259–60
Ackner, Lord 240
Acquaintance rape 110
Adler, P 42
Administrative criminology 111
Advocates, Scotland 282–83
African-Caribbeans 69, 70, 81, 82–83
   See also Minority groups
   policing of communities 82–83
   Yardie gangster gangs 83
Afshar, H 128
Albanese, J 137
Alderson, ... 197
Allen, H 94, 101
Allen, R 59, 60, 61, 62
Alvesalo, A 140, 142
Amir, M 109, 110
Annan, Kofi 158
Anti-Slavery International 159
Anti-terrorism, Crime and
   Security Act 2001 127
Applegate, B 57, 61, 63
Armstrong, P 143
Armstrong, S 116
Ashton, John 21, 32, 183,
                         189, 199
Ashworth, A 203, 204, 206,
                  211, 212, 213,
                214, 215, 271
Association of Chief
   Officers of Probation
   (ACOP) 239, 241
Association of Chief
   Police Officers (ACPO) 192, 194
Audit Commission 54, 194, 195
Auld, Lord Justice 22, 52
Australia
   restorative justice 31
   Safer Streets and Homes 173–74
Aye-Maung, N 86
Ayres, I 140

Bad Girls 74
Baker, Kenneth 194
Baldwin, J 203, 204
Baldwin, R 139, 144, 146
Bali bombings 123, 126, 129
Ball, R 18
Bandalli, S 227

Banton, M 191
Bardach, E 140
Barkan, S 137
Barlinnie Special Unit 259
Barnett, R 267, 268
Bateman, T 229
Bauman, Z 99
Beaumont, B 244
Beccaria, C 5, 154
Becker, Howard 14, 38, 40, 226
Beckett, K 256
Beckford, J 124, 125
Beijing Rules 227
Belmarsh prison 127
Benn, Hilary 243
Benn, M 85
Bennett, T 197, 207
Bentham, Jeremy 154, 251
Benyon, J 87
Bergman, D 134
Berlin Act 1884 159
Bernstein, Marver 142
'Best value' regimes 52
Better Regulation Task Force 143
Beylevald, D 208
Bhopal disaster 117
Bill, The 72
Billington, A 52
Biometric scanning devices 13
Birmingham Six 27, 71
Black, J 139, 140
Blagg, H 225
Blair, Tony 112, 239, 240, 252
   See also New Labour
Blakelock, PC Keith 87
Bloch, A 124–25
Bloomstein, Rex 75
Blowers, A 141
Blud, L 253
Blunkett, David 53, 254
Boot camps 7, 53
Bottomley, AK 206
Bottoms, A 36, 106, 213
Bourhill, M 228
Boutros-Ghali, Boutros 158
Bowling, B 83, 90, 126,
                215, 222, 224
Box, S 67, 134, 146
Braithwaite, John 16, 29, 93, 94,
                140, 146, 270
Briggs, D 58, 59

British Crime Surveys 22, 23, 42,
52, 61, 111, 112
British Society of
Criminology 41, 42
Britton, Nadia Joanne 83, 84, 90
Brixton riots 87, 191, 192
See also Riots
Broadwater Farm riots 87
See also Riots
Brody, S. 208, 210, 237
Brogden, M 111
Brown, S. 106
Brown, W. 257
Brunskell, H. 108
Bulger, James 213, 239, 251
Bullard, R 143–44
Bureaucratic model
of criminal justice 28, 29
Buried 74
Busby, N 280, 283, 285,
287, 293
Bush, George W 256
Butler, AJP 190, 194
Byfield, Toni-Ann 85

Cain, M. 84, 93, 94, 191
Calavita, K. 142
Calvey, D 42
Cambodia 163
Campbell, D. 139
Caporaso, J. 154
Capture theory. 133, 142
Carlen, P 96, 101, 257,
258, 259, 260
Carson, W 142, 143
Casement, Roger 159–60, 161
Cashmore, ... 89
Categorical theory. 98
Causes of crime
biological and psychological
factors 8–10
neo-conservative view 6–7, 12
relative deprivation. 11
sociological positivist view 8, 11–12
strain theory. 11
Cavadino, M 211, 212, 214,
215, 287
Cavadino, P. 21
Cave, M 139, 146
CCTV (closed circuit
television) 13, 70, 116,
175, 197
Chain gangs. 7
Chan, J. 84
Chandler, D 158, 164

Chapman, Jessica 70
Charles, N 114
Chartism 186
Cherney, A 170
Chibnall, S 67
Chicago School 37, 38
Chief Constables. 88, 188, 189,
190, 191, 193,
194, 195, 196
Chigwada-Bailey, R 113, 224, 230
Child curfews 30, 229
Child safety orders 229
Children
See also Youth crime;
Youth justice
in custody 75
sexual offences against 55
Children and Family
Courts Advisory and
Support Service (CAFCASS) 238
Children (Scotland) Act 1995 285
Children and Young
Persons Act 1969 . . . . 225, 228
Children's hearings, Scotland. 284–85
Chomsky, N. 141
Christiansen, KO. 208
Christie, N. 16, 106, 115,
269, 275
Church Jr, T 215
Cicourel, A 111
Civil disturbances
Chartist protest 186
industrial conflict 190, 191–92, 193
riots 69, 71, 83, 84,
87, 191, 192–93
Clark, B 293
Clark, LMG 110
Clarke, J 174, 177
Clarke, Kenneth. 250
Clarke, RV 9, 13, 111
Classicism 36, 154
deterrence and. 4–6
Climbié, Victoria 70–71
Clinard, M 137
Closed circuit television
See CCTV
Cloward, R. 11
Cobb, S. 127
Cohen, AK. 97
Cohen, L 111
Cohen, N 252
Cohen, S 9, 69, 222,
226, 232
Cold War 161
Coleman, C 36

Collier, R 99
Colonisation
  Congo 159–61
  genocide and 155
  the 'other' and 153, 156
Columbus, Christopher 153, 155
Commission on the Future
  of Multi-Ethnic Britain 87, 89, 125
Commissioner for
  Correctional Services 244
Community action 62–63
Community cohesion 11
Community policing................. 197
Community punishment
  order.................... 236, 241, 245
Community punishment and
  rehabilitation order 245
Community rehabilitation order 244
Community safety
  comparative
    understanding of 178–80
  defining 170–71
Community sentences 26, 101, 212,
                              216, 236, 237,
                              241–42, 243,
                              244–45

Comprehensive Spending
  Review 175
Conan Doyle, Arthur 160
Conferencing 269–71
Confidentiality, research and 43
Congo 159–61, 163
Congo Reform Association............ 159
Connell, RW 98
Conrad, Joseph 161
Conscience......................... 7
Consent
  policing by..................... 190
  research and.................. 42–43
Conservatism 6
  See also Neo-conservatism
Conservative Governments 111
  prisons..................... 244, 249,
                          250–52, 253
  regulating corporations 144
Construct theory
  See Social construct theory
Contempt of Court Act 1981 73
Contributory negligence.............. 110
Conway, G 123, 124, 125
Cook, D 82
Coomber, R 42
Cornish, D 9, 111
Coronation Street..................... 76
Corporate crime
  corporate killing..... 134–36, 138–39, 143
  deaths at work 135, 136, 138–39

endowment mortgage frauds..... 136–37
food poisoning................ 135, 136
fraud 136–37, 144
injuries and diseases 134–35, 138–39
language of 134
pollution.................... 135, 136
price fixing..................... 137
regulating corporations........ 138–39
  capitalism and 140–42, 145
  capture theories 133, 142
  consensus theories........ 133, 139–40
  critical perspectives 133, 142–44
  deregulation.................... 141
  neo-liberal theories 133, 140–42
  neo-Marxist theories 143
  privatisation.................... 141
  regulatory agencies 144
  self-regulation 139–40
  under-enforcement........ 133, 138–39
victims................ 116–17, 143–44
violence 134–36
Corporate harm..................... 145
Correctional Services
  Accreditation Panel (CSAP) 243
Cotton, J.......................... 138
County and Borough
  Police Act 1856..................... 187
Courts
  See also Crown Court;
    Magistrates' courts;
    Sentencing
  media representations 73–74, 203
  Scotland 283–85, 286,
                            288–91
Cox, P............................. 222
Crawford, Adam............. 173, 176, 181,
                            212, 242

Crime control
  See also Crime prevention;
    Punishment; Tolerance;
    Treatment
  as industry....................... 16
Crime control model 27, 28, 29, 32
Crime and Disorder
  Act 1998.................... 14, 30, 52,
                          174–76, 177, 195,
                          196, 197, 215,
                          229, 240, 253
Crime and disorder
  reduction................. 169, 171, 174
  local partnerships 175, 176–78
  managerialisation 174–76
  modernisation 174–76
  'what works' 3, 10, 169, 171,
                          174–76, 179, 231
Crime and Disorder
  Reduction Partnerships......... 176, 177

Crime prevention. 10–14, 169–81
   defining 170–71
   left realism. 11–12, 111–13
   Morgan Report 197
   opportunity theory 11
   rational choice theory 4, 5, 12–14, 111
   situational 10, 12–14, 111,
                                  116, 169, 173
   social. 10, 169, 174
   sociological positivism 11–12
Crime and Punishment
   (Scotland) Act 1997 284
Crime rate 23
   notifiable offences 23, 24
   perceptions of 22
Crime Reduction Programme. . . . 37, 175–76
Crime (Sentences) Act 1997 . . . . 213, 214,
                                    241, 253
Crime statistics 36
Crimean War 187
Crimes against humanity 162
Crimewatch UK. 59, 71, 76
Criminal Appeal Act 1995 27
Criminal Cases Review
   Commission. 27
Criminal Justice: The Way Ahead 23
Criminal Justice Act 1948 228
Criminal Justice Act 1967 237
Criminal Justice Act 1982 226
Criminal Justice Act 1988 226
Criminal Justice Act 1991 . . . . . 213, 214, 226,
                                    238, 239,
                                    241, 251
Criminal Justice Act 2003 . . . . 22, 29, 32
Criminal justice agencies 21, 22
   managerialisation 30
Criminal Justice Boards 22
Criminal Justice Council. 22
Criminal Procedure Act 1701 280
Criminal Procedure
   (Scotland) Act 1995 . . . . 288, 289
Criminalisation 14, 15, 53, 68
'Crisis in masculinity'. 99
Critchley, TA 186
Critical criminology 16–17
   corporate crime 133, 142–44
Critical social research 108
Croall, H 32, 116, 137, 143, 146
Crow, I. 81, 211, 250, 251, 260
Crown Court 21, 25
   adversarial process 100
   sentencing in. 22, 25, 204, 205, 214
   Witness Service 21, 26
Crown Court 73–74
Crown Prosecution Service. . . . 21, 24, 86, 89
   lay inspectors. 52
   women lawyers. 99

Cullen, F. 10, 18, 57, 210
Cullen, Rt Hon Lord 139
Cunneen, C 274
Curfews
   child curfews 30, 229
   curfew order with
      electronic monitoring 245
Currie, Elliot 11–12

Daily Mail. 68
Dalrymple, James,
   Viscount of Stair 280
Dalton, A 140
Danner, M 143
Darbyshire, P. 204, 205
Date rape 110
Davies, Edmund 192
Davies, M. 29, 32
Davies, P 46
Davis, AY 256, 260
Davis, C 140, 143
Davis, H. 228
Dawson, S 140
Death penalty 7
Decarceration. 16–17
Decriminalisation 15
'Defensible space' theories 13
Del Castillo, Bernal Diaz. 155–56
Delamont, S. 40
Denham, J 125
Denman, S. 89
Deterrence 4, 207–08
   classicism and 4–6
   criticism of. 12
   general 5–6, 208
   specific 208
Dews, Eileen 240
Dignan, J 204, 211, 212,
                                  214, 215, 287
Disclosure, research and. 43
District Court, Scotland. 283, 288, 289
District Judges
   (magistrates' court) 24, 204, 205, 216
Ditton, J 67
Diversion 15
   See also Tolerance
Dixon of Dock Green 72
Dobash, R and Dobash, R. 111
Doble, J. 54, 57
Dodd, D 109, 110
Domestic violence. 95–96, 110,
                        113–15, 116, 117–18
   feminist analysis 113, 114
   racial stereotyping 113–14
Doran, S. 205
Douzinas, C. 158
Dow Chemicals 117

Doward, J. 60
Dowler, Milly 70
Downes, D 112–13, 237, 256
Drug couriers. 85–86
Drug Court, Scotland 291
Drug offences 83
Drug treatment and
    testing order. 245
Dubow, F 62
Due process model 27, 28, 29, 32, 226
Duff, P 205
Duffy, J 67
Dunbar, I. 208, 214, 237
Durham, A 56–57
Durkheim, E 36
Dutch East India Company 159
Dyer, C 73

East Port House. 291
Eaton, M. 101
Economic and Social
    Research Council. 43
Edgar, JM 194
Edwards, Adam 169, 175, 176,
                              177, 178, 179, 181
Edwards, L 53
Ehrlich Martin, S. 100
Einstadter, W 11, 18
Eisenstein, J 215
Elias, R 115, 116
Empey, La Mar T. 15
Empirical research. 35, 36
    See also Research
Emsley, Clive. 183, 184, 185,
                                   187, 200
Endowment mortgage frauds 136–37
Enron 137
Environment Agency. 136, 138, 139
Epistemologies. 105, 107–08
Essentialism. 96
Ethics, research and. 35, 41–43
Ethnic minorities
    See Minority groups
Ethnography 37–38
Evans, K 56, 61, 101
'Evil'. 69

Facade, B 114
Farrington, D 37, 111, 124
Fattah, EA. 115, 118
Faulkner, Lord. 244
Fear of crime. 51, 52, 54,
                                   60–61, 113
    See also Perceptions of crime
Feenan, D. 43
Felson, M 13, 111

Feltham Young Offenders Institute 75
Feminism 94–97, 98
    See also Gender; Women
    domestic violence, analysis of. . . . 113, 114
    jurisprudence and 101
    liberal 94, 97
    postmodern 96, 97
    radical. 95, 96, 97
    research methods 42
    socialist. 96, 97
Ferrell, J 76
Field, S 83
Fielding, Henry. 184
Fielding, John 184
Financial Reporting
    Review Panel. 137
Financial Services Authority. . . 137, 143, 144
Findley, M 205
Firkins, V 109
Fishman, M 67
Fisse, B 140
Fitzgerald, M. 18, 81, 82,
                                   250, 255
Fletcher, WPC Yvonne 71
Flood-Page, Claire. 135, 222
Floud, J. 209
Floud Report 209
Folk devils 69
Food poisoning 135, 136
Food Standards Agency 135, 136, 139
Fooks, G. 134, 136, 137,
                                   142, 144
Forbes, ... 286
Foucault, M 69, 255–56,
                                   258, 259
Fox, J 117, 118, 143
Francis, P 46
Frankenberg, R 128
Franklin, B 69
Fraud, corporate 136–37, 144
French, M. 139
Friedman, M 140
Friedrichs, D 137, 145
Fuller, Mike 88

Gangs. 87
    minority groups. 83, 85
Garland, D. 9, 36, 54, 56,
                              60, 61, 68, 169,
                              172, 174, 178,
                              236, 256, 273,
                              274, 287, 292
Garofalo, J 111
Gaskell, G 83
Gayford, JJ 110
Gelsthorpe, L 94, 102, 214, 215

Gender
  See also Feminism; Women
  as accomplishment 98
  criminal justice policy and 101
  criminal justice
    profession and 99–100
  essentialism 96
  hegemonic masculinity 98, 99
  masculinity. 97–99
  prison and 257–58
  sex distinguished. 93–94
  sex role theory 97–98
  sexual violence 98, 99
  victimisation and. 99
  victimology and. 95, 101–02
  young offenders 223–24, 226
Genn, H 109, 110
Genocide 153, 157, 158,
                        161, 162
  colonisation and 155
Genocide Convention 1946 162
Gibson, B 21
Giddens, A 98, 178
Gilbert, K 10, 210
Gilchrist, E 61
Gill, M 53, 106, 109, 207
Gillespie, M 59, 68, 75–76
Gilliat, S 124, 125
Gilling, Daniel 181
Gillis, JR 222
Glasbeek, H 140
Globalisation 153, 155–56
  imperialist 155–56
Gobert, J 134, 146
Goldblatt, P 174, 175, 241
Goldson, Barry 75, 145, 222,
                    224, 225, 226,
                    227, 228, 229,
                    230, 231, 232
Goodey, J 99
Gordon, A 261
Gordon, D 145
Gordon, P. 85, 86
Gottfredson, M. 6, 7, 111
Grabosky, P 140
Graham, J 222, 224
Graham, M 60
Gray, J. 84
Greenpeace 117
Greenwood, P 209
Greer, C 67
Grendon Underwood 259
Grigg-Spall, I. 143
Grunwick dispute. 192
Guardian, The 73, 253
Gun crime 83, 85

Haantz, S 143
Hagan, J 101
Hale, C 37
Halifax 136
Hall, R. 111
Hall, S. 67, 83, 222
Halliday Report. 22
Hammersley, M. 40
Hancock, Lynn 55, 56, 58,
                        59, 62, 64
Hanmer, J. 114
Hannah-Moffat, K. 258
Harding, S 128
Harrington, V 223
Harris, R. 143
Harvey, L 108
Hate crime 126–27
Hawker, S 46
Hawkins, G 7
Hawkins, K 139, 140
Hay, C 228
Haydon, D 227, 228
Hayek, F. 140
Hazards 139
Health and Safety Executive 138
Hedderman, C 10, 94, 214, 215
Hegemonic masculinity 98, 99
Heidensohn, F 100, 102, 106, 215
Helms, M. 135
Hendrick, H. 222
Henry, S 11, 18
Herrnstein, RJ. 6, 7, 111
Hertz, Noreena 142
High Court of Justiciary,
  Scotland. 284, 285,
                    286, 289, 290
Hillyard, P 145
Hindelang, MJ 95, 111
Hiroshima 162
Hirschi, T. 6, 7
Hirst, PQ 187
HM Prison Service. 21, 26–27, 29
  See also Prison
  attitudes to. 22
Hobbes, Thomas 156
Hobbs, D 38
Hochschild, A 160–61
Holdaway, S 84, 86, 88,
                    89, 90, 192
Holocaust, the 153, 157
Home Affairs Committee
  on Racial Attacks and
    Harassment 86
Home Office. 21, 22, 23, 32
Home Secretary 189, 195, 196, 241
'Honour killings'. 88
Hood, R 37, 85, 215

'Hooligan' 221
Hope, T 60
Hough, M 57, 58, 59, 60,
61, 63, 64, 68,
111, 208, 254
Howard League for
Penal Reform..................... 223
Howard, Michael 213, 239, 240,
251–52, 253, 254
'prison works'......... 213, 239, 251, 254
Hoyle, C...................... 44, 276
Hucklesby, Anthea 203, 215
Hudson, Barbara............. 9, 17, 18, 82,
111, 210, 215,
50, 285, 293
Hughes, Gordon 3, 32, 36, 111,
116, 169, 170,
172, 175, 176,
177, 178, 179,
181, 200, 225, 293
Hulsman, LHC 16
Human rights.............. 153, 157, 158
international justice............. 159–61
youth justice................... 226–27
Human Rights Act 1998 ...... 227, 252, 285
Hume, David..................... 286
Hutter, B...................... 139, 142

Ignatieff,......................... 255
Imperial Foods..................... 117
Imperialist globalisation........... 155–56
Imprisonment
See Prison
Incapacitation.............. 4, 6–8, 208–09
See also Prison
Independent Monitoring
Boards 52
Indermaur, D.................... 59, 60
Individual positivism 8–10, 36
Industrial conflict......... 190, 191–92, 193
Industrial injuries
and diseases 134–35, 138–39
Informalism...................... 226
Inner city riots............. 69, 71, 83, 84,
87, 191, 192–93
Inquiry into Police Core
and Ancillary Tasks................ 194
Inspectorate bodies............. 26–27, 52,
127, 187, 194
Intensive Control and
Change Programme................. 242
International bodies 157–58
International Criminal Court 161, 163
International relations............. 154–55
Interpretivism........... 107, 108, 117–18
Involvement.................... 52, 53

Ireland, P 143
Islam............................. 123
See also Muslim communities;
Muslim offenders
interpretations of.................. 125
Qur'an 125, 127, 128
researching................... 128–29
Sunni tradition.................... 123
Islamic Human Rights
Commission...................... 127
Islamophobia................... 125, 129
Itzin, C 114

Jacob, H 215
Jacobs, J 196
James, A 23, 27, 32, 52
Jamieson, J..................... 44, 227
Jarvis, FV 243
Jefferson, T...................... 68, 99
Jeffreys, S 110
Jermyn, D........................ 71
Jessop, B......................... 141
Jewkes, Yvonne................ 67, 68, 71,
72, 75, 77
Johnson, G........................ 85
Johnstone, Gerry............. 16, 266, 267,
268, 271, 274,
275, 276
'Joined-up' government 253, 254
Joint Prisons and Probation
Accreditation Panel (JPPAP)......... 243
Joly, D........................... 123
Jones, Abdalla 88
Jones, D 229
Jones, S........................ 100, 116
Jones, T..................... 53, 111, 200
Judge John Deed 73
Judge Judy.......................... 74
Judges..................... 204, 205–06
Scotland 282, 283
Jupp, V........................... 46
Jury service 58, 59
Jury system 73
Jury trial....................... 204, 205
'Just deserts'............. 4, 9, 29, 211, 238
See also Proportionality
of punishment
Justice for All...................... 22, 23
Juvenile delinquency.......... 97, 221, 225
See also Youth crime

Kagan, ... 140
Kane, J 137
Karmi, G 127
Katyn massacre..................... 162
Keith, M......................... 83

Kelling, G 13, 111
Kelly, L 114, 127
Kershaw, C. 61
Keynon, E 46
Khmer Rouge 163
Kidd-Hewitt, D 67, 78
Kilbrandon Committee. 285
King, JFS 243
King, Michael 27
King, R. 46
Kinsey, R. 111
Kitsuse, J. 111
Knowledge, theories of 105, 107–08
Kosovo 161, 162
Kramer, R. 143, 145
Kuper, Leo 157–58
Kutash, I. 127

Labelling. 14, 15, 115
    See also Stereotyping
    racialisation 81
Labour Government
    See New Labour
Lacey, M. 4
Lacey, N 145
Lambert, J 84
Laming, Lord. 70
Landau, SF. 82
Langdon, A. 208, 214, 237
Lange, B 140
Law officers of the
    Crown, Scotland 282
Lawrence, Stephen 72, 87, 191
    See also Macpherson Inquiry
    and Report
Lay magistrates 24, 52, 53, 204–05
    women magistrates. 99
Laycock, G. 170
Lea, J. 11, 111
League of Nations. 157
Lee, R 139
Lee-Treweek, G 46
Lees, S. 99, 101
Left realism 11–12, 111–13
Leishman, F 72, 77, 200
Lemert, Edwin. 14, 226
Leopold II, King of
    the Belgians 159, 160
Levi, M. 136
Lewis, B 128
Lewis, C 174, 175, 241
Lewis, DJ 110
Lex talionis 7
Liberal feminism. 94, 97
Liebling, A. 40
Lifer: Living With Murder. 75

Lighting and Watching Act 1833 186
Lilly, R 11, 18
Linkogle, S. 46
Lipetz, M 215
Livingstone, S 59
Lloyd, C. 208
Lloyds TSB. 137
Local Government Act 1888. 189
Local pressure groups. 62–63
Lombroso. 156
Lord Chancellor's Department 21
Loveday, B 200
Lubans, VA 194
Lukes, S 143
Lustgarten, Laurence 200
Luttwak, Edward 158

MacKenzie, R. 144, 286
Maclean, B 111
Macpherson of Cluny,
    Sir William. 87
Macpherson Inquiry
    and Report. 72, 86–87,
                                    88, 89, 90, 191
McBarnet, D. 140
McCall Smith, RAA. 279, 286, 293
McCarthey, B. 101
McConville, M. 203
McGuire, J 211
McKay, H 11, 36
McKeganey, N. 42
McLaughlin, Eugene 3, 16, 18, 59,
                                    68, 75–76, 134,
                                    171–72, 175, 176,
                                    177, 179, 181,
                                    290, 293
McMahon, M. 10
McWilliams, W. 235, 236, 245
Macey, M 125
Magistrates' court 21, 24
    'bench cultures' 214–15
    court clerks 204
    District Judges 24, 204, 205, 214
    lay magistrates 24, 52, 53, 204–05
    sentencing in. 22, 24, 204, 214–15
    women magistrates. 99
    youth court 24
Magnusson, W 157
Maguire, M. 36, 38, 77, 206
Mahon, R. 144
Mama, A 125
Managerialism. 30
    bureaucratic model
        of criminal justice 28
    New Labour and 30, 174
    new public managerialism. 30

Manning, P. 142, 144
Marital rape 95, 110
Mark, Robert 188, 190
Martin, Tony 203
Martinez Lucio, M. 144
Martinson, R. 9, 210, 237, 250
Marx, Karl 140, 142
Mason, D 83, 90
Mason, P. 72, 74, 77
Matassa, M. 176
Mathiesen, T 17, 254, 255,
256, 259, 261
Matthews, R 12, 55, 58, 59,
60, 257, 260
Mattinson, J 63
Matza, David 226
Mawby, R. 53, 72, 106, 108,
109, 116, 118
Maxwell, Robert 144
May, T 40
Mayhew, P 61, 111, 223
Maynard, M. 128
Mays, R 293
Media
  courts in 73–74, 203
  ethnic minorities in 69, 70, 71, 75
  'evil' 69
  factual portrayals 59, 67, 71,
72–73, 74, 75, 76
  fictional portrayals. 67, 72, 73–75
  folk devils 69
  misrepresentation 67
  offenders 70
  over-reporting of violent
    and sexual crimes 67, 68
  paedophiles 55, 71
  police in 71–73
  prisons in 74–75
  public opinion and. 55–56, 59–60, 72
  racism 69, 70, 71, 75
  representations of
    criminal justice 17, 55–56,
59–60, 67–78
  'self' and 'other' 68–69
  soap operas 59, 75, 76
  victims 70–71
Medical model of
  criminal justice. 28, 29
Mendelsohn, B. 105, 109
Mentally disordered offenders 26
Merton's strain theory 11
Messerschmidt, J 98, 99, 101, 102
Metropolitan Black
  Police Association 89
Metropolitan Police Act 1829 185
Miers, D 95, 109, 272

Milkis, S 143
Miller, J. 99
Miners' Strike 1984/85 193
Minister for Children 70
Minority groups 81–90
  See also Muslim communities;
    Muslim offenders
  African-Caribbeans 69, 70, 81, 82–83
  agents 88–89
  Asians 70, 81, 84
  gangs 83, 85
  gun crime 83, 85
  'honour killings' 88
  media portrayal of 69, 70
  National Survey of
    Ethnic Minorities 124
  perpetrators 85–86
  police and 82–89
    minority officers 88–89
  prison and 86, 124, 125–26,
215, 253, 256
  riots 69, 71, 83, 84,
87, 191, 192
  sentencing and 215
    young offenders 230
  stereotyping 83, 87, 113–14
  suspects 82–85
  unemployment 124–25
  victims 86–88
  young offenders 223–24, 226
Mirrlees-Black, C 57, 58, 63, 86
Miscarriages of justice 27, 71, 73, 87
  Scotland 290
'Mobilisation for youth' 11
Models of criminal justice 27–30
  bureaucratic model 28
  crime control model 27, 28, 29, 32
  due process model 27, 28, 29, 32, 226
  hybrid models 29
  'just deserts' model 29
  medical model 28
  power model 28
  status passage model 28
Modern retribution model
  See 'Just deserts'
Modood, T 124
Monbiot, G. 141, 143
Mooney, J 113, 118
Moore, D 270
Moore, R 141
Moore, S 86
'Moral majority' 68, 69
Moral order 6, 7
'Moral panics' 69, 221, 222, 228
Moran, M. 141
Morel, ED 159, 160

Morgan, J 111
Morgan, R 53, 205, 237,
                                   243, 244
Morgan Report 197
Morris, A 102, 215
Morrison, Wayne 123, 157, 164
Motoring offences 23
Moxon, ... 214
Mubarek, Zahid 75, 86
Muir, H 89
Muncie, John 18, 30, 36, 108,
                               134, 179, 181,
                               221, 224, 225,
                             227, 232, 290, 293
Municipal Corporations
    Act 1835 186
Murray, C. 6
Muslim communities 123–24
    See also Islam
    census data 123–24
    hate crime 126–27
    media treatment 69, 70
    terrorism and 123, 126, 127, 129
    women 126, 127
Muslim offenders 124–26
    age of 124
    in prison 124, 125–26
    unemployment among 124–25

Naffine, N 100, 101
Nagasaki 162
Narey, M. 205, 244
Nash, Mike 235, 237, 239,
                               240, 241, 242,
                               244, 245
National Association of
    Probation Officers (NAPO) 239, 243
National Black Police
    Association 89
National Census 2001 123
National Crime Squad 195, 198
National Criminal
    Justice Board 22
National Deviancy
    Conference 1968 38
National Probation Service 235, 241
National Survey of
    Ethnic Minorities 124
Nationwide 136
Navarro, V 143
Naylor, B 67
Naylor, T 191
Neighbourhood Watch 196
Nelken, D. 136
Neo-conservatism 5, 6–8, 12, 250
New Labour 18, 111, 177
    crime prevention 12, 169, 197

'joined-up' government 253, 254
Justice for All. 22, 23
managerialism 30, 174
New Deal policies 12
No More Excuses 228–29
partnership models 175, 197, 253
prisons and 249, 252–24, 258
public opinion and 52, 54
Stephen Lawrence inquiry 87
Newburn, T 53, 95, 200, 212
Newman, O 196
Newman, Sir Kenneth 194
News of the World 55
Nichols, T. 143
Nijhar, P 111
Nimitz, Admiral 162
Noaks, L 37, 39, 40, 46
Non-governmental
    organisations (NGOs) 159
Norrie, A 145
Norris, A 36
Norris, C 116
'Nothing works' 9, 10, 172, 208
Notifiable offences 23, 24
Nuremberg trials 161, 162

Ocamp, Luis Moreno 163
Occupational culture
    courts 214–15
    police 84, 88
O'Donnell, I 56
Offender accountability 10
Ogus, A 139
Ohlin, L 11
Oliver, Ian 189, 200
Opportunity theory 11
Osborne, R 67, 78
O'Sullivan, E 56
'Other'
    colonisation and 153, 156
    media representations and 68–69
    woman as 96

Packer, Herbert 27
Padfield, N. 214
Paedophiles 55, 71, 240
Pain, R 61, 112
Painter, K 111
Paisley, R 293
Palast, G 141, 143
Paradigms 27
    See also Models of
       criminal justice
    justice paradigm 23, 27
    welfare paradigm 23, 27
Parenti, C 257, 261
Parenting orders 229

Park, A 57, 61
Parker, CS 185
Parker, H 38, 204, 215
Parsons, Talcott 97
Payne, Sarah 55, 70
Pearce, F 136, 137,
                                           141, 143, 146
Pearson, Geoffrey 221–22, 232
Pease, K 206
Peel, Robert 185
Peltzman, S 141
Pemberton, S 138
Penal welfarism 236, 238
Perceptions of crime 22, 51, 52–23
   See also Fear of crime;
      Public opinion
Perez de Cuellar, Javier 158
Performance management 194–95
Petley, J 69
Phillips, C 83, 90, 215
Phillips, J 139
Picciotto, S 134
Pick, D 156
Pillsbury, S 271
Player, E 211
Podolefsky, A 62
Polanyi, K 141
Police 24
   amalgamation of forces 189
   attitudes to 22
   central control 185, 188
   Chief Constables 88, 188, 189,
                                      190, 191, 193,
                                      194, 195, 196
   clearance success rates 24
   community policing 197
   complaints against 188, 189
   due process model
      of criminal justice 29
   history 183–89
   industrial conflict and . . . 190, 191–92, 193
   inner city riots 69, 71, 83, 84,
                                      87, 191, 192–93
   institutional racism 71–72, 87, 88
   local control 186
   media representations 71–73
   minority groups and 82–89
   minority officers 88–89
   National Crime Squad 195, 198
   National Policing Plan 196
   number of officers 24
   occupational culture 84, 88
   performance management 194–95
   policing by consent 190
   policing by objectives 194
   politicisation 191–93
   professional policing 189–91
   racial awareness training 72–73
   recording of offences 23
   Royal Commission on 188, 190
   'stop and search' 24
   unit beat policing 190
   women officers 100
Police Act 1946 189
Police Act 1964 . . . . 188, 190
Police Authority 189, 196, 197, 198
Police Community
   Consultative Groups 52, 53
Police Core and Ancillary
   Tasks Inquiry 1995 194
Police Federation 190, 192, 194
Police and Magistrates
   Courts Act 1994 195
Police Reform Act 2002 . . . . 52, 195–96
Police (Scotland) Act 1967 287
Police Standards Unit 195
Pollak, O 94
Pollution 135, 136
Pontell, H 142
Porridge 74
Positivism 36, 37, 69,
                                      105, 107–08,
                                      154, 156
   individual 8–10, 36
   positivist victimology 95, 107,
                                      108–13, 118
   rehabilitation and 8–10
   sociological 8, 11–12
Postmodern feminism 96, 97
Potter, G 146
Power, M 174
Power model of
   criminal justice 28
Powers of the Criminal
   Court (Sentencing) Act 2000 230
Pratt, J 54, 55, 60,
                                      236, 273
Pressure groups 62–63
Prevention
   See Crime prevention
Priestley, P 211
Principal Reporter, Scotland 285
Prison 26–27
   See also Imprisonment
   abolitionists 259–60
   Belmarsh 127
   boot camps 7
   children in custody 75
   Conservative
      Governments and 244, 249,
                                      250–52, 253
   continuities and
      discontinuities 252, 253
   critical perspectives 255

decarceration 16–17
    effects of 209
    funding 26
    gender and 257–58
    HM Prison Service 21, 26–27, 29
        attitudes to 22
    incapacitation 4, 6–8, 208–09
    Independent Monitoring
        Boards 52
    institutional racism 75
    liberal perspective 254–55
    media representations 74–75
    minority inmates 86, 124, 125–26,
                                    215, 253, 256
    Muslims in 124, 125–26
    New Labour and 249, 252–54, 258
    remand 26
    Scotland 290–91
    size of population 26, 76, 212,
                                    250, 251, 253,
                                    254, 258, 260
    social order and 255–57
    Special Hospitals 26
    United States 7, 256, 257
    women and 93, 253,
                                    257–58, 259
    the working prison 252–54
    young offender institutions . . 26, 228, 230
Prison Reform Trust 51, 254–55
Prison Rules 1964 250
'Prison works' 7, 213, 239,
                                    251, 254
Probation of Offenders
    Act 1907 237
Probation Service 21, 26
    attitudes to 22
    community sentences 236, 237,
                                    241–42, 243,
                                    244–45
    history of 235–40
    Intensive Control and
        Change Programme 242
    national standards 239
    women officers 99
Procurators-fiscal, Scotland 288
Proportionality of
    punishment 9, 10, 21,
                                    211, 238, 265
    See also 'Just deserts'
    youth justice 226
Prosser, T 134
Psychoanalysis 99
Psychological hedonism 5
Public ignorance 75–76
Public involvement 52, 53

Public opinion 51–64
    assumptions about
        criminal justice 75–76
    criminal justice and 56–58
    expression of 56
    fear of crime 60–61
    jury service 58, 59
    liberal unease 55–56
    meaning 56–58
    media influences
        See Media
    perceptions of crime 22, 51, 52–53
    polls 56–57
    punitiveness and 55–56, 61, 68
    reflecting and responding to 53–55
    shaping 58–61
    soap operas 59
Public Order Act 1986 86
Public prosecutors, Scotland 282
Pugsley, L 41
Punch, M 134, 146, 191
Punishment 4–8
    See also Prison; Sentencing
    conservatism 6
    critics of 266–67
    deterrence 4–6, 12, 207–08
    incapacitation 4, 6–8, 208–09
    'just deserts' 4, 9, 29, 211, 238
    justification 4
    lex talionis 7
    mitigation 5, 6
    neo-conservatism 5, 6–8, 12
    'nothing works' 9, 10, 172, 208
    proportionality 9, 10, 21,
                                    211, 238, 265
    purpose of 4
    retribution 4, 7–8, 12, 211
Punitiveness 55–56, 61, 68

Quetelet, A 36
Quinney, R 106
Qur'an 125, 127, 128
    See also Islam

Race Relations Act 1976 87
Race Relations (Amendment)
    Act 2000 87
Racial and Violent
    Crimes Taskforce 88
Racial harassment and attack 86
Racialisation 81
Racism
    institutional 71–72, 75, 87, 88
    media and 69, 70, 71, 75
    police and 71–72, 87, 88
    in prison 75
    stereotyping 83, 87, 113–14

Radford, J 110
Radical feminism 95, 96, 97
Rafter, N 102
Raine, J 23, 27, 32, 52, 204
Raissi, Lotfi 127
Ramazanoglu, C 128
Rape
    See also Sexual violence
    acquaintance rape 110
    contributory negligence 110
    date rape 95, 110
    marital rape 95, 110
    victim precipitation 95, 110
    victim-offender relationship 110
Ratcliffe, P 125
Rational choice theory 4, 5, 12–14, 111
Rawlings, Philip 200
Raynor, P 211
Reagan, Ronald 250
Rebovich, D 137
Recidivism 58, 255, 258
    treatment model and 9
Redmond, Phil 74
Rehabilitation 209–11, 250
    criticism of 8–10, 11, 12
    individual positivism and 8–10
    medical model of
        criminal justice 28, 29
    young offenders 229
Reilly, T 60
Reiman, J 145
Reiner, Robert 59, 69, 72,
                                            77, 191, 199
Reintegrative shaming 15, 29, 31, 270
Reiss, AJ 191
Reith, C 187
Relative deprivation 11
Remand 26
Reparation 211–12, 267–69
    See also Restorative justice
    symbolic 268–69
Research 35–46
    bias 40
    Chicago School 37, 38
    combining traditions 38–39
    confidentiality and disclosure 43
    consent, informed 42–43
    critical social research 108
    development of 36–39
    empirical 35, 36
    ethics and 35, 41–43
    ethnography 37–38
    fieldwork 40
    hierarchy of credibility 40
    interviews 38
    intrusion 42
    Islam 128–29

opinion polls 56–57
politics of 35, 39–41
publication and dissemination 41
qualitative tradition 35, 37–38
quantitative tradition 35, 36–37
safety in 35, 44–45
symbolic interactionism 38
theoretical 36
'Respectable fears' 221–22, 228
Restorative justice 17, 30–32,
                                            212, 265–77
    benefits of 271–74
    community representatives 52
    concerns about 274–75
    conferencing 269–71
    guiding questions 276
    public opinion 54
    reparation 211–12, 267–69
    symbolic reparation 268–69
    victim-oriented justice 269
Retribution 4, 7–8, 12, 211
Right realism 111, 112
Riots 69, 71, 83, 84,
                                            87, 191, 192–93
Risk assessment and
    management 10
Riyadh Guidelines 227
Roberts, J 57, 58, 61, 63,
                                            64, 68, 208
Roche, Declan 269–70, 274
Rock, P 112–13
Roshier, B 67
Roshier, R 5
Rossington, P 139
Royal Commission on
    the Police 190
Rubenstein, R 157
Ruggiero, V 134
Rumgay, J 215
Runnell, R 157
Runnymede Trust 86
Rural Constabulary Act 1839 186
Russell, B 159
Russell, N 53, 205
Rwanda, international
    criminal tribunals 162
Ryan, M 54, 55, 56, 239,
                                            241, 250, 251,
                                            259, 261

Said, E 125
Salmonella 135
Sanders, A 203, 204, 205, 206
Savage, S 200, 237
Scarman OBE, Rt Hon
    the Lord, Scarman Report . . 83–84, 87, 88,
                                            191, 192

Schabas, W. 164
Schlesinger, P. 67
Schur, Edwin 15
Scotland 279–93
    Act of Union 280
    advocates 282–83
    appeals 290
    children's hearings 284–85
    criminal apprehension
        and investigation 287–88
    criminal courts 283–85
    criminal justice process 285–91, 292
    District Court 283, 288, 289
    Drug Court 291
    East Port House 291
    High Court of Justiciary 284, 285,
                                        286, 289, 290
    history of Scots criminal law 280–81
    judges 282, 283
    Justices of the Peace 282, 283
    law officers of the Crown 282
    legal personnel 281–82
    legal profession 282–83
    Lord Justice-Clerk 282, 284
    Lord President 282, 284
    miscarriages of justice 290
    penalties 285, 290–91
    Principal Reporter 285
    prison 290–91
    private prosecutions 288
    procurators-fiscal 288
    public prosecution 288
    public prosecutors 282
    sentencing 285, 290–91
    Sheriff Court 284, 286,
                                        288, 289, 291
    sheriffs 282, 284
    sheriffs principal 282, 284
    solemn procedure 288–89
    solicitor-advocates 283
    solicitors 283
    summary procedure 289–90
Scotland Act 1998 281
Scottish Criminal Cases
    Review Commission 284
Scottish Prison Service 290
Scraton, P 227, 228, 232
Seago, P 205
Secondary victimisation 112
Secret Policemen, The 72
Secure training centres 228
Secure units 228
'Self' and 'other'
    See 'Other'
Self-control 7

Sentencing 206–07
    'bench/court cultures' 214–15
    bifurcation 213
    'cafeteria style' 213
    community sentences 26, 101, 212,
                                        216, 241–42,
                                        243, 244–45
    Crown Court 22, 25, 204,
                                        205, 214
    curfews 30, 229, 245
    discretion 214–15
    discrimination in 215
    District Judges
        (magistrates' court) 204, 205, 216
    effects of 206–07
    gender and 93
    jury trial 204, 205
    Justice for All 23
    'justice by geography' 214
    justifications 207
        deterrence 207–08
        incapacitation 208–09
        rehabilitation 209–11
        retributive 211
        utilitarian 207–11
    lay magistrates 204–05
    magistrates' court 22, 24, 204, 214–15
    mandatory sentences 214, 285
    minimum sentences 214
    minority groups 215
        young offenders 230
    policy 212–13
    practice 213–15
    prison population, size of 212
    Probation Service reports 26
    proportionality 9, 10, 21
    public opinion and 53, 57–58, 59
    public protection and 213
    reparation 211–12
    Scotland 285, 290–91
    serious and persistent
        offenders 213
    women 93
Sentencing Advisory Council 215
Sex role theory 97–98
Sexual violence 98, 99, 101
    See also Domestic violence; Rape
    over-reporting of
        sexual crimes 67, 68
Shapiro, S 144
Sharp, Douglas 126, 183, 189, 199
Sharpe, K 44
Shaw, C 36
Shaw, M 258
Shaw, S 51
Sheehy Inquiry Report 1993 194

Shelden, R 257
Sheldon, David 279, 286, 293
Shell 137
Sheriff Court, Scotland . . . 284, 286, 288, 289
Sheriff, S. 127
Sherman, L. 170, 174
Shiels, RS 289
Shore, H 222
Shover, N 146
Show trials 162
Siddiqui, S 126
Sierra Leone 162–63
Silcott, Winston 87–88
Sim, Joe 101, 145, 250,
                                251, 252, 255,
                                258, 259, 261
Simmons, J. 223
Simon, Jonathan 170
Simon Jones Campaign 139
Simpson, S 139
Situational crime prevention . 10, 12–14, 111,
                                116, 169, 173
Skogan, WG. 62
Skolnick, J 191
Slapper, G 117, 136, 137, 146
Slavery 153, 155, 156
Smart, Carol 101, 110
Smiljanic, N 126
Smith, C 43, 147
Smith, D 84, 140, 225
Smith, R 157, 232
Smith, SJ. 67
Snider, L. 101, 142, 143,
                                144, 145, 146
Soap operas 59, 75, 76
Social class
    criminality and 6, 7, 15
    power model of
        criminal justice. 28
    youth crime and 15, 224
Social construct theory 14–16
Social contract theory 4
Social crime prevention. 10, 169, 174
Social reform 11–12
Social Research Association 41, 44
Social Work (Scotland) Act 1968 285
Socialisation. 7, 97
Socialist feminism 96, 97
Sociological positivism 8, 11–12
'Soft on crime' 12, 68
Soham murder case 70
Solicitors, Scotland 283
Solomon, ... 254
Solomos, J. 83, 87, 90
Soros, G 141
South, N. 261

Sovereignty 153, 156–57
    Treaty of Westphalia 156, 157
Soviet Union, Katyn massacre 162
Spalek, Basia 125, 126, 129
Sparks, R 74, 76, 109,
                                110, 251, 290
Special Hospitals. 26
Spink, P 293
'Square of crime' 112
Stanko, EA. 95
Starsky and Hutch. 72
Statement of Local Objectives
    and Priorities (SLOP) 238
Statement of National
    Objectives and Priorities for
    the Probation Service (SNOP) . . . 237, 238
Status passage model
    of criminal justice 28
Stenson, K 176
Stereotyping. 115
    See also Labelling
    of Muslims 125
    racial 83, 87, 113–14
Stick, N. 72
Stigler, G 141
Stoker, G 62
Stokes, E. 69
'Stop and search'. 24
Strain theory 11
Strang, H 269, 272
Straw, Jack 53, 240, 252, 254
Strong, K 268
Sullivan, A 125
Summary procedure,
    Scotland 289–90
Sun, The 68
Sundra, J 137
Sundt, JL 57
Surette, R 76
Suspects, minority groups 82–85
'Sustaining society' 11–12
Sutherland, E 115, 137, 146
Sutton, Adam. 170, 180
Sweeney, The. 72
Symbolic interactionism. 38
Symbolic reparation 268–69
Szockyj, ER. 117, 118, 143

Tappan, P 115, 136
Tarling, R 208, 209
Taylor, Damilola 70
Tequila Sunrise 75
Territoriality. 13
Terrorism 123, 179
    attacks on United States 123, 126,
                                129, 154

Bali bombings............. 123, 126, 129
 Muslim communities and 123, 126,
                                 127, 129
Thatcher, Margaret 237, 250
Theories of knowledge 105, 107–08
Thomas, D 212
Thomas, J 139
Thorpe, DH 225
'Three strikes' laws 53, 57, 61
Tokyo trials 161–62
Tolchin, M 141
Tolchin, S 141
Tolerance 14–17, 235
 abolitionism.................... 16–17
 critical criminology 16–17
 decarceration 16–17
 decriminalisation................... 15
 deinstitutionalisation 15
 diversion 15
 labelling 14, 15
 non-intervention 14–16
 radical non-intervention............. 15
 social construct theory 14–16
Tombs, S................... 117, 135, 136,
                          137, 140, 141,
                       142, 143, 144, 146
Treatment.................. 3, 8–10, 251
 due process and 9
 individual positivism 8–10
 public opinion..................... 54
 recidivism and..................... 9
 rehabilitation................... 28, 29,
                          209–11, 250
  criticism of 8–10, 11, 12
  individual positivism and........ 8–10
  young offenders................. 229
 risk assessment and management..... 10
Treaty of Westphalia 156, 157
Truman, C 42
Tucker, E 143
Tumber, H 67
Turner, MG 57
Twain, Mark 160
Tweedale, G.................... 135, 143
Tyrer, J 32

Uglow, S........................... 53
United Nations........... 157–58, 161, 162
 youth justice.................. 227, 230
United States
 boot camps......................... 7
 chain gangs 7
 Chicago School 37, 38
 corporate crime 137
 death penalty....................... 7
 International Criminal
  Court and..................... 163

Megan's law 55
 'mobilisation for youth' 11
 prison 7, 256, 257
 right-wing 7
 terrorist attacks........ 123, 126, 129, 154
 'three strikes' laws 57
Unreported crime 111
Utilitarianism 5

Van Kesteren, J 61
Van Ness, D........................ 268
Vennard, J 10
Verdict Is Yours, The................. 73
Victim support 114, 115–16
 Muslim women 127
 Victim Support........... 21, 25–26, 53
Victim-oriented justice 269
Victimisation 95, 105
 corporate crime 116–17
  fraud 137
 domestic violence 110
 experience of 52, 53, 60
 gender and........................ 99
 secondary....................... 112
'Victimless crimes'............. 15, 68, 116
Victimology 95, 105, 106–07
 corporate crime 116–17
 critical.................. 107, 108, 115,
                          116–17, 118
 domestic violence 110, 113–15, 116
 gender and 95, 101–02
 interpretivist........... 107, 108, 117–18
 murders and victims............... 109
 objectivist........................ 112
 politics, role of 115–16
 positivist 95, 107,
                          108–13, 118
 rapists and victims 110
 subjectivist...................... 112
 victim precipitation.......... 95, 109–10
Victims............................ 105
 conceptualisation of
  the term 'victim'.............. 106–07
 contributory negligence 110
 corporate crime......... 116–17, 143–44
 culpability.................. 95, 109–10
 domestic violence.......... 110, 113–15
 gaining knowledge about........ 107–08
 'ideal' victims................. 106, 111
 'innocent victims' 106
 Islam and....................... 127
 media constructions of 70–71
 minority groups................. 86–88
 'natural' victims 13
 restorative justice
  See Restorative justice
 social construction of 106

status of 106
surveys 110–11
typologies 106, 109, 110
victim precipitation 95, 109–10
'victim-blaming' 110
of youth crime 223
Vieira, C 52
Vigilante activity 55
Violence
  See also Domestic violence;
    Sexual violence
  corporate violence 134–36
  dangerousness and 209
  over-reporting of violent crime 67, 68
Virdee, S 86
Virta, E 142
Von Hentig, H 99, 105, 109
Von Hirsch, A 9, 208, 209, 274

Wacquant, L 256, 257
Waddington, David 250
Waddington, PAJ 190, 191, 199–200
Walker, H 244
Walker, N 207, 209, 211, 214
Walker, Robert 154
Walklate, Sandra 36, 42, 56, 61,
                          93, 95, 100, 101,
                          102, 105, 107, 108,
                          109, 110, 113, 115,
                          116, 118, 293
Wallis, Eithne 241
Walmsley, R 258
Walters, R 145
Walton, D 243
War crimes 161–62
Wardhaugh, J 44
Waters, R 82, 85
Watson, H 128
Weatheritt, M 52, 190
Weiss, R 261
Weitekamp, E 267
Welfare
  crime control and 9
  paradigm 23
  youth justice 225–26
Welfare to work 12
Welland, T 41
Wells, C 134
Wells, Holly 70
Wertham, Frederick 107
West Midlands Serious
  Crime Squad 71
Western, B 256
Westmarland, L 100
Westphalian sovereignty 156, 157
'What works' 3, 10, 169, 171,
                    179, 211, 231, 236

Wheelan, C 140
Whitelaw, William 250
Whittaker, B 190
Whynne, A 204
Whyte, D 143, 145
Willan, ... 77, 78
Wilson, David 21, 32, 62, 74,
                          86, 125, 126,
                          183, 189, 199
Wilson, J 138
Wilson, James Q 6, 7, 13, 111, 112, 172
Wincup, Emma 37, 39, 40, 43, 46
Witness Service 21, 26
Wolfgang, M 109
Women
  See also Feminism; Gender
  as criminal justice
    professionals 99–100
  domestic violence 95–96, 110,
                          113–15, 116,
                          117–18
  murder victims 93
  Muslim women 126, 127
  'otherness' 96
  policewomen 100
  prison and 93, 253,
                          257–58, 259
Wonders, N 143
Woodhouse, T 111
Woolfson, C 141, 143
Wootton, B 93, 94
Worpole, K 85
Worrall, A 101, 243
Wright, JP 146
Wright, M 141
Wright Mills, Charles 170
Wright, R 207

Yardie gangster gangs 83
Yeagar, P 137
'Yob' 221
Yorkshire Ripper inquiry 71, 193
Young, A 96
Young, J 11, 12, 18, 56,
                          60, 111, 112, 172
Young offender institutions 26, 228
Young offenders 29–30
  gender 223–24, 226
  minority groups 223–24, 226
  restorative justice 212
Young, R 203, 204, 205,
                          206, 276
Young, W 209
Youth court 24
Youth crime 221
  anti-social behaviour 229
  gender and 223–24

juvenile delinquency 97, 221, 225
minority groups 223–24
'moral panics' 222, 228
offences 223
offenders 223–24
offending 222–23
'respectable fears' 221–22, 228
social class and 15, 224
victims of 223
Youth custody centres 228
Youth justice 224
  age of criminal minority 227
  due process 226
  hybridity 228
  informalism 226
  Intensive Control and
    Change Programme 242
  international rules 227
  justice 226
  'new youth justice' 228
    critical attention 230

custodial detention 230
  intensive intervention 229–30
  No More Excuses 228–29
proportionality 226
responsibilities 227
retribution and punishment 227–28
rights 226–27, 231
United Nations and 227, 230
welfare 225–26
Youth Justice Board 30
Youth Justice and
  Criminal Evidence Act 1999 229
Youth offending boards 52
Youth offending teams 21, 25, 32
Yugoslavia, international
  criminal tribunals 162

Zedner, L 111
Zehr, Howard 268, 270, 276
Zero tolerance 14, 53
Zimring, FE 7